ORIENTAL NEIGHBORS

THE SCHUSTERMAN SERIES IN ISRAEL STUDIES

≡≡≡

Editors | S. Ilan Troen | Jehuda Reinharz | Sylvia Fuks Fried

The Schusterman Series in Israel Studies publishes original scholarship of exceptional significance on the history of Zionism and the State of Israel. It draws on disciplines across the academy, from anthropology, sociology, political science, and international relations to the arts, history, and literature. It seeks to further an understanding of Israel within the context of the modern Middle East and the modern Jewish experience. There is special interest in developing publications that enrich the university curriculum and enlighten the public at large. The series is published under the auspices of the Schusterman Center for Israel Studies at Brandeis University.

For a complete list of books in this series, please see brandeisuniversitypress.com

Abigail Jacobson and Moshe Naor

≡

ORIENTAL

NEIGHBORS

≡

Middle Eastern Jews and Arabs

in Mandatory Palestine

Brandeis University Press | Waltham, Massachusetts

Brandeis University Press
© 2016 Brandeis University
All rights reserved

Designed by Mindy Basinger Hill
Typeset in Adobe Caslon Pro

For permission to reproduce any of the material in this book, contact
Brandeis University Press, 415 South Street, Waltham, MA 02453,
or visit brandeisuniversitypress.com

Library of Congress Cataloging-in-Publication Data

Names: Jacobson, Abigail, 1973– author. | Naor, Moshe, author.
Title: Oriental neighbors : Middle Eastern Jews and Arabs in mandatory Palestine /
Abigail Jacobson and Moshe Naor.
Description: Waltham, Massachusetts : Brandeis University Press, [2017] |
Series: The Schusterman series in Israel studies |
Includes bibliographical references and index.
Identifiers: LCCN 2016017473 (print) | LCCN 2016017694 (ebook) |
ISBN 9781512600056 (cloth : alk.) | ISBN 9781512600063 (pbk.) | ISBN 9781512600070
(epub, mobi & pdf)
Subjects: LCSH: Palestine—Ethnic relations. | Jewish-Arab relations. |
Jews, Oriental—Palestine—Social conditions—20th century. |
Palestinian Arabs—Social conditions—20th century. | Palestine—History—1917–1948.
Classification: LCC DS126 .J27 2016 (print) | LCC DS126 (ebook) |
DDC 305.80095694/09041—dc23
LC record available at https://lccn.loc.gov/2016017473

FOR OUR CHILDREN | Alona, Yehonatan, and Naomi

Contents

Acknowledgments

This book is the culmination of almost five years of collaborative work, which crossed oceans and continents and involved many people and institutions. The research and writing about the complex relations between Oriental Jews and Arabs in Mandatory Palestine began in a period of emerging hopes for historic change in the Middle East. The book developed in parallel to the great vicissitudes in the Arab world, as relations between Jews and Arabs in Israel deteriorated. In many ways, our geographical distance from Israel—living as we did in Boston, Massachusetts, and San Diego, California, during these years—enabled us to write with some emotional distance. This intellectual and scholarly effort, which was also a personal journey that engaged our own identities, was made possible through the support of many colleagues, friends, and institutions, to which we would like to extend our deep gratitude here.

First and foremost, we take this opportunity to express our gratitude and friendship to Tammy Razi at Sapir Academic College, who was involved in all stages of this research, from its very early phases until it was consolidated into a book. We are indebted to Tammy for her work and effort, as well as her scholarly acumen, wisdom, and enthusiasm. Her advice and suggestions inspired us and are apparent throughout the book. We were also fortunate to have wonderful research assistants. We would first like to thank our main research assistant, Dotan Halevy, for his dedication to this project, his enthusiasm and curiosity, and his superb analytical skills. This study could not have been accomplished without Dotan's considerable contributions. We wish him every success in the new phase of his academic journey as a PhD candidate in the Department of History at Columbia University. We also want to recognize and thank our two other very dedicated research assistants, Eli Osherov in Jerusalem and Mano Sakayan in Boston, who helped us tremendously in the latter stages of writing the book. Special thanks go to our translator and editor Shaul Vardi, for his painstaking work and his valuable contribution to this effort.

Several institutions supported and facilitated the research and writing of this book. We are grateful for the generous research grants and financial support that we received from the Center for the Study of Relations between Jews, Christians, and Muslims at the Open University in Israel; the Israel Institute in Washington, D.C.; the Schusterman Center for Israel Studies at Brandeis University; Sapir Academic College in Israel; the Dean's Fund for Professional Development at the School of Humanities, Arts, and Social Sciences of the Massachusetts Institute of Technology (MIT); the Younes and Soraya Nazarian Center for Israel Studies at the University of California, Los Angeles (UCLA); and the Faculty of Humanities and the Department of Israel Studies at the University of Haifa. We also thank the many archivists and librarians who helped us as we conducted research for this book.

The editors at Brandeis University Press and the University Press of New England offered us continuous support and good advice. Sylvia Fuks Fried, the director of Brandeis University Press, was among the first advocates of this project, always willing to share her wisdom and available for a phone conversation or meeting. We would also like to thank Phyllis D. Deutsch, the editor in chief at the University Press of New England, for believing in this collaborative undertaking from its early stages and for providing guidance through the writing and review. We thank Ilan Troen at the Schusterman Center for Israel Studies at Brandeis University, for his insights and support, as well as the three anonymous readers who read the manuscript with a critical eye and whose suggestions were much appreciated.

Parts of the book were presented at various conferences and academic workshops. The comments and ideas we received there were invaluable and advanced our thinking in many ways. We have presented papers at numerous meetings of the Association for Jewish Studies, the Middle East Studies Association, and the Association for Israel Studies, as well as at the annual conference of the Center for the Study of Relations between Jews, Christians, and Muslims at the Open University in Israel. We would also like to thank the participants and commentators at two international workshops: Jewish Thought in Arab Societies (Ben-Gurion University, 2013), and German Orientalism and the Jewish "Arab Question": On the Study of Arabic Language and Culture in the Jewish Community in Mandatory Palestine (Hebrew University of Jerusalem, 2015).

Coauthoring this book was a new and exciting challenge for both of us.

Writing a book together is rarely an easy task, and we are delighted that it was such a meaningful experience for us, both as scholars and individuals. Our on-going exchange of ideas during the writing of different drafts of this book has enriched us and, we hope, has begun to narrow the gap between the disciplines of Israel and Jewish Studies on the one hand and Middle Eastern Studies on the other hand. Writing this book was a joint effort, and we both contributed equally to it. We should also mention here that our names appear on the cover of the book in alphabetical order.

At the end of this journey, we are pleased to recognize and thank many friends and colleagues. Gur Alroey, Moshe Behar, Zvi Ben-Dor Benite, Hedva Ben-Israel, Michelle Campos, Yigal Elam, Yuval Evri, Israel Gershoni, Jonathan Gribetz, Liora Halperin, Liat Kozma, Jessica Marglin, Roberto Mazza, Yonatan Mendel, Derek Penslar, Yona Sabar, Eugene Sheppard, Amy Singer, Reuven Snir and David Tal were always interested in our work and offered helpful comments and suggestions at different stages of its development. Special thanks go to Hagit Lavsky for her careful reading of the manuscript and her important suggestions. Needless to say, any errors are ours alone.

The History Department at MIT was Abigail's academic home for four years, and special thanks go to Lerna Ekmekcioglu for many conversations and fruitful exchanges, as well as to Craig Wilder, Jeff Ravel, Mabel Chin Sorett, Margo Collett, and Chuck Munger for their support and friendship. At the early stages of writing this book, Abigail was a junior research fellow at the Crown Center for Middle East Studies at Brandeis University, where she wishes to thank especially Shai Feldman and Naghmeh Sohrabi. Thanks are also due to the Department of Israel Studies at the University of Haifa, Moshe's new academic home; the Jewish Studies Program at York University, in Toronto, especially Kalman Weiser; Risa Levitt Kohn, of the Jewish Studies Program at San Diego State University, and Maura Reznik, of the Nazarian Center for Israel Studies at UCLA.

Abigail thanks her friends in Boston who provided love, wisdom, and sup-port and made her feel she had a home away from home: Noga Ron-Harel and Tal Harel, Gal Kober and Aaron Shakow, Sarit and Rotem Bar Or, Rebecca Weitz-Shapiro and Daniel Shapiro, Avital and Oren Parnas, Hila Milo Rasouly and Aviram Rasouly, Michal and Uri Sheffer, and Michal Ben Joseph Hirsch. Orli Fridman, Noya Regev, Rivka Neriya Ben Shahar, Naomi Davidson, Varda Halabi-Senerman, Tami Katzir, and Hadas Shintel remain dear and loving friends, even from afar.

This book could not have been written without the endless love and support of our families. Abigail's parents, Cheli and Dani Jacobson; her sister Noa; and the memory of Moshe's late parents, Angela and Sabri, served as inspiration as we wrote this book. Rachel and Avner shared this journey with us at all times, and their love and patience helped us complete the project. Our daughters, Alona and Naomi, were born during the writing of this book. It is our hope that the Middle East in which they will grow up will be different than ours. It is to our children, Alona, Yehonatan, and Naomi, that we dedicate this book.

ORIENTAL NEIGHBORS

Introduction

In June 2009, after President Barack Obama addressed the Muslim world in Cairo, promising a new beginning to the charged relations between the United States and the Muslim world, a group of Israeli intellectuals and artists whose parents had immigrated to Israel from Middle Eastern countries published an open letter calling for a "New Spirit" in the relations between Israel and the Arab world, and for Israeli-Arab reconciliation. The writers emphasized two facts: not only have Jews been an integral part of the region for hundreds of years and contributed to its cultural development, but Arab culture is also an important part of the current Israeli identity. The call for a new spirit in the Middle East and a reconciliation process between East and West was expressed in another open letter published in 2011 by the same group. Following the eruption of popular demonstrations in the Arab world, the new letter expressed the hope that Mizrahi Jews would form a living bridge of memory, reconciliation, and partnership between the different communities of the Middle East. This letter also called for renewing the mutual influences on and relationships between Jewish and Arab cultures and for creating a dialogue between Jews and Arabs in the Middle East, as people who have a common past and future.[1]

The timing of the publication of the 2011 letter was not coincidental. The Arab uprisings in that year that were collectively called the Arab Spring led to a lively discussion about the region's national and geographic boundaries and the role played by Western colonialism in the period after World War I. Israel was also influenced by these uprisings and was forced not only to reconsider its security and foreign policy toward its neighbors, but also to consider its connections and cultural, political, and social links to the Middle East as such. The discussion of Israel's location in the region is not new, of course. Members of the Zionist movement debated similar questions from the beginning of the movement, and since the late nineteenth century various positions, sometimes contradictory, have been expressed about the national and cultural characteristics of the movement and its relation to the East.[2]

Indeed, the New Spirit open letter is part of an ongoing discussion about the nature of Israeli identity in general, and contemporary Mizrahi Jewish identity in particular. The call for the peaceful coexistence of Jews and Arabs is not new either. It was preceded by calls by other movements consisting of Mizrahi, as well as Ashkenazi, Jews for Arab-Jewish cooperation during the late Ottoman and mandatory periods and after the establishment of the State of Israel. Those movements conveyed a historical perception that highlighted the relatively satisfactory conditions in the past of Jews in Arab countries, where they enjoyed relative tolerance and cultural integration. Movements such as Brit Shalom, Kedma-Mizraha, the League for Arab-Jewish Rapprochement and Cooperation, and Ichud all debated the so-called Arab Question. More recently, movements such as Hamizrah el Hashalom (The East to peace), active in Israel in the 1980s, and Hakeshet Hademocratit Hamizrahit (Mizrahi democratic rainbow coalition) also offered, and continue to offer, a critical discourse that examines the connections between the ethnic relations in Israel and its conflict with its neighbors.[3]

This discourse that highlighted the good relations between Jews and Muslims in the history of the Middle East and under the rule of Islam pointed also to the Arab-Jewish cultural symbiosis that existed, according to this discourse, until the development of Arab and Jewish national movements. In recent years, in contrast, a growing discussion in the Israeli public and political sphere has emphasized the status of Jews who immigrated from Arab countries as a minority who had lived in a hostile environment. The history of the Jewish exodus from Arab countries has been described with terms such as the "forgotten refugees" (referring to the Jews from Arab countries) and "the double Nakba" (referring to the argument about population exchanges in the Middle East during and after 1948), and there have been demands for "Justice for the Jews from Arab countries."[4]

These two narratives in the Israeli discourse reflect different historiographic trends. As Mark Cohen and others have argued, in contrast to the utopian and idyllic description of Jewish life in Arab countries and under Islam, a new historical view has emerged since 1967.[5] This new view emphasizes the inferior status of Jews under Islam and focuses on examples of conflict, discrimination, and humiliation. For example, Albert Memmi writes that "never, I repeat, never—with the possible exception of two or three very specific intervals such as Andalusian, and not even then—did the Jews in Arab lands live in other than a humiliated state, vulnerable and periodically mistreated and murdered, so that they should clearly remember their place."[6]

The recent renewed public interest in and discussion of the history of Jews of Arab countries and Jews' relations with the Arabs in their original communities has focused on, among other things, the Zionist movement's role in and effect on the deteriorating relations between Jews and Arabs in Palestine, and the movement's impact on the Middle East as a whole. This discussion demonstrates not only the connection between the Palestinian case study and the Middle East at large, but it also sheds new light on the links between the Jewish-Arab conflict and the situation of Jews of Middle Eastern countries. In addition, it highlights the important role of the Sephardi and Oriental Jewish communities in Palestine regarding the issue of Arab-Jewish relations.

This book focuses on the relations and links between Sephardi and Oriental Jews and the Palestinian Arabs in Mandatory Palestine. One of the main arguments presented here is that examining the relations between Jews and Arabs through the perspective of Sephardi and Oriental Jews sheds new light not only on the complexities and nuances of the Arab-Jewish conflict in Palestine, but also on the Zionist perspective toward it. As this book demonstrates, the Sephardi and Oriental Jewish communities are central in providing a more comprehensive and complex picture of the history of relations between Jews and Arabs in Palestine, and the way the Zionist movement perceived the Arab Question.[7]

The narrative and perspective offered by Sephardi and Oriental Jews during this period differed in many ways from the dominant perspective of the hegemonic Zionist movement and its national institutions, which crystalized mainly in the 1930s under the leadership of Mapai and Labor Zionism. However, in the histories of the Zionist movement and the Jewish community in Palestine, as well as in the vast amount of research dedicated to the roots of the Arab-Jewish conflict, this perspective has been largely neglected and understudied. By focusing on it, on the one hand, this book reveals patterns of close connections, coexistence, and cooperation between Jews and Arabs, and on the other hand, it sheds light on the many points of tension and friction between the two peoples. In fact, we argue that in many instances these close connections—based on geographical, linguistic, and cultural proximity and similarities—increased the tensions. An awareness of the complex dynamic between Oriental Jews and Arabs challenges the conventional narrative, which tends to accentuate the national, social, and military conflict between Arabs and Jews during the Mandate era.

This unique perspective also brings to the fore the different links and connections between Sephardi and Oriental Jews in Palestine and the surrounding

Middle East, both with their own communities of origin and with Arab culture, history, and the Arabic language. This book, then, offers a perspective that enables us to set Palestine and its inhabitants within their Semitic or Levantine surroundings and context, and thus to reconnect Palestine to its surrounding Middle Eastern environment.[8] By doing so, the book challenges the separation between the study of the Zionist movement and the Jewish community in Palestine, on the one hand, and the study of the Middle East and its history, on the other hand. In addition, the book bridges the gap between the political, social, and cultural history of the conflict and the mainly sociological discussion of the Jewish-Arab and Oriental identity. As we will discuss below, this book therefore questions some of the historiographical trends that emphasize the separation between the two communities living in Palestine and shows that there were, in fact, many points of contact between them and affinities of various kinds.

As this book demonstrates, Oriental Jews moved between different locales in the Middle East, crossing both geographical borders and boundaries of identity. Palestinian Sephardi and Oriental Jews maintained cultural, educational, economic, religious, political, and social links with their peers in the Arab world; studied at universities in Cairo and Beirut; taught Hebrew in Jewish schools in Baghdad, Damascus, Alexandria, and other cities; and wrote articles in various newspapers edited by Jews and Arabs in Palestine and other countries in the Middle East. In fact, we argue that Sephardi and Oriental Jews in Palestine lived in a Levantine space and belonged to an intellectual community that encouraged a debate on the nature of past and future relations between Arabs and Jews.

Historiography: Old, New, and Renewed

For years, the predominant trend in the history of relations between Jews and Arabs in Mandatory Palestine has been to focus on the Arab-Jewish conflict and its political and ideological dimensions. As Yaron Tsur shows, Zionism's approach to the relations between Jews and non-Jews was based mainly on the European model and was viewed through the prism of Jewish-Christian relations in Europe, which had been formed by an ongoing crisis with the non-Jewish environment that culminated in the Holocaust.[9] The national conflict with the Palestinians and the Arab countries, which also manifests itself as a clash with a non-Jewish environment, seems therefore to be a natural continuation of the historical relationship of Jews with their surroundings. Yet such an approach ignores the possibility of examining Arab-Jewish relationships in Palestine in terms of an alternative model of integration and cooperation.

Before the 1970s, most studies of the Arab-Jewish conflict and Jewish-Arab relations in Mandatory Palestine were written by scholars outside Israeli academia. The main focus of these works was on the political and military dimensions of the issues, seen through the prism of the national struggle. With the expansion of research dealing with the Yishuv and Zionism in general and the Arab-Israeli conflict in particular, in the 1970s the emphasis shifted to an examination of the interaction between economics, social issues, and ideology during the Mandate period.[10]

It was in this context that the dual-society model developed. According to this model, associated with Dan Horowitz and Moshe Lissak's *Origins of the Israeli Polity*, although Jewish and Arab societies in mandatory Palestine shared a single political framework under British rule, in fact they had two separate political, economic, and cultural systems and mutually exclusive and sometimes contradictory interests and aspirations.[11] The dual-society model was based in part on the British approach and policies, which argued for differences in the political organizations and national aspirations of both societies and portrayed the Jewish Yishuv as European in nature, and the Arab community as Asian.[12] Since then the dual-society model has been followed by two other historiographic schools and approaches: the postcolonial model and the joint-society model, which focused on social and economic aspects and was described by Zachary Lockman as the "relational paradigm."[13] Yet, as Aviva Halamish argued, neither historiographic model in fact argued against the existence of two separate societies in Palestine.[14]

One of the prominent characteristics of the development and trends in research on Jewish-Arab relations is the almost complete neglect of the role played by Sephardi and Oriental Jews vis-à-vis the Arab Question and the relations between Jews and Arabs.[15] In fact, the study of the Sephardi and Oriental Jewish communities in Palestine and the study of the relationships between Jews and Arabs during the Mandate period moved mostly along parallel lines. Moreover, as Tammy Razi suggested, the mainly sociological discussion of the category of Arab-Jews or Mizrahi Jews was in a separate sphere, focusing mainly on questions of ethnic identity, Ashkenazi-Mizrahi relations, and the question of the Sephardi and Oriental Jews' integration into the Zionist leadership and the Yishuv's institutions.[16] Some of this research also discussed the effects of the transition between the Ottoman era to British colonial rule on the Oriental Jewish leadership, and the loss of its political power as the representative of the Jewish Millet during Ottoman times.[17] This transition between empires and regimes had significant implications for the Sephardi and Oriental communities and signaled the transition from the practice of joint citizenship based on Ottoman citizenship into a national-colonial regime based on ethno-national and religious divides, as discussed above.[18]

Despite the fact that it seems only reasonable to combine the debate about the nature of the Yishuv as a dual or joint society with the historical and sociological discussion on Sephardi and Oriental Jews, most of the research on Sephardi and Oriental Jews has not discussed their position regarding the Arab Question or analyzed the diverse cultural, social, and geographic links that existed between Sephardim and Arabs.[19] Itzhak Bezalel tries to explain this void in his important *Noladetem Ziyonim*. Reflecting on Yosef Gorny's suggested typology of the different Zionist approaches to the Arab Question, Bezalel argues that the Sephardi leadership presented an additional, separate approach. Instead of the dichotomies that are so prevalent in the research on Zionism and the Yishuv—such as the new versus the old Yishuv, secular education versus religious education, modern Zionism versus a belief in messianic redemption—Bezalel argues that the Sephardi-Oriental approach did not adhere to these dichotomies, but rather offered a more complex and nuanced approach. This unique approach made it difficult for the dominant historiography to integrate the Sephardi and Oriental Jews into the existing historical models. This book, then, is intended to bridge the gap between these two parallel lines in research and offers ways of connecting them, by focusing specifically on the approaches of Sephardi and Oriental Jews in Palestine to the Arab Question, and by examining the nature of the links and connections between Jews and Arabs in Mandatory Palestine.

Who Were the Oriental Jews?

Bezalel's observation is also significant because it points to the terminology that is used to define the Arab-Jewish identity and, as a result, the different definitions of the group that is the focus of this book. Those definitions include, for example, Sephardim, Mizrahim, Arab Jews, Oriental Jews, 'Edot Hamizrah (Jews of Eastern descent), and Bney Ha'aretz (natives of the land). Which definition should be used, then?

The category of Sephardim was a very common one to use when referring to Middle Eastern Jews. The term "Sephardim" included all the descendants of Jews exiled from Spain who then spread to various countries, especially Italy, Turkey, and the Balkans. It also included the Jews of Middle Eastern descent, especially those from Egypt and North Africa, Bokhara, the Caucasus, Persia, Afghanistan, Yemen, and Palestine. Therefore, the term "Sephardim" included the Sephardi Jewish community and the communities of Oriental Jews (Yehudei Hamizrah), which were also called 'Edot Hamizrah. The English term used for Yehudei Hamizrah by the leadership of Sephardi and Middle Eastern Jewish communities, in their official documents, was "Oriental Jews."[20] In this book we mainly use that term, although we also include some other terms that were used by certain groups or individuals to refer to themselves. To fully understand the richness of this ethno-geographical category, however, it is important to also consider the way these groups were referred to by the British authorities, the Yishuv's institutions, and the Palestinian Arabs.

The demographic composition of the Yishuv and the place of Sephardi and Oriental Jews in it can be found in the statistical data of the Jewish Agency. Overall, the most common ways to refer to this community during the Mandate period and within the Yishuv were Sephardi Jews and 'Edot Hamizrah or Yehudei Hamizrah. The statistical department of the Jewish Agency used the ethnic categories of Sephardim, Yemenites, and Mizrahim. In December 1936, for example, it was reported that the Yishuv numbered 404,000 people, of whom 94,000 were defined as Sephardim and Oriental Jews, according to the following breakdown: 37,000 Sephardi Jews, 18,000 Yemenite Jews, and the others 'Edot Hamizrah.[21] At the end of 1945, in comparison, the Jewish population in Palestine was reported to number 592,000 people (accounting for 32 percent of the population in Palestine at the time), 22 percent of whom were defined as non-Ashkenazi Jews, 7.8 percent were Edot Hamizrah, 9.6 percent were Sephardim, and 4.9 percent were Yemenite Jews.[22]

When considering their numerical significance within the Jewish population, it is important to note that the overall number of those defined as Sephardi and Oriental Jews decreased gradually during the Mandatory years in comparison to the numerical weight of Ashkenazi Jews. The Zionist waves of immigrants from the beginning of the Mandate period until 1948, most of whom arrived from Eastern and Central Europe, increased the number of Jews by 80 percent, with around 81 percent of the immigrants being Ashkenazi Jews.[23] Hence, the percentage of Sephardi and Oriental Jews in the Yishuv decreased gradually throughout the interwar period to only 22 percent, as noted above.

From the perspective of the Yishuv, the Sephardi and Oriental Jews consisted therefore of three main ethno-linguistic groups: the Sephardim, referring to the descendants of those expelled from Spain and the Ladino speakers; Jews of Arab and Middle Eastern countries who spoke Arabic, Farsi, and Aramaic; and the Yemenite Jews, who were considered to be a separate category based on the group's unique cultural and political identity. In addition to these categories, another definition was used: Bney Ha'aretz, which referred mainly to Ashkenazim, Sephardim, and Mizrahim who had lived in Palestine before World War I and held Ottoman citizenship. When we use the term "Bney Ha'aretz," then, we refer to Mizrahi, Sephardi, and Ashkenazi Jews who were natives of the country, had previously held Ottoman citizenship, usually belonged to the educated elite, and were fluent in Arabic and used it regularly. As Menachem Klein demonstrates in his recent study, this sense of a local identity was shared by Mizrahi, Sephardi, and Ashkenazi Jews. People such as David Yellin, Yosef Yoel Rivlin, and Yosef Meyuchas, to mention a few, belonged to this category and often referred to themselves as members of it.[24]

One of the terms that Palestinian Arabs used to refer to this group was *yahud awlad 'arab* (native Arab Jews). Other terms included among them *al-yahud al-'arab* (Arab Jews), *al-yahud al-muwlidun fi Filastin* (Palestine-born Jews), *al-yahud al-'asliin* (original Jews), and *abna al-balad* (local Jews). The latter term was also often used to describe Palestinian Arabs as well.[25]

How did Sephardi and Oriental Jews view themselves and their social and cultural identity and affiliation? In November 1923 the journalist, writer, and Maghrebi activist Avraham Elmaleh (discussed in chapter 3) published an article in *Doar Hayom*, in which he used the term "Sephardim" and divided the Jewish Sephardi youth into three social and cultural categories. The Sephardi Jews who were strongly influenced by the Arab culture and life style he termed "Moriscos," as the Musta'arvim Jews were called.[26] The second category in Elmaleh's typology was the young educated Sephardim, whom he named "Mitarfim" (Europeanized)—those who were educated at the Alliance Israélite Universelle schools and acquired a "Levantine education." The third was the youth who were educated in religious institutions, who were not particularly influential within the Sephardi community.

Elmaleh's article, written to mark the fifth anniversary of the establishment of the Association of the Pioneers of the East (Histadrut Halutzey Hamizrah), an organization that will be discussed at length in this book, reflects the complexity involved in defining the linguistic, social, cultural, and geographical composition of the Sephardi and Oriental Jewish communities in Palestine. The article also alludes to the various tensions within this diverse community. For example, there was ethnic tension between the Ladino, French, and Arabic speakers; and there were generational tensions between the older leaders who had been prominent in the late Ottoman period and the younger generation, whose members reached maturity in the 1930s and became active in the security apparatus of the Yishuv. An additional, related, tension was the geographical one, between the Sephardi Jerusalemite leaders—a notable group—and the younger, and often more radical, generation most of whose members lived in Tel Aviv and Haifa. This book discusses these tensions, including the social and political frictions between the Sephardi elite and the Oriental Jews who lived in the poor frontier neighborhoods in the mixed cities (those whose populations included both Jews and Arabs).[27] It examines how these frictions affected the position of Sephardi and Oriental Jews on the Arab Question and the influence of the frictions within the Sephardi and Oriental Jewish communities.

Crossing the Frontier Borders and the Boundaries of Identity

The mixed cities form one of the arenas for exploring the encounters between Jews and Arabs at the micro level, in popular culture, and in everyday life, with the most obvious and well-researched examples being Jaffa and Haifa.[28] The mixed cities offer a model of a new direction in the historiography of Arab-Jewish relations, which focuses on new research perspectives and examines the connections, cooperation, and mutual influences between Jews and Arabs in various local and national arenas.[29] One of the focuses of this book is the mixed cities in general, and the frontier neighborhoods in particular. It was in these neighborhoods in the mixed cities that Jews—mainly Sephardi and Oriental Jews—lived side by side with Arabs. As will be explored in the following chapters, these frontier neighborhoods, sometimes called Oriental ghettos, embodied aspects of coexistence, cooperation, and neighborly relations, as well as of conflict and hostility. Focusing on the frontier neighborhoods also sheds new light on the socioeconomic similarities between the Jewish and Arab inhabitants of these neighborhoods, which contributed to the neighborly relations but also added at times to the hostility. Moreover, the frontier neighborhoods were the place where a hybrid Arab-Jewish identity developed.

Indeed, one of our arguments in this book is that Sephardi and Oriental Jews formed a hybrid group that bridged not only the dichotomies mentioned by Bezalel, but also the gaps between the Arab and Jewish identities and geographical regions.[30] In other words, Sephardi and Oriental Jews served as mediators not only between the old and new Yishuv, but also between Jews and Arabs. Their position is best exemplified in the case of the frontier neighborhoods, and the ability of Oriental Jews to cross borders in the Middle East in general. The book examines the Sephardi and Oriental Jews' special position as mediators in different spheres, including the political, security, cultural, journalistic, linguistic, and social ones. In so doing the book combines the discussion about the unique Jewish-Arab culture and that about Jewish-Arab relations. It brings the discussion about Jewish-Arab identity, which has been debated in scholarship mainly in relation to Iraq and other areas in the Mashriq, into the Palestinian context and integrates it with the discussion on Jewish-Arab relations in the same context.[31]

In this book we use the term "mediation" to analyze the position of Sephardi and Oriental Jews within the complex matrix of relations between Jews and Arabs in Palestine.[32] The term "mediation" has various meanings according to the context and historical realities. For example, cultural mediation refers to the creation of bridges and contacts between different cultures, whereas political mediators may be viewed as those who act in the context of political conflicts of different types, such as the Israeli-Palestinian conflict. Another form of political mediation has been discussed in relation to the role of minorities as mediators between the colonial state and the indigenous communities placed under colonial rule.

The term "mediation" is used here in its political, cultural, and social contexts. As we argue, these forms of mediation complemented each other and often could not be separated. Moreover, the cultural forms of mediation had political implications, as did social mediation—including its economic and security aspects. As we demonstrate here, the perception (and self-perception) of Oriental and Sephardi Jews as possible mediators was based on, among other factors, their historical roots in the Middle East, even before the rise of Islam.[33] Their cultural and linguistic connections to Arab culture and their fluency in Arabic also made them seen as mediators between the Zionist movement and the Arabs in Palestine. In various Arab countries Oriental Jews mediated between the state and its Jewish communities. However, in Mandatory Palestine the Oriental and Sephardi leaders lost the political status they had held during the Ottoman era, and they were no longer considered by the Zionist leaders as possible mediators between Jews and Arabs. The insistence of the Sephardim and Oriental Jews that they be viewed as mediators during the Mandatory period can hence be understood as both an attempt to return to their historic role and to regain a more dominant social and political position in the Yishuv. Their desire to be mediators, then, should be analyzed as part of an internal power struggle in the Yishuv, not only through the prism of the ongoing conflict and tensions between Jews and Arabs.

Some prominent Ashkenazi figures also viewed the Sephardi and Oriental Jews as possible mediators between the old and new Yishuv, tradition and modernity, and East and West. For example, the author and scholar Joseph Klausner expressed this view in an essay he published in honor of Avraham Elmaleh's seventieth birthday. Klausner characterized Elmaleh as "the Easterner-Westerner" (Hamizrahi-hama'aravi) and wrote: "The Sephardim and the other Oriental Jews argue that the Ashkenazim do not give them a proper role in the national and Zionist work. There is a basis for such an argument. The Zionist leadership should and could have received advice from the Oriental Jews in many aspects, for example on [issues related] to the relations with the Arabs, in which the Sephardim are considered to be experts, as people who lived in the country hundreds of years prior to the Ashkenazim." Yet for Klausner the Sephardi and Oriental Jews could mediate not only between Jews and Arabs, but also between Jews of Oriental and Western descent: "The Zionist Executive slighted (zilzela) the value of the Asian and African Jews. The Jews of the East should act as mediators between East and West in Jewish Eretz Israel: to bring the Sephardi and Oriental Jews closer to the Jews from Poland, Russia, Germany, Italy, England, and the United States."[34]

Oriental Jews' perception of themselves as mediators originated not only from their cultural and linguistic proximity to the Arabs, but also from their geographical proximity, since they lived among Arabs in the frontier neighborhoods in the mixed towns in Palestine. As we will discuss at length in this book, recognizing this physical proximity is crucial to understanding the ambivalent and sometimes contradictory nature of mediation. We argue that the involvement of Oriental Jews in translation projects from Arabic to Hebrew and vice versa, in teaching Arabic to Jewish communities, and particularly in security and intelligence work, served other purposes than their original one of fostering coexistence between Jews and Arabs. The Oriental and Sephardi leaders did not see any contradiction between these aspects of their position as mediators. And as we show, the hybrid space of the mixed Jewish-Arab neighborhoods contained acts of coexistence, conflict, and animosity, which demonstrates the complex connections that existed between Oriental Jews and Arabs at this time. Oriental Jews' Jewish-Arab cultural identity and their deep connections to the Arabs and the Middle East as a whole contributed to their perception of themselves as mediators on different levels.

Oriental Jews were not the only ones to view themselves as mediators and go-betweens in the Yishuv. Indeed, as mentioned above, Bney Ha'aretz referred to Ashkenazi Jews as well, who viewed their role in similar terms, as we will discuss below. However, the unique nature of the Oriental and Sephardi Jews, which included an ethno-cultural and linguistic identity of being in between, also affected their political role and made them different from other groups that claimed to play a mediatory role. These groups included, for example, the German Jewish scholars and intellectuals who helped establish the Institute of Oriental Studies at the Hebrew University in Jerusalem. For many of them, the attraction to the East (and, as a result, to the study of Arabic as philologists and that of Islam as religious scholars) was part of a complex Orientalist approach, which for some translated into both political activism and scholarship.[35]

This book, then, aims to closely analyze this unique view of Sephardi and Oriental Jews. As we will discuss in the following chapters, their political views varied, with some of them active in Revisionist Zionism and others in Labor Zionism. What united them was their deep confidence that they could serve as mediators between Jews and Arabs. This belief did not come at the expense of their commitment to the Zionist movement and to Jewish national goals in Palestine. The question of why this historical mediatory mission of the Sephardi and Oriental Jews failed belongs to "the road not taken" categories of historical enquiries. It is also closely connected to the question of why other organizations that strove during the Mandatory years to promote peaceful coexistence between Jews and Arabs also failed in finding a solution for the Arab-Jewish conflict. These questions were raised during the Mandate period and especially during the Arab Revolt. Indeed, as we show in this book, the period of the revolt was an important turning point in the way the Oriental Jews reexamined their role as mediators between Jews and Arabs. The Arab Revolt also represented an important generational shift, when the younger Oriental generation challenged the older Sephardi leadership and became deeply involved in the security apparatus of the Yishuv.

Understanding the position of Sephardi and Oriental Jews as possible mediators between Jews and Arabs is essential to understanding the complex relations between them and the Arab community in Palestine. In many ways, as we will discuss below, it is this role that enabled them to position themselves as part of Zionist institutions during the Mandatory years. The book examines their special position at the political-institutional level; the cultural, linguistic, and journalistic level; the socioeconomic level; and in the security apparatus. In each of these spheres of operation, the way they acted as mediators enabled them to also maintain their Jewish-Arab identity and integrate it within the national and political project of Zionism.

Each of the following five chapters analyzes a different dimension and sphere of the bridging and mediation activities of the Sephardi and Oriental Jews. The first three chapters discuss the links between politics and ideological, social, and cultural mediation; the fourth chapter focuses on the frontier neighborhoods in the mixed cities and examines interactions between Jews and Arabs in everyday life, from neighborly relations to conflict, as well as instances of border crossing. The idea of border crossing, both in terms of geography and identity, is also discussed in chapter 5, which focuses on the security sphere. Each chapter also looks closely at several individuals and, through their lives and public activities, demonstrates the variety of voices, perceptions, and visions among the Sephardi and Oriental Jewish communities in Palestine.

Chapter 1 begins by examining the role of the Association of the Pioneers of the East and the various political proposals made by this organization, as well as other institutions in the Sephardi and Oriental communities, in regard to the Arab Question and relations between Jews and Arabs. The chapter analyzes the links between the changing position of the Sephardim as a result of the transition from Ottoman to British rule and their loss of political power and their attempts to position themselves as possible political mediators between Jews and Arabs in Palestine. It also discusses how prominent figures in the Palestinian Arab national movement perceived the Sephardim and the Oriental Jews and asks whether they viewed local Jews as a possible alternative to the Zionist leaders. As this chapter shows, there was a clear link between the different political activities and initiatives of the Sephardi and Oriental Jews and their constant need to demonstrate their loyalty to the Zionist project. Their position as political mediators should be examined in light of this constant tension with the hegemonic Zionist, mainly Ashkenazi, leaders.

The discussion of political mediation continues in chapter 2, with the examination of the role played by prominent Sephardi and Oriental activists in various organizations that focused on Jewish-Arab relations in the Zionist apparatus. Such organizations include the United Bureau of the Jewish Agency and the National Council, the Arab Bureau of the Political Department of the Jewish Agency, and the Arab Department of the Histadrut (the General Federation of Jewish Workers in the Land of Israel). The lives and work of figures such as Eliyahu Sasson, Eliyahu Agassi, Zaki Alhadiff, Abraham Khalfon and Yehuda Burla, among others, are examined closely in this chapter, and their attempts to position themselves as mediators and promote rapprochement between Jews and Arabs in the political, social, and economic spheres are discussed in relation to their social, linguistic, and cultural background.

Chapter 3 moves to the cultural, journalistic, and linguistic spheres as venues of exchange between Arabs and Oriental Jews. This chapter scrutinizes the role of the Bney Ha'aretz in writing, editing, debating, and translating Arabic texts, as well as their role in teaching Arabic to different audiences in the Yishuv. The cultural sphere—to which all these activities belong—cannot easily be separated from the political sphere. As this chapter shows, cultural and educational activities often went hand in hand with political and diplomatic ones. This chapter uses the term "cultural politics" to characterize this special form of mediation and looks at the special form of Zionism, as understood by Oriental Jews and the Bney Ha'aretz.

The remaining two chapters move to a different level of hybridity. Chapter 4 looks at the frontier neighborhoods and the Oriental ghettos in the mixed cities as places of social, cultural, and geographical peripheries. These places, often located on the border between the Arab and Jewish neighborhoods, were places where Jews and Arabs lived side by side. Thus, they constitute fascinating case studies in the level of everyday interaction between Jews and Arabs who did not belong to the elite or the middle classes in their respective communities. The chapter focuses on these spheres of common life to examine the delicate line between mixing and unmixing in the context of the intensifying national conflict.

It was in these neighborhoods that a new generation of Oriental youth was raised, whose members played a major role in the security and intelligence apparatus of the Yishuv during the Mandatory years. Chapter 5 examines the security sphere and analyzes the role of Oriental youth as both *mista'avrim* and victims of violent confrontations between Jews and Arabs. Their familiarity with their Arab neighbors and especially their proficiency in Arabic allowed them to play an active role in the paramilitary groups of the Yishuv and in the Zionist security apparatus. The chapter focuses on several individuals and demonstrates how they used their Jewish-Arab identity and familiarity with Arab culture to cross geographical as well as identity borders. These crossings can also be viewed as acts of mediation, though of a very different nature than the previous forms of mediation discussed in earlier chapters.

By examining different spheres of interaction between Oriental Jews and Arabs, the book brings to the fore a set of questions and issues to consider and offers a new dimension to the vast literature on the Jewish-Arab conflict and on Jewish-Arab relations in Mandatory Palestine. The variety of Hebrew, Arabic, and English sources that we used for the analysis, as well as our focus on numerous individuals, allow us to present a range of voices and perspectives from the Sephardi and Oriental Jewish communities. The sources include memoirs, autobiographies, newspapers published in Hebrew and Arabic in Mandatory Palestine and the Arab world, institutional records of many Sephardi and Oriental organizations, and documents about the political debates that took place in the Sephardi and Oriental Jewish communities in Palestine. They all testify to the diverse and rich discussion that took place during the Mandatory years not only about Jewish-Arab relations but also about the role and position that Sephardi and Oriental Jews should play vis-à-vis the Arabs on the one hand, and the Zionist movement on the other hand. As the book argues, this discussion was not confined solely to Palestine, but crossed geographical boundaries and connected Palestinian Jews to other communities in the Middle East.

The attempt to present the links between the Palestinian case and its Middle Eastern context is also what led to the cooperation between the two historians who have coauthored this book. A clear historiographical and sometimes disciplinary split has existed for years between two fields of scholarship: research on the experience and narrative of Jews and research on those of Arabs. The latter generally remained in the hands of scholars specializing in Middle Eastern studies, and the two fields were usually separate.[36] This division reflects a wider disconnection between the study of the history of the Yishuv and Zionism, on the one hand, and the study of the Arabs in Palestine and the Middle East, on the other hand.[37] Our choice to cooperate as coauthors reflects our strong commitment to an interdisciplinary approach to the study of Palestine, Israel, and the conflict between them and to the need to examine the local case of Palestine in its regional historical context.

This book does not offer a monolithic perspective. On the contrary, it aims to present the multiple and sometimes contradictory perspectives on the complex and delicate issue of relations between the Oriental neighbors (Jews and Arabs) offered by Sephardi and Oriental Jews. It highlights the role of a community that has hardly been mentioned in the canonic Israeli narrative, while "bringing to the fore the voices of those who remained on the margins of history."[38]

ONE

═══

The Road Not Taken

*The Ethnic Problem and
the Arab Question*

═══

The entry of the British army into Jerusalem on December 11, 1917, and the surrender of the Ottoman Empire approximately one year later signaled the end of a period of great despair for the civilian population of Palestine. During the war years, Arabs and Jews alike had experienced grave economic difficulties and political persecution. A financial crisis, exacerbated by a plague of locusts, was accompanied by the imposition of political and military measures by the Ottomans that included the expulsion and exile of both Jews and Arabs. The end of World War I also marked the changing political and social status of the Sephardim and the Oriental Jews in Palestine, from a position of relative superiority as recognized Jewish Millet during the Ottoman period to one of a community that needed to struggle for political status and power.

This chapter will focus on this new political and social status and the ideological position of the leadership of the Sephardi and Oriental Jewish communities in Palestine toward the solution of the Jewish-Arab conflict. The political position of this leadership was influenced by its claims of ongoing neglect and discrimination on the part of the hegemonic Zionist leadership toward the Sephardi and Oriental Jews on social, political, and economic issues. Simultaneously, by presenting their historical role as mediators, the Sephardi and Oriental leaders tried to affirm their loyalty to the Zionist movement and the national project and to contribute to the political resolution of the Arab Question.

This chapter will first examine the role and work of the Association of the Pioneers of the East, and will then examine the different political proposals and attempts made by various political and intellectual leaders among the Sephardi and Oriental Jewish communities to address the evolving Jewish-Arab conflict.

It will also discuss how prominent Palestinian leaders perceived the Sephardim and Oriental Jews and assess whether the Palestinians viewed local Jews as a possible alternative to the hegemonic Zionist leaders. As we will see below, the connection between loyalty to the Jewish national movement and serving as mediators was very clear in the formal political activities of the Sephardi and Oriental Jewish elite. Although the Sephardi and Oriental Jews did not present a unified political program for the resolution of the conflict between Jews and Arabs in Palestine, they still viewed their role as unique because of their historic, cultural, and linguistic affinity to Arab culture and society.

National Awakening: Pioneers of the East and Loyal Zionists

On February 20, 1918, some three months after the British army entered Jerusalem, the Association of the Pioneers of the East held its founding meeting in the city.[1] Graduates of the Alliance Israélite Universelle schools and of the Hebrew Gymnasium in Jerusalem, the members of this new organization viewed themselves as Bney Ha'aretz who were in a position to serve as a bridge between the old and new Yishuv. The forming of the association did not only reflect the emergence of a cadre of young political leaders who were beginning to gain prominence in the Sephardi and Oriental communities, including in relation to Jewish-Arab relations. It also signaled the ongoing presence of a circle of Sephardi, Mizrahi, and Ashkenazi intellectuals who, under the leadership of David Yellin, had been active in Jerusalem since the late nineteenth century. The members of this circle, who viewed the Hebrew cultural renaissance as an important component of the Jewish national movement and their own identity, advocated for an ongoing dialogue between Jewish and Arab cultures.[2]

In *Noladetem Ziyonim*, Itzhak Bezalel discussed Yosef Gorny's description of four approaches to the Arab Question that were prevalent in the Yishuv toward the end of the Ottoman period. Those approaches were the altruistic approach, the separatist approach, the approach of the Labor movement, and a neutral liberal approach that Gorny argued characterized some of the leaders of the Zionist Executive. Bezalel suggested a fifth approach, which he argued was unique and prevalent among the Sephardi and Oriental communities in Palestine. In this way, Bezalel positioned the Sephardi and Oriental elite as a key player in Zionist activity during the period before World War I. Bezalel described their position regarding the Arab question as one characterized by tolerance and as an attempt to serve as a bridge for interaction between Jews and Arabs. According to Bezalel, the unique aspect of the Sephardi and Oriental leaders' activities was the adoption of a political position that sought to avoid taking sides in the evolving political divisions between the right and left wing in the Yishuv. Instead, this position emphasized the unique identity of the Sephardim and the Oriental Jews as natives of Palestine who were thoroughly and intimately familiar with the local Jewish and Arab society and felt fully part of both Hebrew and Arab cultures.[3] Indeed, this position was expressed in the work and ideology of the Association of the Pioneers of the East.

Headed by David Avissar, the association was originally called the Association of Young Sephardim in Jerusalem. The adoption of the new name in October 1919 reflected the association's emphasis on its commitment to improving its members' status in Mandatory Palestine and enhancing the integration of the Sephardim and the Oriental Jews in the national and public institutions of the Yishuv.[4] The Association of the Pioneers of the East, which at its peak numbered 300 members, defined its goal as being "to raise the spiritual level of the Oriental Jewish public (*yehudey hamizrah*), to involve Oriental Judaism (*hayahdut hamizrahit*) in the work of national revival, and to unite the Jews of the Land of Israel into a single community."[5] The association's emphasis on cultural and educational activities as a way of raising the level of national consciousness among Sephardi and Oriental Jews was reflected in its offering of evening classes on Hebrew and of lectures on aspects of Jewish history and Hebrew culture.[6] These activities took place at the association's branches around the country, as well as at its central branch in Jerusalem, which was active until the association suspended its activities in 1929.

During the preparations for the first elections to the Assembly of Representatives of the Yishuv in 1920, the Association of the Pioneers of the East joined forces with the Council of the Sephardi Community in Jerusalem (Va'ad Ha'eda Has'fardit Beyerushlaim). The two bodies jointly founded the General Organization of Sephardi Jews (Hahistadrut Haklalit shel Hayehudim Hasfaradim), which advocated a national and spiritual revival among the Sephardim, especially in terms of encouraging Zionist activity and Hebrew education, while emphasizing the need for good relations between Jews and Arabs.[7] Despite the similarity between the goals and activities of the association and the council, they maintained their distinct identities, and the association remained dominated by members of the younger, educated generation. Its leaders were also involved in the organization and activities of the World Confederation of Sephardi Jews (Hahitahdut Ha'olamit shel Hayehudim Hasfaradim).[8]

Advocating for the national revival of Sephardi and Oriental Jews was one of the recurring activities of the Association of the Pioneers of the East, and characteristic of its members' unique form and vision of Zionism.[9] In October 1922, for example, Moshe Atiash (a teacher, a native of Salonika, and a member of the association, he was also the chief secretary of the Yishuv's National Council [Va'ad Leumi], beginning in 1929), described the Sephardim as those who are "unfamiliar with Ahad Ha'am, and barely familiar with Herzl. They have not read modern Hebrew literature and they only have limited knowledge of the Zionist movement." Atiash acknowledged that this group had "a profound sense of natural love of the homeland, but still lacks the corpus of national ideas that the Zionist movement has created over the past 25 years and more."[10] Similar claims were made throughout the Mandatory period. As this chapter demonstrates, such allegations influenced the way in which the leaders of the Sephardi and Oriental Jewish communities in Palestine presented their political and ideological positions in general, and those regarding the Arab Question in particular. Indeed, the desire to avoid defining the Association of the Pioneers of the East as a political party with a clear ideological position and to present it instead as an arbiter and mediator between the various political forces in the Yishuv as well as between Arabs and Jews sparked a profound crisis among the Sephardi and Oriental leaders and raised questions regarding their communities' national and cultural identity and their loyalty to the Zionist movement. The evolution of the Arab-Jewish conflict contributed to this crisis.

Is Every Jew a Zionist? Oriental Jews in the Eyes of Palestinian Arabs

The role of Sephardi and Oriental Jews as mediators and the doubts expressed about their loyalty to the Zionist movement are interrelated. These doubts were felt not only by Zionist leaders and political activists, as will be discussed below, but also by some prominent Palestinian national leaders. Starting in the last years of Ottoman rule, the latter often distinguished between the new Ashkenazi immigrants (who kept their foreign citizenship instead of adopting Ottoman citizenship and who did not speak Arabic) and the local Jews (including the Oriental Jews, who were sometimes referred to as Arab Jews). This distinction was shared by many local Jews. It was based on the notion that Palestine was a shared homeland for its indigenous people, Jews and Arabs alike, and the fact that Palestinian Arabs viewed the Ashkenazi Zionists, mainly the new Russian immigrants (*moskobim*), as foreigners. Related to this distinction and to the one made between Zionism and Judaism by Palestinian Arab leaders was the question of whether the local Jews fully adhered to the Zionist ideology—a question that was raised to create a notion of disunity in the Zionist movement. These issues were discussed in different contexts during the Mandatory years.[11]

In July 1921, a delegation of Palestinian Arabs departed for Europe, headed by Musa Kazim al-Husseini, the chair of the Arab Executive Committee.[12] The delegation met in London with Winston Churchill, then the British colonial secretary, and on Churchill's initiative the members of the delegation met with Chaim Weizmann, the president of the World Zionist Organization, on November 29, 1921. In interviews in the British press, the members of the delegation emphasized their opposition to the Balfour Declaration and to Jewish immigration to Palestine. They quoted Weizmann's statement that "Palestine would become as Jewish as England is English" as evidence of the Zionists' true intentions. Regarding the relations between Jews and Arabs, al-Husseini commented that "the Arabs have never opposed the Jews. We live peacefully and happily with the Jews and there are no grounds to think that this will not be the case in the future."[13] This is an example of the tendency to paint an idyllic picture of Jewish-Arab relations during the late Ottoman period, before World War I and the Balfour Declaration. In this particular instance, the specific claim was that the Sephardi and Oriental Jews opposed Zionism and supported the Palestinian Arabs' position on the future of the country.

The comments made by the Palestinian-Arab delegates were reported to the Yishuv Executive of the National Council at its meeting on August 10, 1921, which illustrated the strong impact of the Arab claims on the Yishuv.[14] The Association of the Pioneers of the East, the General Organization of Sephardi Jews, the Council of the Sephardi Community in Jerusalem, and the Sephardi Chief Rabbinate in Palestine published a joint telegram they had sent to the World Zionist Organization, which was meeting in Carlsbad at the time.[15] The leaders of the Sephardi and Oriental Jewish communities in Palestine rejected the claims that the members of their communities opposed Zionism, protested against the "libel of national betrayal," and declared: "The Sephardim in the Land of Israel vehemently protest the suggestion that they support the Arab delegation. They are completely united with the remainder of Jewry in the Land of Israel in demanding the realization of the promises that have been given to create a Jewish National Home in the Land of Israel."[16]

During this public campaign, the Association of the Pioneers of the East together with other Oriental and Sephardi organizations organized protests in dozens of synagogues around Palestine. Following the gatherings, a statement was published protesting "vehemently against the reports disseminated by the Arab delegation that Sephardi Jewry in the Land of Israel is on its side."[17] The Association of the Pioneers of the East also responded separately to the claims made by the Arab delegation, suggesting that the delegates' intention was to stir up distrust within the Yishuv. However, the association then expressed its confidence that "the revival of Sephardi Jewry in the Arab countries will serve as a model and as proof that the two peoples, the Hebrew people and the Arab people, are brothers in race and can cooperate in order to develop the ancient Land."[18] A similar response was published originally in the English press and translated by Shlomo Kalmi, a member of the editorial board of the newspaper *Doar Hayom* who was also serving at the time as the secretary of Keren Hayesod (the World Zionist Organization's Foundation Fund) in London: "As a Sephardi Jew born in Jerusalem who had lived in the Land of Israel for many years . . . I can promise therefore that there is not a single Sephardi Jew in the country who opposes the Zionist idea."[19] Kalmi, who was involved in arranging diplomatic meetings between Weizmann and Arab leaders following World War I, added in his public letter that the Sephardi Jews in the Land of Israel, and in the Middle East in general, were Zionists and at the same time longed to live in peace and friendship with the Arabs.

The reactions of the Sephardi and Oriental Jewish organizations and leaders to the claims of the Arab delegation were reported extensively in the Palestinian press. The Palestinian newspaper *al-Karmil*, for example, declared: "Let the public not be deceived into thinking that the Arab-Jews are on the side of their [Arab] brothers. The Arabs should learn the meaning of unity and mutual trust from the various sections of the Jews."[20] The newspaper *Filastin* reminded its readers:

> The Sephardi Jews found refuge in Palestine and other Ottoman lands, when they were persecuted in Spain and the other western countries. The Ottoman Empire received them with open arms and did not distinguish between them and the indigenous people. We thought these Jews are our brothers. . . . Those Jews were known during the Ottoman rule for their opposition to the Zionist principle. . . . [The Sephardi response] makes us believe that eventually, every Jew is a Zionist. They ultimately align themselves with the winning side, the Zionists. Once they [the Sephardim] realized that the Zionists control the country, they turned away from the Arabs, and joined their rivals, from their own race, in order to oppose the indigenous residents and their ambitions.[21]

Some of the Palestinian leaders continued to discuss the special status of Arab Jews as an inherent part of Palestine, as well as the effects of the Zionist immigration on Jewish-Arab coexistence in the country. In February 26, 1922, the newspaper *al-Sabah* published Jamal al-Husseini's call to local Jews, on behalf of the Arab Executive Committee, titled "Come to Us." Al-Husseini, then the secretary of the Arab Executive Committee and a prominent politician, was quoted in *Ha'aretz* as writing:

> To our Jewish fellow natives of the homeland (*bney moladetenu hayehudim*), to those who were cheated by Zionism, to those who understand the goals and damage of Zionism—to them we extend our hands today and call: Come to us! We are your friends! You share the same rights and duties in our mother (*imenu*) Palestine as we do . . . because you and we are the sons of the same homeland, whether the Zionists like it or not. . . . Experience shows that the latest events demonstrate that our era is the era of nationalism, and not of religion, and that nationalism forms a stronger bond than religious bonds. . . . We are sorry for your persecution by the Zionists, for the denial of your rights, freedom, and ability to explore your goals and aspirations. We consider this to be an offense against the honor of the Palestinian nation, whose sons you are. Hence, your Muslim and Christian brothers strongly protest against these actions, extend their arms, and call you: come to us!"[22]

In 1923, al-Husseini again issued an appeal on behalf of the Arab Executive Committee to the native Jews (*al-yahud al-wataniin*). He repeated his appeal from the previous year and urged "the Jews of Palestine who lived with us before the war in peace and friendship" not to be misled by the false dream of Zionism, but to stand together with the Arabs in their demand to nullify the Balfour Declaration. "It is our duty as neighbors to warn the Jews who lived with us before the war and loved our neighborliness to get away from Zionism," wrote al-Husseini. He urged native Jews to join the Arab's boycott of the election for the legislative council, which was promoted by the British Mandatory rule but ended in failure. According to al-Husseini, if "Palestinian Jews" joined the Arab boycott, that would "bring back the friendship that has been lost, and erase the hatred that has been created."[23] As will be discussed later in this chapter, al-Husseini would make similar comments in different circumstances throughout the Mandatory years. Similar comments were also made during failed attempts in the early 1920s by the Palestinian national leaders to get local Jews to sign petitions against Zionism.[24]

The local Sephardi and Oriental Jews were placed in a tough position. They were asked to choose between having a local territorial identity—as part of a joint homeland for Jews, Christians, and Muslims—and a Jewish ethno-national identity. The doubts regarding their loyalty and adherence to Zionism highlighted the local Jews' position of otherness vis-à-vis the European, hegemonic, Zionist circles and made them feel obliged to constantly apologize for their own belief that they could be both loyal Zionists and mediators between Jews and Arabs. They also felt defensive about other accusations from prominent figures in the Yishuv and some European leaders, who questioned how loyal the Sephardim and the Oriental Jews were to the Zionist movement.

Defensive Politics: Sephardi-Oriental Zionism and the Arabs

In October 1920, the Hebrew press reported on some remarks made by Louis-Ernest Dubois, a Catholic cardinal who was appointed archbishop of Paris at the end of the year. The cardinal noted that during his visit to Jerusalem, the chief rabbi told him unequivocally that he was opposed to Zionism.[25] In his effort to gain supporters for the Vatican's opposition to the Balfour Declaration, the French cardinal thus embroiled the Chief Rabbinate in Palestine in the debate. In response, Ashkenazi Chief Rabbi Avraham Yitzhak Hacohen Kook issued a public statement declaring that he had never met the French cardinal. Certainly, Kook added, "there can be no person in Jerusalem who can justly call himself a rabbi who has any attitude of opposition to Zionism."[26] Hakham Bashi Nissim Danon, who had served as the Sephardi chief rabbi until the end of 1918, confirmed that he had met a senior French cleric together with two Ashkenazi rabbis who were members of the Ashkenazi Jerusalem City Committee, but Danon denied the comments attributed to him by the cardinal. Danon declared that no Jew would speak ill of Zionism. The two Ashkenazi Haredi rabbis who accompanied Danon denied even meeting Cardinal Dubois.[27]

In August 1921, a new public storm erupted following comments by Raymond Poincaré, who had been the French president between 1913 and 1920 and who would be appointed prime minister in 1922. In an interview published in a French newspaper, Poincaré claimed that the Sephardi Jews in Palestine were opposed to the Zionist movement and aligned with the Arabs. He also declared that he had received letters from Sephardim in Palestine expressing their opposition to Jewish immigration.[28] In response to Poincaré's comments, the Association of the Pioneers of the East published an open letter warning against attempts to portray the Sephardim in Palestine as betraying the Zionist ideal: "Sephardi Jewry was the first to put in place solid foundations for the Hebrew national revival in the Land of Israel. It has suffered lovingly to this day the ills of the Land." After emphasizing the founding role of the Sephardim in the emergence of Zionism and the Jewish community in Palestine, the authors of the letter emphasized their support of the Balfour Declaration: "We, the Sephardi Jewish natives of this country, are bound by a profound bond to the World Zionist Organization and support all its aspirations, which are our aspirations, and its paths, which are our paths, as manifested in the Balfour Declaration and the San Remo decision."[29] Why did the Sephardi and Oriental Jews feel the need to prove their loyalty to Zionism, in light of accusations made about them from Arab and European figures? The answer to this question has to do with the changing position of Sephardi and Oriental Jews in the Yishuv.

"I found it astonishing how the Arabs, with whom we had lived peaceably for centuries, had the audacity to throw themselves on an entire community whose sole desire was to create and to build, and to beat it mercilessly. I was at a loss and did not know where to turn."[30] These were the words used by Yosef Eliyahu Chelouche—a prominent Sephardi Jewish leader and entrepreneur who was one of the founders of Tel Aviv—in his memoirs to describe his reaction to the violent events that erupted in Jaffa in May 1921. As a native Jew, Chelouche attempted to respond to intensifying tension by means that were customary and familiar to him from the Ottoman period—namely, arranging a meeting between Jewish, Christian, and Muslim notables in Jaffa. However, in the new reality of 1921 and in light of the struggle for power in the changing political realities of the Yishuv and the formation of its national institutions, he encountered mistrust not only from his Arab counterparts, but also from the Yishuv leadership.

Indeed, Chelouche's belief in the ability of the politics of notables to bridge the gap between Arabs and Jews was a result of his own background. Born in Jaffa in 1870 to a family of merchants of Baghdadi and Algerian origin, he grew up in an Arab environment and became active in public affairs. As he described it, "I acquired a love for my Arab brethren and I mingled with them, whether in business or in their joys and sorrows."[31] However, the profound changes that occurred during the Mandate period and the deterioration of Jewish-Arab relations impaired the status of the Sephardi notables and their ability to serve as mediators between the two peoples, as is apparent from Chelouche's own story.

Chelouche held various positions, serving as a member of the city councils of Jaffa and Tel Aviv. He saw Sephardi-Oriental Zionism as a bridge for rapprochement between Jews and Arabs and as the adoption of a political approach that did not distinguish between a traditional Jewish identity—rooted in the religious bond with the Land of Israel—and the Zionist ideal. In the final chapters of his memoirs he criticized Labor Zionism: "I am tired of those who prioritize their Zionism over their Judaism, in contrast to us locals, who see nationalism within Judaism."[32] Chelouche's claim that the Sephardi and Oriental Jews had combined Jewish religious belief with practical Zionism even before the beginning of Zionist immigration and were deeply familiar with their Arab neighbors was part of an ideological position that can be termed Sephardi-Oriental Zionism.

Indeed, similar to Chelouche's position, Sephardi-Oriental Zionism is presented as distinct from the other forms of secular Zionism, which developed in Europe, and from religious Zionism. Itzhak Bezalel described Sephardi-Oriental Zionism as different from Ashkenazi Zionism in its goals, characteristics, and vision. The former was a type of Zionism that had developed based on a belief in religious redemption and that signaled a continuation of, and not a rupture with, Jewish tradition. Bezalel also stressed the importance of the Semitic identity to this form of Zionism, the existence of Sephardi-Oriental Jews in the country before the Zionist immigration, and their close familiarity with the East and Arabs.[33] It was a form of Zionism that was closer to practical Zionism than to political Zionism, and that adopted a positive and peaceful attitude toward Arab society and culture: it could be termed inclusive Zionism.[34] The ideological implications and manifestations of Sephardi-Oriental Zionism will be discussed below.

Chelouche planned to travel to Egypt in 1923 with Shmuel Aghrabiya, another member of the Jaffa City Council. The purpose of the trip was to gauge the mood at an assembly of Muslim dignitaries that had been convened to discuss the idea of installing Emir Abdullah as the ruler of an Arab federation, which would include Palestine. The planned journey led to rumors in the Zionist Executive suggesting that Chelouche was disloyal to the Zionist ideal. In his memoirs, he recalls: "When I heard this, I almost lost my mind. I could not forgive this insult to me and my friend, the slander leveled against us and against the Sephardim in general to besmirch our name. . . . I was born in Zion and I have no other homeland; those who slander me were born and raised in Exile."[35] Chelouche chose not to name those who spread accusations against him, but his words referred to a political debate that took place in 1922 on the representation of the Sephardim in the National Council.[36] A letter from Eliyahu Berlin to Yosef Sprinzak sheds more light on the deep offense felt by Chelouche and others: "There is considerable foment among the Sephardim, who now feel themselves to be more offended than ever by their exclusion from the National Council. It has even gotten to the point that they have heard veiled threats that some of them may ally themselves with the Arabs, with the Mufti, and so forth. There are also those who claim that were it not for Zionism they would be living on good terms with the Arabs as had been the case until now."[37]

These allegations echoed perceptions that had also been apparent toward the end of the Ottoman era and during the British military rule.[38] From its early days, Zionist discourse had touched on the subject of the Zionist attitude toward the Orient and the positions presented by Sephardim who advocated bonds between Zionism and the Orient, between the Jewish and Arab national movements, and between Hebrew and Arab cultures. Historians have examined in depth the different positions that could be found in the Zionist movement regarding the integration of Zionism into the Orient, the cultural identity of the Jewish national movement, and its affinity to European and/or Arab culture.[39] As Moshe Behar and Zvi Ben-Dor Benite have recently shown, this trend continued during the Mandatory period.[40] Despite the escalating conflict, Sephardi and Oriental Jewish intellectuals, as we will see in chapter 3, continued to advocate the integration of Zionism into the Orient and the blending of Hebrew and Arab cultures. A similar position was presented by European Ashkenazi Zionists—especially by some of the German Jewish scholars of Islam, who were among those who established the Hebrew University in Jerusalem and its School of Oriental Studies. However, the cultural and social affinity between the Oriental Jews and the Arabs added an additional aspect to their call for Jewish-Arab affinity. This cultural and social affinity was clear to Zionist representatives, who objected to the idea of an integration of Zionism into the Levant or to acultural Jewish-Arab integration. It is not surprising that those in the Zionist movement who negated the Jewish-Arab identity used vocabulary borrowed from the discussion about Jewish emancipation in Europe, such as the argument that a Jewish-Arab affinity might lead to the assimilation of the Oriental Jews among Arabs.[41]

The debate about the Zionist credentials of the Sephardi and Oriental Jews extended beyond the borders of Mandatory Palestine, reaching into the Jewish communities in the Arab countries. In June 1924, for example, following the murder of Jacob Israël de Haan, one of the main figures of the Jerusalem Haredi community who was murdered by members of the paramilitary group Haganah, the important Egyptian newspaper *al-Muqattam* reported on Arab-Jewish relations in Palestine and on the status of the Oriental Jews. The article discussed de Haan's opposition to Zionism, explaining that he had realized the damage the Zionists were causing to the Palestinian people in general and to Oriental Jews in particular. The newspaper emphasized de Haan's observation that a distinction should be made between Zionist Jews and Oriental Jews and added: "The Jews of the East are our brothers, our neighbors, and the sons of our homeland; they have been our brothers for many years and they are our partners in good times and bad. They have never been tempted by the ideas and aspirations of the extremist Zionists."[42]

In addition to the Arabic press, Arabic-language Jewish newspapers published in the Middle East also discussed the status of Oriental Jews in Palestine, focusing in particular on their exclusion from senior positions in the leadership of the Zionist movement. This discussion was closely related to the criticism voiced by some Jewish journalists and intellectuals of Zionist policies toward the Palestinian national movement. As will be discussed in chapter 3, newspapers in Palestine and the Arab world served as forums for lively debates that discussed these interrelated issues. Newspapers such as the Beiruti *al-'Alam al-Isra'ili*, the Iraqi *al-Misbah*, and the Egyptian *Israël* all participated in debates and discussions that tied together the discrimination faced by Oriental Jews in Palestine and the failure of the Zionist movement to take advantage of their potential to serve as a bridge between Jews and Arabs and to promote understanding between the two peoples.[43]

Indeed, the Jewish and Arab press in Palestine and elsewhere in the Middle East was also an important way of keeping Sephardi and Oriental Jews in Palestine in contact with other Jewish communities in the Middle East. Such contacts took place also in the framework of the World Confederation of Sephardi Jews. The confederation issued newsletters in various languages that were published in the local Jewish press and sent emissaries to the Jewish communities in the Middle East to promote the organization's work and hold public meetings. The confederation also collected donations for the Zionist funds such as Keren Hayesod, sent Hebrew teachers to work in communities around the Middle East, and published information about developments in Palestine and opportunities for immigration. It thus served as a pressure and interest group that sought to encourage the Sephardim to increase their influence on the World Zionist Organization, particularly in the allocation of immigration certificates and funds and the appointment of officials. Delegations from the confederation that visited the Jewish communities in Arab and Muslim countries had a clear impact on the ways in which the Arabic-language Jewish press covered developments in Palestine.[44]

In addition to claiming not to be involved in the policy of the Zionist Executive regarding the Arab question, the leaders of the Sephardi and Oriental Jewish communities in Palestine voiced demands, such as for changes in the allocation of funds to education and welfare projects, the distribution of immigration certificates, and the allocation of positions in the Zionist institutions. In particular, leaders argued that young Sephardi and Oriental Jews found it difficult to secure jobs in the two Zionist institutions Keren Kayemet (The Jewish National Fund) and Keren Hayesod. These complaints were raised throughout the Mandatory period in various forums, including Zionist Congresses, sessions of the Assembly of Representatives of the Yishuv, and annual conferences of the Sephardi organizations.[45]

With these issues in mind, in the summer of 1928 a meeting took place between representatives of the World Confederation of Sephardi Jews and officials from the Zionist Executive, Keren Kayemet, and Keren Hayesod. One of the goals of the meeting was to examine the claims made by the Zionist Executive that the Sephardim were operating against the Zionist Executive. The officials from the Zionist Executive were gravely concerned at the damage the allegations had caused to the fundraising work of the Zionist campaigns launched by Keren Hayesod among the Jewish communities in the Arab countries, particularly in Egypt. The meeting focused on trying to reach a middle ground between Sephardi and Ashkenazi Jews, while integrating the Sephardim into the process of nation building. It demonstrated the connection between economic considerations and the inability of the Sephardim to influence the budgets of the Zionist movement, which led in turn to fierce disagreements and accusations of anti-Zionism. At the meeting, Menachem Ussishkin, a prominent Zionist leader and president of the Jewish National Fund, described the Sephardim as apathetic about the public and national life of the Yishuv. In contrast, Meir Laniado—a Sephardi activist, attorney, and one of the main leaders of the Association of Pioneers of the East, who served as president of the Council of the Sephardi Community in Jerusalem in 1932–33—accused Keren Hayesod of waging a propaganda war claiming that the Sephardi association was anti-Zionist and separatist. Laniado added: "A national home must be shared by all of us, or it should not exist at all."[46]

Integral Ideology: Sephardi Politics and Jewish-Arab Relations

Despite their fierce criticism of the Zionist leadership and national institutions, the Sephardi and Oriental leaders held varying positions regarding the political future of Palestine.[47] Their diverse views represented the range of political and ideological streams in the Zionist movement at the time. For example, the Sephardi and Oriental leadership included members of the Hamizrahi religious Zionist movement such as Chief Rabbi Ya'acov Meir and Rabbi Ben-Zion Meir Hai Uziel, who succeeded Meir as chief rabbi in 1939.[48] Several members of the Sephardi and Oriental Jewish leadership joined the centrist General Zionist Party, while others—such as Avissar, Yehuda Burla, and Eliyahu (Lulu) Hacarmeli—joined the Labor Zionist Mapai. Another group, led by David Abulafia, who served as president of the Council of the Sephardi Community in Jerusalem in the late 1930s, identified with the Revisionist Party. The contrast between unified action in the communal organizations and diverse political orientations encouraged debates among Sephardi and Oriental activists about the relationship between ethnic identity and nationalism. As Pnina Morag-Talmon has shown, the dominant principle behind ethnic organization and identity was that of national unity, and this principle determined the activists' specific political and cultural actions in the political system of the Yishuv. The activists' debates also addressed the question of whether the Sephardim had a unique position on the Arab Question.[49] Even though Sephardi leaders expressed a variety of opinions on the Arab Question, in internal discussions and public statements the main Sephardi organizations expressed their belief in the importance of Jewish-Arab rapprochement and their potential as mediators between the two people.

The view of the Association of the Pioneers of the East on Jewish-Arab relations was the dominant one among Sephardi and Oriental Jews at the beginning of the Mandatory period and until the riots of 1929. The work plan prepared by the association's branch in Tel Aviv in December 1924 illustrates the organization's guiding ideology. The main goal of young Sephardi activists was to increase the involvement of their community in the national and public institutions of the Yishuv. Secondary to that was an emphasis on the importance of promoting the study of Hebrew and Jewish history among the Sephardi and Oriental Jews themselves. The plan also mentioned an intention to send Hebrew teachers to Jewish communities in the Middle East and to publish a weekly or monthly journal on cultural affairs. An interesting section of the plan advocated a cultural union of Hebrew and Arab intellectuals, with the goal of promoting the study of both Hebrew and Arabic language and literature.[50] In this respect, the association remained faithful to an approach that had been prominent during the final years of Ottoman rule, which considered the cultural sphere to be one that promoted peaceful relations and mutual understanding between Jews and Arabs. This was accompanied by recognition of the needs for economic cooperation and joint commercial ventures. The emphasis on Jewish-Arab cooperation and association in the cultural and economic spheres was also reflected in Avissar's proposed solution to the Jewish-Arab conflict, made in November 1929, following the August riots. Avissar had been born in Hebron and had worked as director of the Sephardi Talmud Torah in the Old City of Jerusalem and as a teacher at the Alliance School. In addition to serving as the chairman of the Association of the Pioneers of the East, he later represented the Labor Zionist party Achdut Ha'avoda in the National Council.[51] In his proposal Avissar noted that Sephardim had been claiming for years that it was possible to reach an agreement with the Arabs. He argued that it was important to present a clear political program to the Arabs to clarify the true intentions of Zionism. Avissar's position was that a single, joint homeland for Jews and Arabs should be established in Palestine on both sides of the Jordan River. His plan advocated a joint constitution that would lead to an independent, free, and secure life for both peoples, and that would be approved by the peoples of the Orient and the League of Nations. Avissar sought to ensure that both peoples would enjoy national self-determination through the egalitarian allocation of governmental powers and the autonomy of each people to nurture its own life and to develop the country for the benefit of all its inhabitants, without fear of expropriation. Avissar's proposal thus effectively incorporated the concept of national autonomy into a federative political structure, while recognizing the potential for integration and cooperation between the two autonomous entities that would share a single country. Regarding the name given to the country, Avissar rejected the use of the name Palestine and recognized that the name Israel—though sacred to both Jews and Arabs—would provoke disagreement. His plan proposed that each people have its own national flag and anthem.[52]

Avissar criticized the World Zionist Organization, which he argued had abandoned the use of propaganda to influence the Arab public: "All our work and activities have taken place above the heads of the masses, and we have failed to take into account the Arab community that has been present in this land for 1,300 years."[53] Referring to the riots of 1929, Avissar added: "I would not be exaggerating if I said that one of the reasons for the riotous outbreaks was offense at our failure to take them [the Arabs] into account and to negotiate with them as we set out to build the Land following the Balfour Declaration.... We must now turn to the East and engage in vigorous propaganda activities." Like supporters of the central stream in the Zionist movement, Avissar paternalistically chose to emphasize the Jews' economic contribution to the country, noting that the Jews' return to the Land of Israel had saved the country from desolation, revived the spirit of the Arab people, and improved their life significantly: "The Arab people will eventually recognize that it is the Hebrew people that is returning to its inheritance. It is coming to its fellows in race, faith, history, language, and hope. It is coming to the residents of the Land of Israel, in whose veins much Jewish blood flows. Not by might nor by power, but by spirit alone: by the spirit of Hebrew morality to create a kingdom of justice and peace that will be a model to all the nations."[54]

Avissar's plan has some similarities to other programs for the resolution of the Jewish-Arab conflict that were presented following the 1929 riots, such as the binational program of Brit Shalom and David Ben-Gurion's federalist option.[55] Avissar's program stressed the cultural, social, and economic links between Jews and Arabs, and he demanded that the Zionist leaders recognize the importance of having Jews study Arabic language, culture, and history. He had already highlighted these points in the early years of the Mandate, when he encouraged the leaders of the National Council to take advantage of the knowledge and familiarity of Oriental Jews with the Arabic language and culture.

One can learn more about Avissar's ideology from his 1923 plan, titled "The Arab Question."[56] In this plan he discussed the claim that Zionism had had a negative impact on Jewish-Arab relations. He explained that Muslims had tolerated the Jews only because the latter had constituted a minority. It was true that the Muslims had not persecuted the Jews as a nation, but as individuals Jews had certainly suffered under Ottoman rule. He claimed that following the Balfour Declaration and the violent events of 1920 and 1921, the Sephardim "have always lived in brotherhood and friendship with the Arabs, and it is only foreigners who have created conflict between the two peoples." Avissar argued that through the adoption of this argument, the Sephardim "sought to prove the racial and cultural affinity between the Jewish and Arab peoples and the possibility of creating coexistence in the Land of Israel." Nevertheless, this implied that the Balfour Declaration had damaged the relations between Jews and Arabs. Avissar believed that successful coexistence between the two peoples could be promoted by political activists, through cultural and scientific work, and by encouraging joint Jewish-Arab economic activity. In practical terms, he urged the Zionist Executive to publish a newspaper in Arabic and to develop joint economic projects. The importance he attached to the cultural realm was also reflected in his recommendation that Jews study and understand the history of the Arabs, and a parallel recommendation to encourage Arabs to study Hebrew culture.[57]

The manifesto of the Association of the Pioneers of the East similarly advocated cultural integration, mutual spiritual enrichment, and understanding between the two Semitic cultures. These views reflected an approach that was dominant during most of the Mandatory period and that saw the cultural and educational spheres as key components in resolving the conflict and securing peace between the two peoples. In some cases this approach focused on promoting Hebrew-Arab cultural integration, while in others the goal was to have the

Arab and Jewish peoples respect each other's culture. This Sephardi-Oriental Zionist promotion of the idea of social and cultural inclusion of Palestinian Arabs was one of the motivations behind Avissar's recommendations to encourage joint cultural activities and mutual language studies and to establish Arabic-language newspapers.[58]

The Association of the Pioneers of the East ceased to exist in 1929 due to disillusionment about and frustration with the internal struggles in the Sephardi and Oriental leadership and the inability to break through the ethnic barrier and engage in national, cultural, and education action. The sensitive political situation and position of the Sephardim led to the development of a political debate in the Yishuv before the elections to the third Assembly of Representatives in January 1931. The Sephardi leaders in Jerusalem demanded that places for Sephardi representatives be reserved in the Assembly. This was done, but the result was fierce criticism from the National Council Executive and the Labor Zionist movement, which argued that the Sephardi organizations were acting in a divisive and sectarian manner. As a consequence, some of the Sephardi leaders preferred to run in the elections on Sephardi lists affiliated with the main political parties. The elections once again put the issue of ethnic representation on the public agenda, together with accusations that Sephardi separatism was jeopardizing the unity of the Jewish community as a whole.[59]

As noted above, the criticism of the Sephardi leadership voiced by some Zionist political leaders was based on the continued claim that the Sephardim were adopting a separatist approach and refraining from involvement in issues that went beyond their narrow communal interests. It was also argued that the Sephardi leaders were encouraging ethnic divisions in Jewish society. The accusations leveled against the Sephardi leadership also served as a tool in the internal political struggle in the Yishuv. As Hanna Herzog noted, the communal organization of the Sephardim was defined by the Labor movement as separatist and was identified interchangeably with the old Yishuv and with the right wing of the political spectrum. All of this served to delegitimize the Sephardim's political ideology when their interests conflicted with those of the Histadrut and, in particular, those of Mapai. [60]

Accusations that the Sephardim lacked national consciousness were made once again in 1934. The Jewish Agency's Immigrant Absorption Department, headed by Yitzhak Greenbaum, was accused of discriminating against Sephardi and Oriental Jews in allocating immigration certificates. In response to these allegations, Greenbaum declared that migration permits were given "to those who built and who continue to build the Land" and to those that the Land of

Israel needed.[61] Responding to Greenbaum's comments, the Council of the Sephardi Community in Jerusalem emphasized that the Sephardim had been in the country for centuries before Greenbaum's family arrived. A statement by the council accused Greenbaum of a lack of familiarity with the Sephardi community and a lack of awareness of the Sephardim's Zionist activities and their bond with the Land of Israel, which predated the emergence of Zionism. The council protested vehemently about "the misconception among leaders of the Zionist movement such as Greenbaum regarding the national identity and pioneering value of the Sephardi Jews."[62] The council also noted in its statement that the disrespect for the Sephardi public, "which has built the Land over recent centuries with its spirit, body, and money," was apparent in the exclusion of the Sephardim from positions of influence in the national Zionist institutions. The message was clear: "In light of the situation that has emerged in the Zionist movement, the Sephardi public in the Land of Israel would know, from this point on, how to determine its attitude toward those who were placed at the rudder by chance and were granted power."[63]

The Liberal Party and the Peel Commission

With the rise of political tension during the 1930s in general, and in the years of the Arab Revolt in particular, an effort was made to leave behind Sephardi communal activism in favor of activities in the framework of party politics to improve Jewish-Arab relations. Following the outbreak of the Arab Revolt in 1936, a group of Sephardi and Oriental activists who had been active in the Association of the Pioneers of the East established the Liberal Party. Its formation at this juncture reflected the ideological and physical threats that faced the Sephardi and Oriental Jews and their understanding of the urgent need to promote a rapprochement between Jews and Arabs. The new party adopted liberal principles in general, and its goals included developing cultural, social, and economic contacts with the peoples of the Orient and engaging in educational, cultural, and economic activities among the Sephardim. The attempted transition from communal to political activism was short-lived and unsuccessful. Nevertheless, the establishment of the Liberal Party provided a contrast to the apolitical position of the organizations of the Sephardi and Oriental Jews.[64]

Laniado was one of the leaders who firmly supported the political approach. A native of Jerusalem and an attorney by profession, Laniado, as noted above, was one of the leaders of the Association of Pioneers of the East. According to him, the motivation for the establishment of the Liberal Party was the desire of the activists in various Sephardi organizations to break away from the restrictive ethnic framework. He explained that the ethnic-based approach had created a group with the characteristics of an ethnic minority: "This is a minority with all the feelings of resentment that any other minority anywhere in the world feels. This is a minority with all the feelings of inferiority and fear that any other minority anywhere in the world feels. This is a minority with all the feelings of suspicion and awe regarding the majority. This is a minority with a lack of courage and daring. In other words, this is a minority that inevitably reconciles itself to its situation along with a sense of silent resentment."[65]

While it is possible to understand the existence of a Jewish minority with a similar pattern of behavior in the Diaspora, Laniado argued, "it is unthinkable that in the Land of Israel two communities will exist, one of which will stand at the top while the other remains on the bottom. . . . The Sephardim do not belong to a different race or religion, as is the case with other minorities around the world that cannot assimilate in their country of residence, despite their will and aspiration."[66] Laniado's views on the gap between Ashkenazi and Sephardi Jews in the Yishuv and the lower status of the Sephardim are consistent with the Liberal Party's goal of encouraging the Sephardim to think of themselves as part of the whole Yishuv. Another goal of the party was to increase the involvement of the Sephardi and Oriental Jewish leaders in making decisions about the national conflict. However, to do that, the leaders had to form a united political bloc and avoid disputes within their community.

After discussing the low sociopolitical status of the Sephardim in the Yishuv, Laniado criticized the Sephardi leadership. His main argument was that the Sephardim should aspire to integrate themselves into the general society of the Yishuv. However, he continued, what had transpired since the establishment of the Association of the Pioneers of the East was that young Sephardim had turned in the opposite direction: "Instead of encouraging this ingathering for revival, we have fostered the feeling of a discriminated minority. We have fostered a feeling of resentment and sometimes even hatred. We have isolated [the Sephardi community] and prevented it from influencing matters of state. We have distanced it from the broad-based field of political work and confined it to poor and meager local issues."[67] Laniado's trenchant criticism led him to the conclusion that ethnic community organizations had completed their historical duty. He agreed with the general public criticism of the isolationist nature of ethnic organizations and concluded that the process of nation building required "that we cast off the name Sephardi or Ashkenazi or Yemenite."[68]

However, the Liberal Party was in fact an ethnic framework whose activists were exclusively Sephardim. The members of the party were aware of this contradiction. Despite his criticism of the lack of practical political action, and his concern that the party was merely another example of communalism, Laniado saw it as a platform for ideological discussion and development. The main goal, he believed, was to foster political and cultural discourse centering on the revival of Sephardi culture.[69]

One of the main outcomes of the formation of the Liberal Party was the establishment on September 1936 of the Political Council of the Sephardi Community and Oriental Jews that was intended primarily to represent the Sephardi Jews before the Palestine Royal Commission (commonly called the Peel Commission), appointed following the Arab Revolt in 1936.[70] In this way, the idea of adopting a political position was combined with the concept of viewing the Sephardim as political mediators between Jews and Arabs. The establishment of the Liberal Party, against the background of the Arab Revolt, highlighted the crisis in relations between Jews and Arabs, but at the same time it was viewed as an opportunity to cause political awakening among the Sephardim, with the establishment of the Political Council of the Sephardi Community and Oriental Jews, an organization that would represent the Sephardim before the Peel Commission.

The council was established in a conference that was held in Jerusalem on September 1936. The conference had been called by members of the Liberal Party and was attended by leaders of the Sephardi and Oriental Jewish communities in Palestine, including representatives of various Oriental communities such as the Bukharis, Yemenites, Iraqis, and Syrian Jews. The participants complained about the exclusion of the Sephardim from the organized political activities of the Yishuv, and particularly from matters relating to relations with the Arabs. The participants protested that not a single native Jew had been included in the political committee established by the Zionist Executive to present the movement's position to the Peel Commission. The Political Council members sought to represent all the Sephardi and Oriental communities in the Yishuv and present a unified position. The members felt that they were better suited to present the position of the Yishuv regarding the Arab Question than the Jewish Agency Executive, which they argued had shown itself to be inexperienced in this field. The Political Council decided therefore to send a separate delegation on its behalf to appear before the commission and to submit a memorandum that would present the political stand of the Sephardi and Oriental Jews in Palestine.[71]

The Political Council's discussion of the draft memorandum to the Peel Commission, which was prepared by Laniado, expressed the organization's approach to Jewish-Arab relations. One of the points made in the discussion was that the memorandum depicted the Arabs in a negative light and failed to emphasize the real potential for reaching peace. Members of the Political Council expressed their concern that Laniado's draft would create great animosity toward the Sephardim in Palestine and the Middle East in general. Eliyahu Eliachar, the head of the Political Council Executive, was among those who criticized the document. An even sharper criticism came from Meir Hai Ginio, an attorney and prominent Sephardi leader, who warned that the memorandum "is no more than a list of complaints and accusations against the Arabs; it may cause us considerable problems, and may also cause problems for our brethren in the Orient."[72]

One of the activists on the Political Council was Yitzhak 'Abadi, who was born in Jerusalem in 1898 to a family of mixed Damascene and Jerusalemite origin. Like many of his peers in the Sephardic elite he studied at the Teachers' Seminar directed by David Yellin. 'Abadi, who was a member of the Association of the Pioneers of the East, served as the chief mandatory government translator from Hebrew to English and also translated for the Commission, expressed a concern similar to Ginio's during the Political Council meeting, stressing that "it is important to avoid polemics."[73] The Political Council Executive decided to combine Laniado's memorandum with a separate document prepared by 'Abadi. The Political Council also appointed Rabbi Ya'acov Meir, Rabbi Ben-Zion Meir Hai Uziel, Yosef Meyuchas, Laniado, and Eliachar as representatives of the Sephardim to the Peel Commission.[74] The representatives were unable to present their testimony due to bureaucratic reasons relating to the commission's timetable. Despite this, on December 28, 1936, Avraham Elmaleh made a special statement before the Peel Commission as a representative of the Sephardi and Oriental Jews on the National Council Executive.

Elmaleh's statement was coordinated with—and followed—that of Yitzhak Ben-Zvi, the chairman of the National Council Executive. For Ben-Zvi, it was important to present the Sephardi position concerning the situation in Palestine, as well as the need to address the condition of the Jews in the Middle East as a whole.[75] In his testimony, Ben-Zvi emphasized that "the Yishuv is united in its religion, language, shared past, and its common aspirations regarding the purpose of the National Home. In this respect there is no difference between immigrants from Europe and those from the Asian countries."[76] In accordance with this position, Elmaleh's testimony was intended to emphasize the support of Sephardi and Oriental Jewish communities for the position of the National Council and the Jewish Agency Executive and, in particular, to refute the Arab claim that these communities were opposed to Zionism. Members of the Peel Commission expressed surprise regarding the need for a separate statement, but 'Abadi persuaded them to hear Elmaleh's testimony.

The choice of Elmaleh as the spokesman for the Sephardi and Oriental Jews was due mainly to his membership in the National Council Executive during the third Assembly of Representatives. His appointment also reflected his status in the Yishuv in general, and in the Sephardi and Maghrebi leadership in particular. Born in Jerusalem in 1885, Elmaleh served as president of the Maghrebi Committee and was one of the most prominent activists in the various Sephardi organizations that emerged from the Association of the Pioneers of the East during the Mandate years.[77] Elmaleh highlighted his background at the beginning of his presentation before the Peel Commission and linked the Sephardim's (and Maghrebim's) perception of themselves as Bney Ha'aretz to their special role in the relations between Jews and Arabs.[78] Elmaleh began his statement by declaring that "the Sephardi and Oriental Jews (*bnei 'edot hamizrah*) have been in this land for many generations and they are thoroughly familiar with the life of the Orient (*hamizrah*), since they were the first inhabitants therein." Accordingly, he assured the Peel Commission that the Sephardi and Oriental Jews in Palestine identified completely with the Jewish Agency and the National Council. He concluded by saying that "as Jews rooted in the soil of this land for many generations, we believe that the solution to the Jewish question lies solely in Zionism."[79] Thus, Elmaleh argued that Sephardi-Oriental Zionism was inherently an integral part of the Zionist movement and that the Sephardi and Oriental Jews practiced Zionist ideals because of its historical continuity in Palestine in particular and the Middle East in general. These arguments, together with the point that the Oriental Jews had a deep familiarity with the Arabs, were repeated in other testimony and memorandums presented by the Sephardi representatives during the Mandate period.

The memorandum submitted to the Peel Commission by the Sephardi and Oriental Jews also highlighted the strong connection of the Sephardim to the Middle East in general. It began by clarifying that their position was not one of a political party but that of a collective within the Jewish people—the Jews of the Orient (*yehudi hamizrah*)—whose members have "for several generations" had "close and firm ties with the peoples of the Orient."[80]

The memorandum emphasized that the Oriental Jews identified with the Zionist ideal and accepted the authority of the World Zionist Organization and the Jewish Agency. It explained the need for separate testimony by claiming that "our knowledge of, and familiarity with, the natives of this country and of the

Orient, among whom we have lived for centuries, can help the Commission to understand the situation."[81]

After providing a historical review of the origins of Sephardi Jewry, the memorandum described the relations between Jews and Arabs during the final years of Ottoman rule:

> One of the common claims raised by Arab representatives is that prior to the war, when the problem of Zionism had not yet emerged on the agenda in its full force, there was peace in the land and no man spoke ill of his fellow or sought to harm him, and that the two peoples lived together in an almost idyllic atmosphere. The Jews enjoyed a relative degree of generosity and religious tolerance from the [Ottoman] state. In this idyllic era, not only were there no riots or attacks against the Jews, but Jew and Arab lived in complete harmony, and this harmony was particularly noticeable given the persecution and oppression that faced the Jews in the Western countries.[82]

The memorandum continued: "Such a description does not reflect the entire truth."[83] It noted numerous grave attacks by zealous Muslims against both Christians and Jews, who, as a result, required the protection of the Ottoman authorities and the intervention of the European consulates. Nevertheless, the memorandum was careful to acknowledge that there had been many instances of economic and social cooperation between Jews and Arabs. It placed particular emphasis on examples of cooperation in the educational and cultural spheres, such as the study of Arabic in Jewish schools, taught by Jewish teachers.

Private memorandums were also submitted to the Peel Commission by Eliachar and Yosef Meyuchas. Meyuchas enjoyed a prominent status in the Sephardi community and in the Yishuv, due in part to his scholarly work and his public activities. He was the quintessential example of the Sephardi notable who was deeply rooted in the social, cultural, and political realities of the Sephardi community during the Ottoman period.[84] With David Yellin, his brother-in-law, Meyuchas was one of the founders of the Association of the Pioneers of the East, and he was one of the most prominent members of the circle of Sephardi intellectuals in Jerusalem in the late nineteenth century. Meyuchas remained active in public life until his death in September 1942. The numerous eulogies published after his death portrayed him as the ultimate native of the country who was not only merely educated in an Oriental and Arab environment but whose life, mastery of various languages, literary creativity, and cultural actions all embodied the integration of Hebrew and Arabic culture and the ideal of rapprochement between the two peoples.[85]

Meyuchas submitted his memorandum to the Peel Commission as an expert on Arab culture and society, not only because of his intellectual credentials but also because of his identity as the scion of a family that was well established in the country and his having lived as a child alongside Arabs in the village of Silwan.[86] On the basis of this deep acquaintance and academic expertise, Meyuchas sought to present the negative and positive qualities that he believed characterized the Arabs.[87] He argued that the outbreak of Arab violence in 1936 was due to various aspects of Arab mentality. His recommendations to the Peel Commission were based on his close reading of the Arabic press and his knowledge of the curriculum in Arab schools (he had been a teacher at some of the elite schools for Palestinian Arabs). His proposals therefore focused on the educational arena. He highlighted the importance of studying Arabic and Arab culture in Jewish schools, as well as of studying Hebrew language and culture in the Arab schools, and he referred to the Jews' golden age in Muslim Spain as his historical model.[88]

The second private memorandum submitted to the Peel Commission was by Eliachar.[89] This memorandum touched on various issues, including the hostile attitude of the Christian Arab population in Palestine toward the Jews and the contribution Zionism had made to the economic development of the Arab population and the country at large. Eliachar challenged the claim that the Jews were foreigners in the country and insisted on their historical and moral right to the Land of Israel. He also noted his opposition to any restriction on Jewish immigration and discussed the repeated arguments about the actual relations between Jews and Arabs prior to World War I and the Balfour Declaration. The Jews, he claimed, had lived in constant fear of cruel treatment by the Arab population, though good relations did prevail between the Arab and Jewish elites in the cities, particularly in the case of the Sephardim. Eliachar noted that the two elites mingled and engaged in commerce together, thereby creating lasting friendships that extended from one generation to the next. He summarized his position in the following words: "Let us not accept the legend of tolerance and generosity toward us. This tolerance has never existed in any place where the Arabs have ruled. Yemen, Tunisia, Morocco and Algeria prior to the French conquest, or the attitude of Iraq toward the Assyrians—all these are live examples of what Jews and Christians in Palestine can expect if they remain a weak minority bereft of British or other protection."[90]

Despite this somber appraisal, Eliachar emphasized the proximity between Jews and Arabs and the idea that the Jews, as an Oriental people, were returning to the land where Judaism had developed: "Our languages stem from the same source, as do our beliefs, and many aspects of our character are the same."[91] He believed that the future of Palestine lay in the integration of the Jewish National Home into a regional federation with the neighboring Arab countries, under British patronage. Like Avissar, Eliachar advocated the sharing of power by Arabs and Jews in a joint legislative council, based on absolute equality between the two peoples—who would cooperate in politics, industry, agriculture, and other fields of life under British patronage as they developed their shared homeland. And like Avissar, Eliachar supported the unification of Palestine and Transjordan.

Another key point raised by Eliachar had to do with the relations between the Sephardi Jews in Palestine and the other Jewish communities of the Middle East. At the meeting of the Political Council on October 18, 1936, held to discuss the drafting of the memorandum to the Peel Commission, it was decided that both Eliachar and Meyuchas would submit memorandums to the commission. Eliachar claimed that the Jews of the Orient were facing grave distress. He argued that the Sephardi Jews in Palestine must speak out on behalf of their brethren in the neighboring countries, and he made particular reference to the difficult conditions of the Jews of Iraq—who, he claimed, were being held hostage by the Iraqi government. He emphasized that the Sephardim in Palestine must take action to help the Jews in the rest of the Middle East, "since the Jewish people as a whole, which is mainly Ashkenazi, does not take into account the condition of the Oriental communities."[92] In his memorandum, then, Eliachar highlighted the connection between the Sephardi community's public position on the political future of Palestine, the local relations between Jews and Arabs, and the condition and status of Jews in the Arab countries. This connection was also made in the testimony of the Sephardi and the Oriental Jewish communities' delegation to the Anglo-American Committee of Inquiry in 1946 and to the United Nations Special Committee on Palestine (UNSCOP) in July 1947, which will be discussed below.

"Peace Seekers": The Sephardim and the Legacy of Brit Shalom

The Sephardim who had been active in establishing the Liberal Party were also among those who in April 1939 established the Union of Sephardi and Oriental Jews in the Land of Israel (Haihud Ha'artzi Shel Hayehudim Hasfaradim Vebnei 'Edot Hamizrah Be'eretz Israel). This new national initiative, which sought to serve as a single umbrella organization for the various Sephardi and Oriental Jewish communities, only further emphasized the communities' focus on ethic and communal issues. On April 8, 1939, a conference of Sephardi and Oriental

Jews opened in Tel Aviv under the chairmanship of Moshe Chelouche, head of the Association of Sephardi Jews in Tel Aviv (Histadrut Hayehudim Hasfaradim Betel Aviv).[93] The event provided further evidence of the growing status of Tel Aviv as a political center for Sephardi Jews, challenging the traditional leadership role of the Council of the Sephardi Community in Jerusalem. Dozens of participants from around the country, representing a variety of organizations, attended the conference.[94]

The need to organize a national conference highlighted the serious impact of the Arab Revolt on the Sephardi and Oriental Jews, as well as the power struggles that were waged between Sephardim and Oriental Jews in the Council of the Sephardi Community in Jerusalem. The need for a conference and for a united Sephardi and Oriental Jewish organization illustrated the economic and social relations between Jews and Arabs that existed in the mixed cities, and that had been severely impaired following the outbreak of the national conflict, as we will discuss in greater detail below.[95] Members of the Union of Sephardi and Oriental Jews in the Land of Israel also discussed the failure to include Sephardi and Oriental Jews in the delegation sent by the Jewish Agency to the St. James Conference in London, which opened in February 1939, failed to reach a peace agreement in Palestine and ended the following month.

The national conference of Sephardi and Oriental Jews in Palestine also criticized the failure to include Sephardim in the delegation, with the exception of Rabbi Ben-Zion Meir Hai Uziel. The criticism followed the familiar line of alleging that the Sephardi and Oriental Jews had been excluded from policy-making processes in the Yishuv and the Zionist movement. Speaking to participants at the conference, Eliachar commented: "Regarding the Arab question, leading Sephardim came and stated that we should be acting in a different manner, but no one listened to them and we have reached the current state of affairs. It is more than possible that had we adopted a different approach over the past twenty years, we would not have reached the situation we now face."[96]

A similar view was voiced by Oriental Jews in the Arab world, such as Yosef Katawi Pasha, the chief rabbi of Egypt. At a meeting with Elmaleh in Cairo at the end of 1938, Katawi warned of the danger in the continued refusal of the Zionist leaders to listen to the opinion of the Sephardi Jews, "who are thoroughly familiar with Oriental manners, the Arabic language, and with Arab thought." Directing his comments primarily at Weizmann, Katawi rhetorically asked: "Can they imagine that we will remain silent even when we become the victims of their mistakes?"[97] His comments reflected not only resentment at the failure to include Sephardi Jews in the management of contacts between Jews and Arabs, but also the growing concern about the status of the Jewish minority in the Arab countries. Katawi's position, which rejected the Peel Commission's partition plan and endorsed political reconciliation with the Arabs, was similar to that of the Jewish associations in Palestine that supported the binational idea and called for Jewish-Arab rapprochement.

Following the outbreak of the Arab Revolt, in 1936, another association, Kedma Mizraha, was established. Its members included former activists of Brit Shalom; members of the Association of Farmers; municipal leaders such as Zaki Alhadiff, the mayor of Tiberias; native Sephardi and Ashkenazi intellectuals; and former members of the Association of Pioneers of the East.[98] The members of Kedma Mizraha were a diverse group with a range of opinions. As a result, the organization's goals were defined in vague terms as "familiarization with the Orient, the creation of social and economic contacts with the peoples of the Orient, and proper informational activities regarding the project of the Jewish people in its land."[99]

The association, which was active for only a brief period, was especially interesting given the limited involvement of Sephardi and Oriental Jews in other similar associations, such as Brit Shalom, the League for Jewish-Arab Rapprochement, and, later, Ichud. The main Sephardi activists in these organizations were Yitzhak Shamosh; Judge Moshe Valero; and Yitzhak Raphael Molcho, who continued to support the political initiatives of Judah Leon Magnes, the President of the Hebrew University of Jerusalem. Although Molcho supported the idea of a federative union, he opposed any concessions regarding Jewish immigration, as did Eliachar.[100]

A question that naturally arises in this context is why so few Sephardi and Oriental Jews were involved in such associations, which were established to promote cultural rapprochement and closer ties between Jews and Arabs during the Mandatory years. One of the reasons is the social profile of Brit Shalom and its successor associations, particularly the League for Jewish-Arab Rapprochement and Ichud. Numerous studies have described the social and ideological origins of Brit Shalom, which was dominated by German Jews and faculty members from the Hebrew University.[101] Accordingly, it is not surprising that one of the members of Brit Shalom was Yitzhak Shamosh, who taught modern Arabic literature at the Institute of Oriental Studies, established by the Hebrew University in 1925 (Shamosh is discussed in more detail in chapter 3).

Magnes hoped that the institute would help bring Jews and Arabs together. However, Josef Horovitz, who served as its first director, believed that only a scholar who had studied in Europe or the United States would be able to serve as director, and that there were no Oriental scholars who were fully familiar with modern research and pedagogical methods.[102] His view was best illustrated by the rejection of Abraham Shalom Yahuda's appointment as a faculty member at the institute. Born in Jerusalem and a cousin of Yellin, Yahuda was described by Ya'akov Yehoshua as a scholar who was a native of the Orient and a product of Jewish-Arab culture.[103] The rejection of his appointment was perceived as an example of the exclusion of Oriental Jews from positions that potentially could strengthen the cultural and intellectual connections between Jews and Arabs. Indeed, Yahuda criticized the Jewish Russian intellectuals who were active in the Zionist movement and the Zionist leaders who prevented the Oriental Jews from helping address the Arab Question. The reasons for the rejection of his appointment have been debated, but Yahuda was convinced that it was the Zionist European leaders—mainly Weizmann, Ussishkin, and the Zionist leader and author Nahum Sokolov—who were responsible. According to Yahuda, they opposed his views on the Arab Question and the importance of integrating the Hebrew and Arab cultures.[104] As Yehoshua suggested, Yahuda's attempt to "make his expertise available for those who came from the west resulted in great disappointment."[105]

The main reason for the dearth of Sephardim in Brit Shalom, however, was the approach adopted by the association to the resolution of the conflict, particularly its support for restrictions on Jewish immigration and its willingness to accept the Yishuv's constituting a minority in a binational state. In this regard, the Sephardi leaders sought to present a political solution similar to that of the Zionists. In addition, while emphasizing the historical links between Oriental Jews and Palestine and rejecting the proposed restriction on Jewish immigration, the Sephardi leaders also wanted to emphasize the need for Jews to immigrate to Palestine not only from Europe, but also from the surrounding Arab countries. Cultural and social differences were also a factor.

In an article published in *Hed Hamizrah* in November 6, 1942, Yosef Rivlin attempted to examine why "the native Jew, who has been in the country for generations, the Oriental Jew (*ben 'edot hamizrah*), and even the Ashkenazi whose family has been here for generations steadfastly refuse to support Brit Shalom and all its reincarnations."[106] Rivlin sought to understand the reason for the fierce hostility toward those movements that were perceived as promoting peace and understanding among native Jews of all political persuasions. He rejected the hypothesis that the Oriental Jews were indifferent to public affairs and politics and preferred to concentrate on their private concerns. One of Rivlin's assumptions was that Oriental Jews worried that they would be identified as traitors to the national cause and accused of disloyalty to Zionism and the Yishuv, if they openly supported these organizations.[107]

This comment by Rivlin is important, since one of the factors that made the Sephardi and Oriental Jews reluctant to join Brit Shalom and Ichud was the fact that the organizations were not part of the Zionist mainstream. As we have seen, the Sephardi leaders were sensitive to accusations that they had a separatist orientation and sought to disassociate themselves from the Yishuv. However, Rivlin argues that Bney Ha'aretz's special connection with and deep understanding of the Arabs, compared to the Ashkenazi "foreign" Jews, is what stands at the core of the special relations between Oriental Jews, Ashkenazi local Jews, and Arabs—despite the political radicalization among both Jews and Arabs.[108] For Rivlin the most important reason for the Sephardi reluctance was the particular perspective of native Jews, who did not share the European Jews' experience of exile and hence saw no reason to efface themselves before the Arabs:

> The attitude of the Ben Ha'aretz to the Arab is different. He does not view the Arab fellah or the worker with pity. . . . The Jewish Ben Ha'aretz does not pity the Arab. He is in many ways equal to him. The eastern Jewish worker is very similar to the Arab worker, as all are members of the poor social strata among both peoples. They are similar to each other not only in their language, but in the language of their souls (sfat nafsham). . . . Let's have no illusion: many things have changed since World War I [and the fall of the Ottoman Empire]. Political Zionism developed a new spirit among Oriental Jews, who became, it is worth noting, radical Zionists (*tziyoni kitzoni*). 100 percent Zionists. Arab nationalism has developed as well and the [national] demands have grown on both sides. However, where there is one language and one track of mind, there is still some possibility of finding a solution, or at least seeking one, at least many more ways than the "peace seekers" [of Brit Shalom] are seeking.[109]

The ideological stance and political activity of Eliachar may also offer an answer to the riddle of the reservations among Sephardi and Oriental Jews regarding Brit Shalom and Ichud. Eliachar was born in Jerusalem in 1899 and was educated at the Lemmel and Alliance schools in the city. During World War I he served as an officer in the Ottoman army, and he completed his studies at the French College in Beirut after the war ended. In 1922 he returned to Palestine after spending a year in Cairo. Until 1935 he was employed as a clerk in the Commerce and Customs Department of the Mandatory government. In 1947 he was appointed president of the Council of the Sephardi Community in Jerusalem, after a lengthy period of involvement in various Sephardi organizations—particularly the Association of the Pioneers of the East.[110] As Israel Bartal noted, a clear connection can be found between Eliachar's background as a native of Jerusalem and his political position regarding Jewish-Arab relations.[111] Eliachar formulated his views on national issues during the late Ottoman period. To Bartal, he serves as an example of the Sephardi notables who saw no contradiction between the Zionist enterprise and Arab nationalist aspirations, and who indeed saw the Yishuv as a model for national autonomy within a multinational empire. The view that Zionism must integrate itself into the national movements of other ethnic minorities in the Ottoman Empire was shared by the elite Sephardi and Ashkenazi families of the old Yishuv.[112] Eliachar tried to adopt this approach to the new Mandatory era when, as discussed above, he proposed the establishment of a Jewish-Arab federation in Palestine under British patronage.[113]

However, Eliachar rejected the political solutions proposed by Brit Shalom and Ichud, which was established in 1942 by Magnes. Eliachar had a profound admiration for Magnes and even attended the founding conference of Ichud, at which he was elected as Magnes's deputy. However, after Magnes published a plan that would establish a quota for Jewish immigration and accept the principle that Jews would not constitute more than 40 percent of the country's total population, Eliachar resigned from Ichud. Like his peers in the Association of the Pioneers of the East who had remained active in the Sephardi and Oriental Jews' organizations during the 1930s and 1940s, and who were involved in the issue of Jewish-Arab relations, Eliachar opposed any restrictions on Jewish immigration and could not accept the perpetuation of the Jews' status as a minority in Palestine.[114]

Moreover, like Rivlin, Eliachar believed that while the Sephardim and Oriental Jews lived side by side with the Arabs and interacted with them on a daily basis, the members of Brit Shalom and Ichud lacked this experience. Hence, he felt that the members of the two associations reached their conclusions on the basis of an academic and "theoretical" knowledge, not of personal experience.[115] Eliachar repeatedly emphasized the importance of the understanding of another group that is created through close daily contact, personal acquaintance, and shared interests with its members. He felt that the solutions proposed by Ichud were ill conceived and would damage the Jewish future in the country. Instead, he argued, efforts should first focus on creating an atmosphere of understanding and mutual recognition between the Yishuv and its Arab neighbors.[116]

In his numerous articles and his political and other public activities, Eliachar can be viewed as the most prominent example of an approach that might be called "the road not taken." He presented in its clearest and purest form the argument that the marginalization of the Sephardi and Oriental Jews prevented the implementation of their approach, which was one of compromise and mediation. The result was that the leaders of the Yishuv adopted the wrong policy toward Jewish-Arab relations. Eliachar argued that the leaders of the Zionist movement and the Yishuv showed a lack of interest in becoming acquainted with the Arab society and culture and refused to allow the Sephardi and Oriental Jews to manage Jewish-Arab relations. This led the Zionist leaders to make political mistakes that exacerbated the conflict between the two national movements.[117] The fundamental mistake of this leadership, Eliachar believed, was their failure "to create direct relations and contact with our neighbors, to learn to understand them, and to build cultural and economic ties with them. This situation led to the emergence of a terrifying alienation between us and our neighbors that grew deeper every day."[118]

Saving the Jews of the Arab Countries

The leaders of the Sephardi and Oriental Jewish communities in Palestine were well aware of the direct impact that the actions of the local Jews in Palestine and the development of the Jewish-Arab conflict had on the status and future of Jews in the Arab countries. Their seeking to represent the Oriental Jews as a whole was evident in public and political discourse, as was their attempt to promote solidarity and mutual support among the various Jewish communities in the region. This commitment to their fellow Jews in the Arab countries, and the awareness that their actions were scrutinized not only by the leaders of the Yishuv and their own constituents, but also by leaders in other countries, affected the way in which they presented their positions regarding the national conflict in Palestine.

The close link between the situation in Palestine and Jewish-Arab relations in the Middle East in general was highlighted during the 1940s, with the growing concern for the fate of Jews in Arab countries. This concern was reflected in the memorandums that the Sephardi delegations submitted to the Anglo-American Committee of Inquiry, as well as to UNSCOP. Part of the Sephardim's goal in these memorandums was to again prove their loyalty and deep commitment to Zionist ideas. They continued to present themselves as possible mediators between Jews and Arabs, but they also attempted to adhere to the Zionist position vis-à-vis the Jewish-Arab conflict.

The institutional, political, and public criticism of the Sephardim reached its peak following the decision of the Sephardi leaders to boycott the elections for

the Yishuv's fourth Assembly of Representatives that took place in 1944. Eliachar
played the lead role in the decision.[119] The Council of the Sephardi Community
in Jerusalem demanded a change in the electoral system and the adoption of
regional elections. This demand led to repeated claims of Sephardi separatism
and allegations that the demand was based on a communalist approach.[120]

The demand for changes in the electoral system enjoyed the support of organizations associated with the "Civic Circles"—the middle class and bourgeoi-
sie—and the Revisionist Party, thereby positioning the Sephardi leaders not
merely as opponents to the labor movement and the leadership of the Yishuv
but as supporters of the dissenters. Moreover, the alliance between the Sephardi
leaders and the Civic Circles in boycotting the elections strengthened the claim
that the Sephardim belonged to the center right part of the political spectrum in
the Yishuv. Like the Association of Farmers, which also boycotted the elections,
the Sephardi political leadership and elite was seen to be clinging to a narrow
view of the Jewish community. Like the Civic Circles, Labor Zionism identified
the leadership with the urban middle class and with the professional fields of
commerce, law, education, and banking.[121]

The exclusion of the representatives of the Council of the Sephardi Community in Jerusalem from the National Council Executive led to a rift in the
Yishuv and to considerable tension within the Sephardi and Oriental Jews'
communities in Palestine. David Abulafia, who was the president of the Council
of the Sephardi Community in Jerusalem, and Laniado, who were opposed by
the circle identified with Eliachar, entered into negotiations with Mapai, with
the goal of allowing the Sephardim to return to the Assembly of Representatives
and the National Council.[122]

Abulafia and Laniado also headed the Sephardi delegation that testified before
the Anglo-American Committee of Inquiry on March 13, 1946. The delegation
also included 'Abadi, the official translator mentioned above, and Asher Malach,
who before his arrival in Palestine in 1934 had served as a member of the Greek
parliament and as one of the leaders of the Jewish community in Salonika.
Malach was invited to testify about the conditions of the Bulgarian Jewish
community. The members of the delegation represented several organizations:
the Council of the Sephardi Community in Jerusalem, the Association of Sephardi Jews in Tel Aviv, and the Council of the Sephardi Community in Haifa.
The delegation also worked in coordination with the World Confederation of
Sephardi Jews, which at this time was based in New York.[123]

In its testimony before the Anglo-American Committee of Inquiry, the representatives of the Sephardi and Oriental Jewish communities in Palestine chose

to depict the Jews of the Middle East as a community in political, economic, and physical distress, thereby linking the Jewish-Arab conflict in Palestine to the question of Jewish-Arab relations in the region as a whole. The Sephardi delegation also argued that during the committee's visits to Arab countries, its members had been unable to hear the true opinions and positions of the Jewish communities due to their fear for the safety of their communities and their own lives. The Sephardi position was that the Jews of the Middle East must be permitted to immigrate to Palestine. The memorandum presented by the Sephardi delegation characterized the mood among the Jews of the Arab countries as one of terror, particularly in the case of those suspected of maintaining contacts with Palestine or Zionism. However, the immigration of Jews from Arab countries was recommended not only because of their distress but also because of the close ties between Oriental Jews and Eretz Israel, which had existed even prior to the establishment of the Zionist movement in the late nineteenth century.[124]

In his testimony, Abulafia emphasized that he was speaking as the official representative of Sephardi Jewry in Palestine and around the world, and that his positions reflected the ideological position of Sephardi Jews toward Zionism. He emphasized the full identification of the Sephardim with Zionism and with its official and elected representatives, who also appeared before the committee. In fact, Abulafia defined in his testimony the meaning of Oriental and Sephardi Zionism. "Our Zionism stems from the specific historical and psychological circumstances of Sephardi Jewry in the Diaspora," he said. "The Sephardim were among the first Zionists, not only in theory but also in practice, and many of them put practice before theory when they were among the first to immigrate to Palestine."[125] Before declaring that Sephardi Jewry unreservedly supported the position of the representatives of the Zionist movement regarding the creation of an independent and sovereign state in the Land of Israel, Abulafia explained the special status of the Sephardim as mediators: "We carry a special role and destiny of Zionism in terms of nurturing peaceful relations and understanding with the Arabs of this land." However, they could play this special role only if a Jewish state was established. Then, continued Abulafia, "we will be able to perform our duty and provide important assistance in promoting cooperation on the basis of equal relations between the two brother peoples."[126] The written memorandum that was submitted to the committee by the Sephardi leadership further highlighted this role of the Sephardim and Oriental Jews as mediators and described it as their historical destiny:

We further believe that in this particular sphere of overriding importance, namely the maintenance of relations of good neighborliness and friendship with the Arabs amid and around us, Sephardi Jewry will be assigned by history a very special task. It is true, as we have stated above, that until the new racial doctrines have spread their poison among the Arab communities, Jews and Arabs were able not only to understand each other but indeed to live in relations of sincere and genuine friendship. . . . The deterioration in the relations between Jews and Arabs is not at all an inevitable outcome of the Zionist effort in this country. . . . As deputies of Sephardi Jewry, who by our mentality and our way of life are rather closer to the Semitic world, it may be permissible for us to declare before you [based] not only on the strength of our belief but also on the strength of personal experience that the alleged "enmity" between Jews and Arabs is not at all inevitable and that without prompting and incitement from non-Arab quarters, the Arabs would never have come to racial persecutions [of Jews]. If, nevertheless, a very gloomy picture has been exposed in this statement on the plight of Sephardi Jewry in adjacent countries, it is because in our view these new states have found themselves intoxicated by the wine of sudden independence and have taken to emulating the methods of the worst European countries with longer experience then their own.[127]

The Anglo-American Committee of Inquiry also heard testimony from several Palestinian Arab delegates. Once again, Jamal al-Husseini questioned the loyalty of Oriental Jews to the Zionist idea. In his testimony he presented the position of the Palestinian leadership, which rejected any Jewish right to or share in the Palestinian homeland. This approach recognized Judaism as a religion but not the Jews as a nation. Al-Husseini emphasized that the Arab claims had nothing in common with antisemitism. He denied the legitimacy of the Balfour Declaration, which he described as the beginning of the Zionist invasion of Palestine, with the goal of abrogating the Palestinians' rights. He added that before November 1917, "the Arabs had always lived in peace and friendship with the many Jews who settled in Palestine for religious reasons. History does not include any riots or incidents testifying to Arab hatred of Jews in Palestine or elsewhere. On the contrary, the chroniclers testify convincingly to a positive Arab attitude toward Jews whenever Jews were persecuted in Europe. It was only after the publication of the Balfour Declaration, as the Jews began to display political ambitions and to reveal their true and aggressive intentions, which we consider nothing less than an invasion, that concern and opposition grew among the Arabs."[128]

Al-Husseini described the pre-Zionist period as an era of cooperation and understanding between Jews and Arabs: "I could give you numerous examples of the good relations that existed between the Jews of the Orient and the Arabs, and I could clarify how these relations were spoiled as a direct result of Zionism." Thus al-Husseini presented the Palestinian goal of restoring the situation in Palestine to the status quo prior to World War I. He was convinced that "at least 60 percent of the Jews in Palestine, who are currently subject to the power of Zionist coercion, would cooperate with us. For although they are now a small minority, many of them—at least 50 percent—formerly lived together with us and they know that we always lived with them in friendship and peace." Husseini also presented personal information: "As a small child, my father used to take me with him, together with my six brothers, to visit an old Jewish woman and to kiss her hand."[129]

Following Abulafia's testimony, and on the basis of the memorandum submitted on behalf of Sephardi Jewry, 'Abadi and Laniado were asked to respond to questions posed by members of the Anglo-American Committee of Inquiry. In particular, they were asked to address the connection between the Zionist demand for a state and the future relations between Jews and Arabs in the Middle East. An article by 'Abadi titled "A Jewish-Arab Federation" shows his political position on the Arab Question.[130] Although the article was published in 1920, it seems to reflect a position 'Abadi maintained throughout his life, which emphasized the cultural spheres as a way of promoting Jewish-Arab relations. 'Abadi was also a member of Solel, a short-lived association of Jews and Arabs in Jerusalem, who arranged language classes for its members. 'Abadi was the Hebrew teacher, while Khalil al-Sakakini was the Arabic teacher.[131]

In the article, 'Abadi called for a Jewish-Arab union to promote the renaissance of the Orient. Despite their long exile in the West, he maintained that the Jews were an Oriental people: "Even in a Jew who is 'Western' from tip to toe, you will find his original Mizrahiyut [Orientalism], to the point that it is difficult to imagine that he is a son of the West. We are returning now not only to our country, but to ourselves and to our origin. All the attempts to prove that we are Western will thus be to no avail, particularly after we again settle here and the climate of the Land begins to leave its mark on us, as on the other inhabitants of the Land." [132] 'Abadi urged recognition of "true, non-fraudulent Mizrahiyut, pure and distilled." He explained that this Mizrahiyut was more genuine and healthy than "fraudulent Ma'araviyut [Occidentalism]." 'Abadi ended his article by mentioning the golden age of Jewish-Muslim symbiosis in Muslim Spain: "Our meeting with the Arab nation was the most blessed of all our meetings through the course of history. . . . There is no reason to fear that the encounter this time would not be even better than its precursor. A little study of Arab affairs, some good will, and true neutrality will lead us to the genuine understanding that will lead to harmonious unity between Hebrews and Arabs."[133]

Despite the time that passed between the publication of this article and 'Abadi's testimony before the Anglo-American Committee of Inquiry, his strong belief in the importance of Jewish-Arab rapprochement remained intact. This committee sought to clarify the claim by the Sephardi delegation that the status of Jews in Arab countries had deteriorated and that they faced legislation that discriminated against them. Replying to a question as to whether it was not Zionism and the demand for a state that had led to the deterioration in relations between Jews and Arabs in the Middle East, 'Abadi acknowledged that there was some foundation for seeing Zionism as one of the causes of this process. However, he argued that the main factor was the growing hatred of foreigners in most Middle Eastern countries, a phenomenon that was not directed only toward Jews. 'Abadi reiterated the comments in the Sephardi memorandum that Islam had generally expressed tolerance toward non-Muslim minorities, and that in the past Muslims had indeed treated Jews fairly in Muslim countries, although Jews had been considered second-class citizens. "It was a situation of humiliation, but not of discrimination, and Islam should be given credit for this," 'Abadi said. However, he continued, "over the past 20 years, a fanatic nationalism has emerged in the Muslim countries and the Jews have been the first victims of this trend." 'Abadi explained that "we do not deny that Zionism has, to an extent, served as a convenient pretext for the deteriorating condition of the Jews," but "this was just one among a series of reasons for this exacerbation." To the question of whether there were any disagreements among the Sephardi leaders regarding the desirability of Zionism, 'Abadi replied: "There may some-times be profound disagreements. Some Jews who are more assimilated than others adopt this position." However, he reiterated the Zionist position and the demand of the Sephardi delegation to open the gates of Palestine to Sephardi immigration, emphasizing that "Zionism is not just a matter of refugees, but a question of national revival."[134]

The testimony of the leaders of the Sephardi and Oriental Jewish communities in Palestine before UNSCOP in 1947 again emphasized the communities' historical role as mediators. However, the leaders also highlighted the grave situation of Jews in Middle Eastern countries and thus expressed once again the connection between Palestine and the Middle East as a whole, and their own responsibility for the fate of the Jewish communities in the Levant.

The Sephardi delegation to UNSCOP was headed by Eliachar, who had recently replaced Abulafia as president of the Council of the Sephardi Community of Jerusalem. Eliachar's election to that position in February 1947 reflected a shift in the balance of power in the council. For the first time, a majority of the council's members were Oriental Jews from Arab countries, rather than representatives of the Sephardi community in Palestine. Eliachar's election also reflected a renewed attempt in December 1946 to create a national Sephardi organization under the name of the National Representative Body of Sephardi Jews in the Land of Israel (Moetezet Hanetzigut Ha'artzit Shel Hayehudim Hasfaradim Be'eretz Israel).[135]

The composition of the delegation to UNSCOP was coordinated and approved by the National Council Executive and the Political Department of the Jewish Agency Executive.[136] Eliachar also submitted a memorandum he prepared for prior review by Ben-Zvi, Moshe Shertok (Sharett), and Eliyahu Sasson from the political department of the Jewish Agency.[137] The Sephardi delegation included Eliachar; Rabbi Uziel; Elmaleh; Binyamin (Salah) Sasson, head of the Committee of Iraqi Immigrants, whose inclusion reflected the growing involvement of the Oriental communities in the Sephardi leadership; and David Sitton, coeditor of the journal *Hed-Hamizrah*. The delegation was accompanied by Ya'acov Shimoni, a member of the Arab Bureau of the Political Department, and Zvi Schwartz, an attorney. It declared that one of its purposes was "to present our case in order to put an end to slander against the Sephardi public in the Land of Israel and in exile."[138]

In his testimony to UNSCOP, Eliachar noted that good relations between Jews and Arabs in Palestine were impossible under the current Arab leadership of the Mufti, Haj Amin al-Husseini. This view, as we will discuss in the chapter 2, was one of the foundations of the Zionist arguments in the Mandatory years. The Sephardi leadership also expressed its clear rejection of any limitation on Jewish immigration, while emphasizing that it opposed any regime that would force the Jews to remain a minority in Palestine. Eliachar's testimony provides a glimpse into the ways the Sephardi leadership perceived the deteriorations in social relations between Jews and Arabs in the mixed cities, and the weakening of its belief in the ability of Jews to live as a minority among Arabs, as a result of the 1929 riots. Many Arabs condemned the murder of Jews in the mixed cities, and friendly relations with the Jews had rapidly been restored, Eliachar said. Nevertheless, "no longer can Jews intermingle freely in Arab towns and villages, even if they are of Oriental background and indigenous residents. Based on our past experience and recent events in the country, we cannot imagine being dependent on an Arab state. Our bare lives will be in danger and the fate of the Hebron community may be ours too."[139] Referring to Arab-Jewish relations in the Arab countries, Eliachar suggested that the Jews were being held as hostages by the governments of these countries. The Sephardi explanation for the increased anti-Jewish sentiments in the Middle East was a combination of antiforeign sentiment, religious fanaticism, and the nationalism and ignorance of the masses. All those led to the use of the term "a war on Zionism" as a pretext for the deteriorating conditions faced by the Jews.[140]

In his testimony, Eliachar emphasized that he was speaking on behalf of Jewish communities in Arab countries who could not speak freely. He demanded that Palestine be open to Jewish immigration from these countries. He again emphasized his belief that Jews and Arabs could live together, and that the Sephardi and Oriental Jews had a special role to play in achieving this goal: "Having been born in Oriental countries, knowing their customs and languages, their mode of life and their ethics, the Sephardim are called upon to play a greater role in the establishment of harmony and peace through the Middle East." Eliachar concluded his request to secure the political rights of the Jews as established by the Mandate with a statement of his belief that peace between the semitic peoples was a real possibility: "As the indigenous Jewish population of Palestine, we demand the restitution of our rights, by the abolition of the White Paper of 1939 and all it stands for, and the opening of the gates to all those Jews in need of a home whether from East or West. . . . To impose upon Palestine a permanent Jewish minority is to add insult to injury. . . . The courageous establishment of a haven of refuge for the most persecuted people since man was created may bring peace to this country, to the Middle East and to the world, in collaboration with all our Semite and Arab brethren."[141]

During the months following his appearance before UNSCOP, Eliachar visited Europe and the United States in an attempt to draw the attention of the world to the conditions of Jews in Arab countries. During his visit, Jewish-Arab relations in Palestine and in the Middle East as a whole entered a new stage. The Sephardi leadership, which had attempted to position itself as mediators between the two peoples during the Mandatory period, had to make a similar attempt as a result of the 1948 war and the establishment of the State of Israel. The attempt by the Sephardi and Oriental leadership to serve as intermediaries between the majority Jews and the minority Arabs, and between old inhabitants and new immigrants, reflects once again the affinity between the ethnic problem and the Arab Question, and the Sephardi and Oriental Jews' perception of themselves as cultural, social, and political mediators.

TWO

Natives of the Orient

Political and Social Rapprochement

The riots that began on August 1929 signaled the end of the first decade of Jewish-Arab relations in Palestine under British rule. The violent nature of the 1929 national confrontation not only shocked the Sephardi and Oriental Jews, who were severely affected by the events, but also led to a reexamination of the Zionist policy toward the Arab Question and the national conflict.[1] Following the 1929 riots, the Jewish Agency and the National Council established the United Bureau (Halishka Hameuhedet), which was supposed to examine ways of advancing rapprochement between Jews and Arabs in Palestine.

Several prominent Sephardi and Oriental Jewish leaders were active members of the United Bureau. In fact, the United Bureau was the first official organization in the Zionist administration in Palestine in which Sephardi Jews took an active part. Despite its short period of operation, the United Bureau serves as an important example for the special contribution of members of the Sephardi and Oriental communities to Jewish-Arab relations. Other institutions that will be examined in this chapter include the Arab Bureau of the Political Department of the Jewish Agency and the Arab Department of the Histadrut, which was also established following the 1929 riots. The involvement of Sephardi and Oriental Jews in these organizations demonstrates their attempt to influence the political decisions regarding Jewish-Arab affairs, and the way they viewed their unique role as intermediaries between the two peoples. This chapter will focus on their role as mediators in the political and diplomatic spheres, as well as in the socioeconomic one.

Oriental Jews in Arab-Jewish Negotiations

In the early 1920s, as a result of the changes in the region following World War I, Chaim Weizmann, president of the World Zionist Organization, instructed the Information Office of the Zionist Commission to formulate a plan for action toward Palestinian Arabs. The proposed steps included forging an alliance between the Zionist movement and Bedouin sheikhs in the south of Palestine, nurturing friendly relations between Jews and Arabs, and encouraging the Arabic press to publish Zionist propaganda.[2] As natives of the country, and because of their close familiarity with Arab culture and society, the Sephardi leaders viewed themselves as the natural and ideal candidates to manage the political contacts and negotiations conducted during the 1920s between Arabs and Jews.[3] The participants in the negotiations with Arab leaders, led by Weizmann, included Sephardi and Ashkenazi Jewish intellectuals from the cadre that had emerged during the late nineteenth century in the old Yishuv, such as Shlomo Kalmi and Asher Sapir, a native of Hebron who had studied law at Istanbul University. The Sephardi Chief Rabbi Ya'acov Meir also participated in the negotiations, meeting Sherif Hussein Ibn 'Ali and Emir Abdullah in 1924 as part of a delegation that also included David Yellin and Colonel Frederick Kisch, the head of the political department in the Zionist Executive. During the early 1920s some Sephardi and local Jews, such as Nissim Malul (discussed in chapter 3), were also active for short periods in the Arab Bureau of the Zionist Commission and the National Council.[4]

In accordance with the division of responsibilities between the Zionist Executive and the National Council, efforts to address the Arab Question were coordinated by the Zionist Executive's Political Department, despite attempts made by the National Council Executive to assume responsibility for Jewish-Arab relations. As discussed in chapter 1, the Sephardi and Oriental Jewish communities did not have any representatives in the Zionist Executive. The result was the distancing of the communities' leaders from the discussion of the Arab Question and the rejection of repeated requests by the main Sephardi organizations to serve as mediators between Jews and Arabs.[5] The main person who coordinated the political negotiations until 1929 was Haim Margaliot-Kalvarisky. He was the head of the Arab Department of the National Council until it was dissolved in 1923 and was the head of the Arab Bureau of the Zionist Executive in Jerusalem until 1927.[6]

Following the riots of August 1929, the Jewish Agency Executive and the National Council Executive recognized the need for a change of policy regarding the Arab Question This realization led to a greater degree of cooperation between the two bodies and the formation of the United Bureau. The United Bureau was headed by Kisch and Yitzhak Ben-Zvi; its members also included Yellin, Yosef Eliyahu Chelouche, Yitzhak Shamaya Eliachar, Yosef Meyuchas, Shabtai Levy, Zaki Alhadiff, Yisrael Rokach, Meir Dizengoff, and Kalvarisky. The Sephardim were also represented in the new body by A. Laniado, as its secretary, and Chaim Hasson, as its translator from Arabic to Hebrew.[7] Like most of his Sephardi colleagues in the United Bureau, Hasson was a member of the Association of Pioneers of the East, in which capacity he often emphasized the importance of rapprochement between Arabs and Jews and the need for mutual understanding.

The purpose of the United Bureau, as perceived by its Sephardi members, was to improve Jewish-Arab relations. To this end, they made a distinction in the Bureau's work between negative and positive actions. Negative actions included political and journalistic activities intended to turn Palestinian public opinion against the Mufti, Hajj Amin al-Husseini, and to strengthen the Palestinian opposition to him. These included, for example, the publication of articles in the Arabic press advocating cooperation with the Zionists. The positive actions sought to encourage economic and cultural cooperation between Jews and Arabs to promote rapprochement between the two peoples.[8] Discussions in the United Bureau mentioned the need to place educated Arabs in clerical positions in Jewish-owned banks, to include them in commercial and financial companies by providing loans for Arab businesses and investors, and to employ Arabs in other Jewish-run businesses. The cultural sphere was another area that was considered vital for improving relations, particularly studying Arabic and employing Arab teachers in Jewish schools. The United Bureau called for a renewal of the friendly relations between Jews and Arabs that had existed prior to the riots, emphasizing the role of local leaders from both sides and the resumption of visits and other contacts.[9]

The approach advocated by the Sephardi and Oriental activists in the United Bureau was particularly evident in the actions of Alhadiff. Born in 1890, he served as the mayor of Tiberias from 1923 until he was murdered in October 1938, during the Arab Revolt. Alhadiff served as an example for local leaders, who—based on their personal acquaintance with Arab leaders and their familiarity with Arab culture and the Arabic language—believed in the ability of the Sephardim to serve as a bridge between Jews and Arabs. During the riots of 1929, Alhadiff managed to prevent the spread of violence to the mixed city that he governed. In the United Bureau, he strove to develop contacts with Arab dignitaries and prominent Palestinian leaders in the Galilee, with whom he was familiar not only because of his official position but also because he was a native of the country and knew Arabic and the Arab culture.[10]

Alhadiff also supported the idea—prevalent in the United Bureau—that it was important to strengthen the Palestinian opposition to the Mufti, while emphasizing the role played by local Arab leaders in influencing the rural population. To this end he sought to strengthen ties with Arab sheikhs and *mukhtars* (village leaders) and called for the publication of leaflets in Arabic urging rapprochement and peace between the two peoples and trying to reduce the level of incitement in the Arabic press. In keeping with the approach of the Sephardi leadership since the last years of the Ottoman rule, Alhadiff made a distinction between Christian and Muslim Arabs and recommended that the United Bureau work to enhance this division within Palestinian society and exploit it as part of Zionist policy.[11]

One of Alhadiff's colleagues in the United Bureau was Shabtai Levy. Born in Istanbul in 1876, Levy served at the time as a member of the Haifa City Council and became mayor of the city in the 1940s.[12] Levy recommended that the United Bureau promote rapprochement between Arab villages and neighboring Jewish agricultural communities by developing contacts between the leaders of the respective communities and by using the Jewish communities as a base for the provision of economic and medical assistance to their Arab rural neighbors. He also proposed that Arab children be educated in Jewish schools. In the economic sphere, Levy suggested establishing a joint Jewish-Arab chamber of commerce in the mixed cities.[13] As will be discussed later in this chapter, the same approach was adopted by the Arab Bureau of the Political Department of the Jewish Agency.

The role of Alhadiff and Levy demonstrated the changing status of the political leadership of the Sephardi and Oriental Jews during the Mandatory period. After World War I, the Jewish leaders in the Arab world continued to play a mediating role between the colonial rulers, the local royal families, the Arab national leadership, and the Jewish community in their respective countries.[14] In Palestine, by contrast, the Sephardi elite lost this function. The Jewish Agency Executive, which as noted above did not include representatives of the Sephardim, assumed the role of intermediary with the authorities. The Sephardi leaders also found it increasingly difficult to maintain their traditional role as mediators and go-betweens among Jews, Christians, and Muslims since Palestine lacked any shared (Jewish-Arab) government, including legislative and administrative institutions. However, they were able to maintain this role in the municipal administrations of the mixed cities, including Haifa, Jaffa, Jerusalem, and Tiberias. Accordingly, the political power of Sephardi Jewry became concentrated in the local Jewish community committees (*va'ad hakehilah*).

Until it was dismantled at the beginning of 1931, the United Bureau continued to try to strengthen Palestinian opposition groups and establish political parties to oppose the Mufti, who was perceived as the main obstacle to improving relations between Jews and Arabs. The bureau also worked to gather information about developments in Palestinian and regional Arab politics. One of the main figures responsible for these activities was Aharon Chaim Cohen, who headed the Intelligence Service of the United Bureau. Cohen was born in Jerusalem in 1906 to a family of mixed Iranian and Moroccan origin. He worked in a print shop before joining the Haganah, where he was involved mainly with intelligence work. In the United Bureau, Cohen collected and analyzed information from different sources about domestic Palestinian politics and the relations between the Palestinian leadership and the British.[15] Indeed, Cohen's extensive contacts among Palestinians who worked as informants in the service of the United Bureau may serve as an example of the intelligence operations in the Yishuv at the time.[16]

One of the strategies used by Cohen was to exploit for the benefit of the Zionist movement the internal conflicts between the Palestinian opposition and the Mufti and between the rural and urban Palestinian elites. As part of this process, the members of the United Bureau held meetings and maintained political contacts with Palestinian opposition members. Yellin, Chelouche, and Levy, among others, were involved in the bureau's negotiations with Omar al-Bitar, president of the Muslim-Christian Association and mayor of Jaffa, and with Omar Salah al-Barghouti, a former member of the Arab Executive Committee.[17]

During the same period Weizmann met Arab leaders in Egypt and North Africa, with the assistance of his envoy, 'Ovadia Kimchi. Born in Hebron in 1888, Kimchi was a reporter for the newspaper *Doar Hayom* in the early 1920s. In 1930 he arranged a meeting between Weizmann and Abbas Hilmi Pasha, the former khedive of Egypt, who had been deposed at the beginning of World War I. During the 1930s, Kimchi was based in Paris, where he served as the editor of the journal of the World Confederation of Sephardi Jews. In February 1931 he met with Abbas Hilmi Pasha, and later that year he met with Emir Abdullah in Amman on Weizmann's behalf. Kimchi reported that during a visit to Algeria he drew on his experience as a native of the Orient with expertise in mediation and rapprochement between Arabs and Jews to encourage the formation of a joint committee of Jewish and Arab intellectuals. Apart from his diplomatic contacts, Kimchi's chief achievement was the organization of a Jewish-Arab assembly in

Algiers in March 1931, where he talked about the common semitic origins of Jews and Arabs and on the similarities between Hebrew and Arab cultures.[18]

The United Bureau was also involved in the organization of a Jewish-Arab association under the name of the Semitic Federation (Hahitahdut Hashemit).[19] The federation was proposed by Kalvarisky as a cultural association of young people who supported Jewish-Arab cooperation in the fields of economics, commerce, health, agriculture, and education, with the goal of promoting athletic competitions between Jews and Arabs and the study of Hebrew and Arabic.[20] The federation was launched in Nablus as a joint initiative of Akram Tukan, an activist in the Arab Agrarian Party, and Kalvarisky. Meetings were held at the Nordia Hotel in Jerusalem between Kalvarisky and groups of young Arabs, including teachers, clerks, and students, to promote the idea. The next stage included two meetings of young Jews and Arabs, held on April 15 and 19, 1930, at the Amdorsky Hotel in Jerusalem. The meetings were attended by Malul, Kalvarisky, and A. Laniado, in addition to eighteen Arab participants led by Tukan.[21]

The meetings resulted in the establishment of a joint committee to promote fraternal relations between the two peoples. The committee met at the home of one of its Jerusalem members, and the participants included Meir Laniado, David Avissar, Chaim Hasson, Yosef Rivlin, Eliyahu (Elias) Sasson, Eliyahu Epstein (Elath), and Reuven Zaslani (Shiloah).[22] The organization was short-lived and essentially served to strengthen the Palestinian opposition to the Mufti. Kalvarisky sought to establish additional branches of the Semitic Federation as an Arab political party. These attempts had a clear political orientation and attracted considerable criticism in the Arabic press. Moreover, the Arab participants did not come from the senior ranks of the Palestinian social and political circles.[23] Nevertheless, some of the Jewish participants in the meetings would later play a crucial role in the contacts between Jews and Arabs under the auspices of the Arab Bureau of the Political Department of the Jewish Agency. Those included Sasson, Epstein, and Shiloah.

As noted, Cohen served as coordinator and fieldworker for the United Bureau, remaining active until well into the 1930s. Until 1937 he continued to manage the contacts between the leaders of the Jewish Agency and the Palestinian leaders, as well as the Arab national leaders elsewhere in the Middle East.[24] In this capacity he supervised the contacts between Moshe Shertok (Sharett), head of the Jewish Agency's Political Department, and Emir Abdullah before the outbreak of the Arab Revolt. Cohen also accompanied David Ben-Gurion, chairman of the Jewish Agency Executive, in some of the meetings and discussions he held in 1934–36 with Arab and Palestinian leaders.[25] Some of the

Sephardi leaders reacted to these activities with suspicion, questioning Cohen's ability to manage diplomatic contacts with Palestinian national leaders as part of a broader criticism of the policy of the national institutions regarding the Arab Question. For example, Yitzhak Molcho commented in 1936 that the way Cohen managed the contacts of the Yishuv with the Arabs was a fiasco.[26] However, the practical nature of Cohen's work positioned him as one of the founders of the Haganah's Intelligence Service (Sherut Yedi'ot, or SHAI), which developed during the 1930s, and finally etablished in 1940. Indeed, Cohen's case demonstrates the multiplicity of orientations that existed among the Oriental Jewish leaders, as well as the different facets and versions of rapprochement attempts. Sasson provides another such example.

Eliyahu Sasson and the Arab Bureau

The change in the Zionist leadership following the elections to the third Assembly of Representatives of the Yishuv and the elections to the Zionist Congress had a clear effect on Jewish-Arab relations, as well as in other areas. In August 1931, Chaim Arlozoroff was appointed head of the Political Department of the Jewish Agency, while Yitzhak Ben-Zvi assumed the position of chairman of the National Council Executive. Arlozoroff sought to change the approach to the Arab Question and to emphasize economic and social aspects, along with the diplomatic contacts that were already under way. He consulted regularly with Yehuda Burla, Alhadiff, and Avraham Elmaleh and appointed Shertok as coordinator of the Arab Bureau of the Political Department of the Jewish Agency.[27] Arlozoroff's activities highlighted the division of responsibilities between the Jewish Agency's Political Department, which focused on diplomatic contacts, and the Haganah, which concentrated on collecting information on security-related issues.[28] Following his assassination in 1933, Shertok assumed responsibility for the Political Department, including its contacts with Arab representatives. He brought two new staff members into the department: Epstein, a graduate of the American University in Beirut, and Shiloah, who was sent in 1931 (to collect intelligence for security purposes) by the department to work as a Hebrew teacher in Baghdad after graduating from the Teachers' Seminary in Jerusalem and while studying at the Hebrew University.[29] In 1934, Sasson also joined the department.

Born in Damascus in 1902 to a merchant family of Baghdadi origin, Sasson attended the Alliance Israélite Universelle primary school. After completing high school at the Azaria Christian school in Damascus, he traveled to Beirut to attend St. Joseph's College. In his memoirs, Sasson described the cultural atmosphere in his parents' home and at St. Joseph's as one characterized by Jewish-Arab integration. His portrayal of his father's warm social and commercial relations with his Arab friends and of the role his father played as an arbitrator and mediator in various affairs seems to echo the way Sasson saw his own public position as an adult. Sasson described his days at Azaria School and St. Joseph's as a time when he met and became friends with many Muslims and Christians from Syria, Lebanon, and Iraq. As adults, his friends played leading roles as politicians and journalists in these countries. Sasson was active in the Zionist organization Hathiya (Renaissance) but was also a member of the Arab Club and closely connected to the Arab national activists who supported King Faisal's rule in Damascus.[30] In many ways, Sasson was the most prominent example of the hybrid Jewish-Arab identity, as we will argue below.

The first encounter between Sasson and the Sephardi elite of Jerusalem and Palestine took place in Damascus during World War I.[31] Sasson's upbringing and early years in Damascus, his work in both Arab nationalist and Zionist circles, his personal connections with prominent figures of the Arab national movement, and his journalistic work all were part of his complex and hybrid Jewish-Arab identity as a member of the Jewish intellectual community in the Levant. His Jewish-Arab identity played a significant role in his political and diplomatic work in the Arab Bureau of the Political Department of the Jewish Agency. Starting in 1934, when he joined the department, Sasson became the central figure in the negotiations and contacts between Jews and Arabs in Palestine in particular, and in the Middle East in general.

Before joining the department Sasson had expressed his political views in various articles published in the Hebrew and Arabic press in Palestine and elsewhere in the Arab world. He was one of the most prominent exponents of the view that the Oriental and Sephardi Jews were ideally placed to serve as mediators between Jews and Arabs and to help promote understanding between the two peoples. Like Avissar, Burla, Laniado, and Molcho, however, Sasson believed that acting within organizations that included only one ethnic group would weaken, rather than strengthen, the Sephardi position. Sasson did not join the various Sephardi organizations that were active in the Yishuv in the 1920s, nor was he among the Sephardim in the United Bureau during that decade. In addition, he criticized the Jewish Agency Executive's policy regarding the Arab Question. What, then, were Sasson's motivations in joining the Jewish Agency's Political Department in 1934?

The explanation for the change in Sasson's position may lie in the appointment of Arlozoroff as head of the department and the recruitment of Shertok to it. Sasson's involvement in the Zionist establishment began at about the same time as the convening of the General Islamic Congress in Jerusalem in December 1931, on the initiative of the Mufti. As noted above, Arlozoroff customarily consulted with Sephardi leaders, and Sasson was brought into this circle alongside Alhadiff, Burla, and Elmaleh. On November 24, 1931, Arlozoroff described a meeting with Sasson in his diary: "Sasson came to us in the evening. He has received an invitation from the Mufti to visit him. The contacts between this young Damascene Jew and the Arab nationalists date back to his period of involvement in the Syrian independence movement. He is acquainted with the nationalist activists in Syria and publishes articles in their newspapers."[32] It seems that both the Mufti and Arlozoroff were interested in hearing Sasson's opinions and his analysis of the intentions of the other side. "Is this the way to criticize a friend?" the Mufti asked Sasson at their meeting, referring to an article Sasson had published in the Damascus newspaper *Alif-Ba* in which he had criticized the Mufti.[33] The first meeting between Sasson and the Mufti took place in November 1928 during an interview for a newspaper article, but the Mufti's reference to Sasson as a friend alludes to the period when both men were active in Damascus during King Faisal's regime.[34] This comment underscores the way Sasson became an expert in Middle Eastern diplomacy in the service of the Zionist movement, while never forgetting his own identity as a native of the Orient.

In an open letter of June 20, 1932, to Tawfiq Mizrahi, his close friend and colleague in Damascus, Sasson described his change in attitude toward the Jewish Agency Executive: "I will not, I believe, be revealing a secret if I note that until recently, that is to say until the point at which Colonel Kisch completed his work in the [Jewish] Agency, I was also among those who criticized the Executive for its inefficient attitude to the Arab Question and its failure to find a way to reach peace and understanding that would benefit the Executive itself. Today, however, under the chairmanship of Dr. Arlozoroff, I have changed my opinion completely, and instead of attacking the current Executive I find that it is my duty to stand alongside it and to struggle on its behalf."[35] Sasson ended his letter to Mizrahi by declaring that the time has come "for the two brothers, the Oriental and the Western [Jews], to work together for the sake of the ideal. This will reopen the longed-for golden age in the life of the Israeli nation, which will also lead to the path of understanding with the Arabs."

Sasson's work in the Jewish Agency began during the Arab Revolt and continued through the early days of World War II. As a result of the activities of the United Bureau, contacts between the leaders of the Yishuv and Palestinians opposing to the Mufti continued during the years preceding the Arab Revolt. During the revolt, the Jewish Agency Executive monitored the meetings between the group of the Five, as they were known—headed by Magnes, and several Palestinian figures, while at the same time holding its own meetings with two members of the Arab Higher Committee, Ragheb Nashashibi and Hussein al-Khalidi. During the Arab Revolt, the Jewish Agency Executive also held meetings with members of the Syrian National Bloc, and once again the idea was raised of including Palestine and the Yishuv in a pan-Arab federation. Following the publication of the conclusions of the Peel Commission, Palestinian Arab leaders also met in the United States, Britain, and Switzerland with Jewish individuals who did not represent the Jewish Agency Executive. The Jewish Agency Executive itself was involved in the contacts between Kalvarisky and al-Barghouti and Hulusi al-Kheiri, a member of the Istiqlal Party.[36]

Sasson attended some of these meetings, and he continued to promote the Zionist policy of supporting the opposition to the Mufti. As part of these efforts, Sasson arranged meetings and other contacts between members of the Zionist movement and Fakhri al-Nashashibi—who, until his assassination in 1941, was the most senior figure opposing the Mufti. After the Mufti fled to Beirut in 1937, Sasson moved there for several months, making frequent trips to Damascus and Jerusalem. During this period, Sasson contacted Palestinian exiles, visiting the cafés frequented by the Mufti's associates and monitoring his activities in the city. Damascus and Beirut were also the cities in which Sasson nurtured his contacts with the leaders of the Syrian National Bloc.[37]

During the Arab Revolt, Sasson continued to follow the Syrian National Bloc's struggle for independence and to examine the attitude of the Syrian leaders vis-à-vis the Zionist movement. During his meetings with former Lebanese President Emile Eddé, Syrian Prime Minister Jamil Mardam, the Syrian opposition leader 'Abd al-Rahman Shahabander, and others, Sasson sought to understand if their positions toward the idea of an Arab federation included acceptance of a Jewish state and tried to strengthen the relations between the two national movements. In the years before World War II, Sasson also visited Iraq, where, as in other places, he established a network of informants, read local newspapers, and held meetings with journalists and senior politicians. In particular, he met Iraqi Prime Minister Nuri al-Said, who was one of the prominent members of King Faisal's regime in Damascus. In the 1940s, the attention of Sasson and the Political Department shifted to Egypt, the home of the Arab League. During this period, Sasson also developed closer ties with Emir Abdullah and managed the contacts between the Department and the emir's envoy, Muhammad al-Unasi.

Sasson also continued his meetings with 'Awni 'Abd al-Hadi, the leader of the Palestinian Istiqlal Party.[38]

Ezra Danin, one of the founders of the Haganah's Intelligence Service, mentioned that he joined Sasson at more than one meeting with Arab leaders in Beirut and Damascus during the early 1940s: "Eliyahu Sasson's contacts in Beirut were absolutely incredible. No door there was locked for him, and he was always welcomed with warmth and affection. He was truly at home in both these Arab capitals."[39] Danin, who was born in Jaffa in 1903 to a family of mixed Polish and Iraqi origin, spoke fluent colloquial Arabic, but he refrained from participating in the discussions because he realized that his use of colloquialism would impair his social standing in the minds of those with whom he met. In contrast, Sasson had a perfect command of Arabic and led the meetings and discussions in Arabic with the Arab leaders, with most of whom he had been personally acquainted since his student days and his activities in the circle around King Faisal in Damascus. While Danin preferred to meet with Palestinians from all ranks of society, Sasson concentrated on the elite, among whose members he felt most comfortable.

Sasson's frequent trips to Syria and Lebanon during the Arab Revolt illustrate the freedom with which he moved around the Middle East, particularly between Beirut and Damascus. In his memoirs he recalls arriving in Beirut on October 4, 1937: "As I got out of the car in Beirut, several Arabs, presumably from Palestine, surrounded me and asked me for news about the country. They assumed I was an Arab as I was wearing a tarboosh and speaking Arabic."[40] During the Arab Revolt and the early stages of World War II, Sasson thus moved between Jerusalem and Beirut, shifting from one identity to another, contacting friends and acquaintances among the Arab nationalist leadership and the local Jewish communities alike, and establishing networks of informants who provided him with the latest political updates concerning local and regional developments. In this mission, Sasson remained faithful to his view that the Jewish Agency's Political Department should focus on the Arab elite. Sasson attached little importance to the Arab masses, who he believed would follow the example of the urban notables. The Arab elite, including Arab intellectuals, constituted the target of Sasson's diplomatic actions and, to a certain extent, the cadre to which he himself belonged.[41] His connections reflected the diplomatic orientation of the Political Department, as well as the collection of political intelligence that would expand later in the 1940s along with the activities of the Haganah's Intelligence Service.

The sociologist Gil Eyal describes the tension within the Israeli intelligence agencies between academic and military analysis, and between those who specialized in the collection of information and those responsible for analyzing it. Eyal notes the connection between the Israeli academic world and the Israeli intelligence agencies. This connection reflects an approach encapsulated in the expression "know your enemy," embodying a distant standpoint vis-à-vis Arab society that, it could be argued, includes a measure of Orientalism.[42] Eyal distinguishes between two types of Orientalist (*mizrahan*) expertise that developed in Palestine between the Arab Revolt and the 1948 war. The first type was that of academic experts who were affiliated with the Institute of Oriental Studies at the Hebrew University, many of whom were connected with Sasson in his work at the Political Department of the Jewish Agency.[43] This connection between academic expertise and more practical political work and knowledge would develop further after the establishment of the State of Israel. According to Eyal, the second type of Orientalist expertise was that of the Arabists, Jews who mastered Arabic and served as advisors of different kinds to the Yishuv's political leadership. The Arabists included merchants, guards, mukhtars of Jewish settlements, and others who maintained regular connection with Arabs.[44] Members of this group were recruited for intelligence purposes, but at the same time they considered themselves to be mediators between Jews and Arabs.[45] People like Sasson, Alhadiff, and others discussed in this chapter had a hybrid Jewish-Arab identity and demonstrated the complex matrix of relationships between the ethnic and national components of this identity.[46]

The involvement of Oriental Jews in diplomatic activities, which is presented in the literature as an essentially intelligence-oriented pursuit, was also the product of these individuals' attempts to create cultural and linguistic bridges between Jews and Arabs and to enhance the Oriental Jews' involvement in Zionist institutions and their influence on Zionist policy. As we will see in the following chapters, the young Oriental Jews who were part of the new generation that emerged during the 1930s and 1940s in Palestine, and who became involved in the security apparatus of the Yishuv, continued this trend. However, their hybrid identity led them in a different direction, as they became more clearly integrated into the national struggle of the Yishuv. One of these figures was Moshe Sasson, Eliyahu's son, who was born in Damascus in 1926 and who, after serving in the Haganah's Intelligence Service, followed in his father's footsteps by entering the Israeli diplomatic service. In an interview many years later, Moshe Sasson was asked whether he was an Orientalist (*mizrahan*). He replied that he was a "native of the Orient" (*ben hamizrah*).[47] This comment sums up most of Eliyahu Sasson's life and work as well. His activities in the diplomatic and intelligence fields, which were motivated by his deep commitment to Zionism, enabled him to maintain his Jewish-Arab identity. His self-identification as a native of the Orient influenced his work within the Jewish Agency and was also apparent in his proposals for resolving the conflict between the two peoples.

Promoting Neighborly Relations

Beginning in the last stage of the Arab Revolt and during World War II, Eliyahu Sasson drafted three detailed documents that specified the working plan of the Arab Bureau that he was heading. These documents were submitted to Ben-Gurion and Shertok and demonstrated the way Sasson combined the political and security sphere with the enhancement of relations between Jews and Arabs in Palestine and the Middle East in general. These plans also highlighted the special place and role of Middle Eastern Jews in Jewish-Arab relations and their attempts to influence the political decision-making process.

The first document was submitted by Sasson in April 1939 to Ben-Gurion and outlined a proposal for improving Jewish-Arab relations. The goal was to maximize efforts to reach agreement with elements of the local and regional Arab population whom Sasson characterized as "responsible." He argued that the agreement that could be sought through these contacts would be based either on the establishment of two states in Palestine—one Arab and one Jewish—or on the formation of an Arab federation that would include an independent Jewish entity. In keeping with the dominant methodology employed by the United Bureau, Sasson's plan recommended intensifying propaganda and outreach efforts and encouraging the publication in the Arabic press of articles supporting a Jewish-Arab agreement; increasing the funding for the Arabic-language newspaper of the Arab Department of the Histadrut, *Haqiqat al-Amr*, and having the Political Department publish booklets in Arabic on political, economic, and social issues.[48]

In the political realm, Sasson recommended that the Political Department strengthen its ties with Arab activists—not on the basis of baksheesh (bribes), but making the point that relations between Arabs and Jews were in the interests of all the peoples of the Orient. In the economic sphere, the plan demonstrated the importance Sasson attached to combating the Arab boycott and to involving Arabs in Jewish commerce and industry. For example, he recommended that Arab merchants sell produce grown by Jewish farmers. On the basis of the experience of foreign companies that had become active in the Arab economy, Sasson suggested that Arab merchants be appointed as consultants in Jewish companies. He also advocated visits by Jewish economic delegations to Arab countries in an effort to promote commercial, agricultural, and industrial ties. In particular, Sasson proposed the development of direct contacts with the chambers of commerce in Arab countries.

In the social sphere, Sasson's memorandum suggested activities that would promote rapprochement between Jews and Arabs in the fields of sport and culture. The memorandum also emphasized the need to provide assistance for the Arab villages in Palestine by strengthening their ties with the adjacent Jewish communities, including the provision of loans and medical and agricultural assistance for the Arabs. Sasson also advocated meetings between the leaders of Arab and Jewish communities.

In political terms, Sasson's recommendations were similar to those of the Sephardi leaders active in the United Bureau. The failure of the contacts between Jews and Arabs to produce a peaceful resolution to the national conflict had led Sasson to the conclusion that there was little chance of cooperating with the Mufti and his supporters, and that rapprochement would be possible only with the Palestinian opposition circles. In his memorandum, Sasson mentioned the attempts made during the Arab Revolt to strengthen relations with Ragheb Nashashibi and other members of the opposition and argued that such actions must be coordinated and based on a political program. In this context he noted the activities of associations in the Yishuv that attempted to promote contacts with Arabs outside the official framework of the Zionist movement, adding that such actions might create the impression among the Arabs that the Jews were divided and that the Jewish Agency was not interested in rapprochement.

Sasson's memorandum does not specify what associations he meant. Nevertheless, based on previous correspondence we are reasonably certain his comments were directed at Magnes and Kalvarisky. In criticism of their activities, Sasson chose to emphasize the negative attitude of the Palestinian leaders toward Magnes. In a letter sent in April 1941 to Shertok and the members of the Jewish Agency Executive, Sasson warned that any negotiations with the Arabs that did not include a clear demand for the establishment of a Jewish state could damage the position of the Yishuv in its diplomatic contacts.[49] Sasson's position indicated a power struggle, but it was also held by the majority of the Sephardi leaders, as noted in chapter 1. The political part of Sasson's memorandum of April 1939 also discussed the question of supporting the French policy of encouraging separatist movements among the different ethnic and religious groups in Syria. Sasson believed that the idea of a federation of minorities in Syria could be used by the Zionist movement to argue against Arab rule in Palestine. He ended his memorandum by emphasizing that the implementation of his plan would require the mobilization and training of personnel. "Not every individual who has a command of Arabic is also qualified to be active among the Arabs, and not everyone who is familiar with Oriental affairs is competent to manage Oriental affairs," he wrote.[50] He suggested that Hebrew University graduates with a background in Islamic studies should be recruited for diplomatic work and efforts to promote rapprochement between Jews and Arabs.

This memorandum served as the foundation for an additional plan for strengthening relations between Jews and Arabs in Palestine that Sasson submitted to Shertok in April 1940. Drafted by Sasson and Zaslani, the plan focused mainly on the economic sphere, in which they believed Jews and Arabs had a common interest. Sasson and Zaslani argued that the agricultural sector was the most suitable for such cooperation, and accordingly they recommended the establishment of a joint Jewish-Arab rural organization. They also suggested that the Histadrut should expand its activities among Arab workers, particularly those employed on the railroads, in international factories, and in other sectors where Jews and Arabs worked alongside each other. The plan emphasized the importance of providing medical assistance and loans for Arab workers. Sasson and Zaslani also proposed that the number of Arabs employed in the Jewish economy should increase, and that cooperation between the two groups in the industrial and commercial sectors should also be considered. The plan advocated closer links between Jewish and Arab sports organizations and the study of Arabic by Jews, particularly in rural settlements. The authors argued that the Political Department should appoint Arabic teachers to work in the rural communities, who would also represent these communities in contacts with neighboring Arab villages.[51] As will be discussed below, these suggestions and plans were the basis for the activities that the Arab Bureau tried to promote and organize with the cooperation of the Arab Department of the Histadrut.

Sasson was also involved in the work of the Yishuv's formal Committee of Investigation of the Relations between Jews and Arabs (Hava'ada Leheker Hayahasim Bein Yehudim Ve'aravim). This committee was established in 1939 following the Zionist Congress by the Jewish Agency Executive and the National Council Executive. The committee was headed by Shlomo Kaplansky, then director of the Technion (the institute of technology in Haifa) and former director of the Settlement Department in the Zionist Executive. Sasson was the secretary of the committee and supervised it on behalf of the Jewish Agency Executive. The other members were Magnes; Ya'acov Tahon, former chairman of the National Council; Kalvarisky; Daniel Auster, deputy mayor of Jerusalem;

Michael Assaf, a journalist with *Davar* and a member of Mapai; and Sephardi Chief Rabbi Ben-Zion Meir Hai Uziel. The committee's discussions focused on the subject of diplomatic contacts between Jews and Arabs and the formulation of a proposed solution to the conflict between the two peoples. The committee also sought to submit proposals for rapprochement between Jews and Arabs in the social and economic spheres. To this end, it invited various experts—including Elmaleh; Judge Moshe Valero; and Shabtai Levy, by now mayor of Haifa—to suggest proposals.[52]

The participation of Rabbi Uziel in the committee reflected the recognition of his extensive activities during the Mandatory years in the areas of Jewish-Arab relations and the Sephardi community. Born in Jerusalem, Uziel was chosen for the position of the Sephardi chief rabbi in 1939. Before that he served as the Sephardi chief rabbi of Salonica and later of Tel Aviv. Uziel was a member of a circle of Sephardi religious activists identified with the Hamizrahi movement who were active in the bureaucracy of the chief rabbinate and the religious courts.[53] He held numerous positions in Sephardi organizations, including honorary president of the Council of the Sephardi Community in Jerusalem and of the World Confederation of Sephardi Jews. In the field of Jewish-Arab relations, Uziel served as the Sephardi representative to the St. James conference in 1939. He also maintained close connections with the leaders of Jewish communities throughout the Middle East and participated in several delegations sent by the Sephardi community in Palestine to visit the Jewish communities in Arab countries.

As a member of the committee, Uziel focused mainly on the need for economic and social rapprochement between Jews and Arabs. He refrained from offering opinions on diplomatic and political matters and abstained from a vote in November 1942 to approve the committee's political recommendation.[54] Nevertheless, during the committee's deliberations he expressed clear opposition to the binational idea and to the partition of the country, and he strongly supported the establishment of a Jewish state. Uziel did not believe that it would be possible to reach an agreement with the Palestinians under the leadership of the Mufti, and he expressed willingness to integrate Arabs in the administrative and governmental bodies of the state.[55]

According to the committee, relations between Jews and Arabs were characterized by cultural estrangement, social and economic segregation, and political opposition. By emphasizing cultural and social aspects, the committee hoped to overcome feelings of alienation, competition, and mistrust.[56] Many Oriental and Sephardi leaders also emphasized these aspects (as discussed in chapter 3), as did organizations such as Brit Shalom, Ichud, and the League for Jewish-Arab Rapprochement.[57] A similar emphasis on the importance of economic, social, and cultural rapprochement was also clear in a special meeting on May 13, 1943, that focused on the work of the Political Department regarding the Arab Question. Ben-Gurion initiated the meeting; some of the other participants were Assaf, Abba Hushi (who was the secretary of Haifa's Workers' Council and later became the mayor of Haifa), Ze'ev Sherf (a member of the Haganah command), Shartok, and Sasson.[58]

A similar approach was presented by Sasson. Toward the end of World War II he published another memorandum addressing the regional and local changes that had started to emerge as a result of the war, as part of his continued emphasis on the possibility of achieving agreement between Jews and Arabs. He submitted this memorandum to Shertok on March 5, 1944, around the time when the Arab League was established. The document focused mainly on a proposal to establish a network of informants in the Arab world who would collect political information for the Political Department. Sasson also recommended the expansion of propaganda efforts in Arabic, including the publication of articles in the Arabic press. The third item in his plan repeated a theme from his previous memorandums: he recommended fostering closer economic and social ties between Jews and Palestinian Arabs by reinforcing the existing contacts with Arabs maintained by orchard owners, the Association of Industrialists, sports organizations, merchants, Hadassah, Hebrew University, and the Histadrut. In the diplomatic sphere, Sasson argued that official talks should be undertaken with the Arabs with the goal of solving the Palestine problem through mutual agreement. The memorandum expressed a more optimistic position than in the past regarding the chances of securing Palestinian Arab, and perhaps even Syrian, agreement that a peaceful solution for the Arabs in the Middle East could be achieved if the Yishuv's demands were met.[59]

As Sasson's memorandums noted, the Arab Bureau was supposed to promote activities to dissipate tensions between Jews and Arabs and in general to improve relations between the two peoples. To achieve this goal, the Arab Bureau was interested in engaging in economic, cultural, and social activities as well as diplomatic contacts. To this end, it organized Arabic language classes in Jewish agricultural settlements, attracting some 500 Jewish participants a year—including adults from the settlements and workers in security agencies. The Arab Bureau paid for the classes and supervised the teachers; inspected their work; and provided study materials, books, newspapers, and Zionist propaganda. The idea was that the Arabic lessons would provide Jews in these communities with a basic grounding in Arabic to prevent friction between the Jews and their Arab neighbors. The Arab Bureau also supported evening classes for adults in the cities. And, as will be discussed in chapter 3, the Arab Bureau was involved in training courses for Arabic teachers, in cooperation with the Education Department of the National Council.[60]

Another institution that the Arab Bureau established was the Institution of Arab Studies (Hamosad Lelimudim 'Aravim), whose purpose was to train Jewish mukhtars and guards in the Jewish settlements. The purpose of the institution and its training courses was to avoid misunderstandings between the Jewish inhabitants in the agricultural settlements and their Arab neighbors in conflicts over water, borders, and areas of pasture. The goal was to encourage visits between villages and settlements, the study of colloquial Arabic, and getting to know Arab society. The original purpose of the Institution of Arab Studies was to train Jewish mukhtars and guards, training that began at the end of 1939 in an initiative of the Agricultural Department of the Histadrut. Sasson, Assaf, Danin, and Eliyahu Agassi (discussed in more detail in chapter 3) were among those who participated in the training courses and seminars.[61]

At the beginning of 1941 the responsibility for these training courses was handed to the Arab Bureau of the Political Department and the Agricultural Department of the Histadrut.[62] Starting in August 1944 the courses were held in the Institute of Arab Studies, which was established on Mount Carmel not too far from Haifa, and was headed by Danin and Yehoshua Palmon. Each course lasted for two months.[63] Other than learning colloquial Arabic, the students heard lectures about criminal law, land laws, and taxes; the responsibilities of the different law enforcement bodies; and the role of the mukhtars. They also studied the history of Palestinian Arabs and their political and economic organizations. Danin and Palmon worked mainly with the mukhtars and the guards, assuming that they could later gather intelligence. Indeed, the mukhtars, who had daily contact with their Arab neighbors, played an essential role in the Haganah's intelligence network.[64] Danin also sought to collect intelligence in places where Jews and Arabs interacted, including governmental offices, businesses, and British military camps.[65]

Another area in which the Arab Bureau was involved was the establishment of committees to encourage contacts between Jews and Arabs. The Committees for Neighborly Relations (Hava'adot Leyahasey Shkhenut) were organized by the Political Department with the goal of developing neighborly relations between Arabs and Jews, particularly in rural settlements but also in the mixed towns.[66] Such committees were established, for example, in 'Ein Harod, Safed,

'Afula, Nahalal, Hadera, and the Hula Valley. Their members were the settlements' mukhtars, guards, secretaries, and others involved in various aspects of Jewish-Arab relations.[67] The committees were active in promoting links and cooperation in different areas between Jews and Arabs; encouraging the study of Arabic; and organizing visits of Jewish students to Arab villages, the development of social ties between neighbors, and joint activities in various areas.

Despite the involvement of the Arab Bureau and the important cooperation and support from the Arab Department of Hashomer Hatza'ir, the committees did not always manage to carry out their aims.[68] Yehoshua Havoushi, for example, who was born in Iraq and immigrated to Palestine in 1933, taught Arabic and organized the committees in the Hula Valley area. He remembered that many Arabs visited the kibbutzim out of curiosity and sometimes to get assistance, but they were often pushed away by the members of the kibbutzim.[69] The committees tried to appease the members of the kibbutzim who rejected the hospitality of their Arab neighbors. Havoushi's comments also reveal the stereotypes involved in the relations between Jewish and Arab neighbors. For example, the Arabs clearly distinguished between Jews of Arab countries, who were called "Arabs," and Ashkenazi Jews, who were portrayed as occupiers.[70]

As was the case with other projects that Sasson initiated and was involved with, these committees were also intended to gather intelligence for the Political Department of the Jewish Agency and the Haganah's Intelligence Service.[71] In a meeting that took place in Nahariyah in October 1942, attended by Sasson, Danin, and Palmon, some of the questions that were debated had to do with how to gather information on Arab villages, including the atmosphere there and the political tensions in Arab society. Other issues that were addressed in this meeting had to do with requests from Arab villagers to get medical assistance in Jewish settlements and whether or not to integrate Arab students into Jewish schools.[72]

The fact that the committees were used not only for their alleged aim of developing neighborly relations between Jews and Arabs but also for security and political purposes was a topic of a debate among the committees' members.[73] The combined work of Danin and the Haganah on the one hand and of Sasson and the Arab Bureau on the other hand was reflected in the work done by the committees. Unlike the Arab Bureau, the Haganah and its Intelligence Service focused mainly on security and military efforts.[74] The Arabs who cooperated with the committees were often perceived as collaborators with Zionists. The narrow line between fostering Jewish-Arab relations and taking advantage of these relations for security purposes raised questions among the members of the committees and their Arab counterparts about the meaning and nature of the committees' activities. Some of these questions were resolved by Jewish attempts to foster Arab opposition to the Mufti and encourage Arab-Jewish cooperation on a socioeconomic and cultural basis.[75]

Committees for Neighborly Relations were established in the cities as well. The committee in Tel Aviv, which was headed by the Tiberias-born Judge Bechor-Shalom Sheetrit, was particularly active in promoting economic and social contacts between Jews and Arabs during this period.[76] The committee's work involved activists among the Sephardi community, who also emphasized the importance of advancing cooperation and joint interests between Jews and Arabs, and of Jews' familiarizing themselves with Arab culture. These ideas were expressed, for example, in a speech by Judge Zidkiyahu Harkabi at an October 1942 conference in Tel Aviv.[77] His presentation reflected his life story as an Arabic teacher who completed high school in Damascus. His son, Yehoshafat, would become a prominent figure in the academic and security circles in Israel.

In addition to the work done by the Arab Bureau of the Political Department discussed above, the bureau also focused on the identification, recruitment, and training of Oriental and Sephardi youth who would work to advance relations between Jews and Arabs in general and between Jewish and Arab co-workers. Sasson viewed the Oriental youth as disconnected from Zionist reality and lacking both national and general education. The Political Department therefore embarked on extensive activities among this group of young people. The goal was to fill in the gaps in their general and Zionist education, engage them in the department's activities, and train them to help the Zionist movement in its future contacts and relations with the Arabs.[78]

Mobilizing the Oriental Youth

The mobilization of the Jewish community in Palestine for the war effort, including volunteering for service in the British army, revealed political and ideological tensions within the Yishuv. In addition to disagreements within the Labor Zionist movement about enlistment in the British army as opposed to serving in the ranks of the Haganah or Palmach, its elite unit, there were disputes about the involvement of Oriental Jews in the mobilization effort and claims that the members of the Sephardi elite were evading the draft, while those who reported for service came from the poorer sections of the Oriental population.[79] Allegations that the Sephardim were failing to respond to the draft led to demands for apologies and proposals to take a census to examine the recruitment figures and prove the level of response of Sephardim to the draft. In addition, there were complaints about the failure to recognize the historical role of Oriental Jews in the Jewish Legion and the Ottoman Army during World War I.[80] These complaints were a direct response to the allegations we discussed at length above that Sephardim and Oriental Jews were not loyal to Zionism and lacked national awareness.

Chaim Shar'abi was one of the main activists among the Jewish Yemenite community in Palestine who addressed the volunteering for military service of Oriental Jews in general and of Yemenites in particular. In an article published in *Davar* in May 1945, Shar'abi discussed the history of Jews in the Arab armies and the stereotypical view that they avoided the military professions and the draft under the Ottoman Empire. According to Shar'abi, the change in the attitudes of the Sephardim to military service and to war in general that took place after their immigration to Palestine went beyond historical and national circumstances and had social, cultural, and gender dimensions. It was important for Shar'abi to note that almost a thousand members of the Yemenite Jewish community in Palestine joined the British army, while another thousand served in the defense forces in Palestine.[81] Ya'acov Yesh'ayahu—another Jewish Yemenite activist and a member of the Sephardi Labor Organization (Histadrut Ha'ovdim Hasfarardim)—also protested against the prevalent and damaging tendency in the Yishuv to claim that the Sephardim had failed to make an adequate contribution to the military effort. He demanded that the Jewish Agency appoint a special committee to examine the number of people who responded to the draft, including their ethnic affiliation.[82]

In addition to efforts to increase Oriental youth's military involvement during World War II, there was an increased attempt to encourage their involvement in Zionist institutions. The Political Department of the Jewish Agency sought to consolidate the Oriental communities, promote awareness of the special problems they faced, and integrate them more fully into the Zionist enterprise. As part of this effort, at the end of August 1942 the Arab Bureau of the Political Department organized a meeting in Tel Aviv, attended by dozens of young Jewish immigrants from Aleppo, Syria, to discuss their role in the Zionist movement. The speakers at the meeting included Yitzhak Shamosh, who talked about the need to promote nationalist sentiments and a commitment to mutual assistance among Oriental youth. Sasson addressed the meeting as well, in his capacity as head of the Arab Bureau. He claimed that the Jewish Agency was interested in organizing Oriental immigrants within the framework of the Zionist movement.

His comments focused in particular on the need for Oriental Jews to help the Zionist movement in at least one area: the Arab Question.[83]

The Council of the Sephardi Community in Tel Aviv was another organization that focused on organizing young Oriental immigrants, mobilizing them to participate in the national project and uniting the various organizations representing the Sephardi and Oriental Jews in Tel Aviv and Jaffa. Most of the council's members were from the Sephardi and Oriental middle classes, including judges, members of the Tel Aviv and Jaffa city councils, physicians, lawyers, bank managers, and merchants.[84] Headed by Sheetrit, the new council challenged the dominant status of the Council of the Sephardi Community in Jerusalem and organized cultural activities for Oriental youth to encourage them to become acquainted with Zionist and national activities. In their cultural and national activities for Oriental youth, members of the Tel Aviv council sought the support of Sasson and the Arab Bureau.[85]

Sasson's approach to the issue of Oriental youth revealed his critical view of the Council of the Sephardi Community in Jerusalem, under the leadership of Eliyahu Eliachar—who, Sasson claimed, encouraged ethnic separatism among the Sephardim. The debate that took place between Sasson and Eliachar was certainly colored by a considerable degree of personal animosity, but it touched on the complex relations between Oriental Jews and Sephardi Jews in the leadership of the Sephardi and Oriental Jewish communities in Palestine. As Yitzhak Levi observed in his research on the political activity of the Sephardim that this period marked a change in the balance of power among the Sephardi organizations, with the decline of the hegemonic power of the Council of the Sephardi Community in Jerusalem and with the growing power of the councils of Tel Aviv and Haifa.[86] This struggle represented not only an ethnic division between Oriental Jews from Arab countries and the Sephardi elite in Jerusalem, but also a generational difference between the old Sephardi notables based in Jerusalem and the younger generation based in Tel Aviv. Sasson claimed that he had no desire to deny or break the bond between Oriental and Sephardi Jews, but at the same time he strongly opposed the hegemonic role played by the Council of the Sephardi Community in Jerusalem at the expense of the Oriental communities in issues related to social, cultural, and political work. Moreover, Sasson saw the Sephardi leadership, particularly Eliachar, as a group that sought to challenge the status of the Jewish Agency Executive. He explained that "it is an open secret that a large section of the Sephardim have an apathetic stance toward many of our institutions and endeavors and I do not wish to see my fellow Oriental immigrants follow in their footsteps."[87]

In response, Eliachar declared that he had no desire to divide the Zionist camp and that the Sephardim were an integral part of the Yishuv and the Zionist movement. Eliachar's criticism focused on the lack of representation of the Sephardi public in Zionist institutions and on the claim that the Jewish Agency had alienated the Sephardim and failed to support their youth organizations. He argued that Sasson's work with Oriental youth, including his speech at the conference for young immigrants from Aleppo, actually reflected a "divide and rule" approach toward the Sephardi leadership. In an article titled "Divide and Rule," Eliachar demanded that the leaders of the national institutions work to organize Sephardi youth through the Sephardi leadership.[88] This was Eliachar's attempt to maintain the position of power of the Sephardi leadership in Jerusalem in spite of the growing influence of the Sephardi council in Tel Aviv.

Indeed, the tension and mutual suspicion between Sasson and Eliachar went much beyond the question of who would influence Oriental youth: it was rooted in the debate about the policy of the Zionist movement toward the Arab Question. During a discussion chaired by Ben-Gurion on May 13, 1943, about possible actions among the Arabs, Sasson explained the motives behind his activities among Oriental youth and, in so doing, fiercely criticized Eliachar. Sasson argued that the connection between Eliachar and Magnes in the framework of Ichud was jeopardizing and damaging the political contacts between the Jewish Agency Executive and Arab leaders. His criticism included the claim that Eliachar's activities among Oriental Jews were disastrous and negative. Sasson argued that young Oriental Jews were exposed to positions that opposed the Jewish Agency Executive and called for "preemptive action to prevent this scourge; just as these youth may present a danger, so they can constitute a blessing if we are able to train them, draw them closer to us, and engage them in action."[89]

The Arab Bureau's activities with Oriental youth in 1943 took place alongside efforts to create a general national framework for Sephardi and Oriental youth. On January 21, 1943, a national conference of Sephardi youth was held in Jerusalem. The speakers at the conference included Yitzhak Shamosh, who was elected president of the organization, as well as Moshe Chelouche and Eliachar. The conference attendees decided to establish a new body to be known as the National Center of Sephardi Youth Organizations in the Land of Israel (Hamerkaz Haartzi shel Irguney Hano'ar Hasfaradi Be'eretz Israel). Its main function would be to organize public and national activities among Sephardi youth, including attempts to persuade them to enlist in the military. The conference attendees also demanded that Sephardi representatives be included in the Rescue Committee that was established during the war by the national institutions.[90]

One of the main movements that were active among the Sephardi youth was the Degel Zion (Flag of Zion) youth movement, which became one of the bases of the Sephardi leadership in Tel Aviv and the country. The establishment of Degel Zion in 1938 was initiated by the Association of Sephardi Jews in Tel Aviv, under the presidency of Chelouche and the chairmanship of Aryeh Turgeman.[91] Chelouche was born in Jaffa in 1892, and his education was similar to that of the Sephardi elite in the city: he attended the Alliance Israélite Universelle School and the French College in Jaffa (Collège de Frères de Jaffa) and the School of Commerce in Marseille, France. Along with most of the Sephardi leaders, he had been exiled to Damascus during World War I. Chelouche headed the Palestinian-French chamber of commerce and served as the Bulgarian consul general in Palestine. He was also a member of the Association of the Pioneers of the East and, after being elected as a member of Tel Aviv city council in 1928, he continued to represent the Sephardi cause in various positions.[92]

Turgeman was another figure who was prominent in organizing Oriental and particularly Sephardi youth. Like Chelouche, Turgeman was a member of the Sephardi elite in Jaffa who had received an education preparing him for both commercial and public positions. Turgeman was born in 1910 to a family of Moroccan and Ashkenazi origin, whose members were active in the Jewish community in Hebron and Jaffa. His father, Yitzhak Turgeman, was the Jewish mukhtar of Jaffa.[93] Aryeh Turgeman was one of the founders of the Battalion of Defenders of the Hebrew Language in Tel Aviv (Gdud Meginey Hasafa Betel Aviv), chairman of the Jerusalem branch of the Association of Hebrew Youth that was founded at the Zionist Congress in 1923, a leading member (together with his brother, Raphael Turgeman) in the Sephardi Labor Organization in Tel Aviv and—as noted above—chairman of Degel Zion.

Under the leadership of Chelouche and Turgeman, Degel Zion attracted hundreds of young men and women as members. They attended social meetings and listened to lectures in its club in Tel Aviv, which also housed a library. Degel Zion organized activities around the country and work camps in the kibbutzim. However, its activities were impeded by financial difficulties, and it did not resume its operations until toward the end of World War II. One of Degel Zion's objectives was to spread Zionism among Oriental youth. It also had a soccer team, with the goal of encouraging the sporting spirit among Oriental youth. Degel Zion sought to change the urban character of Oriental Jews by providing agricultural training and seeking to establish new agricultural communities.[94]

One of Degel Zion's main goals was to draw Oriental youth into the service of the national institutions of the Yishuv.[95] Yet Degel Zion was not the first youth movement established among Sephardi and Oriental youth during the Mandatory period. The Association of the Pioneers of the East devoted most of its energies to fostering the national idea and Hebrew revival among the youth in the mixed cities. Under its auspices, youth organizations were established in Jerusalem, and a youth organization called The Young Hebrew (Ha'ivri Hatza'ir) was active in Tel Aviv in the 1920s. With the goal of cultural and national awakening in mind, these movements focused on educational and social activities, including weekly meetings, lectures, and excursions.[96]

Degel Zion sought to work among youth in the spirit of the Association of the Pioneers of the East. Its center was in Tel Aviv, and it focused on Oriental youth who had grown up mainly at the frontier neighborhoods in the mixed cities at the time of the 1929 riots and the economic, social, and cultural deprivation of the 1930s. The call to rescue this youth from protracted neglect and to enhance their integration into nationalist and Zionist activities was reinforced following the outbreak of the Arab Revolt. The Oriental youth was the subject of extensive and lively public debate. The group was described as "apathetic and hostile to the entire revival project," but the Sephardi leaders argued that the youth had been ignored by the Yishuv and the Zionist institutions, and that "the Zionist Executive stood by and did nothing to raise them from the depths."[97]

This situation led to calls to provide vocational education for Oriental youth and increasing efforts to organize Oriental youth and integrate them into the activities of the Yishuv. As we saw earlier in this chapter, one of the bodies that began to work among the Oriental youth was the Arab Bureau of the Political Department. As part of the Histadrut's efforts to reach out to the unorganized Oriental and Sephardi youth, it encouraged them to join the Hano'ar Ha'oved (the working youth) youth movement. The Sephardi Labor Organization was also involved in the effort to organize the Oriental youth, as well as to promote Arab-Jewish rapprochement by focusing on economic relations between the groups.

Labor Struggle and Economic Rapprochement

World War II was a period of gradual economic revival, during which various industrial, agricultural, and merchandise projects were begun to support the British war effort. Together with the cultural, educational, and political realms, the economic realm was perceived as a sphere for Jewish-Arab cooperation. Joint activities in the merchants' associations, cooperation in agricultural matters, and work in places in the public or private sector that employed both Jews and Arabs encouraged the groups' interaction. Different organizations, such as the Arab Bureau and the Arab Department of the Histadrut, were involved in supporting economic growth, as well as in enhancing Jewish-Arab relations.

The Arab Department was established by the Histadrut Executive at the end of 1930 as a department to be in charge of labor relations between Jews and Arabs. Its establishment was one of the results of the 1929 riots, and its creation was part of a broader discussion in the 1920s on the status of the Histadrut as a joint Arab-Jewish labor union and on its policy toward the Arab Question.[98] The Arab Department also coordinated and supervised the activities of the Palestine Labor League (Brit Po'aley Eretz Israel), which was founded in the early 1930s as a separate Arab section within the Histadrut and became the most important institution in the Arab Department.[99]

Yehuda Burla, a writer and educator, was in charge of the Arab Department in the beginning, under the supervision of Dov Hoz. Burla was born in Jerusalem in 1886. After his military service in the Ottoman army during World War I he served as principal of the Hebrew school in Damascus. When he returned to Palestine, he became one of the prominent intellectuals and public figures in the Sephardi community. Choosing him as head of the Arab Department indicates the orientation of the department in its early days and Burla's political affiliation with the labor movement and Mapai. Burla focused on promoting Arab studies and tried to create links between economic, political, and cultural activities of the Arab Department.[100] One of the department's first activities was promoting and coordinating the General Workers' Club in Haifa. The Haifa Workers' Council established the club in 1925, and it was headed until 1927 by Abraham Khalfon and his Christian Arab assistant, Philip Hassun.[101]

Khalfon, who served as the first secretary of the Union of Railway, Postal and Telegraph Workers, was born in Tiberias in 1900 and grew up in Haifa as part of a Ladino-speaking Sephardi family of Moroccan origin.[102] Khalfon was one of the main Sephardi activists in Haifa. He was a member of the Association of the Pioneers of the East and, after 1927, served as the secretary of the municipality of Haifa. He was also the secretary of the Jewish Local Committee in Haifa and chair of the Council of the Sephardi Community in the city. He was typical of the Sephardi Jews who were natives of Palestine, proficient in Arabic, and active during the Mandatory period in efforts to enhance relations between Jews and Arabs. Raised in the Harat al-Yahud neighborhood of Haifa, Khalfon described the neighborly relations between Jews and Arabs in this neighborhood as good, even during the events of 1929.[103]

Khalfon's work as the secretary of the municipality of Haifa demonstrates the important role of the municipal sphere in Arab-Jewish political cooperation. It is in this sphere that figures like Alhadiff in Tiberias, Yosef Eliyahu Chelouche in Jaffa, Shabtai Levy in Haifa, and Yitzhak Shmaya Eliachar in Jerusalem were active.[104] After Khalfon left the Histadrut, Philip Hassun continued to be the secretary of the General Workers' Club in Haifa until 1932.[105] He was replaced by Agassi.

In March 1931 the Arab Department submitted its proposal to promote Jewish-Arab relations to Weizmann. The proposal highlighted the importance of fostering joint economic and professional interests and links between Jews and Arabs, while establishing workers' clubs similar to the General Workers' Club in Haifa. That club demonstrated the outlook of Burla, the director of the Arab Department of the Histadrut, that the social and cultural realms, involving class struggles and social and professional contacts, were possible bridges between Jews and Arabs. The Haifa club was open to every worker who was at least eighteen. During its first period of operation, there were about 138 Arab members, the majority of whom were Christians. The activities included social meetings, Hebrew and Arabic classes, and sports activities. The main aims of the club were to create solidarity among Arab and Jewish workers and to enhance the economic, cultural, professional, and physical situation of its members. Among other things, the club served as a liaison between the workers and the municipality, British administration, and possible employees, and it supported the workers in various struggles to improve their work conditions.[106] The Arab Department needed economic support to establish similar clubs in Jaffa, Jerusalem, and Tiberias. It also hoped to expand its activities to rural areas and other areas of operation, including cultural, linguistic, and journalistic activities. Some of its activities in these areas, including the study of Arabic and training of Arabic teachers, will be discussed in chapter 3.[107]

In the second half of the 1930s Agassi was the most active member of the Arab Department. Born in Baghdad in 1909, Agassi immigrated to Palestine in 1928 and studied at the Hebrew University of Jerusalem before joining the Histadrut.[108] Agassi's cultural and journalistic work will be discussed in chapter 3; in addition to that, his work at the Arab Department focused mainly on the activities of the Palestine Labor League.[109] The league's work in the three main branches—in Haifa, Jaffa, and Jerusalem—serves as an important example for the work of the Histadrut among Arab workers.[110]

The Palestine Labor League was very active in the General Workers' Club in Haifa. In that mixed city, Jews and Arabs cooperated in various spheres, including in the municipal administration, the Mandatory governmental institutions, and various organizations and businesses.[111] The league was active in organizing Arab workers into trade unions, and it supported labor struggles of the Arab workers and strikes of Arabs workers who were employed by the Mandatory administration or by Jews.[112] In its work among Arab workers, the league competed both against the Palestinian Communist Party and the Palestinian Arab Workers' Society, which was established in 1925 by Arab workers.[113]

The Haifa office of the Palestine Labor League was directed in the second half of the 1930s by Shlomo Alafia, who was born in Damascus in 1911 and also served as the assistant of Abba Hushi, the secretary of the Haifa Workers' Council. Alafia tried to assist Arab workers who sought the help of the Histadrut in finding jobs, as well as helping organize Arab workers in Jewish-owned factories. Alafia also joined Hushi in meeting Druze leaders in Palestine and Syria and helped collect political and security information about Arab society.[114] Yet the work of Alafia, Burla, and Agassi signaled mainly the involvement of Sephardi and Oriental figures in the work of the Arab Bureau of the Political Department of the Jewish Agency and the Arab Departments of the Histadrut, as well as in the Arab Department of the Palmach, an issue that will be examined later in the book.

Zachary Lockman portrayed the attitude of most of the Histadrut leaders toward the Arabs as paternalistic and arrogant, writing that the leaders lacked any respect for the Arabs and saw them as ignorant and culturally inferior.[115] He also discussed the roles of the Sephardi activists in the Histadrut and of Khalfon. Specifically, Lockman wondered if Khalfon tried to mislead the Arab railway workers in Haifa about the real nationalistic intentions of the Histadrut.[116] However, Khalfon's actions may be interpreted in a different light. In fact, if Khalfon is seen as one of the Sephardim who tried to work as intermediaries between Jews and Arabs as part of their personal, political, and ideological agendas, and not only as a member of the Zionist circles that Lockman criticized, Khalfon's character and work become much more complex and nuanced.

However, in their work as part of the Histadrut's Arab Department, Khalfon, Burla, Agassi, and Alafia followed the Histadrut's policies of establishing a separate Arab workers' union. Thus, they supported the Zionist policy that institutionalized the separation of Jews and Arabs in the labor market.[117] The ideals of Oriental-based solidarity among Jewish and Arab workers were abandoned in favor of the ideal of Hebrew labor and to promote the success of the Zionist project. This approach was especially clear in the attempts of the Arab Department to decrease the effects of the general Arab boycott in the early years of the Arab Revolt. Here, too, people like Khalfon, who were heavily influenced by their social and cultural affinity to the Arabs, became an intermediary group that was supposed to develop that affinity—but, at the same time, they had to take account of the changing political and security realities and conform to the policies of the Zionist institutions led by Labor Zionists, which often helped increase the separation between the two peoples.

During World War II, the Arab Department began to cooperate more closely with the Arab Bureau and the Arab section of Hashomer Hatza'ir.[118] The connection between these organizations reflected the attempts of the Histadrut to expand its operations to other cities beyond Haifa, in light of its competition with the Palestinian Communist Party and the Palestinian Arab Workers' Society.[119] As discussed above, the work of the Arab Department focused not only on economic aspects but also on cultural and educational ones.[120]

The attempt to organize Arab workers as part of the Palestine Labor League, which also involved collecting intelligence for the Arab Bureau and the Haganah, continued despite the opposition of the Palestinian Arab Workers' Society. In World War II the Haifa branch of the Palestine Labor League coordinated the work of thousands of Arab workers.[121] This connection continued, with less impressive numbers, after the end of World War II until the 1948 war. In fact, in April 1948 Alafia wrote a leaflet on behalf of the Haifa Workers' Council that urged Arab residents to stay in Haifa. The leaflet was distributed in the city by members of the Palestine Labor League.[122]

The economic problems facing Oriental Jews following the outbreak of the Arab Revolt, and their unique position between the Jewish and Arab workers, led to the establishment of the Organization of Sephardi and Oriental Workers in Jerusalem (Irgun Ha'ovdim Hasfardim Vebney 'Edot Hamizrah). Another organization, established in Tel-Aviv by Moshe Chelouche and David Benvenisti and headed by Raphael and Aryeh Turgeman, was the Sephardi Labor Organization in Tel Aviv (Histadrut Ha'ovdim Hasfaradim Betel Aviv). In 1940, the two organizations, the Organization of Sephardi and Oriental Workers in Jerusalem and the Sephardi Labor Organization in Tel Aviv, decided to establish a joint national committee and to found the Sephardi Labor Organization in the Land of Israel (Histadrut Ha'ovdim Hasfaradim).[123] Both organizations conducted various activities, including addressing union issues, setting up work and study programs for youths, assisting new immigrants, helping find jobs, improving conditions of employment, and establishing credit institutions and social aid programs.[124]

Raphael Turgeman was one of the founders of the Tel Aviv branch of the Association of the Pioneers of the East and, as noted above, was one of the main leaders of the Sephardi Labor Organization in Tel Aviv. In the latter capacity he devoted most of his efforts to improving the financial condition of Sephardi workers and the advancement of Oriental youth, but he also worked to strengthen Jewish-Arab relations. Under Raphael and Ariyeh Turgeman's leadership, the organization attached great importance to promoting cooperation between Sephardi and Oriental Jewish workers and Arab workers. Raphael Turgeman was a fierce critic of the Zionist establishment and argued that the Sephardi and Oriental Jews were discriminated against by the Zionist movement. The Sephardi Labor Organization, as a uniting the two organizations from Jerusalem and Tel Aviv, was established to challenge this discrimination and demand a change in the economic, social and political status of the Sephardim in the Yishuv. Part of Raphael Turgeman's criticism had to do with the special role of mediators with the Arabs that the Sephardim could play.[125] Moshe Chelouche supported Turgeman on this issue and argued that "the Sephardim play an important role especially in the political national aspects that are related to our relations with the Arab peoples and the East."[126]

In a speech at the second conference of the Sephardi Labor Organization, held in Jerusalem on October 23, 1942, Raphael Turgeman focused on the subject of Jewish-Arab relations. He advocated cooperation between the Sephardi Labor Organization and Arab workers' committees on issues relating to labor, economics, and culture.[127] The conference adopted a resolution calling for the Jewish Agency Executive and the National Council to include Sephardi representatives in activities intended to improve Jewish-Arab relations, arguing that the Sephardim could make an important contribution in this area: "It is a pity that on such an important issue as the regulation of relations with the Arabs, the relevant institutions have not involved the Sephardi public, which could make an important contribution to solve this problem. The Sephardi Labor Organization empowers its leaders to find proper ways to promote cooperation with those among our neighbors who are willing to build fair and neighborly relations in the areas of labor, economics, and culture."[128] Turgeman's speech should also be understood in the context of the establishment of the Arab Workers' Congress in Haifa, which included Arab workers' organizations from the British military camps, the port, refineries, and the transportation sector. The congress demanded that working conditions for Arab and Jewish workers be made equal and an end to discrimination against Arab workers in the military camps.[129] Interestingly, the Sephardi Labor Organization demanded that the Zionist movement and the Jewish Agency equalize the working conditions of Sephardi and Ashkenazi workers and stop discriminating against the Sephardi and Oriental workers.

On October 22, 1944, the Palestinian communist newspaper *al-Ittihad* published a memorandum allegedly sent by the Sephardi Labor Organization to the chief secretary of the Mandatory government in July 1943. The memorandum, which had been forwarded to the newspaper by the Association of Arab Workers in Jerusalem, stated that "the Oriental Jews in Palestine oppose the Zionist movement and demand the cessation of Jewish immigration."[130] The Sephardi Labor Organization quickly denied sending such a memorandum. Hence, it emphasized its unconditional support for Jewish immigration and the establishment of a Jewish state.[131] The attempt of Palestinian organizations to present the Sephardim as anti-Zionists should be understood as part of the attempt to distinguish between the Sephardim as natives and the Ashkenazim as immigrants, as discussed in chapter 1, and also as part of the struggle between the Sephardi organizations and the Histadrut.

The Sephardi Labor Organization organized diverse activities, including lectures for the general public on cultural and political topics, and also established a clinic and a labor bureau.[132] These activities competed directly with those of the Histadrut and the Political Department of the Jewish Agency, which accordingly opposed the union's initiatives. Yet there were other sources for the confrontation between the Histadrut and the Sephardi Labor Organization and once again raised questions regarding the attitude of the Sephardim toward Zionism.

Despite the central role of Raphael Turgeman and the emphasis of the Sephardi Labor Organization on Jewish-Arab rapprochement, it had no Arab members and was not a joint organization. It tried not to compete with the Palestine Labor League or the Arab workers' organizations and focused its efforts within the Jewish socioeconomic context and on attracting workers who were not affiliated with any other workers' organization or union in the Yishuv. Among the workers who joined its ranks were the sanitation and cleaning workers of the Tel Aviv municipality, carpenters, shoemakers, construction workers, and other nonprofessional workers. In its early years it included 1,500 men and women, and by its final years it had 4,000 members.[133] Like other Sephardi organizations in the Yishuv, the Sephardi Labor Organization refrained from affiliating itself with any political party in the Yishuv. Despite the criticism that it operated as an ethnically segregated organization, it continued to represent and support the Sephardi workers as well as immigrants from Arab countries who were looking for jobs and to help caring for abandoned children, many of them of Oriental descent.[134]

The confrontation between the Sephardi Labor Organization on the one hand and the Histadrut and Mapai on the other hand continued until 1943, when the Labor Department of the Jewish Agency recognized the organization and invited its representatives to participate in the Central Labor Bureau.[135] As a result, the Sephardi Labor Organization called on its members to participate in the 1944 elections for the Assembly of Representatives.[136] At the same time, the Histadrut became more active among Sephardi workers and established the Department of Oriental Jews (Hamahlaka Le'edot Hamizrah). Among the department's members were Eliyahu Hakarmeli, a teacher and former member of the Association of the Pioneers of the East; Avraham 'Abbas, a leading member of the Hahalutz movement in Syria; and Shlomo Alafia.[137] The involvement of Alafia in both the Arab Department and the Department of Oriental Jews was therefore another expression of the status of the Sephardim not only in the Histadrut but also in the Yishuv.

As discussed above, doubts about the loyalty of the Sephardim to the Zionist movement and their adherence to its principles continued well into the 1940s, as an inherent part of the political struggles in the Yishuv. At the same time various efforts to encourage social and economic rapprochement between Jews and Arabs continued, led by different organizations and associations. However, most of these efforts were short-lived. Similar efforts took place, lasted much longer, and also reflected the unique approach and hybrid identity of Oriental Jews in the cultural, linguistic, and journalistic spheres, to which we turn in chapter 3.

THREE

≡≡≡

Cultural Politics

Journalistic, Cultural, and Linguistic Mediation

≡≡≡

On December 17, 1912, with criticism of the Zionist movement increasing in the Palestinian Arabic press, Haim Ben 'Attar, the editor of *Haherut*, a newspaper in Jerusalem, published the following lines: "Our [political] activists from Jaffa made a big mistake because they were unable to do whatever is needed to protect us in the country. If there was an Arabic-Hebrew newspaper, our enemies (*zorerim*) would have been quiet and would not have dared to test their faked 'patriotism.'. . . If we had an Arabic newspaper we could have distributed it well among the Muslim readers, and could have highlighted in it what we did and what we do for the benefit of the homeland (*moledet*) . . . to bring our Muslim neighbors closer to us."[1] Ben 'Attar's article was part of an ongoing debate which took place in *Haherut* and in the Yishuv in general before World War I about the relations between Jews and Arabs in Palestine and the best ways to reduce the tension between the two groups. One of the issues that was debated was the possibility of establishing a bilingual (Hebrew-Arabic) newspaper or an Arabic newspaper that would be distributed among the Arabs in Palestine. The aim of such a newspaper would be to expose Arab readers to the intentions of the Zionist movement and the Jewish community in the country. Such a newspaper, it was hoped, would serve two purposes: it would prove the loyalty of the Jews in Palestine to the Ottoman Empire (referred to in Ben 'Attar's article as "the homeland"), and it would respond to and eventually reduce the criticism of the Zionist movement that was often published in the Arabic press. This short quote from the article also demonstrates the criticism of "the [political] activists from Jaffa," the heads of the Zionist office (Hamisrad Ha'eretz Israeli) in Jaffa, as well as the Zionist activists who were Ashkenazi, arrived in the second wave of Jewish immigration, and were, according to Ben 'Attar and other Sephardi activists, detached from the Arab population and the Ottoman polity in the country. The criticism of the Zionist Ashkenazi activists is also connected to their inability to converse in Arabic, to the fact that most of them were not Ottoman subjects and hence were unable to participate in the political life of the country, and to their resulting inability to fully integrate themselves into Palestine and the Ottoman Empire.[2]

Obviously, Ben 'Attar's piece was published in a different political context— the years before World War I, during the final years of Ottoman rule—than the one discussed in general in this book. As has been noted above and will be discussed below, Sephardi and Oriental Jews had a different sociopolitical status in the two periods. However, many of the points that Ben 'Attar addressed remained very relevant in the Mandatory period, when the debate about publishing a Hebrew-Arabic or Zionist Arabic newspaper, the related discussion about the importance of learning Arabic by Jews in Palestine, and the criticism of the Zionist (mainly Ashkenazi) leadership all continued.[3]

This chapter will address many of these issues, while focusing on exchanges between Oriental Jews and Arabs in the journalistic, cultural, and linguistic spheres during the Mandatory period. Examining the different forms of writing, editing, debating, and translation of Arabic texts; the format of articles, newspapers, scholarly journals, and books; and the teaching of Arabic to different audiences in the Yishuv reveals the Arab-Jewish hybrid identity of the Oriental Jews and the way they perceived themselves as possible mediators between Jews and Arabs during the years of growing tension between the two groups in Palestine.[4] The cultural sphere where all these activities took place cannot easily be separated from the political sphere, however. As this chapter shows, cultural, educational, political, and diplomatic activities often went hand in hand. The chapter suggests that they were all representations of "cultural politics," as Bney Ha'aretz perceived it, as well as of the Oriental Jews' own special understanding of Zionism.[5]

The chapter is divided into two parts. The first part focuses on the Hebrew-Arabic (or Zionist Arabic) newspapers published in Palestine and looks specifically at their role, connections to other newspapers published elsewhere in the Arab world, and many of their Oriental writers and editors. One of the arguments in the chapter is that the participation of various intellectuals, political activists, and journalists in debates taking place in the Arabic-Hebrew press about Zionism, the special role of the Sephardi and Oriental Jews in the complex matrix of Zionist-Arab relations in Mandatory Palestine, and those

Jews' relations with the Arabs demonstrate the role that such newspapers, as well as their editors and writers, played in the intellectual exchange and discussions in the mixed Jewish-Arab environment of the Levant during the Mandatory years. The role of these newspapers in cultural and political exchanges between Oriental Jews around the Middle East, as well as between Jews and Arabs in Palestine, will also be discussed below. As a case study, the chapter will discuss a 1932 debate taking place in the Arabic Zionist press about a possible Arab-Jewish conference, in which local and Middle Eastern Jews at large were supposed to serve as mediators between the Zionist movement and the Arabs.

The second part of the chapter examines the cultural and linguistic spheres of exchange and different kinds of mediation between Jews and Arabs in Palestine. We look mainly at the discussions about studying and teaching of Arabic among Jews in Palestine, as a way of examining the special role of Sephardi and Oriental Jews in the Zionist establishment. We focus on the work of Yisrael Ben-Ze'ev, the inspector of Arabic in the Department of Education of the National Council and examine the discussions and debates about Arabic teaching for Hebrew-speaking students, the ways of advancing the study of (mainly colloquial) Arabic, the writing of textbooks, and the work of translating works from Arabic into Hebrew.

Arabic-Zionist Newspapers as Sites of Political and Cultural Mediation and Exchange

The print media in Palestine played a major role in the debates about the developing national conflict between Jews and Arabs in the country. Much of the research on the press of that time has focused on the ways the Arabic and Hebrew press presented the Arab Question and the Zionist policy toward the Arabs, as well as on the ways Arabic newspapers in Palestine and elsewhere viewed the Zionist movement and the Jews.[6] From a Zionist perspective, the press was viewed as a tool for presenting the Zionist project to the Arab community in the country and was considered to be an effective way to potentially influence the Arabs in Palestine and in the neighboring countries. The publication of an Arabic newspaper, supported by the Zionist movement, was had already been discussed and debated within the Zionist national institutions and others during the final years of Ottoman rule in Palestine, as the article by Ben 'Attar quoted above demonstrates.

The national institutions of the Yishuv and the Zionist movement published and funded several Arabic newspapers that operated for different periods of time. These included *al-Akhbar* and *al-Salam*, both edited by Nissim Malul, as well as *Ittihad al-'Ummal* and *Hakikat al-Amr*. Those newspapers are often viewed by various scholars as solely propaganda tools used by the Zionist movement to expose Palestinian Arabs to the Zionist project and the ways it could benefit them and the country as a whole.[7] Discussions about the best ways to influence Arabs in Palestine and the larger Arab world and explain to them the purpose of the Zionist movement took place quite often within Zionist institutions, especially during or after periods of violence. In relation to this, Liora Halperin argues that *Hakikat al-Amr*, for example, was part of the evolving Zionist tradition of advocacy (*hasbara*), or of explaining the Zionist project to the Arabs. The publication of an Arabic newspaper, and the emphasis placed on the importance of studying Arabic, is viewed by Halperin and others as a means of both persuading the Arabs of the benefits of the Zionist project and connecting Jews to Arabs, and is hence viewed not as advocacy but as pure propaganda.[8]

But was that the case? A look at the writers and editors of these newspapers—many of whom were local, Sephardi, or Maghrebi Jews—and a consideration of the newspapers not only as political tools but also as part of a much larger cultural and social project may reveal patterns of dialogue and mediation beyond propaganda. In fact, Sephardi and Oriental Jews—such as Malul, Shimon Moyal, Avraham Elmaleh, Sasson, Yehuda Burla, Eliyahu Agassi, Tuviya (Tawfiq) Shamosh—attempted, through their journalistic, editorial, and translation work, to bridge the growing gap between Jews and Arabs on the basis of direct links and contacts, based specifically on a common language, Arabic, and on shared culture and historical ties.

Malul, for instance—born in Safed in 1892 to a family originally from Tunisia—had been one of the main advocates for the publication of a Hebrew-Arabic newspaper even before World War I, and he was one of the main intellectuals who stressed the importance and centrality of Arabic in the Yishuv. With his friends and colleagues Shimon Moyal and Esther Azhari Moyal, he published the short-lived newspaper *Sawt al-'Uthmaniyya*, and in 1911 he began working as a translator at the Zionist office in Jaffa.[9] Malul and Shimon Moyal, as well as other prominent Sephardi and Maghrebi activists, were among the founders of Hamagen association in Jaffa, which tried to improve the relations and increase the links between Jews and Arabs through the publication and translation of articles in the Hebrew, Arabic, and Turkish press.[10]

Malul continued to be active in the journalistic and political arenas following World War I. He returned to Palestine once the British occupation began, and in the early 1920s he was a member of the Arab Bureau in the National Council. He wrote articles for *Barid al-Yawm* (the Arabic version of *Doar Hayom*) and founded two Arabic newspapers, *al-Akhbar* (which he edited until 1920) and *al-Salam*, both funded by the Zionist movement with the goal of explaining its aims and activities and preaching in favor of Jewish-Arab understanding.[11] In 1927 Malul moved to Iraq, where he served as the principal of a Jewish school in Hillah, near Baghdad.[12] He published various essays in Arabic, including two plays, and translated works from Arabic into Hebrew. Malul was like other people discussed in this chapter who had cultural, linguistic, and historical ties to the Arab world and the Maghreb in that his work bridged the journalistic, educational, literary, and political spheres and was conducted in different places in the Middle East—in his case, mainly in Jaffa, Cairo, and Baghdad. Like many other members of his generation and sociopolitical and intellectual circles, Malul was involved not just in Palestine but in the Middle East as a whole: he had studied at the American College in Tanta and wrote for the Egyptian newspaper *al-Muqattam*. Like many others, he worked on behalf of the Zionist movement as a translator but was also very critical of Zionist policies regarding the Arab Question. He often accused the Zionist leadership of ignoring the growing animosity toward Jews among Palestinian Arabs and overlooking the developing tensions between the Zionists and the Arabs. All these seemingly contradictions existed within him, and among other members of his milieu, simultaneously, and did not in fact conflict with each other.[13]

Al-Salam was published irregularly, first in Cairo and then in Jaffa, Haifa, and Jerusalem in Judeo-Arabic and Arabic. In addition to its purpose of exposing the Jewish communities in the Arab countries to the events in the Yishuv, it had two main aims: to promote peace and understanding between Jews and Arabs in Palestine, and to expose its Arab readers to the benefits that Jews brought to the country.[14] In his book on the Arab press in Mandatory Palestine, Ya'akov Yehoshua described *al-Salam* as the only newspaper that tried to promote understanding between the different races and classes in Palestine.[15] The newspaper was partially funded by the Zionist Executive, but it constantly suffered from financial difficulties, and Malul had to struggle to keep publishing it. The newspaper resumed publication after the 1929 events in Palestine, and with the support of the United Bureau it regularly published 700 copies of each issue, with 115 subscriptions in Arab countries.[16] Like other newspapers, it paid some Arab writers to write pro-Zionist pieces for it.[17] When the newspaper resumed publication, it was written that "*al-Salam*'s journalistic ethics, when it was established ten years ago, were honest reporting and serious journalistic investigation. It will continue following these rules, without worrying about the complaints and resentment toward it. *Al-Salam* is returning today to serve the homeland."[18]

Malul was also the editor of the Arabic workers' newspaper *Ittihad al-'Ummal*. This newspaper had been published since 1925 by the Histadrut; its first editor was Itzhak Ben-Zvi. The newspaper's goal was to represent the interests of Jewish and Arab workers in Palestine, promote joint labor struggles, and promote the role of the Histadrut as the protector and representative of the workers. The newspaper saw itself as an important organ for Jewish and Arab workers and an advocate for cooperation between them. Between 1928 and 1936 the Histadrut did not publish any newspaper in Arabic. But in 1937 *Haqiqat al-Amr* resumed publication, with new editors.

Haqiqat al-Amr was published by the Arab Department of the Histadrut. It is another example of an Arabic newspaper with the clear goal of promoting the ideas of the Zionist movement and the Histadrut among the Arabs in Palestine. As mentioned above, Halperin uses this newspaper as her prime example for demonstrating that newspapers were used for propaganda.[19] However, the situation was more complex.

First published in March 1937, *Haqiqat al-Amr* was the organ of the Palestine Labor League. Its editors were Michael Assaf and Agassi, while the author Tuviya (Tawfiq) Shamoush served as the newspaper's secretary. Originally from Poland, Assaf was a journalist specializing in Arab affairs and Jewish-Arab relations. Fluent in Arabic, he was a member of Hashomer Hatza'ir and later of Mapai, as well as a prominent editor of and writer for both Hebrew and Arabic newspapers, including *Haqiqat al-Amr*, *Davar*, and (after 1948) *al-Yawm*, an Israeli Arabic newspaper. He also published extensively on the history of the Arabs in Palestine. Shamosh was born in Aleppo, Syria, in 1914 and immigrated to Palestine in 1934. Like his two brothers, Yitzhak and Amnon, he was a renowned author and translator from Arabic, in addition to his editorial and journalistic work for various newspapers.[20] Agassi was born in Baghdad in 1909 and immigrated to Palestine in 1928. He was the Arab affairs correspondent for *Doar Hayom*, a Hebrew newspaper, and, as noted above, led the Arab Department of the Histadrut and the Palestine Labor League. He published extensively, translated stories and novels from Arabic into Hebrew, and was the editor of several Arabic newspapers, including some for children.[21] All three, especially Shamosh and Agassi, demonstrate the links between the political and cultural spheres and the ways Arabic was used—through writing, publishing, teaching, and translating—to promote connections between Palestine and the Middle East as a whole, as well as between the Jewish communities in the larger Middle East and the Jewish community in Palestine.

Haqiqat al-Amr included a literary section, with translations of works from Hebrew and Yiddish into Arabic; several news sections that dealt with news from Palestine and elsewhere in the world; a Hebrew-teaching section; a section called "Palestinians Debating," in which Jewish and Arab readers exchanged views; letters to the editor; and a political section devoted to Zionist activities in Palestine. In a report to the Histadrut after the first year of the newspaper's publication, its editors wrote that around 3,000 copies of the newspaper had been distributed, of which about 200 were returned from teachers in government schools. According to the report, many of the Arab readers were threatened by the Palestinian national leadership and hence were unable to read the newspaper in public.[22]

To expose more Arab readers to the newspaper, it was reported that the newspaper was sent to Jewish workers in various institutions where Jews and Arabs worked together, such as at the Jerusalem municipality. Jewish workers shared the newspaper with their Arab co-workers, without the Arabs being listed as subscribers to the paper. The newspaper was also read in cafés, which increased its audience. One of the popular sections of the newspaper was the Hebrew-teaching section, which the Arab readers enjoyed and benefited from, according to the report. A reader from Bethlehem, for example, was quoted as writing: "I thank you for starting a new section: teaching Hebrew to the Arabs. Your newspaper not only benefits society, but also is essential for the beginning of understanding between cousins. Only in this way will we be able to reach our important goal—understanding one another—and only by this will real peace be able to exist in the hearts of both people."[23]

The Sephardi and Oriental Jews used newspapers as much more than a propaganda tool. They used the press to express their Arab-Jewish cultural hybrid identity, to mediate between Jews and Arabs in the country, and to connect Palestinian Jews to their surrounding Arabic-speaking environment. As Reuven Snir suggests in his analysis of Jewish participation in Arabic journalism throughout the Arab world, the cultural approaches and characteristics of such involvement varied across Iraq, Palestine, Egypt, and Lebanon, to mention just some of the countries he discusses. In the case of Palestine, Snir argues that the reason for Arab Jews to publish Arabic newspapers in Palestine was to change the Arab perception of such Jews. With regard to the limited support of the Zionist institutions for such publications, as can be seen in the case of Malul's

Al-Salam, Snir writes: "It seems that these organizations did not trust the independent activities of Arab Jews in this field—perhaps simply the result of a patronizing Ashkenazi attitude toward them."[24]

The sense of mistrust that Snir discusses is demonstrated in the discussions taking place in the national institutions about the possible publication of an Arabic newspaper with the support of the Zionist Executive. When David Ben-Gurion heard in 1930 of the possible inclusion of Eliyahu Eliachar, Yosef Eliyahu Chelouche, David Yellin, Haim Margaliot-Kalvarisky, and Meir Dizengoff in the editorial board of such a newspaper, he vetoed the idea and said "we will not accept any of them or [any] of those similar to them."[25] His reservation about the participation of local Jews, Sephardi and Ashkenazi (and mixed, like Yellin) alike, was primarily because of their different position on the Arab Question and possibly because they did not identify politically with Labor Zionism and its political organ, Mapai.

Indeed, the Sephardi and Oriental Jews had already begun to use the press to express their criticism of the Zionist leadership in the final years of Ottoman rule. By so doing, they contributed to the multivocality of views of the Zionist position on the Arab Question that were prevalent in the Yishuv in the 1920s.[26] As noted above, their knowledge of Arabic and their cultural and geographical proximity to the Arabs were central to the way Sephardi and Oriental Jews viewed themselves as possible mediators between Jews and Arabs. And the reason why they perceived and introduce themselves as mediators was because their political and social status had changed from the days of the Ottoman Empire. As Ottoman subjects, they had had a special role and a position of power and influence in the Zionist circles. However, the transition to British rule enhanced the position of the Zionist leaders, many of whom were Ashkenazi Jews, and Zionist waves of immigration from Europe increased the proportion of Ashkenazi Jews in the Yishuv. Having lost their previous political status, the Sephardi and Oriental Jewish leaders looked for ways to increase their political power that would be based on their cultural identity—such as their suitability as cultural mediators.

Many local Jews were enthusiastic (though often also critical) Zionists, supporters of both the Zionist movement and the Zionist work in Palestine. At the same time, they viewed themselves as cultural, linguistic, and political mediators between the two national and ethnic communities in the country. As mentioned above, although these notions may seem contradictory at first sight, local Jews saw them instead as their unique form and interpretation of Zionism and as a way of connecting ethnic and national questions.

As this chapter demonstrates, the Palestinian and Arabic press was one site of political and cultural mediation. Alongside the Arabic-language press, the Hebrew journal *Hed Hamizrah* (known as *Hamizrah* until 1942) served as another important channel of expression for the Sephardi and Oriental Jewish communities during the Mandatory period. Edited by Eliachar and David Sitton, *Hed Hamizrah* covered aspects of Oriental and Sephardi life in Palestine, reviewed developments in the Jewish communities of the Middle East, and published articles examining Arab life and culture in Palestine and the neighboring countries. Its writers were among the main figures active in the field of Jewish-Arab relations, including Elmaleh, who also edited the journal *Mizrah Uma'arav* (East and West), which focused on Arab literature and culture and on the history and cultures of the Jewish communities in the Middle East. *Mizrah Uma'arav* was published between 1920 and 1932 and attempted to focus on Middle Eastern Jews as part of a regional national cultural revival.[27] *Hed Hamizrah* and *Mizrah Uma'arav* were among the main sites for examining the relations between Oriental Jews and Arabs in the Middle East, thereby playing a role similar to that of the Jewish newspapers published in Arab countries.[28]

Many Sephardi and Oriental Jews who were involved with the Zionist-Arabic press in Palestine also wrote for other Arabic newspapers in the Arab world, both those owned by Jews and those owned and edited by Arabs.[29] Malul and Moyal, for example, contributed articles to the Egyptian newspapers *al-Manar* and *al-Muqattam*, and translations of their articles were published in the local Palestinian newspapers *Filastin* and *al-Karmil*. Other venues for publication included newspapers in Arabic that were owned by Jews and that tried to connect the local Jewish community to the Palestinian locale. In Iraq, the Jewish newspaper *al-Misbah*, edited by Anwar Shaul, followed the condition of Iraqi Jews in Palestine and their status in the Zionist movement.[30] In Egypt, the newspaper *Israël* focused on the relations between Jews and Arabs in Palestine while criticizing the way the Zionist movement dealt with the evolving conflict. *Israël* called on the Zionist leadership to make use of Oriental Jews, with their knowledge of Arabic and their familiarity with the Arab world, as possible mediators between Jews and Arabs.[31] In Beirut, in 1932 the weekly Arabic-language Jewish newspaper *al-'Alam al-Isra'ili* published an article on a planned Arab-Jewish conference. The news of this conference, which never took place, sparked a debate about the role and position of the Sephardi and Oriental Jews in the Zionist movement and the evolving national conflict.

The Arab-Jewish Conference: Cultural and
Political Mediation through the Press

Al-ʿAlam al-Israʾili, owned and edited by Selim Eilyahu Mann, was the only newspaper of the Jewish communities in Syria and Lebanon. It was established in 1921 and stopped publication in 1948, following two years of publication under the name *al-Salam*[32] Its main aims were to serve as a voice for the Syrian and Lebanese Jewish communities and Lebanon and to cover aspects of Jewish life and community activities. It also covered events in Palestine and was engaged in Zionist advocacy and propaganda, but of a different kind than that of the Palestinian Arabic-Zionist newspapers mentioned above. Those newspapers were aimed at Arabs in Palestine, but *al-ʿAlam al-Israʾili* was mainly addressed to the Jewish communities outside of Palestine and tried to enhance their connection to the Zionist movement and the Jewish community in Palestine. It also targeted Arab readers in an effort to expose them to the Zionist movement. Like some of the newspapers discussed above, it was partially supported financially by the Jewish Agency and the United Bureau and published articles on their behalf.[33]

However, *al-ʿAlam al-Israʾili* should be examined from another perspective as well. Many of the writers and editors of the Palestinian-based newspapers discussed above also wrote for *al-ʿAlam al-Israʾili* including Malul, Azhari Moyal, Elmaleh, Yitzhak and Tuviya Shamosh, Sasson, and Agassi. In many ways, the discussions that took place in the newspaper reflected the issues facing these Jewish intellectuals: the debates and tensions regarding their national and cultural identity, Zionism and the evolving national conflict, and questions about the position and influence of the Sephardim within the Zionist establishment. The debate over the 1932 Arab-Jewish conference, which we will turn to next, encapsulates many of these issues and hence can serve as a case study of the roles of the press and local Oriental Jews, as cultural and political mediators.

On May 16, 1932, an article titled "The Arab-Jewish Conference: Understanding between Jews and Arabs in Palestine" was published in *al-ʿAlam al-Israʾili*. The article reported on an attempt by "local Jews" (*al-Isarʾilin al-Watani'in*), those who lived in Palestine and elsewhere in the Middle East, to organize a Jewish-Arab conference to discuss the Zionist Question and the relations between Jews and Arabs in Palestine. At the conference, the article reported, the local Jews would serve as mediators between the Arabs and the Ashkenazi Western Jews (*al-Israʾiliin al-Ashkenaz al-Gharbi'in*). The article further explained that the Ashkenazi Jews did not fully understand the Arabs or their traditions and customs, whereas local Jews (meaning in this case the Sephardi and Oriental Jews) could more easily reach an understanding with Palestinian Arabs because of their cultural, linguistic, and geographical proximity.[34]

The article reported that in preparation for the conference, a meeting had taken place in Jaffa with the participation of representatives of leading local Jews (*zu'ama al-yahud al-watani'in*). The aim of the Jaffa meeting was to discuss the organization of the Arab-Jewish conference, whose purpose was viewed as twofold: reaching a compromise between Arabs and the Zionist Arabs (*al-Sahyuniya al-'Arabiya*) and demanding that the Zionist movement grant rights to the Jews of the Orient (*hukuk Isra'ili al-Sharq*). As would be later mentioned in the newspaper, the people behind that meeting were various lawyers, physicians, journalists, and public figures from Palestine, Egypt, Syria, Lebanon, and Iraq. They included Yosef David Farhi, Salim Harari, Yosef Dashi, Yosef Laniado, Yosef 'Atiya, Anwar Shaul, and Tawfic Mizrahi, all of whom were central figures in their respective communities. Farhi and Harari, for example, were among the heads of the Jewish community in Beirut; Laniado was a member of the Syrian parliament and of the Syrian National Congress; Shaul was the editor of the Jewish Iraqi newspapers *al-Misbah* and *al-Hasid* and a central figure in Iraqi literary circles; and Mizrahi, as noted above, was a close friend and colleague of Eliyahu Sasson during his days in Damascus and became a journalist after moving to Beirut.[35]

This conference was hotly debated between May and August 1932 in *al-'Alam al-Isra'ili* and the Hebrew newspaper *Ha'aretz*, published in Palestine. The timing of the debate is not coincidental. After the 1929 riots in Palestine, members of the Zionist movement realized the urgency of the evolving national conflict and its possible consequences. It was also around this time that several attempts were made to reach an agreement between Jews and Arabs in the country, as discussed in previous chapters. The conference discussed here should be viewed in this larger context.

The Arab-Jewish conference that was the subject of so much debate ended up not taking place. However, a large number of interconnected issues came up during the debate about it. They were, first and foremost, the possible role of Oriental Jews from Palestine and the Levant as mediators between Jews and Arabs. Other issues included the question of the Sephardi and Oriental Jews' loyalty to the Zionist movement; the relations between local Jews and the Zionist leadership; and the representation of Oriental Jews in Zionist institutions. The participation of Palestinian Oriental Jews and other public figures from the Arab world in the debates also demonstrates the existence of a Jewish intellectual and cultural community that was active in the Levant, and whose members maintained cultural, literary, educational, political, and journalistic links with each other.

One of the first reactions to the original article about the conference in *al-'Alam al-Isra'ili* was in an article in *Ha'aretz* by its editor, Moshe Glikson. Criticizing the original article, he wrote:

> We, of course, have no objection to any negotiation or conference which would try to reach an agreement [with the Arabs] (as long as such an agreement does not conflict with our needs and national awakening). However, for such a negotiation [to take place] we have national institutions, the Jewish Agency and the National Council. Our brothers the Oriental natives of the country (*yelidei haaretz haMizrahim*) can and should play an important role in this [effort]; they can advise our national institutions based on their knowledge and experience, but they cannot carry out their own external politics. Moreover, they cannot do anything that may harm our national solidarity. . . . There is no doubt that there is an anti-Zionist intrigue here, an attempt by the Arab leaders to break our national unity, and to reach an agreement with the "Oriental Jews," bypassing their Ashkenazi brothers and against them (*me'al lerosh acheihem haashkenazim venegdam*). Our brothers the Oriental Jews (*bney ha'edot hamizrahiyot*) are part of the people of Israel and must conform to our national unity. They cannot carry out their own political activities.[36]

This response refers to the local Jews as "the Mizrahi Oriental" or Mizrahi "natives of the country." In the original article in *al-'Alam al-Isra'ili* they were referred to as the "local Jews" (*al-Isar'ilin al-Watani'in*), and the "Zionist Arabs" (*al-Sahyuniya al-'Arabiya*), two terms that would be used throughout this exchange for describing the Sephardi and Oriental Jews in Palestine. As noted above, additional terms often used in Hebrew by the Sephardi and Oriental Jews in Palestine were Bney Ha'aretz (natives of the country) and Bney Hamizrah (natives of the Orient). These different references indicate the way Oriental Jews viewed themselves—as Jews who rooted in their local Eastern environment—and the way they were viewed by others.

In his response Glikson addressed concerns about a possible cooperation between those local Jews and the Arabs, over the heads of the Ashkenazi Jews and the Zionist movement. He even expressed his concern about a possible intrigue and even a set-up of the Oriental Jews by the Arabs, in an attempt to break the Yishuv's national unity. In other words, the local Jews were viewed as possible collaborators with the Arabs, and their loyalty to the Zionist movement was questioned. As mentioned above, what made them act separately from the Zionist institutions—which led to questions about their loyalty—was closely connected to the growing frustration of many local Jews regarding their own position in the Zionist movement and with what they viewed as the failed Zionist policies related to the Arab Question. This frustration was expressed in different venues and contexts throughout the Mandatory years.

Several writers responded to the accusations and doubts that were raised by Glikson. Aharon Ya'acov Moyal and Baruch Uziel—two prominent Zionist activists and public figures of Maghrebi and Greek descent, respectively—published their responses in *Ha'aretz*.[37] They emphasized the loyalty of Sephardi Jews to the national revival of Jews in the Land of Israel and to Zionism. At the same time, they expressed their disappointment in the failure of the national (Ashkenazi) leaders to make use of the Sephardi Jews to improve relations with the Arabs.

According to Uziel, the Zionist leaders have been at fault in not taking advantage of the merits and virtues that Sephardi Jews have, in order to improve the relations between Jews and Arabs. The common culture (between Sephardim and Arabs), the trust between one Eastern man and another, all these are crucial factors that an external expert cannot understand. "Is it a secret how much damage did our "Orientalist or Oriental diplomats" create [*hadiplomatim hamizrahanim o hamizrahiyim shelanu*]? he asks. The Sephardi Jews are loyal Zionists and would not cooperate with any anti-Zionist intrigue (Uziel alludes here to the conference), and they would not try to act independently from the national institutions. The possible organizers of the conference may be among the unworthy natives of the country, who are not part of the Sephardi masses, he claims. [38]

Uziel's piece goes against what he calls the Sephardistic separatist ideology (*idiologiya Spharadistanit*),[39] which supported the separation of the Sephardi activists from the national institutions. The Sephardi leadership, he argues, is hence also to be blamed for not taking enough responsibility and initiative in changing the Zionist establishment from within, and in preferring a separatist venue. In addition, Uziel points to possible tensions between the Sephardi elite (Ladino speakers) and the non-Sephardi local Jews, who, according to him, had taken the initiative to organize the conference. The latter were perceived by him (and others) as inferior.[40] Interestingly, as noted above, Uziel was not born in Palestine, but he was part of the Sephardi elite.

Another intriguing response to the original report of the conference came from Malul, the Jaffa-based Maghrebi journalist and Zionist activist who was discussed above. The goal of the Jewish-Arab conference is not merely "mediation," he wrote. Oriental Jewry (hayahadut hamizrahit) is part of Zionist Jews worldwide, despite the fact that it had long been neglected and were still not taken into account by "its sister, the Western Judaism" (hayahadut hama'aravit). Despite this ongoing neglect, tens of thousands of Middle Eastern Jews had immigrated to Palestine and not returned to their countries of origin. In fact, even though Middle Eastern Jews felt constantly underrepresented in the Yishuv's institutions and did not take part in the decision-making process of the Zionist institutions, they still believed in the national awakening and were active in the national revival project of Jews in Palestine. Malul concluded by saying: "Those who are for national obedience and national revival of the people of Israel in their country—join us!"[41] As in other instances, Malul expressed in this article his complex perspective, as a passionate, though critical, Zionist and a strong advocate of the role of Oriental Jews in the Zionist national project.

Another prominent writer in *al-'Alam al-Israe'ili* Eliyahu Sasson was also among the main commentators in the discussion of the Jewish-Arab conference. Similar to Malul in his personal history and his political, journalistic, and diplomatic activism, he represents the position of Oriental Jews as mediators and the constant tension in their Oriental hybrid identity and position, as discussed above. It is worth looking at him and his contribution to this debate more closely.

Eliyahu Sasson and the Hybrid Arab-Jewish Identity

As discussed in chapter 2, Sasson was in many ways a product of the period of Arab cultural and literary renaissance in the Middle East called the awakening (*al-Nahda*), as well as of Arab nationalism. His upbringing in Damascus was pivotal for his political and cultural development. Indeed, Damascus was a cultural and political center for local Jews in Palestine, especially those who were deported to the city during World War I, and temporarily joined the Damascene Jewish community. In many ways, Damascus served as a place and a historical meeting point where their Jewish and Arab political and cultural identities could fully coexist, and as a vibrant center of political, cultural, and educational activities.[42]

The Jewish community in Palestine had developed contacts with the Jews of Damascus prior to the outbreak of the war, and Elmaleh was particularly active in this field. He had been born in Jerusalem in 1885 to a family that had migrated to Morocco following the expulsion of the Jews from Spain.[43] After serving as the secretary to the Ottoman Hakham Bashi (chief rabbi) Haim Nahum Effendi, Elmaleh was appointed secretary of the Jewish community in Damascus in 1910. The appointment was initiated by Elmaleh's father-in-law, Ya'acov Danun, who served as Hakham Bashi in Damascus. One of Elmaleh's first steps in his new position was to establish the first Hebrew school in the city in 1911. He also served as the first principal of the school and its adjacent Hebrew kindergarten until 1913, when he returned to Jerusalem.[44] The school was a platform for cultural and educational contacts between Jerusalem and Damascus, and Elmaleh employed Hebrew teachers from Palestine—including the teacher and writer Yitzhak Shami, a native of Hebron.[45]

During World War I, Elmaleh returned to Damascus as part of a group of Jews who were exiled to the city by the Ottoman authorities. The first wave of exiles, numbering some 2,000, arrived in Damascus in October 1917, and several hundred more arrived in December of the same year. The Palestinian exiles to Damascus included Sephardi dignitaries and intellectuals from Jerusalem, most notably David Yellin. The Yishuv Migration Committee was also active in the city under the direction of Dizengoff.[46] One of the main outcomes of the presence of the exiles in Damascus, as the historian Yaron Harel pointed out, was the dissemination of Zionist ideas and the Hebrew language among the local Jewish community, by means of Hebrew classes, the opening of a library, and the marking of events relating to the Zionist movement. The main frameworks for these activities were the Zionist society Hathiya and the 'Ivriya committee, both of which were founded by teachers at the Hebrew school in the city and headed by Yisrael Eitan, a teacher from Jerusalem. Another society established in Damascus was Kadima, whose members were students at the Alliance Israélite Universelle school in the city.[47] Following the war, Burla was appointed principal of the boys' school, while Yosef Yoel Rivlin was appointed principal of the girls' school.[48]

Like Elmaleh, Sasson was inspired by this atmosphere of Zionist national and cultural foment. In 1915, at the age of thirteen, he met Jewish officers from Palestine who were serving in the Ottoman army (one of whom was Moshe Shertok) as well as the Jewish exiles in the city during World War I, including Yellin, Ya'acov Chelouche, Elmaleh, and the Jewish political activist and community leader Albert 'Antebi.[49] During the war, Sasson and his fellow students from the Alliance Israélite Universelle School formed part of the group that developed around Eitan and Yellin. Together with other youths, Sasson became part of the Zionist circle in the city. The youths were also active in the local branch of Maccabi and in the Kadima society, and played a part in organizing cultural and Zionist activities in Damascus.

Until his departure from Damascus in 1922, Sasson was a dominant figure in the younger generation of Jews in the city, joining the two principals of the Hebrew schools in the city, Burla and Rivlin, to encourage the study of Hebrew. Himself fluent in Hebrew, Arabic, and French, Sasson began writing in

Hebrew newspapers such as *Doar Hayom* and *Hadshot Ha'aretz*, as well as in other newspapers such as the bilingual Arabic-Hebrew newspaper *Hamizrah/ al-Sharq* and *al-'Alam al-Isra'ili*. He also founded and became the editor of *al-Ittihad*, a newspaper that was published in 1920 in Damascus.[50] As discussed above, these Hebrew-Arabic newspapers were engaged in promoting dialogue and connections between Jews and Arabs and were the result of a Jewish national and cultural revival movement inspired by the Arab awakening. This movement supported the cultural integration of Jews into their Arab environment and encouraged the learning of the Hebrew language and culture.[51]

From 1922, when he left Damascus, until he joined the Political Department of the Jewish Agency in 1934, Sasson's public and journalistic work can be characterized by his attempt to be a bridge between Jewish and Arab nationalism, and between Jewish and Arab cultures, and to bring together Jews and Arabs in Palestine. However, he was never an active member of the Sephardi leadership or the various Sephardi organizations that were active in Mandatory Palestine.[52] Until he joined the Jewish Agency, he was also a fierce critic of its policies vis-à-vis the Arab national movement. At the same time he also criticized the political positions of the Arab Executive Committee regarding Zionism. He published articles in Arabic in several newspapers during the 1920s and 1930s that focused on the special role of Sephardi and Oriental Jews in relationship to the Arabs and within the Zionist movement, in light of the evolving national conflict.

In 1927 Sasson settled in Jerusalem and resumed writing about the Jewish-Arab conflict. In December 1927 he published an article in *al-'Alam al-Isra'ili* in which he argued that Ashkenazi Jews did not want to reach peace and understanding with the Arabs in the same way that Sephardi Jews did. In the article, where he also criticized the Zionist political leadership, he wrote:

> For ten years the Ashkenazi Jews looked at Europe, which confused them with its promises. The Sephardim looked at them, tried to explain their mistake, but were ignored [by the Ashkenazim]. . . . It is bad that the political leadership is in the hands of Ashkenazi Jews, and that the leaders are foreign to the country's ways (*darkhey haaretz*) and are not familiar with its language. . . . They should work with us toward a religious understanding with the Christians and Muslims and gain their [the Arabs'] trust and understanding of our national aspirations. . . . Much responsibility for our national revival lies on the shoulders of Sephardi Jews who speak Arabic.[53]

In the same article, Sasson presented his political vision: "The Palestinian country will not gain its freedom and independence unless all forces—Jews,

Christians, and Muslims—unite to free it from foreign powers. The Sephardi Jews know that one group cannot operate without the other, and that opposition among them results in a constant domination of foreigners on Palestinian land."[54] Sasson also criticized the Ashkenazi Zionist leadership for relying on European forces for the national revival of Jews in Palestine. Oriental Jews, born and raised among Arabs, are capable of speaking to the Arab villager, worker, peasant, writer, or intellectual in a way that Western Jews would never be able to, he argued in one of his commentaries in 1932, and thus Oriental Jews should become more involved in political life. An agreement with the Arabs could not be achieved without their involvement, he argued.[55]

In his view of Palestine as a joint homeland for Jews, Muslims, and Christians, Sasson departed from the Zionist approach that recognized the national rights of the Jews over the country and did not view the local Sephardi Jews as opposing Zionism. In contrast, according to Sasson, it was the Oriental Jews (*al-yahud al-sharqiin*), who were aware of the growing national sentiments among Palestinian Arabs, who would be able to fully understand the Arab position. Regarding the 1932 Jewish-Arab conference, he claimed, its goals were not to challenge the authority of the Zionist movement but rather to make the important voices of the local Jews heard.[56]

In addition to his criticism of the Ashkenazi Jewish leadership of the Zionist movement, Sasson also criticized the Arab Executive Committee and the Supreme Muslim Council. Following the departure for London in 1930 of the Palestinian delegation (headed by Jamal al-Husseini and 'Awni 'Abd al-Hadi), to present the Palestinian Arab views on the 1929 riots in Palestine, Sasson published several articles in *al-Hayat* in which he called for "Jewish-Arab cooperation and Jewish-Arab unity which would remind the British that they are here to lead the inhabitants toward complete self-governance and independence."[57] To defend his idea of Jewish-Arab understanding, he returned to the early history of relations between Jews and Muslims and tried to apply it to the situation in Palestine:

I am well aware of the equal treatment the Jews received during the rise of Islam and afterward during the reign of the caliphs. Jews were more than happy with the rise of this [Muslim] empire based on rights, equality, and fraternity. . . . What is the harm to the Arabs if they let the persecuted Jewish people come and assemble in this spot on the planet so that they can pursue a free and decent life? . . . Do you honestly think that the Jewish agenda is set on exterminating the Arabs and their language? And if that is part of their agenda, don't you think that they realize that they can never achieve that knowing that there are millions of Muslims who would fight to the last drop of blood for Palestine? I would like to end by restating that Jews should seek an understanding with their Arab brothers to build this nation and bring prosperity and independence to our people.[58]

Unlike the Political Department of the Jewish Agency, which tried to foster the development of an alternative political leadership to the Arab Executive Committee, Sasson acknowledged that the committee represented Palestinian Arabs. The right thing to do is not to try to replace this organization, he argued, but rather to try and influence it to reaching a Jewish-Arab understanding.[59]

In July 1930 Sasson, who was described by the Hebrew newspaper *Davar* as a "Jewish-Arab journalist,"[60] published a letter in *Filastin* in which he argued that mutual understanding between Jews and Arabs in Palestine would be possible only if both national groups recognized each other's full rights. "The view that only the Arabs are the owners of the land and that the Jews are only visitors is a radical view," wrote Sasson. To create mutual understanding, it was important to establish a Jewish-Arab committee that would explore the question of how to create a joint homeland and would result in a Palestinian Jewish-Arab union in which each group recognized the other's national existence. Sasson also called on the Arabic press to explain to its readers the Jewish perspective on Jewish immigration and asked the Hebrew press to recognize the right of "this noble Arab nation in this country" and the existing bonds between Jews and Muslims on the basis of their Semitic and Eastern origin.[61]

Sasson's article received various responses in *Filastin*. For obvious reasons, his recognition of the national rights of the Jews and their equal rights in Palestine created much opposition in the newspaper, which viewed the Jews' renouncing their national aspirations as key for a Jewish-Arab understanding.[62] Indeed, these responses challenge Sasson's view that reaching a Jewish-Arab partnership in Palestine must be based on mutual recognition of national rights. In his future work in the Political Department of the Jewish Agency, Sasson would try to suggest ways of reacting to these challenges.

Sasson's open criticism of the policies of the Zionist leadership created some angry reactions to him from Zionist circles as well. The idea of organizing a Jewish-Arab conference was raised by Sasson in 1928. Michael Assaf, then a journalist for *Davar* specializing in Arab affairs, criticized the plan to convene an "Oriental-Israeli conference" in the same year, claiming that familiarity with Arabic and Arab culture alone could not lead to an understanding between Jews and Arabs in Palestine. Additionally, he criticized Sasson's distinction between the Sephardim and the Ashkenazim and referred to Sasson's Arabic writings on these issues as irresponsible.[63] The debate between Assaf and Sasson was renewed in 1932. On June 27 of that year Sasson argued again that no one other than Oriental Jews could reach an understanding with the Arabs, based on their familiarity with the culture and the people. In fact, he observed that since 1918 Western Jews had been trying unsuccessfully to solve the conflict with the Arabs. Since Western Jews were in charge of political negotiations, Oriental Jews could not use their beliefs and knowledge in support of the Zionist goal.[64] A few weeks later, Sasson also strongly denied the charge that Oriental Jews had conspired to betray the Zionists and repeated his argument that Oriental Jews had advantages that the Western leaders of the Zionist movement did not.[65]

Assaf responded to the idea of the Arab-Jewish conference and to Sasson's arguments once more, writing that the Arab leaders were not willing to cooperate with the Zionists and were willing to negotiate only if the Jews would give up all their national ambitions. There was no need for peace with the Arabs if the price for such peace and negotiations was humiliation to the Jews, Assaf added. The convention of the planned conference would undermine the Jewish and Zionist stance. Assaf acknowledged that Oriental Jews had only limited influence on the Zionists' policies toward the Arabs. However, the Zionist movement had been established in the West and remained a Western-based movement, according to Assaf. How could Oriental Jews carry out their Zionist ideology in the same way as European Jews could? Arab politicians understood this reality and preferred to negotiate with the Zionist minority, not the Zionist majority, claimed Assaf, but they should be ready to negotiate with the majority, the Western Jews. He ended on an optimistic note, hoping that all Jews would unite in their national aims, and once again he argued that a Jewish-Arab conference had no chance of succeeding.[66]

Sasson's response came a few days later. He replied to Assaf in an angry tone:

> It hurts me to know that, as the editor of the Eastern Department of an important newspaper [*Davar*], you don't know a lot about the issues of the Orient (*Masa'el al Sharq*) and the Arab Zionist movement. You, my friend, represent the danger that we wish to avoid: Western mentality (*a'aqliya gharbiya*), views and logic coupled with arrogance trying to solve an Oriental issue (*qadiya sharqiya*), interest, mentality, and policy. You have claimed that the Eastern conference that is being discussed by Arab Jewish writers (*kuttab al-'Arab min al-Isra'iliyin*) is asking to accept the terms and conditions set by the Arabs during the negotiations. There is no one among the Oriental Jews who would accept such defeat or humiliation. So far, the

Zionist committee has not taken concrete steps in building good relations with our brethren, the Arabs. Is it a sin if we, as Oriental Jews, want to live peacefully with our brothers in our homeland? Do you seriously think that the Arabs will run toward us the moment we invite them to hold talks and negotiations with them? Of course not! This would take time and special circumstances that should be set before any serious negotiations can start.[67]

A few weeks later, Sasson addressed Assaf again and clarified the way he viewed the convention of the conference:

We do not want to build an alliance with the Arabs based on the humiliation of our nation. . . . The Jews of the Orient (*yahud al-sharq*) have faced so many hardships throughout their history and were able to surpass them all and to keep their heads high no matter what. Our message to our Arab brothers is that no one can change our allegiance to our cause. Following the past fourteen years, we have come to the conclusion that it is our duty to build closer ties with the Arabs so that we can live peacefully with them. The cooperation between Jews and Arabs will save Eretz Israel from any upcoming perils and will solve its political and economic problems. The Arabs are completely right when they refuse to hold talks with you if they have never heard any praise or positive remarks on their struggle for freedom from your party. We [Oriental Jews] have an advantage over you in these matters [holding talks with the Arabs]. If you [the Zionist movement] create an understanding with the Arabs, then the Oriental Jews will be able to announce their allegiance to the Zionist movement just as proudly as the Western Jews do in the West.[68]

Sasson's criticism appeared in his political work as well. As discussed in chapter 2, in 1934, when he joined the Arab Bureau of the Political Department of the Jewish Agency under the leadership of Shertok, he decided to divert his work to the institutional track.[69] In many ways, his joining the Jewish Agency signaled the beginning of a new phase of his career and activism, in which he combined political, diplomatic, journalistic, and security-related work. From the mid-1930s until the end of the Mandatory period, Sasson met with hundreds of Arab leaders in Beirut, Damascus, Cairo, Amman, Baghdad, and Palestine to discuss possible political solutions for the Zionist-Arab conflict.

As also discussed in chapter 2, some would argue that Sasson really became a *Mizrahan*, an Orientalist, using his knowledge of Arabic and his connections in the service of the Zionist movement.[70] However, we argue that Sasson's Jewish-Arab identity, as ben hamizrah, affected his ideas about how to resolve the conflict between the two groups. In the different proposals that he presented to

Ben-Gurion and Shertok between 1939 and 1944, he emphasized the need to develop connections and to cooperate with the local Arab population in the economic, social, cultural, and political arenas, among others. As we will see below, he was also deeply involved in the discussions taking place about another sphere of cultural and linguistic exchange between Oriental Jews and Arabs—namely, the discussions about the position of Arabic in the Yishuv.

Linguistic and Cultural Mediation: The Role of Arabic Teaching

On October 7, 1942, Gershon Barag, a psychoanalyst from Tel Aviv and a prominent member of the Palestine Psycho-Analytical Society, wrote a letter to Yisrael Ben-Ze'ev, the inspector for Arabic in the Department of Education of the Jewish National Council, asking him to recommend an Arabic teacher in Tel Aviv. According to Barag, he had been studying Arabic for quite some time and could read a newspaper or an easy book with the assistance of a dictionary. He had first learned Arabic from Abraham Levy, a young teacher originally from Tiberias, and later studied in a small group that was led by Malul. He wished to continue studying Arabic, but in Tel Aviv he had heard only about Arabic courses taught by Europeans. He wrote Ben-Ze'ev: "I insist on and wish to study only with a native of the Orient (*ben hamizrah*), because I am native to the country myself (*yelid haaretz*) . . . I am writing to ask if you can refer me to an Arabic study group in Tel Aviv that is guided by a teacher who is of Oriental descent (*'eda mizrahit*), or an Arabic teacher, that I may join."[71]

Ben-Ze'ev received such requests during his tenure as the inspector of Arabic at the Department of Education of the Jewish National Council, a position he held from 1938 until his retirement in the mid-1960s. He was in charge of enhancing the teaching of Arabic in Jewish schools in Palestine, organizing training seminars and meetings for Arabic teachers throughout the country, and developing a curriculum and writing textbooks for the teaching of colloquial and standard Arabic. Ben-Ze'ev was part of a group of scholars and teachers that emphasized the importance of learning Arabic in light of the growing physical and psychological distance between Jews and Arabs in Palestine. For him, Arabic was more than just a language, though. He considered the knowledge of Arabic to be essential for Jews living in Palestine and viewed using the language as a way of creating contacts and links between Jews and Arabs in Palestine, both in daily life and in cultural exchanges.[72]

"Learning Arabic is a part of Zionism," wrote Shlomo Dov Goitein in 1946. A professor of Oriental studies at the Hebrew University of Jerusalem, Goitein was also a senior education officer for Hebrew schools in the Department of Education of the Mandatory government from 1938 to 1948.[73] And indeed, debates about the place of Arabic in the Yishuv—as well as about its uses, perceptions of it, and the ways to study it—had already begun in different Zionist circles at the end of Ottoman rule in Palestine.[74] Those debates took a different turn as a result of the transition to British Mandatory rule, the institutionalization of the Zionist movement, and the intensification of the Jewish-Arab conflict. Considering the debates taking place in the Yishuv during the Mandatory years in particular, Halperin identifies three major views of Arabic. The first—a view held mainly by the scholars at the Institute of Oriental Studies at the Hebrew University—is that Arabic is a romantic nationalist tool, and that the study of Arabic is a way of familiarizing and connecting the Jews to their semitic past. The second view is that Arabic is a modernizing tool that the Zionist movement in Palestine can use to encourage positive encounters between Jews and Arabs to produce Arab cooperation with the Zionist project. The third view is that Arabic is a strategic and practical tool to use in developing a body of knowledge about the Arabs, collecting intelligence about them, and identifying and predicting Arab activities.[75] None of these views pays special attention to the perspective of local Jews, which, we argue, could shed a different light on the study of Arabic as a form of mediation between Jews and Arabs.

As the discussion below suggests, throughout the Mandatory years there was a growing tension between two approaches for studying Arabic, one that viewed the study from a cultural perspective, as a tool for rapprochement, and one that viewed the language as a practical, political tool. Yonatan Mendel, in his discussion of the early history of Arabic studies in Palestine, calls these the "language of the neighbor" and the "language of the enemy" approaches. According to Mendel, during the Mandatory years, and especially following the Arab Revolt, the study of Arabic became much more associated with the latter approach as a result of the security and political needs of the Yishuv.[76]

While these two approaches to the study of Arabic existed during the 1930s and 1940s, the discussion below shows that this seeming dichotomy was much more nuanced. Mainly, it discusses the role of local Jews—the native speakers of Arabic—as educators, teachers, translators, and promoters of Arabic, and the role of Yisrael Ben-Ze'ev and other members of the Arabic teaching committees. Halperin calls the approach taken by Ben-Ze'ev and this group of local Jews "the pro-communication approach," which stressed the practical benefits of contacts

with Arabs because of the assumption that such contacts led to peaceful relations.[77] This approach suggests another type of linguistic or cultural mediation
that was led by local Jews, fluent in Arabic, who felt that using the language could
enhance contacts between the Jewish and Arab communities in Palestine and
link Palestine to its surrounding Middle Eastern environment. Hence, figures
like Ben-Ze'ev, Elmaleh, Rivlin, Yellin, Tuviya Shamosh, and Sasson, discussed
in this chapter, were not only active in Arabic teaching but were also engaged
in translating literary texts from Arabic into Hebrew and vice versa, teaching
Hebrew in Jewish schools in the Arab world, and maintaining contacts among
Jewish and Arab teachers and intellectuals.

Born in Jerusalem 1899 to a family of rabbis, Ben-Ze'ev (Wolfensohn) was a
local Jew of Ashkenazi descent. His family was among the founders of the Meah
She'arim neighborhood and of several of its important religious institutions
but was not among the well-off and notable Jewish families in Jerusalem. Like
many other families of local Jews in Jerusalem, Safed, Tiberias, and Hebron,
Ben-Ze'ev's family had long-lasting ties with Arab families. He grew up in an
Arab-speaking environment and had many Muslim neighbors and friends. In
addition to Yiddish, he spoke Hebrew, Arabic, German, English, and French.
He also held Ottoman citizenship and felt embedded in the Palestinian and
Ottoman environment.[78] In 1919 Ben-Ze'ev began studying in Dar al-Mu'alimin
in Jerusalem, with some members of the local Arab elite members. He re-
ceived training as an Arabic teacher and became very comfortable with both
colloquial and standard Arabic as well as with various prominent local Arabs.
He decided in 1922 to continue his PhD studies in Arabic and Islam at the
Egyptian University in Cairo. Studying in Cairo, Beirut, or Damascus was not
uncommon among local Oriental Jews, as we saw above in the cases of Malul,
Shimon Moyal, Sasson, and others. As Aviv Derri-Weksler suggests, Ben-
Ze'ev's decision to study in Cairo reflected both his socioeconomic status and
his identity as an intellectual who was strongly connected to the local Arabic
culture and language.[79]

Ben-Ze'ev later studied for a second PhD degree at the University of Frank-
furt. Like Malul, he returned to Cairo in 1933 to teach at the Egyptian University
and Dar Al-'Ulum; published extensively in Arabic and Hebrew; and wrote in
such Arab dailies as *al-Muqattam* and *al-Ahram*.[80] In addition to his academic
research and teaching, Ben-Ze'ev was also very active in the Zionist circles in
Cairo: he was the first president of the Hebrew Club and was involved in the
establishment of the Society of Young Egyptian Jews (Association de la Jeunesse
Juive Egyptiene).[81] He kept hoping to enroll in the Hebrew University's Institute

of Oriental Studies but was never able to do so. He returned to Jerusalem in 1938 and became the inspector for Arabic in the Department of Education of the Jewish National Council.[82]

Going back to Barag's letter to Ben-Ze'ev, it seems that Barag was not unique in insisting on studying Arabic only with a local Jew who was fluent in Arabic. Indeed, during Ben-Ze'ev's time at the Department of Education there were many debates regarding the position of local Oriental Jews as Arabic teachers, and whether they had any advantage over Ashkenazi teachers who were not as fluent in colloquial Arabic. For Ben-Ze'ev, the study of colloquial Arabic was as important as the study of standard written Arabic, and hence the teacher's accent, his or her ability to speak Arabic in class, and the degree of comfort with the language were extremely important.

Ben-Ze'ev identified a difference between the periods before and after World War I regarding the nature of Arabic study, from the perspectives of both teacher and student. Prior to the war, Jews in Palestine were familiar with colloquial Arabic as part of their daily interactions and close relations with Arabs, and hence there was no need to pay special attention to colloquial Arabic in the curriculum of Jewish schools. Following the war, however, with the increasing Jewish immigration from Europe and the growing national tension, the study of Arabic became much more challenging, Ben-Ze'ev claimed. Many Jewish students had no contact with Arabs and were unable to communicate in Arabic, and it was hence essential to expose them to colloquial Arabic, including the language's sound and dialects, even before they learned to read Arabic, he argued.[83] Indeed, as Halperin shows, before the war Arabic was regularly taught in Zionist elementary schools, but after the war only about 15–20 percent of Jewish students studied Arabic, mainly in the Gymnasia. In many of the kibbutzim Arabic was taught either as part of the curriculum or as an extracurricular activity.[84] From the perspective of the teachers, before World War I most of the Arabic teachers were Arabs, who graduated from Al Azhar University, many without any pedagogical training. After the war, Arab teachers stopped teaching in Jewish schools, and the Jewish teachers, especially those who came from Europe, were unable to speak with a proper accent, and had difficulty in writing as well.[85]

Who were the Arabic teachers? Addressing the participants in a meeting of Arabic teachers in Tel Aviv in 1939, Goitein reported that there were forty-two Arabic teachers in Jewish high schools. Goitein divided the teachers according to their ethnic background: eighteen were Sephardim and those who are not local Ashkenazi Jews; ten were Iraqis, and one was Syrian; ten were Ashkenazi Jews from abroad (probably Europe); and three were local Ashkenazi Jews.

However, among the Sephardim mentioned, many had studied in Hebrew schools and could be viewed as Ashkenazi, Goitein added.[86] In this group of teachers, then, local Jews—including Sephardim, Ashkenazim, and immigrants from Arab-speaking countries—made up the majority.

Indeed, many local Jews served as Arabic teachers in various schools, including David Avissar (Boys' School, Jerusalem), Avraham Sha'ashua (Sharoni) who wrote an Arabic-Hebrew dictionary and taught in Tiberias and Deganya; he will be discussed in chapter 5), Rivlin (Hebrew Teachers' College and Rehavia High School, both in Jerusalem), Ben-Ze'ev (Bet Hakerem High School, Jerusalem), Yosef Mani, Ezra Mani (various schools in Tel Aviv and Kfar Saba), Yellin (Hebrew Teachers' College, Jerusalem), Yehoshua (Bagrut High School, Jerusalem), Yitzhak Navon (Bet Hakerem High School), Moshe Piamenta (Bet Hakerem High School), and Yosef Meyuchas (Ezra Teachers' College).[87] As we will see below, some of these teachers were also involved in security-oriented activities. Many of the teachers were also engaged in other forms of Arabic teaching, writing, and translating. Such was the case with Yehoshua, for example, who wrote extensively in the Hebrew and Arabic press and published monographs and memoirs about the Sephardi community in Jerusalem and the history of Arabic press in Palestine. Avissar, a Hebronite writer and teacher who was also a poet and a publisher and was active, as noted above, in the Association of the Pioneers of the East; Yellin, who was a prominent intellectual, teacher, and writer, fluent in Arabic, and active in the intellectual milieu of Jerusalem and a teacher of Hebrew and Hebrew literature at the Hebrew University, as well as being one of the main advocates of the revival of Hebrew; and Meyuchas, a member of one of the prominent Sephardi families in Jerusalem, who was a researcher and a teacher of Hebrew, Arabic, and French, as well as being a leading figure of the Sephardi community. According to Ben-Ze'ev, most Arabic teachers were Eastern born (*'edot ha-mizrah*).[88] In addition, around 70 percent of the participants in the Arabic teachers' seminars that were initiated and organized by Ben-Ze'ev "belonged to the Oriental communities."[89]

Some of these teachers were also members of different committees that were established by the Department of Education of the Jewish National Council to discuss how to teach Arabic in Hebrew schools,[90] Along with Ben-Ze'ev the members of these committees included representatives from the Arab Department of the Histadrut, the Arab Bureau of the Political Department of the Jewish Agency, and the Department of Education, as well as faculty members of the Institute of Oriental Studies at the Hebrew University.[91] Prominent local Jews on these committees included Yitzhak Shamosh, Agassi, Rivlin, Yehoshua,

Assaf, and later Sasson, as part of his role as the director of the Arab Bureau.[92] As we will see below, the views expressed by these prominent figures differed considerably from one another.

Ben-Ze'ev's commitment to the teaching of colloquial Arabic was very apparent in the discussions taking place both in the Department of Education and in the training seminars that he organized between 1937 and 1944. Those discussions focused on the school curriculum for teaching colloquial and standard Arabic, textbooks that could be used, pedagogical methods used by teachers, and the level of the teachers. One of the issues discussed was what qualities were desirable in a teacher. Another was the differences between teachers who were native speakers of the language and those who were not. While there was a general consensus among the members of the Arabic committees regarding the importance of studying colloquial Arabic, views about the quality of teachers and students who came from Arabic-speaking countries varied.

Michael Dana, who taught Arabic in Hebrew high schools in Haifa, wrote several Arabic textbooks and an Arabic dictionary. He argued that only a native speaker of Arabic could teach the language. Colloquial Arabic should be taught while using Arabic script, without transliterating the text to Hebrew, just as it was taught elsewhere in the Arab world, he argued.[93] A different view was voiced by Yitzhak Shamosh, born in Aleppo to a prominent family. The brother of Tuviya and Amnon Shamosh, Yitzhak studied law and Arabic literature in Beirut and published frequently in literary journals in Syria, Lebanon, and Egypt. He was a passionate Zionist, was involved in Syrian politics, and was one of the Jewish candidates for election to the first Syrian parliament. He immigrated to Palestine in 1937 following an invitation from the Hebrew University to teach Arabic literature. The rest of his family immigrated to Palestine after him.[94] Speaking in Arabic (which he said was "the language that I feel more comfortable speaking in than Hebrew") during the 1941 convention of Arabic teachers who taught in the kibbutzim, Shamosh argued that it would be wrong to assume that every Arabic speaker could also teach the language. In fact, he claimed, the majority of the Arabic teachers in Palestine were not fit to do their jobs.[95] At a different meeting, while discussing the curriculum for Arabic teachers' seminars, David Zvi Banet, a professor of Arabic language and literature at the Hebrew University, asked whether teachers from Iraq, Syria, and Egypt should participate in the seminars. "Are these teachers even able to understand the pedagogical and the general educational principles?" he asked in a paternalistic tone, adding that "maybe it would be better to leave the schools without teachers, than to bring bad teachers to them."[96]

In contrast, in September 1942 Ben-Ze'ev reported that the majority of the Ashkenazi Arabic teachers, most of whom were graduates of the Hebrew University, had difficulty pronouncing Arabic with a good accent; some also did not have enough knowledge of the grammatical rules. Ben-Ze'ev also mentioned that the teachers who were native speakers needed more practice in speaking clearly.[97] As for the students, Ben-Ze'ev suggested taking advantage of students who spoke Arabic and could demonstrate the correct pronunciation of words.[98] It is clear, then, that the debates about the role of local Jews as potential teachers involved not only their professional skills (or lack thereof, according to some) but also their general knowledge and pedagogical and other abilities.

The debate about the use of Arabic-speaking teachers and their potential advantage in the classroom raises the question of why there was a lack of Arab teachers employed in Hebrew schools, especially since their numbers shrank considerably with the transition to British rule. Mendel argues that this process is linked to what he calls "the Zionisation" or the "political Judaisation" of Arabic, which included a clear preference for Jewish teachers of Arabic and the encouragement of Jewish scholars to write Arabic textbooks.[99] According to Mendel, Ben-Ze'ev explained the lack of Arabic teachers as a result of their lack of Hebrew knowledge, their lack of proper pedagogical training, and the fact that their methods were "not appropriate for the nature and cultural level of our pupils."[100] This Zionization process, Mendel argues, might be caused by the attempt to comply with Zionist ideology in employing Hebrew-speaking Jewish teachers and by the growing hostility between the two communities. It might also be connected to security needs and considerations, especially following the Arab Revolt, when the study of Arabic became closely connected to security and political considerations.[101]

Interestingly, however, training seminars included several Arab teachers who were very successful, according to Ben-Ze'ev's reports. Examples were Jeriyis Mansour (who taught Arabic literature), 'Adel Jabre (classical Arabic literature), Faiz al-Gul (Arabic syntax, writing, and conversation), Yassin al-Khalidi (writing and conversation), and Rabahi Kamal (newspapers).[102] Ben-Ze'ev stressed the need to employ Arab teachers, because the Institute of Oriental Studies at the Hebrew University did not provide strong enough candidates for the training seminars. He also encouraged the participation in the seminars of teachers from Iraq, Syria, and Egypt.[103] Some of those teachers did participate. For example, Murad Mikha'il, the principal of the Baghdadi Shamash School and one of the prominent Jewish writers in Iraq, participated in a 1943 seminar.[104]

The attempt to create connections and to exchange ideas between Jewish teachers in Palestine and their colleagues from neighboring Arab countries—especially Egypt—was partially successful. For example, Avissar and Yellin organized several visits of Eretz-Israeli teachers to Egyptian schools and universities, the first of which took place in March 1926 with 90 teachers and Zionist activists participating. A month later a group of 112 teachers and principals, who represented the Egyptian Ministry of Education, visited Palestine. Among other places, they visited the Herzlia Gymnasium in Tel Aviv, the Reali School in Haifa, and the agricultural school Mikveh Israel.[105] In April 1935 a group of 240 Jewish teachers, authors, physicians, and intellectuals from Palestine participated in another visit to Egypt, as part of the celebrations of the 800th anniversary of Maimonides's birth. Their visit received much attention in the local Jewish press, and its aims were defined as "getting to know the land of Egypt, its inhabitants, to visit its different schools and to exchange knowledge between us and the Egyptian teachers." Ben-Ze'ev, who also wrote a biography of Maimonides in Arabic, was on the committee that organized the visit and was in touch with the Egyptian Ministry of Education and with Sheikh al-Azhar about it.[106]

In connection to his focus on cultural and intellectual exchange, and with the financial support of the Jewish community in Cairo, Ben-Ze'ev established in Jerusalem an Arabic library for teachers, where he hoped to collect Arabic textbooks from the neighboring Arab countries, dictionaries, and Arabic literature. This library was intended not only for teachers, but also for the Jewish and Arab communities in Jerusalem. Its purposes were to enhance the links between the Jewish community in Palestine and the neighboring Arab countries and to expose Jews to Arab culture.[107] The notion of cultural exchange was mentioned by the representative of the Jewish community in Cairo, who said that Ben-Ze'ev was either the Egyptian cultural attaché in Eretz Israel, or the Eretz Israeli cultural attaché in Egypt.[108] The importance of Arab teachers and the establishment of the Arabic library in Jerusalem as a bridge between people, cultures, languages, and communities show that the Zionization of Arabic was not complete and was much nuanced.

Why was it important to study Arabic, and mainly colloquial Arabic? Views on this question varied as well. Yellin, for example, argued that for Jewish students to be able to be around Arabs ("*Lavo besviva 'Aravit*") it was necessary to study colloquial Arabic, and only later should standard Arabic be taught, for students who would like to read and write the language. Alexander Dushkin, who established the Department of Education at the Hebrew University and was the first superintendent of Jewish schools in the Mandatory government, added that it is very important so that "our child would not feel like a stranger in his surrounding environment."[109] Eliyahu Habuba—an Arabic teacher who was born in Damascus, wrote two Arabic textbooks, and was a prominent member of the Sephardi community in Haifa—suggested encouraging the study of Arabic in schools by arranging visits to Arab villages and towns, establishing an Arab club that would offer lectures and seminars by Jewish and Arab teachers, and visiting Arab cultural institutions.[110]

We Are Similar in the Language of Their Souls: Orientations in the Study of Arabic

Starting at the beginning of the 1940s, the Arab Bureau of the Political Department of the Jewish Agency, headed by Sasson, began to financially support the work of the Arabic committees at the Department of Education. As part of a broader effort that was discussed in chapter 2, the Political Department supported some of the teachers' seminars that Ben-Ze'ev organized, with a special emphasis on the training of teachers who could teach in the Jewish agricultural settlements, the kibbutzim and *moshavim*. From a very practical standpoint, Sasson explained that "it is known from experience that the lack of knowledge of Arabic among the Jewish settlers is not conductive in forming honest neighborly relations to the minimal degree necessary, and may cause needless clashes between the Jewish settlements and the surrounding Arab villages."[111]

As Halperin indicates, the emphasis put on the agricultural settlements, where Jews and Arabs often had daily contacts and interactions, demonstrates one of the functions of the study of Arabic during this time: it was a way of responding to Jews' feeling of isolation within the Arab-speaking environment.[112] More relevant in this context, though, is Mendel's argument that the growing involvement of the Political Department of the Jewish Agency indicated the gradual shift in the orientation of Arabic studies to political and security concerns, which involved the use of Arabic for propaganda, surveillance, and other security-oriented projects.[113]

But were there indeed two separate views of the study and teaching of Arabic—as a political undertaking or for its cultural and educational significance? We argue that the local Jews, in their different activities as teachers, intellectuals, writers, and translators, blur the line separating between these seemingly different orientations. This blurry line is nicely demonstrated by the discussions taking place at the February 1941 conference of Arabic teachers who taught in the kibbutzim and were funded by the Arab Bureau of the Jewish Agency. In addition to the teachers, many of whom were of Middle Eastern descent, attendees at the conference included Sasson, Assaf and Agassi as the two supervisors of Arabic teaching in the kibbutzim, Ben-Ze'ev, and other guests.

The discussion in this conference was part of the effort, led by the Arab Bureau, to create the Committees for Neighborly Relations. The conference also included discussions typical of those during World War II on cultural, political, and social ways to improve relations between Jews and Arabs. Assaf, for example, welcomed the participants to the conference and explained the need for such a meeting at that particular time:

> This is a time of emergency. We fell behind in teaching Arabic to our students, and need to correct it now, in a period that provides us with some political opportunities. We should realize that a closer contact (*hitkarvut*) between us and the Arabs would not change the positions and claims of both people regarding this land. However, during this relatively calm period [in terms of Jewish-Arab relations] Jews can get closer to the Arabs. It is true that good neighborly relations would not establish a political movement [among the Arabs], but there is no doubt that an Arab community that is resentful of the Jews would ease the work of the inciters and instigators. It is hence our duty to make the lives of these instigators more difficult."[114]

Assaf viewed the study of Arabic as a political tool and as an aid to creating better relations and reducing tensions between Jews and Arabs. He was clearly part of a growing group in the Zionist establishment, including members of Mapai and representatives of Hashomer Hatza'ir, who were active in cultivating personal relationships with Arabs in the hope that they would transcend the political conflict.[115]

Agassi, then a member of the Arab Department of the Histadrut, spoke after Assaf. He emphasized the importance of teaching colloquial Arabic to create "a way of life (*havay*) of Arabic language":

> The teacher should give his students the feeling that they entered an Arab way of life (*nichnesu letoch havay 'Aravi*). The study material should include conversations, stories, fables, and jokes that are closely related to the lives of the Arabs. The first priority should be given to the lives of the fellaheen, then to the lives of the Bedouin, and only then should the study material represent urban life. The lessons should be aimed not only toward knowledge of the language, but also toward understanding the Arab way of life. The student will familiarize himself with the Arab fellaheen at work, in the field and vineyard, in daily life, and in celebrations (*bemesibot holin*

ubemesibot kodesh). . . . You [the teachers] should visit your Arab neighbors with the students, and make sure that you meet with them often, learn their ways of life, and write down their stories and fables. . . . The Arab fellaheen in Eretz Israel are not homogeneous . . . the study of the language should be as heterogeneous as possible to interest the student.[116]

Agassi continued his introduction with a discussion of some of the methodologies and books that should be used in the classroom. The priority that he gave to the study of the peasant and the Bedouin, before that of the urban dweller, was based on the idea of improving the relations between the kibbutzim and Arab villages. It also reflects what Gil Eyal describes as an image and idea that was expressed in the Zionist discourse—and used by Ben-Gurion—and that viewed the Bedouin and the peasants as the "authentic and real Arabs."[117] It also alludes to questions of class and socioeconomic differences. The peasants were the subject of ethnographic works by scholars and other authors, including Meyuchas and Yitzhak Shami, the Hebronite author.[118] Agassi and other Middle Eastern Sephardi intellectuals were mainly in touch with their counterparts in Arab society—the intellectuals and elite among Palestinian Arabs. As we discuss in other contexts in chapter 4, the lower classes, both Jews and Arabs but mainly those residing in the mixed cities and border neighborhoods, had a completely different hybrid identity and set of links.

Agassi was very clear in his preference for colloquial Arabic over standard Arabic. According to him, "the purpose of the training seminar is to be able to speak and understand simple Arabic, to read a report from an Arabic newspaper. Reading an article from an Arabic newspaper is secondary to reading a note written by a peasant, which is written usually in colloquial Arabic."[119] At the end of the discussion, Sasson emphasized the links between the teachers and the Jewish Agency, which funded and otherwise supported their work. Some teachers were acting independently, without notifying the Political Department, he observed. For example, he had heard of a teacher who visited neighboring Arab villages and another who invited Arabs to his kibbutz without the local residents' agreement. All teachers should notify the Political Department of any interaction with Arabs and get its permission, Sasson insisted, and every activity that involved Arab neighbors should be carried out with agreement from the board of the local kibbutz.[120]

Assaf, Agassi, and Sasson presented a clear political agenda for the study of Arabic but also emphasized that there was a strong connection between learning Arabic and political and social rapprochement. Ben-Ze'ev and some other members of the Arabic teaching committees believed the study of Arabic to have mainly educational and cultural value and to be a way of creating links and dialogue between people. Ben-Ze'ev mentioned the different views of learning Arabic when he asked for some more money to support the work of the "Fund for the Development of Arabic" in the Department of Education. The fund was supposed to support the training of Arabic teachers and establish a publishing house that would focus on Arabic textbooks. Expenditures from this fund were supposed to be made in close coordination with the Arab Bureau and with Sasson in particular. The Jewish Agency had a political interest in this fund, argued Ben-Ze'ev, whereas he and his colleagues in the Department of Education had only an educational or cultural interest in it. In his views, the two approaches were different but complemented each other.[121]

Discussing these two approaches, Mendel argues that Ben-Ze'ev and others were torn between their initial instinct to view the teaching of Arabic in an integrative and scholarly way and their understanding of the growing insistence within the Zionist movement on the urgent need to teach and study Arabic for practical political purposes. The balance between the integrative and security-focused rationales for teaching Arabic was tipped in the direction of the latter, argues Mendel, as a result of the heightened tensions between Jews and Arabs.[122] However, instead of looking at these two rationales as dichotomous, and at Ben-Ze'ev as being torn between them, we argue that the two rationales were tightly connected and reflected the way local Jews viewed their unique role, as people involved in both the political and cultural spheres.

This special approach was nicely defined by Moshe Solovichki, the director of the Department of Education of the National Council, as "cultural politics" (*politika tarbutit*). In a party held as part of the Arabic teachers' conference in August 1945, he made a speech to the teachers and special guests (who included Ben-Ze'ev; the lawyer and activist David Moyal, Shimon Moyal's brother; Dana, Tzidkiyahu Harkabi, who years later would become the chief of Israeli military intelligence and a professor of international relations at the Hebrew University; and the author and Zionist activist Moshe Smilanski one of the supporters of Brit Shalom and the binational option in Palestine. Solovichki mentioned the two significant values of the Arabic study program headed by Ben-Ze'ev. The first was what he termed the "cultural political significance" of entering the Arab cultural world and locating common ground, without losing the Jewish independent development. The second was the educational significance of mastering Arabic in schools.[123] In his turn, Ben-Ze'ev addressed the audience and reported on the training courses for Arabic teachers. Twenty-eight participants were

Sephardi and Oriental Jews, and twenty-two were Ashkenazi Jews. Besides the usual skills of grammar, syntax, and speaking, he emphasized the extracurricular lectures on Arab folklore, Islamic law, and Muslim women that were delivered by Arabs. He also updated the audience on his own efforts, discussed above, to establish a library of Arabic books in Jerusalem, with the support of the Jewish community in Cairo.[124]

Some of the guests at the party spoke as well, including Smilanski, David Moyal, and Harkabi. These three greeted the participants and added their own perspectives on Ben-Ze'ev's work. "I was raised in this country and grew older here," said Smilanski, "and always knew that the destiny of our country is dependent upon our ability to make peace between the two peoples who live here together. Peace would be possible only by a common work and a common culture, hence Ben-Ze'ev's work of studying Arabic and creating common understanding is so important."[125]

Moyal also praised Ben Ze'ev's work and said: "We live among the Arabs, are related to them, and are committed to having work and cultural relations with them. It is impossible to do all this without learning Arabic and without knowing this people ('am). I appeal and ask [you] to try and uproot the hatred of the Arab people and its language, and to deepen the study of Arabic language, culture, and poetry."[126] Harkabi addressed the audience as a former Arabic teacher who had studied in an Arabic school in Jerusalem and later in a Hebrew school in Damascus. "Arabic helps us create links with the Arabs and live peacefully with them, to an extent that even in days of tension I feel comfortable among Arabs," he said.[127]

As Derri-Wexler argues, Ben-Ze'ev was by no means naive or idealistic in his approach to the importance of the study of Arabic and the role it should play among Jews in the Yishuv. In the different projects he was involved in, including his role as an inspector for Arabic in the Department of Education, he continued to view the Arabic language not from a scholarly distance (as was often the case with some of the scholars at the Institute of Oriental Studies at the Hebrew University) but intimately, as part of the local and regional culture and history. Instead of supporting the dichotomy of "language of the neighbor" versus "language of the enemy," Ben-Ze'ev insisted on the way Arabic can connect people, neighbors, and cultures, even at a time of high tension and violence.[128] His background as a local Ashkenazi Jew, educated and deeply embedded in the Arab world, enabled him to view the language is this way and to influence the perception of the study of Arabic during the Mandatory years.

A large group of intellectuals, writers, and political activists shared Ben Ze'ev's view of the political and cultural spheres as closely connected and believed they had a role to play as possible mediators between Jews and Arabs, and between Palestine and the rest of the Arab world. Some of these intellectuals—such as Yitzhak, Tuviya, and Amnon Shamosh; Agassi; Rivlin; Meyuchas; and Yellin—were also all involved in translating Arabic literature into Hebrew, in addition to writing academic publications and conducting research about Islamic studies, Arabic literature, and Middle Eastern history. Some, such as Agassi, also founded publishing houses to produce translated Arabic novels and short stories.[129] Another important translator from Arabic was the renowned Russian-born scholar Menachem Kapeliouk, who in 1932 translated the autobiography of the important Egyptian writer and intellectual Taha Hussein. In addition, Kapeliouk translated a variety of scholarly books; selections of mainly Egyptian literature, including two books by the Palestinian historian 'Aref al-'Aref; and stories of the renowned Egyptian authors Tawfik al-Hakim and Naguib Mahfouz.[130] Translations from Hebrew into Arabic were not as common. David Tidhar's *Hoti'im Vehatai'im Be'eretz Israel* was one of the few Hebrew books that were translated into Arabic—in this case, by Malul.[131] Arabic, then, was not only used for political purposes, but also served as a bridge between two cultures.

The discussion about the potential role of local Jews as mediators between Jews and Arabs continued throughout the Mandatory period. The debates discussed here, about the role of the press and the study of Arabic in the Yishuv, demonstrate many of the views that were expressed throughout this troubled time. Many local Jews continued to write for Hebrew, as well as Arabic, newspapers and to express their views on the national question, the relations with the Arabs, and the Zionist movement. Some, like Sasson, used their knowledge of Arabic and their personal connections with central figures in the Arab world and became active in the political, security, and diplomatic arenas. The attitudes of this group of people were in no way homogeneous. As discussed in chapter 2, they held different political opinions, but they all agreed about two things. Bney Ha'aretz and the hegemonic Zionist leadership, dominated in the 1930s and 1940s by Labor Zionists, differed in their attitudes toward the Arabs, and Bney Ha'aretz were potentially able to serve as a bridge between Jews and Arabs.

This idea was expressed nicely in an article by Rivlin that was published in *Hed Hamizrah* in November 1942. The article was discussed in chapter 1, but it is worth mentioning again how Rivlin differentiated between the patronizing attitude of the activists of Brit Shalom and Ichud toward the Arabs and the attitude of Bney Ha'aretz, both Sephardim and Ashkenazim (the group he considered himself to be part of), which was based on a sense of equality and true understanding.

As he wrote, "the attitude of Ben Ha'aretz to the Arab is different. He does not view the Arab fellah or the worker with pity. . . . The Jewish Ben Ha'aretz does not pity the Arab. He is in many ways equal to him. The eastern Jewish worker is very similar to the Arab worker, as all are members of the poor social strata among both peoples. They are similar to each other not only in their language, but in the language of their souls (*sfat nafsham*)."[132]

In many ways, Rivlin's words echo many of the nuances that have been discussed in this chapter. It is what Rivlin called "the language of the soul" (*sfat hanefesh*) that influenced the way Bney Ha'aretz viewed the Arabs and their own role in the complex matrix of Jewish-Arab relations in Mandatory Palestine.

FOUR

Mixing and Unmixing in
the Oriental Ghettos

In April 1934, Moshe (born Musa) Levi Nachum was elected as the Jewish representative in the Jaffa municipality. Levi was elected thanks to the support of the Jewish and some of the Arab residents of two neighborhoods that stood on the frontier between Jaffa and Tel Aviv: the Yemenite Quarter (hereafter Kerem Hatemanim, which literally means the Yemenite vineyard) and Neve Shalom. Levi listed three main goals for his term in office: to support and protect poor and abandoned children; to guarantee the social and cultural rights of the Jewish inhabitants of Jaffa in return for the municipal taxes they paid; and to strengthen the relations between Jews and Arabs, which could be achieved by mutual understanding and the Jews' knowledge of Arabic.[1]

Levi had served as the mukhtar of Kerem Hatemanim since 1925 and was a well-known figure and local leader in the Yemenite community in Jaffa and Tel Aviv. Among other things, he was known for his work with poor and abandoned children and for his good relations with the British authorities, as well as with many Arab and Jewish public figures in Jaffa, Tel Aviv, and elsewhere in Palestine. In 1936 he established a printing house called Malan (an approximate acronym for his name, Moshe Levi Nahum) and the newspaper *Mizrah* (East), whose goal was to represent Oriental Jews and discuss their special problems.

Levi was born in the Al-Sharaf District in Yemen and at an early age lost both his parents. He arrived in Jaffa in 1905 after encountering many hardships on his journey through Eritrea and Egypt. In his early years in Palestine he struggled to survive.[2] He moved from one place to another in search of work, until he settled in the Karton Quarter, often referred to as Kerem Hatemanim, on the border between Jaffa and Tel Aviv.[3] From his early days as a leader in the Yemenite Jewish community, Levi was very active in the struggles of the Yemenites, as well as in addressing the harsh realities of abandoned children who turned to crime as a last resort. Almost certainly his dedication to those children and his efforts to get them to study or acquire a skill were influenced by his own experience and hardships as an orphan. From his early days in Palestine he was also very aware of the different experiences of Oriental children and Ashkenazi children in Tel Aviv. In 1925, when he was elected mukhtar of Kerem Hatemanim, he competed against an Ashkenazi candidate who won the support of Meir Dizengoff, then mayor of Tel Aviv. "The Ashkenazim still believed that neither a Yemenite, nor anyone else of Eastern descent, would be able to hold a public position. . . . It saddened the residents of this neighborhood that our brothers viewed us as not less inferior than the way we were treated in the Diaspora," Levi wrote later.[4]

As part of his position, Levi was often asked to mediate between relatives or neighbors in various family or communal conflicts. As he later recalled, "making peace and giving advice is one of the duties of respected people, rabbis, and public figures. In my case, I was active not only among Jews [who lived] in the Kerem [Hatemanim] as well as the few who live outside of it, but also among many Arabs, either those who lived in the Kerem or those who lived in Jaffa."[5]

He remembered, for example, that he was asked to come to the home of a well-known Arab family whose sons had had a fight and threatened to kill each other. The parents were afraid of their two sons, but Levi managed not only to win their trust and prevent violence, but also to pacify everyone over lunch and coffee at his house.[6] In other cases, he was asked to help the police locate thieves, hashish traders, or murderers—both Jews and Arabs—who were active around Kerem Hatemanim, especially in the nearby Hacarmel Market. Because he won the trust and respect of the residents, he was able to prevent many fights and conflicts. His house served as a safe haven during periods of conflict and unrest between Jews and Arabs. According to Levi, in times such as during the Arab Revolt, because of the trust and loyalty many Arabs felt toward him and their other Jewish neighbors, they protected the property of those neighbors when the Jews fled their homes.[7]

Among the responsibilities Levi had as mukhtar was to intervene in cases of Jewish girls and young women who wanted to convert to Islam. Cases of conversion from Judaism to Islam or Christianity were delicate matters and were often discussed in the local press. In 1940 and 1941, for example, it was reported that eight Jewish women converted to Islam and two converted to Christianity (through the Greek Orthodox Church). According to the report, all women were 19–23 years old and lived in the frontier neighborhoods or in Jaffa. In 1941 there were also two cases of Christians' converting to Judaism. It was also reported that there was an increase in the number of Jewish girls who married non-Jews (some were Christian soldiers who served in Palestine during World War II). One possible explanation for the mixed marriages is that poor Jewish women could not pay the dowry expected from them when marrying a Jewish man.[8] Cases of Jews' converting to Islam were not unique to Tel Aviv and Jaffa, of course. In Hebron, the Jewish community tried to urge a young Sephardi Jew who had converted to Islam to leave the country for Egypt, where he had relatives.[9] In Haifa several Sephardi men and women converted to Islam, and their cases reached the rabbinical authorities in the city, as well as the National Council.[10]

The cases that Levi dealt with were those of fatherless girls, typically poor, who fell in love with Muslims. The girls' mothers were often unable to support their daughters. As the mukhtar, Levi was asked to approve these conversions, but he generally managed to talk the girls out of it or to convince the Muslim judge (*qadi*) or the municipal authorities not to carry out the conversion. In one instance he talked with the qadi and told him that all the girls who wanted to convert were prostitutes. The conversion of the girl in that case was canceled as a result. In another case a young Muslim orphan asked Levi to support his conversion to Judaism. Levi asked one of the Muslim qadis of Kerem Hatemanim to help the young man and to prevent him from converting. The young Muslim started crying, saying that he was hoping to find refuge in Judaism, a compassionate religion. "If you do not want to accept me, I will go to the Christians," he said and left Levi's house. Levi and the qadi were both saddened by this incident and the hardships of abandoned and orphan children. This incident strengthened the relationship between him and the qadi, concluded Levi.[11]

Levi used the connections he made with Arabs for other purposes as well. When invited to various parties and other events, he remembered that "some Arabs, because we became close, would share important security information with me, and at the same time would say 'too bad you are not an Arab.'"[12] Indeed, during the 1940s, Levi took advantage of his role as mukhtar to support the fighters in different Jewish paramilitary groups, mainly members of the Stern Group (Lehi) and the Irgun, but also members of the Haganah. He shared information with them and hid weapons and fighters in his house. According to Levi, many members of the Irgun and Lehi were Yemenites or of Middle East descent who had joined the organizations either as an outlet for their frustration or to find new challenges and courses of action. In contrast, his impression was that the Haganah had a smaller proportion of Oriental Jews as members. "It seems to me they [the Haganah] did not trust the residents of the neighborhoods, and viewed them as irresponsible and ignorant," argued Levi.[13] The complex connection between the special position of Oriental Jews vis-à-vis the national institutions and the mainly Ashkenazi leadership on the one hand, and the Arabs on the other hand, is demonstrated here as well.

In many ways, Levi's work, experiences, and challenges in Kerem Hatemanim and the adjacent Manshiyya neighborhood demonstrate many of the complexities and contradictions that also characterized the frontier neighborhoods in other mixed cities in Palestine.[14] The frontier neighborhoods—also known as the border or periphery neighborhoods—such as Kerem Hatemanim, Neve Shalom, and Manshiyya between Tel Aviv and Jaffa; Ard al-Yahud and Harat al-Yahud in Haifa; and Nachlaot in Jerusalem were all located on a border between a Jewish neighborhood and an Arab village or neighborhood. In some cases the neighborhoods' populations were also mixed, with both Jewish and Arab residents. These neighborhoods and the experiences of their inhabitants, mainly Oriental Jews and Arabs, are the focus of this chapter. As will be discussed below, these neighborhoods, in which Jews and Arabs lived side by side and interacted on a daily basis, serve as a microcosm to use in examining the complex relations between Oriental Jews and Arabs during the Mandatory years. These relations were full of contradictions and shifted between neighborliness and hostility, as Levi's experience in Kerem Hatemanim shows.[15] The frontier neighborhoods represent the illusional nature of the mixed cities and show that they were simultaneously mixed and divided. On the one hand, as this chapter demonstrates, the frontier neighborhoods were a place where social, cultural, religious, and economic interactions of different kinds occurred between Jews and Arabs, but on the other hand, they were also sites of political and national confrontation. In addition, they were sites of political, ethnic, economic, and cultural marginality for both their (mainly Oriental) Jewish and Arab residents.

This chapter begins by discussing the illusional nature of the mixed cities in Palestine, focusing mainly on the frontier neighborhoods or the Oriental ghettos, the way they were formed, and their socioeconomic profile.[16] It will then move back to Kerem Hatemanim, Neve Shalom, and Manshiyya to examine closely the crossing and uncrossing of boundaries in the frontier neighborhoods and the double marginality experienced by their inhabitants. The last part of the chapter will examine various sites of interactions between Jews and Arabs in these neighborhoods such as the playground, school, beach, café, and cinema.

The Illusional Nature of the Mixed City

"Modern urban spaces are, by definition, mixed," Daniel Monterescu and Dan Rabinowitz state at the beginning of a collection of essays they edited on mixed towns in Mandatory Palestine and Israel.[17] These spaces combine different classes and diverse ethnic and national groups and subcultures. Therefore, as many writings on the modern city have demonstrated, they are simultaneously sites for ethnic, social, and cultural conflict and sites for social change, coexistence and intercommunal collaborations.[18] In the Israeli-Palestinian context the term "mixed cities" specifically refers to cities and other urban localities in which both Arabs and Jews live, even though the term has been criticized for creating an illusion of a "mutual membership while ignoring questions of power, control and resistance."[19] In many ways, therefore, these heterogeneous urban environments have embodied and symbolized the Israeli-Palestinian conflict since its early days.[20]

Mixed cities in Mandatory Palestine were at the same time reality and a metaphor of the existence of two communities—Jewish and Arab—on the same land. Since at least a third of the Jews and a third of the Arabs who lived in towns before 1948 were in mixed cities, understanding this urban setting is key to understanding the dynamics and relations between these two communities.[21] However, in the context of Mandatory Palestine "mixed cities" was a somewhat paradoxical term. It was coined by the British Mandatory government to define cities in Palestine whose population, according to the government's understanding, was anything but mixed. In fact, these cities were defined by the Mandatory authorities as divided between two separate and deeply antagonistic ethnic and national communities.[22]

Thus the term "mixed cities" both embodied and reproduced the basic concept of a dual society in Palestine. The use of the term in the Jewish and Arab discourse in Palestine during the Mandatory period discloses, however, that the British definition was largely ignored by the Arabs, who viewed cities such as Jaffa, Haifa, and Tiberias as Arab cities, while Jews used the term mainly to discuss the status and implications of a Jewish minority living in cities under an Arab majority rule, such as Jaffa, or to refer to the mixed municipalities in these cities.[23]

Until recently, most historians of mixed cities in Mandatory Palestine more or less accepted the British definition of the term as a faithful description of life in the cities. According to Tamir Goren, for example, such cities consisted of "a space shared by two dominant communities who were in conflict, influenced by national and ethno-religious differences," and although the communities shared a municipal government and to a certain extent economic and commercial interests and activities, they lived mostly in separate neighborhoods and had separate social, religious, and cultural institutions.[24]

Researchers accepted the notion that both communities had little or no interest in assimilation or integration and in fact viewed the urban space they shared as playing a central role in the national quest for domination and the expulsion of the other group. In this sense, urban life in general and in mixed cities in particular prior to 1948 is viewed almost universally through the lens of the national conflict.[25] Even works that stress elements of cooperation and coexistence—whether on the individual or collective level, and whether in commercial and economic sites or social and cultural ones—mostly do so within the boundaries of the dual-society framework. In such works, these sites are usually discussed as places where transgressions of set boundaries occur, as a "twilight zone" or "no man's land," terms that reinforce the concept of a dual society.[26] Monterescu and Rabinowitz, for example, state that although "urban space was being constantly drawn along national lines . . . paradoxically . . . nationally espoused boundaries were constantly challenged by more cooperative spirits and practices," a fact they attribute mainly to the "color-blind logic of capital consumption and production," as well as to new residential contact zones.[27]

However, not all of the scholars writing on mixed cities in Mandatory Palestine agree that the term accurately describes the nature of the relations between the two communities in these cities, to say nothing of the changes in these relations. For example, Eli Nachmias suggests that in the case of Haifa, the Jewish and Arab population was not mixed but rather lived in a state of cohabitation, meaning a "cooperation between two sides merely in order to achieve specific objectives," since both sides realized they would gain more from maintaining a state of stability than from living in a state of conflict.[28] Nahum Karlinsky claims that the term "mixed cities" ignores the fundamental changes during the Mandatory period in Jerusalem, Haifa, Jaffa, and Tel Aviv, the main urban centers, and suggests three different and dynamic models—polarized, divided, and partitioned—as a more accurate analysis of the process of national segregation.[29] Like other scholars, Karlinsky focuses almost exclusively on the political level while ignoring other important aspects such as everyday life, and overlooks the perspective of the Sephardi and Oriental Jewish urban communities while stressing the ethnic differences between Arabs and (European) Jews.

In recent years, with the growth of local history of the Yishuv and as part of the turn from political, national, and institutionalized macro history to social, gender, and cultural micro history, quite a few publications on cities in Mandatory Palestine have appeared, most of them dedicated to mixed cities such as Haifa, Jerusalem, and Jaffa.[30] Much less was written on urban life and social history in the peripheral cities, such as Acre, Beit-Shean, Tiberias and Safed.[31] The increasing interest specifically in mixed cities in historical as well as in social scientific scholarship can be attributed to a growing understanding that the relations between Arabs and Jews at the local urban level both reflect and challenge those at the national level, especially in light of the violent clashes in mixed cities during the last ten years of the Mandatory period.[32]

Most of the writing on mixed cities in Mandatory Palestine uses a national or "conflict based" narrative (as Karlinsky terms it),[33] which does not take into account the fact that national categories themselves were historical and not always present. This narrative also largely ignores the perspective of Sephardi and Oriental Jews and overlooks other important components of the relations and dynamics between Jews and Arabs such as ethno-cultural identity or class (social and economic status).[34] It is to these questions that we turn to next.

The Oriental Ghettos and the Frontier Neighborhoods

Although the number of Sephardi and Oriental Jews in the general Jewish population in Palestine decreased during the Mandatory period, their average proportion in the mixed cities remained relatively high.[35] In Tiberias, for example, the Sephardi and Oriental Jewish communities constituted 72.6 percent of the Jewish population throughout the Mandatory period, and in Safed, they constituted 40.6 percent. In Haifa, with the waves of immigrants from Europe, the Sephardi and Oriental Jewish communities shrunk from a majority of 61.3 percent of the Jewish population in 1919 to only 13 percent in the late 1930s.[36] The Sephardi and Oriental Jewish community in Palestine had been predominantly urban since its early days under Ottoman rule, when most of these Jews lived in the four holy cities of Jerusalem, Hebron, Tiberias, and Safed—where they made up the majority of the Jewish community until the beginning of the nineteenth century.[37] During the late Ottoman period there were also very small communities of mostly Sephardi and Oriental Jews living in the Arab cities of Acre, Nablus, Gaza, Ramle, and Beit-Shean. Of these, only the ones in Acre and Beit-Shean remained by 1936.[38]

Most of the Sephardi and Oriental Jews lived in the frontier neighborhoods in the mixed cities. One of the most frequent ways these neighborhoods were referred to in Jewish public discourse during the Mandatory years was as Oriental ghettos. They were characterized by their residents' extreme poverty; high density of population; and general backwardness in terms of housing conditions, livelihood, education, and social development. An article in *Davar* in 1936 described the Oriental Jews in these neighborhoods this way: "Most of them are concentrated in their own special neighborhoods and live in poverty and destitution. The families are burdened with many children and live mostly in one room. They are unemployed, depressed and wretched. Their children are neglected and have gone astray."[39]

Statistics from the 1930s and 1940s confirm that the vast majority of Oriental Jews and many of the Sephardi Jews were living in extremely poor conditions either in mixed neighborhoods in the oldest parts of the mixed cities, such as in Tiberias and Haifa, or in newer neighborhoods that were either mixed or bordered Arab neighborhoods and quarters. Those included, for example, Manshiyya on the southern border of Tel Aviv; Jorat al-'Anab near the Jaffa Gate and the Nachlaot neighborhoods in Jerusalem, the latter located near the Arab village of Sheikh Bader. In surveys such as those conducted by the demographer and statistician Roberto Bachi and the Statistical Department of the Jewish Agency in the first half of the 1940s, the very low standard of living of the majority of Oriental Jews was disclosed in terms of income, occupations, housing conditions, and level of education.[40] The majority of the Arabs in these mixed neighborhoods or in nearby Arab neighborhoods also had poor living conditions, density of population, lack of basic infrastructure, and generally low socioeconomic status.[41] The Arab frontier neighborhoods of Jaffa included Manshiyya and Abu Kabir on the border between Jaffa and Tel Aviv, and Tel al-Rish and South Jebaliyya on the border between Jaffa and the Jewish cities of Holon and Bat-Yam. Among the residents of these poor Jaffa neighborhoods were Arab immigrants, especially from southern Syria.[42] The demographic and socioeconomic similarities between the majority of the Oriental Jews and the Arabs were discussed in the Yishuv usually both in terms of ethnic or cultural affinity and in economic or social terms. Hence, for example, poor Oriental families were often portrayed as living in an Arab environment, suffering from ignorance about the Zionist national project, and often as people with a low moral level. All these, according to this view, led to their development as a separate community within the Yishuv.[43] The socioeconomic similarities between the Oriental Jews and Arabs who lived in these neighborhoods were less emphasized in comparison to the national commonalities, or conflicts.

The patterns of immigration from Middle Eastern countries during the Mandatory period show that the majority of Jews arriving from these countries settled in the frontier neighborhoods in the mixed cities, such as Kerem Hatemanim in Tel Aviv or Nachlaot in Jerusalem. Many of the Jewish neighborhoods in the mixed cities had residents who all came from the same ethnic and geographical community. These patterns of settlement and immigration created a continuation of the traditional forms of life, in terms of communal and religious organizations or establishments, as well as family and other social ties.[44] Setting aside the issues of poverty and economic deprivation, residential patterns in these neighborhoods largely replicated those of the Jewish neighborhoods in the Arab countries and in large Arab cities throughout the Middle East. For the residents, this was a familiar and well-known Oriental space, for better or worse.

The mixture created in many of these neighborhoods of new immigrants from Arab and Muslim countries and Jews from other mixed cities—whether Bney Ha'aretz or newly arrived immigrants—attested to the nature of the internal migration patterns of Sephardi and Oriental Jews and to their tendency to settle down in mixed cities and neighborhoods. Contrary to the claim that these communities demonstrated a low degree of geographic mobility, it seems that there was a constant movement within and between the cities—mostly from Jerusalem, Tiberias, and Safed to the southern neighborhoods of Tel Aviv, but also to Haifa. Hundreds of families, as well as many hundreds of single immigrants, migrated during these years, mainly in search of work during periods of economic crisis; because of the escalation of the national conflict; or due to some other crisis, such as the great flood in Tiberias in 1934 or the economic crisis that was caused by the beginning of World War II. Among the single migrants were many young men and women, as well as adult men who migrated on their own to work in the cities, leaving their wives and families behind.[45] Sometimes children moved on their own to these cities in search of work, and they became a matter of great concern to the different welfare institutions that tried to assist and protect them or send them back to their parents. Children who moved with their families to the mixed cities often wandered the streets and were referred to by the social authorities as abandoned children.[46]

Men moved, not only internally between the mixed towns, but also externally to neighboring countries, and some abandoned their families and returned to the cities they had originally immigrated from. One example is a man who moved to Tiberias from Cairo in 1935 with his wife and four children and was unable to find a job. He then returned to Cairo and disappeared, without sending his family money as he had promised to do. In such cases of abandoned wives of Oriental families, the local welfare departments and other institutions usually suggested that the wife and children also return to their countries of origin, either to the husband or to another man in the extended family, who could take care of them. Sometimes men would go temporarily to a neighboring country to find work to support their families, and they would send money to their wives. During periods of economic crisis, Arab men also sought jobs in neighboring countries to support their families at home.[47] These patterns of temporary or permanent migration to neighboring countries indicate that Arabs and Jews interacted not only in mixed cities in Palestine, but in the Middle East as a whole.

During particularly violent periods—especially during the riots of 1921, 1929, 1936, and 1948—many Jews who lived in the Oriental ghettos fled, becoming refugees in other communities—a situation that contributed to the existing tensions not only between Jews and Arabs, but also between Oriental and Ashkenazi Jews. What were the main challenges faced by Oriental Jews and Arabs who lived in these neighborhoods? What was the relationship between these neighborhoods and the neighborhoods or cities they were on the margins of? The example of Kerem Hatemanim and its mukhtar, mentioned above, can serve as an interesting example of the ambivalent nature of mixing and unmixing in a frontier neighborhood.

Double Marginality: Kerem Hatemanim, Neve Shalom, and Manshiyya as Frontier Neighborhoods

Kerem Hatemanim and Neve Shalom were two of the Jewish neighborhoods that were established in northern Jaffa in the late nineteenth century. They preceded Ahuzat Bayit, considered to be the first neighborhood of Tel Aviv. The establishment of these northern Jewish neighborhoods was motivated by the desire of some Jews to move out of the heart of Jaffa.[48] The first such neighborhood, Neve Tzedek, was established in 1887, and Neve Shalom was established three years later. Zerah Barnett, who started building in an area southwest of Neve Tzedek, was responsible for the establishment of Neve Shalom.[49] Both Neve Tzedek and Neve Shalom were located near Manshiyya—the northern, mainly Arab, neighborhood of Jaffa that had been established at the end of the 1870s. Another neighborhood that was adjacent to Neve Shalom and Manshiyya was Harat (Sakinat) al-Tank, a poor neighborhood whose residents were mainly Arabs and Yemenite Jews.[50]

Kerem Hatemanim was the third neighborhood outside of Jaffa. It was established by Yemenite Jews who had immigrated to Jaffa in the early 1880s. It was established in 1905 near Harat al-Tank and on the northern edge of Manshiyya, on lands purchased by the Sephardi entrepreneurs Ahron Chelouche, Haim Amzaleg, and Yosef Moyal from an Arab named Karton. In various publications the quarter is referred to as the Karton Quarter or Kerem Karton.[51] The Karton Quarter was part of Jaffa, while Kerem Hatemanim, which was adjacent to the Karton Quarter, was part of Tel Aviv.[52] According to a report from 1943, the Karton Quarter—where Levi, the mukhtar, lived—was part of Manshiyya, and there were 2,000 Muslims and 7,000 Jews living in it. The total number of Manshiyya residents (including Karton and Irshid) was 28,030.[53] In practice, the residents of Karton and Kerem Hatemanim considered themselves as part of one neighborhood, regardless of the municipal divisions. Levi viewed himself as the representative of both quarters, and in his official correspondence with the Tel Aviv municipality he presents himself as the mukhtar of Kerem Hatemanin.[54]

The character of Kerem Hatemanim, which was one of the main centers of the Yemenite Jewish community in Palestine, was based on its unique cultural and political identity. In 1936 there were 18,000 Yemenite Jews in Palestine. A new wave of immigration of Jews from Yemen began in 1943, bringing over 5,000 new immigrants within a period of a few years; in 1945 the number of Yemenite Jews had increased to 29,000.[55] Their immigration led to increasing claims that the national and local institutions of the Yishuv were neglecting Yemenite immigrants. The Yemenites were unique within the Yishuv in terms of their organizations. The Yemenite Association, founded in 1923, maintained its independent character throughout the Mandatory period, which led to a perception of the Yemenite community as an autonomous entity with a historical and cultural heritage distinct from those of the other Jewish communities from the Arab and Muslim countries.[56] The high concentration of Yemenite Jews in certain neighborhoods, such as Kerem Hatemanim, added to the unique character of the community relative to the other Oriental Jewish communities. As a result, the Yemenite community acquired a reputation for insularity and separatism and for preserving its unique cultural identity. In part this was due to the Yemenite traditions regarding prayers and religious life.[57]

The borders between Manshiyya, Neve Shalom, and Kerem Hatemanim, and the way people understood them, changed in the 1920s and 1930s as a result of the national tension and the changes in the border between Tel Aviv and Jaffa. For example, Neve Shalom and Neve Tzedek were called Manshyyia al Yahud (Jewish Manshiyya) by the Arabs of Jaffa.[58] Furthermore, Kerem Hatemanim included some small Jewish neighborhoods such as Mahne Yehuda and Mahne Yisrael. The municipality of Tel Aviv, in contrast, referred to Manshiyya as Arab Neve Shalom.[59] In his analysis of the history of Neve Shalom, Or Aleksandrowicz convincingly argues that until the late 1920s, Neve Shalom was the name used in Hebrew to describe Manshiyya, even though in most accounts these two neighborhoods were considered to be separate. In the 1930s, he argues, the Jewish spatial understanding of the area changed, and a separation between an Arab neighborhood called Manshiyya (which included parts of Neve Shalom and Harat al-Tank) and the Jewish neighborhoods that surrounded it began to appear. In fact, as Aleksandrowicz and others demonstrate, in reality there was no separation between Jews and Arabs in these neighborhoods, as they were nationally and ethnically mixed.[60]

When Tel Aviv was established in 1909, it was part of Jaffa. In May 1921 Tel Aviv was granted the status of an autonomous township, which gave it more independence though administratively it was still part of Jaffa. The 1921 border between Tel Aviv and Jaffa attempted to separate Arab Jaffa from Hebrew Tel Aviv. However, in 1931, 14 percent (around 7,749 people) of the inhabitants of Jaffa were Jews. The number of Jewish residents in the frontier neighborhoods on the south border of Tel Aviv that were part of Jaffa was around 18,000 at the end of the 1930s, and the number had grown to 30,000 by 1947.[61] The residents of the Jewish neighborhoods of Jaffa that had been established in the 1920s adjacent to Tel Aviv paid municipal taxes to Jaffa, although in practice they received services and assistance in such fields as education, welfare, and health from Tel Aviv. Their demand that their neighborhoods be annexed by Tel Aviv sparked a dispute that involved the Mandatory authorities and the municipalities of Tel Aviv and Jaffa.[62]

The border between the two cities continued to be contested, even after Tel Aviv was granted full municipal independence in 1934. This border—which Deborah Bernstein calls a "zigzag line" and Aleksandrowicz calls a "paper boundary"—left several neighborhoods or parts of neighborhoods outside the jurisdiction of the Tel Aviv municipality and within Jaffa's municipal zone.[63] In fact, the border went through Neve Shalom and Kerem Hatemanim, as well as through other neighborhoods such as Florentine and Maccabi. It is clear, however, that until the late 1940s all three neighborhoods were mixed and contained Jews and Arabs living side by side, in the same street and sometimes in the same house or compound. A similar situation occurred in other mixed cities. In Haifa, for example, around 3,500 Jews and 17,000 Arabs lived in the mixed neighborhoods during the 1940s.[64]

The borders between Jaffa and Tel Aviv and between Jews and Arabs were much more complicated and much less clear before 1948 than afterward.[65] In Kerem Hatemanim, for example, Arabs owned houses and lived side by side with Jews.[66] As mentioned above, a report about Manshiyya from 1943 mentions Levi as the Jewish mukhtar of the neighborhood, because he lived in the northern part of Manshiyya, in the Karton Quarter.[67] Another interesting piece of evidence of the mixed nature of Manshiyya appears in an article published in *Davar* in May 1936 by Rivka Aharonson, who wrote about the Jewish refugees who fled Manshiyya during the Arab revolt:

The 700 people who lived in Manshiyya in Jaffa had to leave the neighborhood due to insecurity. . . . The land and house owners of the neighborhood are mostly Arabs. Its residents are mixed. The Arab, the house owner, lives together with his Jewish neighbors. . . . As one gets closer to Jaffa, the number of Jews decreases, although even in the remote edges of the neighborhood one can still meet Jewish families. Who are the Jewish inhabitants of Manshiyya? First and foremost, they are new immigrants from the Eastern countries ('edot hamizrah). They had no economic or moral guidance as they immigrated to Palestine and naturally they went to an Arab environment. It is by no coincidence that they live in Jaffa: the living conditions of that environment are closer [more familiar] to them than those of the Hebrew Yishuv, and affect them more. Many in Manshiyya are also natives of the country (yelidey haaretz), born in Jerusalem, Safed, and Tiberias. These are our "Bedouins," who emigrate from one place to the other. Some live permanently at the expense of the collective. . . . Family life is horrible. The wife has no rights at home. The husband beats her and treats her disrespectfully. On the other hand, there are women who look at the free life of the European women, are attracted to it, and [practice] it with prostitution. . . . The most urgent problem right now is the question of housing, because it is better to starve than to return to Manshiyya. It would have been better for the refugees if the neighborhood had been burned down. And it is worth mentioning that among the refugees there were hardly any Ashkenazim. Not because those do not live in mixed neighborhoods, but because they have the realization that one does not leave a place. Clearly, no Manshiyya refugees should return to their neighborhood. Others need to live in this corner on the border.[68]

Indeed, as Norma Musih argues, Aharonson's tone is condescending toward both the Jewish and the Arab inhabitants of Manshiyya. She considers them to be inferior to the rest of Tel Aviv's Jewish residents, views them as a weak social group and a burden on Tel Aviv, and completely ignores the existence of some upper-class Arabs of the neighborhood.[69] This notion of clear socioeconomic and ethnic divisions between Jews who lived in the frontier neighborhoods and those who lived in Tel Aviv, as well as the mention of prostitutes, will be discussed below.

Aharonson's description was not unique; it was part of a discourse that took place in the Yishuv especially during periods of security tensions, when thousands of Jews left the frontier neighborhoods in the mixed cities and became refugees. This phenomenon revealed social, religious, and class tensions and created points of conflict and friction between populations that had limited contacts with each other during periods of peace and quiet. The Jewish leaders in Tel Aviv, for example, described the encounter with the residents of the frontier neighborhoods as one with the unfamiliar world of the Oriental ghetto. This encounter was colored by ethnic distinctions and images, since the residents of the border neighborhoods were identified mainly as Oriental Jews. In June 1936, for example, an activist in the labor movement described her encounter with Oriental refugees in the following terms: "Now we understood just how great the differences are within the communities that everyone refers to as 'the Oriental communities.' They include groups of cultured Jews who are devoted to the people and the land, as well as groups that are closer to our neighbors—and not to the best among them—than to ourselves."[70] Similar descriptions were used during the 1948 war by members of the departments of the Tel Aviv municipality responsible for taking care of the thousands of Jewish refugees who sought asylum in the center of the city.[71] The situation in Haifa, where most of the Jewish refugees from the frontier neighborhoods were Oriental Jews, was similar.[72]

Neve Shalom, Kerem Hatemanim, and Karton are interesting cases of frontier neighborhoods, with a status of double marginality due to their municipal status vis-à-vis Tel Aviv and Jaffa and to the composition of their populations, with their large proportions of Yemenites (in the case of Kerem Hatemanim) or people from other Middle Eastern countries. As mentioned above, parts of these neighborhoods were in Jaffa, and residents paid their taxes to that city even though they received many services from Tel Aviv. With the escalation of national tension, and especially after the beginning of the Arab Revolt, they appealed to the Tel Aviv municipality, asking it to annex their neighborhoods. The reasons for annexation were the growing feelings of insecurity and the ongoing neglect of the neighborhoods by the Jaffa municipality, despite the taxes that were paid to it. However, the residents were constantly reminded by Tel Aviv municipality that they were in an inferior socioeconomic position, and their requests for annexation were not granted.[73] Various appeals from the residents of these neighborhoods, made over a period of more than ten years, reveal the double marginality that they faced.[74] The borderline neighborhoods of Tel Aviv, with around 30,000 inhabitants, developed therefore as the geographical, social, and cultural margins of the city and the Yishuv. There was little contact between the residents of these neighborhoods and those of central and northern Tel Aviv, and the leaders of the borderline neighborhoods who were active in the Jewish Neighborhoods of Jaffa Committees were excluded from positions of political influence and power in Tel Aviv. In this respect, they shared the broader fate of Jews from the Arab and Muslim countries in the institutions of the Yishuv during the Mandatory period.

Neve Shalom, which was divided between Jaffa and Tel Aviv, faced problems similar to those described by Levi in Kerem Hatemanim. Sanitary problems of different sorts had been mentioned in an appeal to the Tel Aviv government as early as March 1927.[75] During the Arab Revolt, the chair of the Committee of the Quarter of Neve Shalom, Abraham Barnett, sent several appeals to the Tel Aviv municipality, describing the effects of the violence and the national tension on the neighborhood and its residents and stating that many of them were poor and could not afford to live in any of the northern neighborhoods of Tel Aviv. Many of the shopkeepers and house owners who lived and worked on Jaffa Road—which separated the Jewish and Arab areas—could not return to their shops and houses due to their fear of the Arabs, claimed Barnett. Many of the houses were empty, and the quarter's residents were in despair. Despite the unique difficulties in the quarter, which bordered Jaffa, the Tel Aviv municipality had insisted on increasing the taxes. Barnett argued that it should reconsider its decision and take into account the harsh conditions of the neighborhood.[76]

An appeal to the Jewish Agency in August 1939 uses the same notion of Neve Shalom as a physical barrier between the Arab neighborhoods and Tel Aviv. The inhabitants of Neve Shalom stood bravely against the Arabs who tried to enter the neighborhood, according to the writer, and in this way prevented the Arabs from reaching the center of Tel Aviv. Now, after a year of relative calm, Neve Shalom needed all the help it could get to restore the neighborhood and life in it. The writer appealed to the Jewish Agency because of the urgency of the matter. Among other things, houses that had been damaged or burned down during the years of violence needed to be renovated or rebuilt, so that they could be made to meet the needs of the middle class—which would make them appeal to more people.[77] As Bernstein argues, the residents of the frontier neighborhood demanded recognition for their role as "gatekeepers" of Tel Aviv and the guardians of the frontier.[78] However, this demand never quite materialized.

The various appeals discussed above by representatives and residents of the frontier neighborhoods point to the growing animosity between Jews and Arabs and to a sense of danger and insecurity experienced by the neighborhoods' residents. The goal of the appeals is to separate from the Arabs, whether those living in the same neighborhood or those living in Jaffa. However, the frontier neighborhoods did not create a separation between Jews and Arabs, or between Tel Aviv and Jaffa. In fact, they often served as sites for various forms of interactions, crossing and mixing between Jews and Arabs, both within the neighborhoods themselves and in Jaffa or Tel Aviv. The beach, the café, and the market, among other sites, served as crossing points and sites for interactions between people of different nationalities, ethnicities, and genders. The mixing of mainly Arab men and Jewish women in cafés and brothels or on the beach was especially alarming to the municipal and social authorities in Tel Aviv, who kept reporting its dangers and the risks.[79]

Levi's work among Jews and Arabs as the mukhtar of Kerem Hatemanim was discussed above in this chapter. On the one hand, his relationships with the Arabs were sincere and honest, based on friendship, respect, and trust; on the other hand, they were affected by national tensions. As noted above, Levi supported the paramilitary struggle and the Jewish national struggle. His security-related activities and his role as a mediator between Jews and Arabs were apparent during periods of high national tension. Such was the case, for example, in the summer of 1947, when a meeting of Arab leaders from Manshiyya took place at his home after tensions on the border between Tel Aviv and Jaffa.[80] Indeed, Kerem Hatemanim was one of the main frontier neighborhoods that was targeted by Arab terrorist attacks, and, as will be discussed in chapter 5, its Jewish residents were also involved in terrorist attacks on Arabs. As Levi's work shows, the frontier neighborhood was a site of Jewish-Arab interaction not only with respect to personal conflicts and issues about religious conversion, but in other contexts as well.

One site that serves as an example of mixing and unmixing between Jews and Arabs along the border between Kerem Hatemanim and Manshiyya was Hacarmel Street and the market located there. Hacarmel Street was one of Manshiyya's main streets, which connected Manshiyya with Kerem Hatemanim.[81] Following the 1917 Russian Revolution, a group of twenty wealthy Russian Jewish families immigrated to Palestine. In 1920, with the blessing of Mayor Dizengoff, they established a fruit and vegetable market on the lots they had purchased in 1913. The Carmel market, located on the line separating Jaffa and Tel Aviv, served as a meeting space for Jewish and Arab merchants and vendors; a site for interaction in cafés; and a meeting point for prostitutes and their clients, Jews and Arabs alike.[82]

In Levi's experience, the market demonstrated the connections between the ethnic and national struggles. Tel Aviv authorities did not view with favor the trade being conducted in the market, which was based on Arab and Jewish vendors who resided mainly in the frontier neighborhoods. According to Levi, he and other Jewish merchants from Kerem Hatemanim tried to do whatever they could to increase the Jewish presence in the market and push the Arab merchants toward its Manshiyya end, but Tel Aviv authorities constantly tried to narrow their influence in the market. The Yemenites, in return, established a poultry market.[83] As a compromise, Levi suggested allocating some shops to the residents of Kerem Hatemanim in the new Betzalel market, but when that market opened there was no place in it for the merchants of Kerem Hatemanim or other traders from the frontier neighborhoods, and the market was run by Ashkenazi Jews only. "I viewed this as a non-Jewish and non-national attitude on behalf of the municipality, [as a proof] of its disregard for our loyalty and value as Jews, exactly the opposite from our attitude toward the Ashkenazim. . . . The way the municipality treated the market is evidence of the way it treated the neighborhoods," claimed Levi.[84]

The Carmel market was often mentioned in other contexts as well. The sanitary conditions in it concerned some of the people who frequented it. In a letter from November 1933, a Jewish woman who visited the market daily complained about the trash that was thrown into the street, the pieces of rotten meat, and the Arabs selling their produce in the market who had dirty hands.[85] A café near the market, between Hacarmel and Gedera Streets, is described in 1946 as a substitute for the Arab cafés in Jaffa that were mostly frequented by Oriental Jews. The café near the market was full all day long, and its location reminded its clients of the atmosphere in Jaffa, some argued.[86] Arabs sitting in cafés near the market are also mentioned as "impudently disturbing" the girls of Kerem Hatemanim as they passed through the market at night.[87] In other words, the market was seen as a symbol of Arab and Oriental culture that stood in contrast to the European values of the Hebrew city.[88]

The national border was also crossed by Jews, who visited Jaffa for various purposes.[89] The cafés and restaurants in Jaffa attracted many Jews, men and women alike, on the holy day of Yom Kippur. On the eve of Yom Kippur in 1933, for example, it was reported that many young Jews had come to the Arab cafés and restaurants in Jaffa, especially those on Jaffa Road. It was estimated that around 10,000 Jews had visited Jaffa on that day. Similarly, it is reported that on Yom Kippur in 1934 Jaffa became "Jewish."[90] Even if these reports were exaggerated, Jaffa continued to attract Jews from Tel Aviv and the frontier neighborhoods at other times as well. In March 1940, for example, it was reported that the cafés in Jaffa were full of Jews, including those who had returned to their apartments in Jaffa after leaving them during the violent years of the Arab Revolt.[91]

Prostitution led to other interactions between Jews and Arabs, which often also involved British soldiers and soldiers of different nationalities. The increase in the number of prostitutes was a source of concern for the authorities in the municipal and social services in Tel Aviv. The neighborhoods of Neve Shalom, Kerem Hatemanim, and Manshiyya; the beach front; and other main streets, like Hayarkon and Allenby, are often mentioned as areas that had many brothels, cafés, and hotels and served as meeting places between mainly Arab men and Jewish women.[92] Along Jaffa–Tel Aviv Road, on the border between the two cities, there were three brothels: two were operated by Arabs and one by Jews. Jews and Arabs formed a joint organization to shut the brothels down.[93]

Many of the Jewish dancers, prostitutes, and visitors to the cafés in Jaffa or on the border between Jaffa and Tel Aviv were of Middle East descent. They often came from poor families and sometimes moved between the two cities.[94] For example, Sarah Mizrahi, originally from Tiberias, was a dancer in the Zarifa café and cabaret in Jaffa. She and an Arab Christian dancer were murdered by a twenty-four-year-old Arab as they were working in the café on May 1947. Mizrahi had been orphaned and was working in the cabaret to support her brothers.[95] Cases of Jewish-Arab romantic relations that crossed not only the municipal borders between Jaffa and Tel Aviv but also the borders of nationality and identity were mentioned in reports of the Lehi's intelligence department from January 1948. The reports provide a list of Arab men in Tel Aviv who had converted to Judaism and who were involved in criminal activities such as selling hashish or trading in weapons. The Lehi reports also focused on Jewish women who were dating Arabs and who were reported as returning from Jaffa to Tel Aviv wearing Arab clothes. All of the people listed lived in the area around Kerem Hatemanim and Manshiyya, and all of the women were of Middle Eastern descent.[96]

The frontier neighborhoods discussed above point to the connection between the national and ethnic struggle in the context of the mixed neighborhoods in Jaffa and Tel Aviv. With most of their Jewish residents originally from Middle Eastern countries, these neighborhoods demonstrate the ambivalent and illusional nature of mixing, not only in the national sense (mixing between Arabs Jews), but also in the ethnic one (between Oriental and Ashkenazi Jews). Despite their residents' continuing desire to have them become an integral part of the "white city" of Tel Aviv, the frontier neighborhoods remained on its ethnic, national, and socioeconomic margins, and its residents were unable to truly mix.[97] However, despite their residents' attempt to separate themselves from and unmix with Arabs, both their next-door neighbors as well as those living in Jaffa, the cases discussed here show that in various spheres mixing, either forced or voluntary, continued even during periods of heightened violence.

The situation in other cities in Palestine, such as Safed, Tiberias, Jerusalem, and Haifa, was in many ways similar to what we have described above in Tel Aviv and Jaffa. As we demonstrate below, life together in the frontier neighborhoods led to interactions of different kinds among Jewish and Arab children, women, and men. Hence, the house compound and street, the neighborhood playground, the cinema, and the school were sites in which the limits of mixing and interaction were constantly challenged and checked.

Sites of Interaction in the Frontier Neighborhoods

The overcrowded housing conditions and general poverty of both the Arab and Jewish residents in the frontier neighborhoods created different types of shared living spaces and close neighborly connections. In certain areas, mostly in the historic old neighborhoods but also in some of the newer ones, Arab and Jewish families shared houses, living on separate floors. In many of these cases Arab landlords were renting to Jewish families. A living space in one of the poor areas might be no more than a stuffy basement or a former stable. Some of these shared spaces were rented out and converted mostly to shops, which created a mixture of residential and commercial spaces that was quite common in these areas. In many cases Arab and Jewish families did not share the same house or living space but lived on the same street or alley, at times literally wall to wall, or courtyard to courtyard, or on separate but nearby streets.[98]

From the memoirs of Jews and Arabs, we know that their close neighborly connections in the frontier neighborhoods, which were strong in the late Ottoman period, often continued well into the Mandatory period and resumed even after periods of violence and national tension. These memoirs depicted the physical proximity in the domestic sphere and the resulting interactions in terms of an actual blurring of ethnic or national identities, a blurring based on the combination of physical proximity and common customs and language, "so there was no difference between Jews and Arabs."[99] Thus, for example, Karl (born Khalil) Sabbagh heard from an Acre-born Palestinian he met at a refugee camp in Beirut in the 1980s about the close ties his family had developed with the "Arab-Jews" who shared the same house: "we lived upstairs; a Jewish family lived downstairs." As an example of their close relationship, he told Sabbagh about the time when his sister was born and his mother asked her Jewish neighbor if she could look after her daughter. "'Of course, she is our daughter too,'" was the neighbor's response.[100] In other instances, Arab midwives delivered Jewish babies, as in the case of Simha Tzuri's mother in Acre, or of Adel Maman's (born Toledano) mother in Tiberias.[101]

Arab and Sephardi Jewish women who breast-fed infants of women in the other group were described as creating an actual blood relation known as brothers by milk or brothers by suckling. Such instances were much more common in mixed areas during the late Ottoman period than they were during the years of the British Mandate. This could indicate a general change in the relations between Arabs and Jews living in these areas, as these stories were always told as proof of the close relations between the Jewish and Arab natives of Palestine under Ottoman rule.[102] However, these early blood ties were at times seen as the basis for a lifelong and cross-generational connection. Eli'ezer Matalon, chair of the Degel Zion Sephardi youth movement who was born in Jaffa and studied in Beirut, recalled the story of his grandmother who had breast-fed both her own son Mussa (Moshe) and a Muslim baby, Omar, the son of their neighbor in Jaffa whose mother could not nurse.[103] According to Eli'ezer Matalon, this experience served as the basis for the continuation of the good relations between the two families into the Mandatory period and even when Omar grew up to be one of the leaders of the Palestinian national struggle. It is important to remember, though, that some of these descriptions were politically motivated and intended to emphasize both the difference between the Sephardi and Oriental Jewish natives and the Ashkenazi foreigners and the connection between the former and their Arab neighbors. Such descriptions also often blamed Zionism for destroying the good relations that existed between Jews and Arabs in Palestine under Ottoman rule. Still, they are important and add to our understanding of the often intimate connections between Jews and Arabs in these mixed locales.

Neighborly interactions seemed to be stronger among the younger generation, and not only among brothers by milk. The easiness with which children sharing the same houses or streets befriended one another and felt at home at each other's houses—especially since in both homes Arabic was often spoken, similar dishes were served, and similar customs were followed (such as respecting the patriarch)—was an indication of the significance of age and physical and cultural proximity.[104] A sense of blurring of national and ethnic distinctions is given, for example, in Leila Khaled's memoirs of her early childhood days in the Wadi Salib neighborhood in Haifa in the mid-1940s. Khaled, who would become the feminine symbol of the Palestinian national struggle and armed resistance, recalled the good relations her family had had with their Jewish neighbors, and how she had met and befriended "many Jewish kids." Among them was Tamara, who was one of her best friends, "but I knew that there was no distinction between us. I was conscious of being neither Arab nor Jewish." Tamara's family lived in the Jewish neighborhood of Hadar, but as Khaled's and other memoirs reveal, daily interactions between Arabs and Jews were not limited to mixed neighborhoods, neither socially nor in terms of work and leisure, as will be discussed below. Like other memoirs of Palestinian national activists, Khaled's are not devoid of political context and meaning.[105]

Khaled's description of her childhood in Haifa before the Nakba and her connections with Jewish neighbors was similar to such descriptions by other members and leaders of the Palestine Liberation Organization (PLO). In his memoirs, Ahmad Al-Shukeiri, the first chairman of the PLO, described his encounter in the summer of 1942 with a Mr. Cohen, the Jewish owner of a restaurant in Tiberias, where Al-Shukeiri had lunch with a friend. He recalled that the restaurant owner "was serving us the food with tears in his eyes. I asked him what was wrong. He said: I am not a Zionist. I am a Jewish Arab. My family has been living in Tiberias for 400 years. Before that, they used to dwell in Damascus." He told Al-Shukeiri and his friend of the rumors that the Germans were on the verge of reaching Alexandria. He then continued: "Go and kill the Zionists. Confiscate their property. Just leave us Arab Jews alone. I beg you. We are Arabs! Arabs! We are just like you!"[106] The use of the name Cohen to refer to the Oriental Jew and the use of the term "Arab Jew" were part of the idyllic narrative that was promoted by Palestinian Arab leaders during the Mandatory period and by PLO members after 1967, and that idealized Muslim-Jewish relations under Islam and before Zionism.[107] Regardless of its political aims, Al-Shukeiri's story also tells a tale of the ongoing daily interactions and connections between Arabs and Oriental Jews in the mixed cities, throughout the Mandatory period and in spite of the national confrontation.

Jewish and Arab memoirs indicate that friendships were created in the mixed neighborhoods not only between Arab and Oriental Jewish children but also between Arab children and children of Jewish immigrant families from Europe. In her memoirs about the upper-middle-class Jerusalemite Qatamon neighborhood during the 1940s, Ghada Karmi describes the neighborly relations her sister Siham had with David and Aviva, two children in a Jewish European family living on the same street in Qatamon. Karmi cited her sister's explanation of the difference between "our Jews" and other Jews: "I don't remember any feelings of animosity towards Jewish people . . . they were friendly and we all got along quite well. We knew they were different from 'our Jews,' I mean the Arab Jews. We thought of them more as foreigners from Europe than Jews as such."[108] Like many other Palestinian Arabs during the Mandatory period, Karmi distinguished between the Zionist European Jews and the non-Zionist Oriental Jews—or, as she called them, "our Jews."

Another example is Benyamin Gayger's memoirs. Born in 1924 to one of the indigenous Ashkenazi families of Safed, Gayger remembered his friendship with the children of the neighboring Shakhrur family in the mid-1920s. Such relations and the blurring of ethnic and national identities also occurred in the older quarters in the mixed cities among Ashkenazi Jews who lived for generations among the Arabs, like Gayger's family. Gayger wrote that "most of my childhood and youth I had passed in the alleys of both the Jewish and Arab quarters."[109] Indeed, Ashkenazi Jews were also among the Buey Ha'aretz (*Abna al-Balad*).[110]

However, some childhood memories of other native-born Jews paint a different picture. In his autobiography, Judge Gad Frumkin—who was born in the old city of Jerusalem in 1887—argues that in spite of the close physical proximity and the shared lives of Jews and Arabs in the old city in the late nineteenth century, Arab and Jewish children were "worlds apart without any mental or cultural affinity," causing the interactions between the two groups of children to consist mainly of throwing of stones at each other.[111] In Ya'akov Yehoshua's memoirs of his childhood days in Jerusalem in the first decade of the twentieth century, the experiences of being worlds apart and of throwing stones applied to Sephardi boys, like him, and Arab Muslim boys. Such street fights took place in the alleys of the old city as well as in the new neighborhoods outside the gates. Like Arab boys, the Sephardi children "were experts in throwing stones."[112]

Daily interactions of the younger generation in the streets and alleys of the mixed neighborhoods, whether friendly or violent in nature, became more common in the 1930s and 1940s. The rapid growth of the population, the high proportions of young people among Arab and Jewish families of Sephardi and Oriental origins, and the high percentages of Arab and Jewish children who did not attend schools at all or did so only for a short period of time and thus roamed the streets and were sometimes involved in criminal activities—all contributed to the increase in interactions.[113]

Alarming data concerning the rates of neglected children among Sephardi and Oriental children published in the mid-1940s indicated that in Jerusalem alone there were close to 2,400 Jewish children of school age who did not attend school at all (only 300 of them were of Ashkenazi origins), in Jaffa–Tel Aviv there were around 2,000, in Haifa there were more than 1,000, and in Tiberias there were hundreds of such children. Statistics indicated that only 20 percent of the Jewish children in the cities completed eight years of elementary education, and there was a marked discrepancy in favor of Ashkenazi children (76.3 percent of those boys and 54.8 percent of those girls completed eight years) as well as differences between the Sephardi and Oriental children, in favor of the former (23.4 percent of the Sephardi boys and 30.3 percent of the girls, compared to only 17.2 percent of the Oriental boys and 13.1 percent of the Oriental girls, completed eight years).[114] According to Yossef Vashitz, the majority of Arab children were illiterate, despite a steep rise in the number of Arab children attending schools—from 25,000 in 1920 to 105,000 in 1944, with marked differences between Christians (58 percent of whom were literate in 1931) and Muslims (19 percent).[115]

Efforts to address the problem of street children in the mixed cities through creating an intentionally joint recreational environment for Arab and Jewish children were rare. An exception was a group of playgrounds funded by the philanthropist Bertha Guggenheimer and operated and supervised by the Hadassah Zionist women's organization, starting in the mid-1920s and continuing throughout the Mandatory period. The Guggenheimer-Hadassah playgrounds, which followed the model of playgrounds first established by Robert Owen in England and later in the United States, were intended to combine free play with organized games and sports supervised by trained guides; the playgrounds were either added to school playgrounds or located nearby. With the goal of addressing the problem of stray Sephardi and Oriental children—or neighborhood youths (*no'ar hashchunot*), as they were often called—the first playgrounds were established in poor mixed neighborhoods or those bordering Arab neighborhoods or villages. The first playground was established in 1925 on the border of the Jewish quarter in the old city of Jerusalem. It was soon followed by another playground in the Mahane Yehuda neighborhood in Jerusalem, which was by then densely populated by poor Oriental Jews who shared the market and other commercial activities with Arabs from nearby villages.[116] Moshe 'Adaki, a *mista'arev* of the Syrian department of the Haganah, described the joy he and the other neighborhood youths felt when the playground was opened, as they were not accustomed to joy and playfulness or to being treated "with affection and understanding," as they were treated by the guides there. Among the people 'Adaki mentioned in his memoirs was Rachel Swartz, who headed the playground. 'Adaki described how greatly the children admired her. Swartz also taught in a mixed kindergarten in the old city and lived with her family in the early 1920s in the Arab neighborhood of Musrara, near the old city.[117]

In 1934 *Doar Hayom* reported that Arab children were among the hundreds of children visiting the playgrounds daily, which by then had opened in Tel Aviv, Haifa, and Safed (and were soon to be opened in Tiberias). The report mentioned that at the Mount Zion playground in Jerusalem, almost half were "Arab and Armenian children."[118] Indeed, having Arab and Jewish children play together and share educational and recreational activities on a daily basis, in the belief that such ties would lead to better connections between Arabs and Jews in general, was part of the ideology of the playgrounds' founders.[119]

However, not everyone was happy with the national mixture in these playgrounds. Some parents protested against the mixed playgrounds, and in the early 1930s, some attempts were made to create separate spaces for Jewish and Arab children.[120] Such attempts were rejected by Henrietta Szold, a Zionist activist and the founder of Hadassah, who was also a cofounder of Ichud and thus an advocate of Jewish-Arab rapprochement. She declared that the playgrounds were politically important and made a significant contribution to promoting understanding and tolerance between the two national communities.[121] However, protests against the playgrounds continued. For example, in 1940, the Committee of the Jewish Community (*va'ad hakehila*) in Safed voted against allowing Arab children to use the playgrounds. The decision was explained by their deep concern regarding the dangers posed to "our girls" by the "depraved" Arab children, and the fear of immoral and sexual misconduct.[122]

Like other sites in the mixed Jewish-Arab neighborhoods during the Mandatory years, the Guggenheimer-Hadassah playgrounds were places of interaction and mixing of Jewish and Arab children that were not necessarily harmonious and peaceful, as the sites' idealistic creators originally envisioned. Nor were the sites disconnected from or unaffected by the realities of the time and the intensified national tension, as can be seen from the memoirs of Sami Hadawi. Born in 1904, Hadawi was a leading expert on land issues in Palestine who grew up in a Christian compound outside the Damascus Gate in Jerusalem. In his memoirs he describes the "fraternity" existing between Muslim, Christian, and Jewish boys, who came from the nearby wealthy Musrara neighborhood to play in an improvised playground, as reflecting the "harmony and tolerance enjoyed between the members of the different communities in Jerusalem at the time." However, he also describes a quarrel between a Muslim boy and a Jewish one that "foretold what the future had in store for the inhabitants." The Jewish boy "blurted out in a fit of anger, 'You wait. Who do you think you are? This country belongs to us, and you Arabs must get out. You belong to the desert. Palestine is the homeland of the Jews, and we intend to have it.' None of us who heard this outburst understood or paid any attention as to its meaning. The incident came back to my mind in 1920 when the first riots broke out between Arabs and Jews following knowledge of the Balfour Declaration."[123]

The threatening aspects of unorganized, restless Oriental youth roaming the streets and mixing with Arabs in cafés, the market, and elsewhere, as well as of distressed youth who were greatly affected by the escalation of violence and the grave economic consequences of the Arab Revolt, led to increased activity by youth movements in the Oriental ghettos. The youth movement that targeted Oriental youth in particular was Degel Zion, which—as noted above—was established in 1938. Degel Zion committed itself to "organizing abandoned youth in the suburbs of the city, left without organization or education, in order to imbue them with national awareness and involve them in the project of national construction."[124] One of the goals of Degel Zion was to improve the condition of Oriental youth through finding jobs for them and their families. In this capacity, Degel Zion competed against another youth movement, Hano'ar Ha'oved, which was affiliated with the Histadrut. Hano'ar Ha'oved provided vocational courses for youths in the peripheral neighborhoods, particularly to prepare them for jobs in metalworking, the diamond industry, and glass factories. However, the involvement of Hano'ar Ha'oved in the frontier neighborhoods of the mixed cities was negligible. The competition among different youth movements—including Beitar, which was affiliated with the revisionist movement—was partly because many members of youth movements later became involved in one of the underground paramilitary organizations. For example, many members of Degel Zion joined the Irgun.[125] Like the youth movements, Arab and Jewish boy scouts operated as two distinct movements, after failed attempts were made to bring them together. Muslim and Christian scouts were unified under the auspices of the British Mandatory administration, but the Jewish scouts had no official status or funding.[126]

The Communist youth movement also became active in the border neighborhoods in particular. This movement targeted mainly immigrants from Syria and Yemen and competed against Degel Zion, which perceived the Communists as a clear threat to its national goals and to its attempt to educate the Sephardi and Oriental youth about Zionism and the national project.[127] One of the famous activists in the communist youth movement, who later became a prominent figure in the Palestinian Communist Party (PCP), was Simha Tzabari. Born in 1919 to a Yemenite family in Kerem Hatemanim, Tzabari lost her mother when she was two, and she and her three older sisters were raised by their father under great economic difficulties. She was first active in the scouts, and she was recruited to the Communist youth movement at the age of fourteen. Tzabari joined the PCP, where she was one of only two Yemenite activists. In 1934 she became the partner of Radwan al-Hilu, a Christian Arab who was one of the three main leaders of the PCP. In 1936, Tzabari, who supported the Arab Revolt, was active in violent operations against British targets.[128] Jews from Arab countries, such as Tzabari, enjoyed a special position in the PCP and were perceived by its leaders as potential mediators between Jews and Arabs and as people who could contribute to the Arabization of the party. Sephardi and Yemenite workers were hence targeted by the party and were viewed as a possible bridge not only between Jews and Arabs but also between Oriental Jewish and Ashkenazi workers. Indeed, in 1934, when al-Hilu became the party's secretary, he invited two local Jews, Meir Slonim and Simha Tzabari, to join him as the party's leaders. That was a significant step toward promoting Arab party members. The fact that Tzabari and Slonim were local, not European immigrant Jews, also helped the party resolve the tension between the local version of Communism and the view that European Jewish activists were part of the colonialist process. The operation of the PCP and its youth movement in the border neighborhoods, and its work among local Oriental Jews, can be better understood in this context.[129]

Although the Jewish and Arab school systems in Mandatory Palestine were mostly separate and were seen by both communities as a vital tool of national indoctrination of the younger generation, some mixed and joint educational frameworks existed in the mixed cities. As noted by the Peel Commission's report of 1937, mixed schools were not part of the formal Jewish educational system of the National Council or of the Arab educational system, most of which was part of the British system.[130] Indeed, some missionary schools, which were ran mainly by Anglican missionaries, served as meeting places of Sephardi and Oriental Jews from low socioeconomic backgrounds and Arabs in the mixed cities. These schools, such as the Jerusalem Girls' College (which in 1919–20 was reported to have 206 Christian, 22 Jewish, and 12 Muslim students), the St. George's Boys' School in Jerusalem, and the English High Schools at Jaffa and Haifa, attracted some the underprivileged students because they provided free education.[131] As Liora Halperin shows, the number of Jewish students in these schools, where the main language of study was English, was tiny in comparison to other schools, both the Zionist ones and the foreign schools that operated in Palestine.[132] However, as she argues, these schools became a subject of great concern for Zionist educators, advocates of the use of Hebrew, and municipal institutions. The Yishuv's anxieties about these schools had to do with their religious aspects, but even more to do with the opportunities that studying in English provided the students. These anxieties stood, as Halperin explains, at "the interface between an increasingly monolingual Hebrew Yishuv and a world that demanded—for some and in certain circumstances—skills, in this case skills particularly associated with women's employment, which could not be provided by a fully nationalist and in the main monolingual educational system."[133]

The Jewish children who attended these schools, many of whom were of

Oriental background, were described as "rootless Levantines, people who deny the original cultural foundation, who won't find their place in our revitalized country, who will be foreigners in our world and foreigners in their own world."[134] In Haifa, for example, pulling the Sephardi students out of missionary schools was described as part of the cultural work of the Council of the Sephardi Community in Haifa.[135] In Tel Aviv and Tiberias, cases of Oriental families who were considering sending their children to missionary schools due to their poor socioeconomic condition were recorded and created much alarm as well.[136] Here, too, Oriental youth were viewed as a potential risk and element of instability within the Yishuv, as "rootless Levantines" who create much concern on the part of representatives of the Yishuv's educational, municipal, and other political institutions. In contrast, some missionary schools, such as the French Collège des Frères in Jaffa attracted Sephardi Jewish students from higher economic status.[137] This was also the case with the Tabeetha Missionary high school in Jaffa, which educated middle-class women.[138]

There were, of course, other schools in which Oriental and Sephardi Jews interacted closely with Arabs, but they targeted a different social group than did the missionary schools. The other schools included the Alliance Israélite Universelle schools in Jerusalem, Haifa, Tiberias, and Safed, where children of the Sephardi and Arab elites studied; the German Lemel school in Jerusalem, in which David Yellin and Yosef Meyuchas, among others, taught; and prominent Arab private schools such as the famous Al-Dusturiyya School established by Khalil al-Sakakini in 1909 in Jerusalem.[139] Some Arab children also studied in Jewish schools, such as in the Hebrew Gymnasium in Tel Aviv; the children included as the sons of Muhamad Siksik of the Nashashibi family, who, according to Chelouche, "started speaking Hebrew just like you and me, with no accent at all."[140]

Jews and Arabs interacted in the cities and neighborhoods in other contexts as well. For example, in Tiberias, the hot baths attracted visitors from Palestine and the neighboring countries and turned the city into a local and regional tourist attraction. Buses ran on a regular basis from Tiberias to al-Hama, Syria, bringing Jews and Arabs into and out of the city.[141] Sephardi Jews also bathed in Al-Hama, as Abraham Khalfon describes in his memoirs.[142] The flood of tourists resulted in a large number of cafés and clubs in the city, frequented by Jews and Arabs alike, where alcoholic beverages were sold.[143] There were some complaints from residents of the city about the operations of cafés on the Jewish Sabbath, in particular about a band playing during the Sabbath. Interestingly, some of the owners of these cafés were Jews of the prominent Toledano family in Tiberias.[144]

Public baths (*hamams*) were a meeting place for Jews and Arabs in Jerusalem, as well as in Acre, Nablus, and other places. In Jerusalem, the hamam was described as a place where friendships were created, business deals were made, and Jewish and Arab women met.[145] Public spaces such as parks, beaches, and municipal gardens were also meeting places of Jews and Arabs in Haifa, Tiberias, Jerusalem, and Jaffa. The municipal garden of Tiberias served as a meeting place for young Jews and Arabs, as well as for mothers who were picnicking with their children.[146] The beaches in Haifa and Jaffa served as a site of recreation, leisure, and meeting. For example, the Khayat Beach in Haifa attracted Jews, Arabs, and British.[147]

Jews and Arabs met in the movie theatres as well. Cinema 'Eden in Tel Aviv, located near the border with Jaffa, attracted Arabs as well as Jews. "On Sundays the big Jaffa sailors came to the cinema, with their smelly dirty feet. They often shouted in the cinema in response to the movie played. We stopped visiting the cinema on Sundays," recalls Yivneel Matalon, writing about his early childhood in Tel Aviv.[148] In Ramat-Gan, the Rama cinema screened "movies for Arab speakers," which attracted many Jewish boys and girls from Tel Aviv. According to a report, "the movies are primitive, and there are unwelcomed meetings that are taking place in the cinema, as well as in the adjacent café. These movies should be stopped."[149] In Safed, Jews and Arabs watched silent movies together in a theatre that was owned by Arabs. It was first located on the rooftop of the house of the wealthy Khouri family, and then, in 1944–45, a cinema was built on the border between the Jewish and Arab quarters. The new cinema not only served as a meeting place for Jews and Arabs, but it was also owned jointly by Idel Meiberg, a Jew, and Mustafa Najib, an Arab. In 1946, as part of the Arab boycott of Jewish products, Arabs stopped frequenting the cinema.[150]

Mixing and Unmixing, Interaction and Conflict

As this chapter has demonstrated, the Oriental ghettos and the mixed cities, served as fertile places for Jewish and Arab interactions of different kinds. The close proximity of the two groups, often living on the same street or in the same compound, and the close and intimate relationships developed between families and neighbors, often enabled the crossing of the national divide. Jews of Oriental descent and Arabs met in markets, playgrounds, cafés, cinemas, schools, and public baths, among other places, as well as in different youth movements. The borders between the Jewish and Arab parts of a neighborhood or a city were often crossed by men and women, both Jews and Arabs, for different purposes, as we have seen in the example of Kerem Hatemanim. Encounters between the groups were full of ambivalences and contradictions, as this chapter has demonstrated, and in many ways reflected the complex and challenging realities of the Mandatory years.

However, as we have argued in this chapter, many of the Jews and Arabs who lived in these particular neighborhoods belonged to the same socioeconomic group—a point not often discussed in the literature. As we demonstrated in the cases of Kerem Hatemanim and Manshiyya, the sense of marginality was not only geographical (vis-à-vis the city of Tel Aviv, in this case) but also socioeconomic. Oriental Jews who lived side by side with Arabs in these neighborhoods shared certain realities and challenges, based on their similar socioeconomic status in their respective national groups. However, these common realities led to activities of a very different nature, which we will show in chapter 5.

FIVE

≡≡≡

Crossing the Lines

The Security Border between Jews and Arabs

≡≡≡

The outbreak of the Arab Revolt in April 1936 presented the Sephardi and the Oriental Jewish leaders with new challenges. As we have seen in previous chapters, their leadership sought to formulate their position on the Arab Question while addressing the subject of their political status in the national institutions of the Yishuv. This process took place at the same time as the increasingly important Sephardi leadership cadre in Tel Aviv sought to challenge the traditional Sephardi leaders based in Jerusalem. However, the most significant social and political transformation in the late 1930s in the Sephardi and Oriental communities was the rise of a younger generation, whose members played an integral part in the security operations of the Yishuv during the decade before the establishment of the State of Israel.

In her book on the attitude of Labor Zionism toward the use of force, the historian Anita Shapira describes the Arab Revolt as a period that marked the transition from a defensive ethos to an offensive one in the Yishuv.[1] As natives of the land, the Sephardi and Oriental Jews participated in security activities side by side with the generation that was sometimes called the generation in the land (*dor ba'aretz*) or the 1948 generation. Those activities intensified in response to the Arab Revolt, World War II, the struggle against British rule, and finally the 1948 war.

The combination of rising nationalist sentiments and military and anticolonial activism was not unique to Palestine but could be found among the younger generation of Jews, Muslims, and Christians who grew up in the 1930s and 1940s across the Middle East and joined the anticolonial struggle. However, the involvement of young Sephardi and Oriental Jews in security-related activities in Palestine had some unique dimensions that were the product not only of the nature of the national conflict and the local anticolonial struggle, but also of the economic, social, and physical situation of the Oriental and Sephardi population in the country and of questions related to the shaping of their cultural and national identity. As we will discuss in this chapter, integration into the security establishment became an additional way in which Oriental Jews attempted to define their national and Zionist identity and strengthen their social and political status in the Yishuv.

Like other areas of activity, the security sphere highlighted the self-perception of Oriental Jews as cultural and political mediators between Jews and Arabs. However, the involvement of Oriental and Sephardi Jews in the security sphere complicates the question of their role as mediators and their hybrid Arab-Jewish identity. In contrast to previous chapters of the book, where we discussed this hybrid identity in social, cultural, and political terms, in chapter 4 and this chapter we discuss it in terms of daily interactions and as the consequence of living side by side with Arabs in the frontier neighborhoods. Thus, as we suggest in this chapter, the involvement of members of the young Oriental Jewish generation who grew up in these neighborhoods in the security establishment of the Yishuv enabled them to maintain a relationship with Arabs whose importance went beyond issues of politics or defense. The security operations of various organizations—particularly in the field of military intelligence and as Mista'arvim, but also terrorist operations—highlighted the existence of the hybrid Jewish-Arab identity and of contacts between Jews and Arabs during the Mandatory period, including not only violent interactions but also instances of cooperation and coexistence. Their background in the frontier and border neighborhoods in the mixed cities left its mark on the younger generation of Sephardi and Oriental Jews, and while crossing physical and identity boundaries in their security missions, they simultaneously mediated between Arab and Jewish identities and between Jewish immigrants and the native population, Jewish and Arab alike.

"Twin Cities, Not Mixed Cities"

On April 15, 1936, armed members of the Izz a-Din al-Qassam group stopped vehicles on the road between Tulkarem and Nablus. The armed men stole money from the travelers, claiming that it was needed to finance the group's operations. After they realized that the passengers in one of the cars were Jews, they shot them. Seventy-year-old Yisrael Avraham Chazan was killed on the spot, while Zvi Danenberg died from his injuries a few days later. On Friday, April 17,

Chazan was buried in Tel Aviv. He was a native of Salonika who had worked as a poultry merchant. After the funeral, clashes erupted between the mourners and the British police; dozens of Jews were injured and arrested.[2]

The situation in Tel Aviv remained tense on the following day, as Jewish youths attacked Arabs working in the city as peddlers and shoe shiners. Two Arabs were murdered in Kfar Saba by members of the Irgun paramilitary group.[3] The series of reprisals and counterreprisals along the border between Jaffa and Tel Aviv reached a peak on Sunday, April 19, when seven Jews were murdered by Arab rioters, and two Arabs were shot dead by the British police. Hundreds of Jewish clerks, merchants, and workers who came to their places of business in Jaffa were attacked by Arabs armed with stones and knives. As in similar instances in the past, alongside the murderous attacks (which were blamed on Arab workers who came originally from Houran in southwestern Syria), many Jews were rescued after they took refuge in government buildings such as police stations, joint Jewish-Arab businesses, and the private homes of Arab residents of Jaffa. The riots and the murders of both Arabs and Jews along the border between Jaffa and Tel Aviv continued the next day. In the frontier and border neighborhoods, particularly in Kerem Hatemanim and Manashiyya, violent clashes erupted between Jewish and Arab youths. Dozens of Jewish homes, workshops, and warehouses were set on fire.[4]

At a mass funeral held in Tel Aviv on April 20 for the Jewish victims of the clashes, the crowd of mourners demanded revenge.[5] Their demands contrasted sharply with the moderate eulogy given by the Sephardi chief rabbi of Tel Aviv, Ben-Zion Meir Hai Uziel, who urged the Jewish population to refrain from acts of murder and violence. This tension between calls for revenge and calls for moderation characterized public debate within the Jewish population during the following three years. After the outbreak of riots along the border between Jaffa and Tel Aviv, thousands of Jewish residents left their homes in Jaffa and in the border neighborhoods and sought refuge in central Tel Aviv.[6] Similar behavior was seen in other mixed cities at this time, and a similar pattern had been seen during the riots of 1921 and 1929. The phenomenon of Jews' abandoning their homes, combined with physical attacks, damage to property, riots in other mixed cities, and the declaration of a general strike by the Arab Higher Committee marked the beginning of the Arab Revolt and were key features of its three-year course.

On April 30, 1936, the Levant Fair (Yerid Hamizrah) opened. This was the second international fair held at the Exhibition Gardens in Tel Aviv. The emblem of a flying camel and the dozens of international companies that participated gave the fair the character of a regional economic event, with cultural and social features that went far beyond the confines of the Yishuv and Palestine. The Levent Fair sought to portray a shared economic domain in the Levant, challenging approaches opposed to this internationalist spirit, including the emphasis among Jews on buying Jewish products, on the one hand, and the Arab boycott of Jewish products, on the other hand.[7] At the same time, the fair, which operated until May 1936, despite the intensification of violence between Jews and Arabs, still underscored the fragile nature of the concept of regional economic cooperation in general, and between Jews and Arabs in particular. As the Arab Revolt continued and intensified, it had extensive economic ramifications. The first victims, and those who suffered most, were the residents of the mixed neighborhoods and the border areas between Jaffa and Tel Aviv; between Hadar Hacarmel and the lower city in Haifa; and between Jewish and Arab neighborhoods in Tiberias, Jerusalem, Safed, and Beit Shean.

Historians have discussed at length the reasons for the outbreak of the Arab Revolt and analyzed its course and impact on the Yishuv. Considerable attention has also given to the political debate between the left and right wings within the Yishuv about the desired balance between restraint and reaction and about whether to accept the 1937 partition plan.[8] One of the aspects of the Arab Revolt that has been the subject of extensive discussion is the importance of this period as a turning point in the development of the Yishuv, the Palestinian national movement, and the Jewish-Arab conflict. Equally, however, it has been argued that the most significant turning point in terms of the pattern of segregation between Jews and Arabs actually came several years earlier, during the 1929 riots.[9] The scholars who made this argument focused not only on economic segregation, but more particularly on physical segregation, in the form of the flight of Jews from Jaffa and neighborhoods in other mixed cities.[10]

The claim that segregation increased during the 1929 riots is also based on the perception that in this period there was a loss of trust between Jews and Arabs and a sense that the security situation in the mixed cities was deteriorating. Historian Hillel Cohen addressed this aspect in his latest book, in which he depicts the 1929 riots as a key moment in the process of separation between the two peoples.[11] Cohen argues that the violent clashes illustrate a process whereby the Palestinian Arabs came to associate the native Jews of the country, and specifically members of the Sephardi and Oriental communities, with the Zionist movement. He uses detailed testimonies to support this argument, particularly the eulogy delivered by her brother for Mazal Cohen, who was murdered in Safed during the riots. The brother's comments highlight the profound crisis in neighborly relations and coexistence in the mixed cities that resulted from the murders:

> For half a century I have spoken their [Arabs'] language, studied their literature, and learned their ways and customs. I have observed their habits and manners, but I have not known them. For half a century I have made friends with them; many of them have been visitors to my home. On Sabbaths and festivals we have exchanged visits of camaraderie and friendship. Daily encounters, bows and greetings, and discourse. But I have not known them. . . . For half a century I have lived among you [Arabs], enjoyed your company, and strived to know your inner feelings and thoughts—but I have not known you.[12]

Menachem Raphael Cohen, Mazal's brother, was thoroughly familiar with Muslim culture and engaged in the study of Islam. He was born in Safed in 1890, studied at the Alliance Israélite Universelle school, and taught Hebrew and Arabic in the Jewish settlements in Upper Galilee. He later worked as a clerk in the Anglo-Palestine Bank, while serving as treasurer of the Hebrew Language Committee and the Israeli Oriental Society. Cohen published numerous articles about Islam in the Hebrew press, including the newspapers *Davar*, *Hapo'el Hatza'ir*, and *Hed Hamizrah*. His book *Mecca and Medina*, published in 1923, was based on his own studies and his translations of Islamic literature into Hebrew. In the 1960s he published an additional volume of translations, including a collection of his writings on Islam and Arabic language, literature, and poetry.[13]

Cohen's eulogy near his sister's grave thus drew on his knowledge as a scholar of Islam and Arab culture, yielding the following sad testimony of a native of Palestine:

> I always argued that you [Arabs] considered the native Jews of the land as your brothers, loved and respected them, since you and they shared the same language and words, and that your complaints were directed solely at those who have just now arrived to seize shovel and plow. . . . You rejected and found fault with them, saying that these are newly arrived foreigners who will not become part of our community or know our language. We desire only you, the natives of the land. Only of you are we not jealous, for we and you share the same drive to cling to the land. Yet how did you, the murderers of Safed, now turn like wild animals solely on the natives of the city, who have made it their home for generations . . . killing people whose mother tongue is the same as yours, and whose lifestyle is your lifestyle, so that only religion separated you—people with whom you had forged the alliance of 'bread and salt.'"[14]

Although the riots of August 1929 seriously damaged the fabric of Jewish-Arab relations and brought an increasing tendency toward segregation, mistrust, and insecurity in the following years, Jews and Arabs still lived together and maintained relations of both neighborliness and confrontation in the mixed cities. This was apparent from the scale of the damage sustained by the civilian population in the mixed cities during the Arab Revolt and in the 1948 war and the commemorations of the Jewish civilians who were killed in the Arab Revolt and the 1948 war.

During the Arab Revolt, Arab terrorists made no distinction between Zionist and non-Zionist Jews, between the old and the new Yishuv, or between Sephardim and Ashkenazim. Victims of violent clashes included, for example, Avinoam Yellin, a scholar the Orient and an official in the Mandatory government's Education Department, who was the son of David Yellin. At the beginning of the Arab Revolt, Avinoam Yellin had eulogized Levy Billig, a scholar of Islam and a professor at the Hebrew University, who was murdered in the Talpiyot neighborhood of Jerusalem. Ya'acov Chelouche's son Gavriel was murdered in 1938 after shots were fired at him from an ambush while he was driving his car in the city of Ramle. Zaki Alhadiff, the mayor of Tiberias, who had headed a joint Arab-Jewish city council for fifteen years and whose city was a model of Jewish-Arab cooperation on the municipal level, was assassinated on one of the city's main streets in October 1938. This assassination—together with that of his Arab deputy, Ibrahim al-Yusuf, a year earlier—underscored the damage caused by the violence to attempts to build peaceful bridges between Jews and Arabs. Tiberias also saw one of the bloodiest incidents of the Arab Revolt, when nineteen Jewish residents of the Kiryat Shmuel neighborhood were murdered on October 2, 1938.

One of the outcomes of such acts of violence was a demand for separation between Jews and Arabs in the mixed cities. This demand was made in April 1936 in an article by Itamar Ben-Avi. Under the title "Twin Cities, Not Mixed Cities," Ben-Avi called for the establishment of buffer zones and other types of physical segregation between Jewish and Arab neighborhoods. However, the editors of *Doar Hayom* were quick to disassociate themselves from this call, noting that "the editors' opinion is that in bad times, as in good times, a way must be found for the two peoples who live in this country to work together. It would be a grave mistake to exacerbate the existing gulf between them due to the short-sighted politics of our leaders, no less than the short-sighted character of the Arab leaders."[15] Alongside the Arab acts of terror that led to calls of segregation, there was also Jewish terrorism during the Arab Revolt. Like the

Arab terrorists, the Jewish terrorists made no distinction between combatants and civilians, and they made none between supporters and opponents of the Mufti. Neither were they always able to distinguish between Oriental Jews and Palestinian Arabs.

Crossing the Moral and National Borders of Identity

On November 14, 1937, the Irgun launched a series of terrorist operations against the Arab population. The actions reflected the organization's decision to reject the policy of restraint announced by the national institutions of the Yishuv. The Irgun's decision to disobey the instructions of the national institutions, together with the ideological debate within the Yishuv at the time about the recommendations of the Peel Commission, reflected the increasingly strong ties between the Irgun and the Revisionist Movement. The Irgun's operations, one of whose aims was to challenge the authority of the Labor Zionist leaders, reached a peak in July 1938, following the execution of Shlomo Ben-Yosef by the British authorities.

The Irgun's terrorist activities in the summer of 1938 included shootings of civilian targets; throwing grenades at civilians; and placing bombs in public meeting places—including cafés, bus stops, and markets—in the centers of the Arab areas in Jaffa, Jerusalem, and Haifa. These actions sparked a fierce public debate about moral and political issues. This debate touched not only on the political identity of the perpetrators, but also on their ethnic identity. In the *History of the Haganah*, which represents the views of Israeli historiography in the 1950s and 1960s, Yehuda Slutsky explains that those chosen to commit terrorist actions among the Arabs were "in most cases young men who knew Arabic from the Oriental Jewish communities, who would dress themselves in the style of Arab peasants, enter Arab streets while walking innocently, place the bomb, and then attempt to return to the Jewish area." Faithful to the perspective of the Labor Zionist movement, Slutsky goes on to explain that most of these youths "were very young, and had been prepared for their dangerous mission by protracted education in Beitar and by the romanticism of the underground."[16] Although this description of the Irgun's terrorist operations is colored by political criticism, it provides an accurate portrayal of these actions. The Irgun indeed preferred to use youths of Oriental origin who spoke fluent Arabic and could mingle safely among the Arab population.

One of the Irgun's terrorist activists was Ya'acov Sika Aharoni. On July 6, 1938, Aharoni placed a bomb in the Arab vegetable market in downtown Haifa.[17] The attack, in which Aharoni's brother was also involved, killed twenty-five Arabs, injured dozens more, and sparked a violent Arab response that culminated in the lynching of four Jews on a street in Haifa. On July 25, Aharoni placed a bomb in a market frequented by Arabs on Hamelachim Street (now known as Independence Road) in downtown Haifa, killing forty-five Arabs and sparking a series of bloody reprisals in the city.[18] The attacks and the general deterioration in the security situation in Haifa led to the evacuation of Jewish residents from the neighborhood of Ard al-Yahud, the first Jewish neighborhood built outside the walls of the old city of Haifa, which over the years had developed into a mixed Jewish-Arab area.[19]

Aharoni, "the dark-faced, black-haired youth known as 'the King of the Blacks,'" carried out his attacks under various disguises, including that of a shoe shiner.[20] He operated under the authority of the Irgun commander in Haifa, Binyamin Zironi. One of ten children, Aharoni was born in the Meah She'arim neighborhood of Jerusalem. His father had immigrated from Isfahan, in Persia, and his mother was a native of Jerusalem. Aharoni grew up in the Nachalat Achim neighborhood of Jerusalem (now known as Nachlaot) and attended the religious school Doresh Zion. He left school at the age of sixteen and began to work, while at the same time attempting to complete his high-school education in evening school. He joined the Beitar youth movement and a year later was recruited to the Irgun.[21] Following the establishment of the State of Israel, he became a teacher, high school principal, poet, and writer.

Aharoni would walk the streets of downtown Haifa and visit the local cafés and mosques before placing his bombs. He disguised himself as a rural Arab with keffiyeh and 'aqal, and carried an Arabic newspaper.[22] Aharoni was also active in the next wave of terrorist attacks launched by the Irgun. On February 27, 1939, he took part in placing bombs at the eastern railroad station and the Arab market in Haifa; twenty-seven Arabs were killed in the attacks. Aharoni stated that his fluent command of Arabic, his knowledge of Arab social customs, and his external appearance all made him ideal for such missions. In 1941 he was one of a group of Irgun members, under the command of David Raziel, who traveled to Iraq to conduct sabotage operations on behalf of the British army.

Aharoni belonged to the Mahatz unit of the Irgun, whose members were Arabic-speaking Jews of Oriental and Yemenite descent. The unit was involved in collecting intelligence and in undertaking sabotage and terrorist operations against Palestinian Arab and British targets.[23] Most of the members of the unit were born or raised in the border neighborhoods of the mixed cities, particularly Jerusalem. Aharoni was not the only member of the unit who grew up in the dense network of dozens of small neighborhoods adjacent to the Mahane Yehuda Market, which at the time was home to the largest concentration of Oriental Jews in Jerusalem. These neighborhoods were founded when Jews first moved outside the walls of the Old City in the late nineteenth century. They expanded in the 1920s and 1930s as Jews arrived from the countries of the Middle East, resulting in a population of some 17,000 Jews who lived in conditions of severe poverty and overcrowding.[24] Like the frontier neighborhoods of Jaffa and Tel Aviv, these neighborhoods were among the main bases for the recruitment of Oriental, Sephardi, and Yemenite Jews to perform in intelligence and sabotage work in the paramilitary organizations of the Yishuv, as will be discussed in greater detail below.

One of the Irgun members active in terrorist operations against the Arab population in Jaffa was Aharon Cohen, a Jew of Yemenite descent who was a member of Beitar. Cohen's family came from Aden to south Tel Aviv in the early 1930s, after spending several years in Egypt. On August 26, 1938, the eighteen-year-old Cohen disguised himself as an Arab porter and detonated a forty-kilogram bomb in the vegetable market close to the Clock Tower in Jaffa. Before carrying out the attack Cohen stayed at an apartment in Florentine neighborhood in south Tel Aviv. The team that assisted him in the attack included Eliyahu Beit Tzuri, who undertook reconnaissance visits to Jaffa while disguised as an Arab; Binyamin Zironi, who assembled the bomb; and Aryeh Yitzchaki, who commanded operations of this type in Jaffa. The explosion killed twenty-four Arabs and injured dozens more.[25] As was the case with other terrorist attacks, the Arab public in Jaffa reacted violently. Several Arab demonstrators were killed by British forces. Such attacks also exacerbated Arabs' suspicion of Jews of Oriental appearance who came to the Arab markets for commercial reasons. The attacks therefore were one of the factors that hindered commercial ties between Jews and Arabs during the Arab Revolt and heightened the trend toward segregation.

Cohen frequently crossed the border between Tel Aviv and Jaffa while disguised as an Arab, dressed in loose pants (*sharwal*) and a striped shirt, a look that was perceived as typical of the Arab population of Jaffa.[26] As he crossed the Abu Kabir neighborhood and Salameh Street, his Arabic appearance raised suspicions among Jews and Arabs alike. Cohen's journeys into Jaffa as an Arab and his returns to Tel Aviv demonstrate the ways young Oriental Jews operated in the Irgun as part of its activities in the mixed cities. These young men and women, who grew up along the border between two cultures and two communities, were hence recruited to cross this border to commit acts of murder and sabotage.

In Jerusalem, Unit 81 of the Irgun, under the command of Ya'acov Eliav, was responsible for the placement of bombs. The unit's members included Ya'acov Raz (Ras), born in 1919 in Afghanistan, who arrived in Jerusalem with his family at the age of ten. Raz attended the Bney Zion Talmud Torah and began to study at the Alliance Israélite Universelle school, but he dropped out. He subsequently worked as a milkman and in 1937 joined the Irgun. Many other youths chosen for Irgun's terrorist missions had also dropped out of school to help support their families. On July 26, 1938, Raz planted a bomb in the Old City of Jerusalem while disguised as an Arab porter. When he later arrived at the Damascus Gate, he was stabbed and seriously wounded by Arab porters who recognized him. Raz died in the hospital from his injuries a few days later. He was immortalized by Uri Zvi Greenberg in his poem "The Legend of Ya'acov Raz," which was published in 1939.[27]

Another figure who inspired the young members of the Irgun, and who the organization's own history describes as its first prisoner and a model of Hebrew heroism and female sacrifice for the sake of the national ideal, was Rachel Habshush.[28] Born to a Yemenite father and Moroccan mother, Habshush lived in the Rouhama neighborhood of Jerusalem, close to Mahane Yehuda. On May 29, 1939, she participated in an Irgun operation during which a bomb was planted at the Rex Cinema in Jerusalem. On June 9, 1939, Habshush set out on another mission for the Irgun wearing traditional Arab women's dress. She arrived at the yard outside the entrance to the main prison in the Jerusalem Russian Compound with a bomb concealed in a basket of food. Her task was to place the device among the family members of Arab prisoners who gathered at the prison gates. The Arab dialect she spoke, the heavy weight of the basket, and the manner in which the device was concealed all aroused the suspicion of a young Arab man and led to her arrest.[29]

Habshush was tried before a British military court. The Hebrew and Arabic press reported extensively on the proceedings, partly because it provided an opportunity to expose the individuals behind the Irgun's terrorist campaign.[30] Newspaper reports described Habshush, who had adopted the family name Ohevet 'Ami (lover of my people) as "a short young woman with black hair in large curls and a round face that did not easily betray her emotions."[31] This description highlights the qualities that led Habshush to be chosen for the mission, but it also touches on a question that became the focus of the court hearing: her true age. The discussion in court revealed racist assumptions concerning biological distinctions between Europeans and Orientals. In an effort to save Habshush from a possible death sentence, her attorney argued that she was seventeen, and not nineteen—as the prosecution argued. He based this position on a claim that X-rays were made to fit the bones of Europeans, and when used for an Oriental Jew they failed to determine the person's exact age. The court accepted the defense's argument and sentenced Habshush to life imprisonment instead of death, to be served at the main women's prison in Bethlehem. Seven years later, she was pardoned by the British high commissioner. During the public campaign to secure the pardon, in which women's organizations identified with the right wing in the Yishuv played a prominent role, her supporters based their request not only on Habshush's young age, but also on the claim that she had become involved in terrorist activities after her relatives were killed in the riots in Hebron in 1929.[32]

Rachel Habshush (Ohevet 'Ami) was not the only figure who illustrated the combination between underground and subversive activities and ethnic affiliation. Two other women who played a prominent role in similar activities, though representing the opposite political stands, were Simha Tzabari and Geula Cohen, both of whom were of Yemenite origin and grew up in Kerem Hatemanim. As mentioned in chapter 4, Tzabari was a member of the Palestinian Communist Party; her partner Radwan al-Hilu, a Christian Arab, shared her ideological leanings and served as secretary of the party. In 1936 Tzabari placed bombs at the Workers' House in Haifa and at the Levent Fair in Tel Aviv. Rachel Tzabari, Simha's sister, was a member of the Haganah and later served as a member of the Knesset for Mapai. Simha Tzabari's unusual biography underscores the small number of Mizrahim who were active in the Palestinian Communist Party. Geula Cohen later served as a member of Knesset for the Likud Party and became one of the most prominent spokespeople for the Israeli right wing. After being arrested by the British due to her activities as a broadcaster on the clandestine radio station of the Lehi (established in 1940 as a result of a split in the Irgun), she managed to escape from the women's prison in Bethlehem. Cohen was hospitalized and escaped, disguised as an Arab woman, with the assistance of the members of an Arab family from the village of Abu Ghosh, whose residents collaborated with the Lehi.[33] Yitzhak Hasson, who commanded the escape operation, noted that the affair illustrated that it would have been possible to develop a joint Jewish-Arab struggle against British colonialism.[34]

Just as the Irgun and Lehi's terrorist operations blurred the distinctions between Jews and Arabs, so did the profiles of the victims of these activities. On the morning of July 25, 1938, an incendiary device exploded in the vegetable market close to Hamelakhim Street in Haifa, killing forty-five Arabs and injuring dozens more. In response to this attack, which as noted above was perpetrated by Aharoni of the Irgun, reprisals were carried out in various parts of Haifa, particularly in the neighborhoods around the Hadar neighborhood. Arabs attacked Jewish passers-by, and three Jews were murdered in cold blood. The fourth Jew to be killed in Haifa on that morning was Moshe Mizrahi, who was killed by three bullets fired by two members of the Irgun. Mizrahi was born in 1914 in Safed and grew up in Acre. After a bomb was thrown into his apartment, in a building inhabited by both Jews and Arabs, Mizrahi left Acre and moved to a rented apartment in Haifa, working in a quarry and as an assistant driver.[35] Like other Oriental Jews of his generation, Mizrahi was in the habit of wearing a tarboosh. His Arab dress, external appearance, and place of residence all led the Irgun assassins to assume that he was in fact an Arab. Eliyahu Rappaport, one of the two assassins who fled the scene, was apprehended by Jewish passers-by, taken to the Haganah forces in the city, and subsequently handed over to the British secret police.[36]

The Irgun activists who violated the official Yishuv policy of restraint and conducted terrorist operations were sometimes referred to by Labor Zionists as *mitpartzim*,[37] a term that might be translated as "secessionists" but that in Hebrew has implications of immodesty and even sexual licentiousness. In her study of prostitution in Tel Aviv during the Mandatory period, Deborah Bernstein discusses the use of the related word *prutza* (prostitute) to describe female prostitutes who crossed not only boundaries of moral and legal propriety but also the national divide between Jews and Arabs.[38] On more than one occasion, this crossing of boundaries had a tragic end. Jewish women of Oriental origin who lived among Arabs and maintained friendly relations with them during periods of tension and violence, such as the Arab Revolt and the 1948 war, were sometimes attacked and murdered, and were subsequently described as *prutzot*.

On April 22, 1936, the police announced that Esther Sheetrit, a "Sephardi Jewish woman" (according to the statement by the police), had been murdered by her Arab neighbor in the mixed Jewish-Arab neighborhood of Ard al-Yahud in Haifa. The statement emphasized that the motive for the murder was personal rather than political.[39] As mentioned above, Ard al-Yahud was the first Jewish neighborhood established outside the walls of the Old City in Haifa and had become a mixed Jewish-Arab area. The police were careful to emphasize the fact that the victim, a forty-six-year-old married woman with six sons and three daughters, was a prostitute. Mendel Singer, a reporter in Haifa for the newspaper *Davar*, wrote about the murder and argued that the motive was indeed political. Singer described the relations between the families of the victim and the murderer in Ard al-Yahud and waged a public campaign to clear Sheetrit's name and secure her recognition as the first Jewish victim of the Arab Revolt in Haifa. Singer documented his public campaign in a booklet he published in Sheetrit's memory.[40]

Yitzhak Hasson, who headed the Lehi's intelligence department, was among those who later discussed the significance of mistaken identity as a reflection of the affinity between Oriental Jews and Arabs in the mixed cities. Hasson himself was born into a middle-class Sephardi family of Turkish descent. He grew up in a Ladino-speaking home in the Neve Tzedek neighborhood of Tel Aviv and studied at the Alliance Israélite Universelle School and the High School for Commerce.[41] He was a member of the Nationalist Cells (Hata'im Haleumi'im) youth movement, which recruited educated youths who had close links to the Beitar youth movement and the Revisionist Party. At the age of fifteen, Hasson joined the Irgun. When he published his memoirs in 1993, he was chairperson of the Israeli Secular Humanist Society. In his memoirs Hasson criticized the Irgun for its inability to cooperate with Arab forces in a common anticolonial struggle against the British Mandatory government.[42]

Hasson recalls one of his first missions for the Irgun, under the command of Yitzhak Jeziernicky (Shamir), who replaced Aryeh Yitzhaki as commander of one of the Irgun's companies. Shamir later became one of the commanders of the Lehi, and in the 1980s he was prime minister of Israel. Hasson's task was to undertake surveillance of Arab passers-by in the border area between Tel Aviv and Jaffa. He was instructed to observe who was coming and alert the assassins he was working with when a potential Arab victim approached. Hasson described his mission in the following terms:

> Tuesday—six o'clock: three Arabs riding on donkeys and heading for Jaffa. Ten after six: two Arabs approach from Jaffa. Quarter to seven: a shady-looking man dressed in a cream-yellow colored tunic with a tarboosh on his head and prayer beads in his hand. He's coming from the direction of Jaffa (unclear whether he is an Arab or a Jew). He doesn't really look like an Arab to me. But how can we really know for certain who is Arab? There are so many Jewish Arabs, and even my own father, who is Turkish rather than Arab, could definitely pass for an urban Arab. He has some photographs from Turkey that show him wearing a tarboosh. But you don't have any doubts when a rural Arab comes, because of the traditional clothes, keffiyeh, and 'aqal cord.[43]

It is unclear whether this report was written by Hasson at the age of sixteen or represents his views as an elderly man and devoted humanist. In any case, it may be seen as an example of the unique anticolonialist perspective that was dominant in the Irgun and later in the Lehi. The description also demonstrates the existence of a hybrid Jewish-Arab cultural identity during the Mandatory period among Oriental Jews.

The Oriental Neighborhoods and Anti-Arab Violence

On May 23, 1939, following the resurgence of the Irgun's wave of terror, the Council of the Sephardi Community in Jerusalem issued a statement urging Sephardi and Oriental youth to obey the instructions of the national institutions, to remain calm and disciplined, and not to be swayed by "the storm on the street." The statement ended with a call to the Arab people: "Our brothers in race! Even now and here, our hand is stretched out to you in true peace and cooperation—but an honorable and lasting peace. The course offered by the Mandatory government in its great confusion is leading to the desolation of this land, to the impoverishment of both peoples—Hebrew and Arab—and not to construction and revival."[44]

The desire to prevent Jewish reprisals and terrorist attacks also led a number of leading figures among the Sephardi community to sign a statement titled "Lo Tirzah" (Thou shall not commit murder). The statement was published in *Davar* on July 7, 1939, on the initiative of intellectuals and political activists associated with Labor Zionism.[45] Eliyahu Eliachar's response to Jewish terrorist actions was typical of the views of the mainstream Sephardi leaders. Eliachar was opposed to the official policy of restraint, which he believed the Arabs were liable to misinterpret as weakness, thereby discouraging the Arabs who opposed the position of the Mufti. At the same time, Eliachar was opposed to Jewish terrorist actions, which he condemned in clear terms on both political and moral grounds.[46]

The identification of Sephardi and Oriental Jews with the Revisionist Movement, and of Oriental Jews with the Irgun's terrorist operations, weakened the status of the Sephardi leadership and portrayed it as a secessionist force and a partner in efforts to challenge the authority of the national institutions. The involvement of Oriental youth in the Irgun's terrorist operations brought the Sephardi leadership into conflict not only with Mapai but also with the British Mandatory government. As we have seen, throughout the Mandatory period Sephardi and Oriental Jewish leaders had been forced to respond to allegations regarding the loyalty of the members of their communities to Zionism. The Labor Zionists, in particular, had also been sharply critical of what they saw as the separatist political tendencies of the Sephardi leaders. The leaders now faced renewed criticism as a result of the identification of the Sephardim with the rejection of the official policy of restraint. They were quick to condemn Jewish terrorist actions in an attempt to stave off this criticism. In addition to political condemnations, however, efforts were also made to understand the reasons for the involvement of Oriental youth in these actions. These attempts focused on an analysis of the socioeconomic problems and educational and cultural deprivation facing Oriental youth.

One of the reasons for the condemnation of terrorist actions by the Council of the Sephardi Community in Jerusalem was the accusation by members of Mapai that the reactions of the Oriental communities to the events in Jaffa in 1936 served as the immediate catalyst for the Arab Revolt. Leading Labor Zionists also claimed that the Oriental youth who carried out terrorist attacks or were engaged in anti-Arab violence, against the policy of restraint adopted by the national institutions of the Yishuv, were the victims of manipulation by the revisionist right wing.[47] Members of Mapai and the Labor Zionist movement presented their policy of restraint as a manifestation of the moral superiority of Jews over Arabs. Accordingly, the implication was that those who violated this policy, particularly Oriental youth, thereby revealed themselves to be as immoral as the Palestinian Arabs. Eliezer Rieger, a professor of education at the Hebrew University, claimed that Oriental youth had a primitive attitude toward the Arab Question. He argued that they shared the Arabs' disdain for the weak and the relationship between the colonizer and the colonized in Palestine.[48] Conversely, others argued that European Jews had adapted the model of Jewish-Christian relations in Europe to the context of Jewish-Arab relations in Palestine. According to this argument—made, for example, by Yehoshua Heshel Yeivin of the revisionist Brit Habiryonim group—the policy of restraint was not merely a sign of weakness but also proved that the Yishuv leaders saw themselves as if they were in the Diaspora.[49] Alongside cultural explanations relating to the adoption of tribal or religious concepts of blood feuds or an eye for an eye, social factors such as educational, economic, and social deprivation and neglect were used by some in the Yishuv, as noted above, to explain the involvement of Oriental youth in violent attacks against Arab civilians.

Against Terror was a collection of articles, notes, speeches, and statements edited by R. Binyamin (the pseudonym of Yehoshua Radler-Feldmann) and Ya'acov Peterzeyl and published in August 1939.[50] A particularly interesting article in the collection, written by Hannah Thon, was titled "Education of Youth in the Oriental Communities." Thon began her article by mentioning several incidents following the outbreak of the Arab Revolt in which Oriental youth had attacked Arab passers-by and vandalized Arab property. She added that these incidents left her with the impression that "the hatred against Arabs in the Oriental neighborhoods goes far beyond the anti-Arab sentiments found in certain Ashkenazi circles." According to Thon, the animosity shown by Oriental youth toward Arabs was not the product of chauvinistic nationalism or a specific political position, but rather of primitive racial hatred. This hatred was in turn the product of "an instinctive and unfounded sentiment—perhaps the remnant of previous generations of persecution, of ancestors who lived in constant fear and self-defense—a tendency to disdain those who are different and therefore perceived as inferior."[51]

Thon mentioned two key arguments that were often used to explain anti-Arab violence by Oriental youth. The first was historical resentment due to the inferior status of the Jews in the Muslim countries; the second was the inferior and neglected social, economic, and cultural status of Oriental Jews in Palestine in general, and in the frontier and peripheral neighborhoods in particular. In her attempt to understand why the hatred of Oriental Jews for Arabs made such a strong impression on "the Ashkenazi observer," Thon offered another observation that she felt might explain the violence shown by Oriental youth—namely, the cultural affinity between Oriental Jews and Arabs: "We find a considerable similarity between the characteristics and customs of certain Oriental Jewish communities and those of their Arab neighbors, and in many cases constructive forces actually seem to be stronger among the Arabs." She suggested that the disdain shown by the Oriental Jews toward the Arabs was the product of foolish and blind racial hatred, "combined in the case of most of the youths in the Oriental neighborhoods with a passion to torture weaker individuals who fall into their hands." This passion was reflected in part in the desire to abuse Arabs, "who find themselves left open to the violence of Jewish children in the Oriental neighborhoods." Thon was careful to acknowledge that instances of cruelty could also be encountered in Ashkenazi neighborhoods. However, in the Oriental neighborhoods such incidents constituted a veritable phenomenon that was not condemned or addressed by the local community. Thon warned that racial hatred of Arabs was liable to spread, and that those who committed hate crimes against Arabs might become role models, as was indeed the case with Habshush, "who has now become a national role model among children in circles close to her worldview."[52]

Thon, who was born in Germany in 1886, suggested ways to reform the condition of Oriental Jewish youth based on her experience as a social worker and women's activist. In 1936, she initiated the establishment of vocational training centers for women, clinics for women and children, and centers for the study of

Hebrew in the Shimon Hatzadik and Nachalat Achim neighborhoods of Jerusalem, two strongholds of the city's Oriental community. The neighborhood centers sought to encourage women to launch their own initiatives, and to provide a refuge for children who had dropped out of school.[53] Based on her experience as a social worker, Thon suggested the establishment of educational and assistance centers "in the centers of the Oriental Jewish proletariat." She was convinced that such facilities would provide an opportunity for volunteer educators to develop among the Oriental youth practical and moral bonds between Jews and Arabs. She argued that "only outreach reflecting an effort to help these members of our people in their distress, and to guide them in the path of a spiritual bond with the entire Yishuv," could overcome their feelings of hatred and destructive urges. She felt that this approach could provide an important goal for Oriental youth, "who are much closer to the Arabs in terms of language, lifestyle, and thought than the Ashkenazim or the educated Sephardim."[54] Thon's indictment of the Yishuv leadership was stark and uncompromising: "Had we not condemned the children of poor and ignorant Oriental families for many years to neglect and lack of guidance, damning them to degeneration, we would not have created such a broad opportunity for inciters to hatred and violence. We exiled these families to a ghetto in which they abandoned the culture they had brought from their countries of residence in the Orient, but we have yet to draw them into the new culture or involve them in the responsibility for the Yishuv."[55]

The public debate during the Arab Revolt regarding the involvement of Oriental youth in terrorism and violence continued until the outbreak of the 1948 war. The debate included the specific allegation that most of the terrorist operations of the Irgun and the Lehi were committed by Jews of Yemenite descent. During the struggles that developed in 1947 between the Labor Zionists, under the leadership of Mapai, and the Revisionists; and between the Haganah, on the one hand, and the Irgun and Lehi, on the other hand (a period known by historians as the Lesser Season)—it was repeatedly claimed that Mizrahim in general, and Yemenite Jews in particular, were involved in terrorist acts against British and Arab targets.

On January 3, 1947, Agence France-Presse reported from London that at a meeting on January 2, 1947, David Ben-Gurion had explained to British Colonial Secretary Arthur Creech Jones that Yemenite Jews were mainly responsible for acts of terrorism in Palestine.[56] Ben-Gurion denied making the comments and asked the news agency to publish a correction to its report. In a letter to the news agency, Ben-Gurion claimed that his comments had been distorted and that "the Yemenite community is poor, peace loving, and hard-working and has suffered both in Palestine and in Yemen."[57] On January 14, 1947, after Yemenite Association had released a statement on the affair, Ben-Gurion spoke to representatives of the association and again denied making the comments attributed to him. The association's statement had declared that the Yemenite public "is known as a quiet and peace-loving element that has no part in terrorist actions, and even if isolated individuals among its number have been dragged into terrorism, as have youths from other communities, an entire community should not be accused or singled out."[58]

The Irgun also responded to Ben-Gurion's alleged comments about the Yemenite Jews. On January 4, 1947, *Herut*, the Irgun's newspaper, declared:

> We do not know whether or not Mr. Ben-Gurion commented to the British minister that the "terrorist acts" are committed by "certain Yemenites." This is not the main point. The fact is that the "official" institutions and newspapers ceaselessly claim that the Irgun is composed mainly of members of the Oriental communities. Naturally, these comments reached the ears of the [British] secret police. . . . The collective informers, these "democrats," seek to malign us—Oriental communities go to them, youths from "the neighborhoods"—this is not somewhere where youths from good families should be found. Is this the only fault you could find in us, you hypocrites? You should know that everyone comes to us—from your spacious homes and from the lowliest huts. There is no monopoly on love of the homeland. But we do not deny that we are particularly proud of our poor and humiliated members, who through our fighting family become proud and rich: rich in an unparalleled possession—idealism and faith.[59]

The Irgun's response reflects the political debate that raged during the 1940s concerning the role of Oriental Jews in its ranks. It is worth noting here that the press of the period includes various references to serious attacks on Arabs attributed to members of the Yemenite community. On August 18, 1947, for example, the newspaper *Mishmar* reported that a gang of "scoundrels" described as Yemenites had attacked an Arab employee of a Jewish-owned cobbler's shop in Tel Aviv and stabbed him to death in Kerem Hatemanim.[60] This murder was presented as being a reprisal for a murder at the Hawaii Garden Café in the city a week before. Together with press reports of similar incidents, the situation led the newspaper *Davar* to warn against the tendency to blame Yemenites: "People often talk about the role of Yemenites in the secessionist organizations; does anyone really imagine that only Yemenites are present in the secessionist organizations?"[61]

The Yemenite Association responded forcefully to the claims, warning that they could lead to attacks on Yemenites by Arabs or the British army. The border neighborhoods—particularly those in south Tel Aviv such as Kerem Hatemanim, Hatikvah, Ezra, and Maccabi—were indeed the target of a series of detention operations launched by the British army. In January 1947, for example, a curfew was imposed on Kerem Hatemanim, and the British Sixth Division searched the area, arresting some fifty people in a hunt for Jewish terrorists. Similar operations took place in other areas with a large concentration of Yemenite Jews, such as the Sha'arayim neighborhood of Rehovot. The local council complained about the behavior of the soldiers, who acted violently and damaged property during the course of their searches, but was at pains to emphasize that it did not support acts of terror and condemned such actions in the names of all the residents.[62]

The British and Arab press also reported on the involvement of Jews of Yemenite origin in the Irgun's terrorist operations. The British press claimed that the perpetrators of one attack belonged to a "Black" company of the Irgun composed of Yemenite Jews.[63] The Palestinian Arab press also claimed that Yemenite Jews were involved in violent attacks against Arabs. The tendency to automatically attribute any attack to Yemenites was illustrated after the murder of five Jewish young men at the Hawaii Garden Café in Tel Aviv in August 1947. Although the men were actually murdered by armed Arabs, the newspaper *Filastin* reported that the attack had been carried out by Yemenite Jews opposed to socializing between young Jewish women and Arab men.[64] The allegations leveled against the Yemenite community created concerns about attempts by Palestinian Arabs to launch terrorist attacks on the main centers of the community, such as Kerem Hatemanim in Tel Aviv, and concern among the leadership of the Yemenite community in Palestine that the result could be a worsening of the condition of the Jews in Yemen.[65] The position of the Council of the Sephardi Community in Jerusalem against terror attacks was expressed by Eliachar: "we have acted immediately to condemn insane and damaging actions, no matter by whom they were perpetrated."[66] The council called for an improvement in the cultural, social, and economic condition of the Oriental communities and warned that blaming the Sephardim for terrorist attacks could widen the gulf between the Zionist institutions and the majority of the Sephardi population.

Following the report claiming that Ben-Gurion had mentioned the involvement of Yemenite Jews in terrorist activities, *Mishmar*—the newspaper of the Hashomer Hatza'ir —remarked in January 1947 that anyone "who reviews the names of [Jewish] terror activists injured or arrested reaches the conclusion that the terrorist groups have enjoyed considerable success among the Oriental communities."[67] The newspaper went on to note the tragic paradox that many of the residents of what it called the "suburban neighborhoods" in the main cities, who the newspaper felt naturally belonged on the Left, had actually voted for the Revisionist Party in the recent Zionist Congress elections. The newspaper hence urged the Labor Zionist movement to intensify its activities in the frontier neighborhoods, noting that the Histadrut's efforts in this field had focused mainly on social assistance, rather than on educational and political work. *Mishmar* added that the youth movements affiliated with the labor movement had virtually no presence in the neighborhoods. The work of Hano'ar Ha'oved had contributed little to improving the situation, in the newspaper's opinion, since its activities were confined mainly to vocational issues. The small number of educational groups initiated by the cooperative settlements were also unable to function as a "serious force given the thousands of youths left to their own devices or to absorb the atmosphere of the streets."[68]

The combination of the feelings of neglect and discrimination prevalent among the residents of the poor neighborhoods and their exclusion from the national institutions of the Zionist movement and the Yishuv contributed to the national friction that erupted along the border between the Yemenite neighborhoods and the Arab-dominated ones. Terrorist acts against these neighborhoods, such as the planting of a bomb by Arabs in the courtyard of a school for Yemenite children in the Kerem Yisrael neighborhood of Tel Aviv, close to Manashiyya, during the early stage of the Arab Revolt, were among the factors that fueled the mutual acts of revenge and violence along these borders.[69]

The arguments surrounding the connection between Yemenite Jews and the terrorist actions of the Irgun and Lehi even led to violent exchanges between members of the Hashomer Hatza'ir and Yemenite youths. Indeed, the Hebrew press depicted the political and ethnic tension that erupted in February 1947 as a battle between Hashomer Hatza'ir and the Yemenites.[70] The clashes began after Yemenite youths from the Neve Shalom neighborhood, just outside Natanya, were beaten by members of Hashomer Hatza'ir from Kibbutz Eilat. The attackers justified their actions by claiming that a member of Hashomer Hatza'ir who was removing an Irgun poster in Natanya had been beaten by Yemenite youths.[71]

On February 12, dozens of youths armed with Molotov cocktails attacked clubs belonging to Hashomer Hatza'ir in Rehovot and Tel Aviv, causing extensive damage.[72] The Hebrew youth movements, including the Sephardi Degel Zion, condemned the attack, which Hashomer Hatza'ir described as a manifestation of fascist tendencies in the Yishuv that gravitated toward the Irgun.[73] Following this outbreak of violence, the Irgun circulated a pamphlet with a statement warning that the British were attempting to foment civil war in the Yishuv. The Irgun emphasized that it had not been involved in the attack on Hashomer Hatza'ir's clubs and added that "there are inciters who are interested in encouraging mutual hatred and in sparking a civil war that will divert attention from the main issue—the war of liberation—to shameful internal squabbles."[74] This was not the first conflict between the secessionist organizations and Hashomer Hatza'ir. During the 1940s, various clashes between members of Hashomer Hatza'ir and "Hebrews of Yemenite origin and non-Yemenites"—to use Menachem Begin's definition—and between members of the kibbutzim and residents of the frontier neighborhoods illustrated the ethnic and political nature of the growing social tension between the right-wing organizations and the Labor Zionist movement.[75]

Against this background, and as part of the attempt to expand the activities of the labor movement and the Histadrut among Oriental youth, a gathering of Oriental activists was held at the Histadrut's building in Tel Aviv. Using the slogan "let our weapons be pure," the event emphasized the need to accept the authority of the national institutions of the Yishuv and to engage in outreach activities among the Oriental communities to "open their eyes to the dangers inherent in the actions of the secessionist organizations." The participants emphasized the urgent need to organize Oriental youth in the neighborhoods and suburbs and engage them in Zionist activity.[76] As on similar occasions, participants suggested that the neglect and poverty facing the young residents of the frontier neighborhoods encouraged them to resort to violence and terror.

Ya'acov Riftin expressed a similar opinion at a meeting of the Hashomer Hatza'ir Council in March 1947: "This pattern is exemplified by the exploitation of the feeling of inferiority among the members of the Oriental communities, who have been neglected for many years—neglect that is unforgivable—to engage them in actions contrary to the supreme national authority. This is a typical fascist rebellion that nurtures delusions of grandeur and victory, but that ultimately leads the people to doom."[77] In a speech in June 1947 to the Council of Hashomer Hatza'ir Party, Yehuda Dranitzky, a senior figure in the Histadrut and in Hashomer Hatza'ir, also noted that the Histadrut constituted a small minority in the "congested and impoverished suburbs." These suburbs, he explained, "do not rest on their laurels. There is constant foment there, and it is there that we find the main bases of Jewish fascism."[78] These "suburbs"—that is, the borderline and frontier neighborhoods—thus increasingly became the target for activities by both right-wing and left-wing parties and a key arena in the political struggle between the two camps. These neighborhoods were also the location of efforts to recruit Oriental youth into the ranks of the Irgun, the Lehi, and the Palmach.

Mizrahanut *and Revisionism: An Anticolonial Struggle*

Israeli historians have examined the affinity between the Irgun and the Oriental communities as part of their broader examination of the status of the Mizrahim in the State of Israel, including the discussion about the political support of these communities for the right-wing Israeli Herut Party and later the Likud.[79] Various factors may explain what has become known as the alliance of the downtrodden (*ahvat hameduka'im*)—the coalition forged among various social and political groups that were excluded by Mapai and its associated institutions. The theories proposed include voting as a form of protest, patterns of nationalist extremism, attempts by the Mizrahim to distance themselves from their Arab identity, and reactions to the changing status of Jews and Muslims as the minority and majority groups in Israel. Yet, as Uri Cohen and Nissim Leon have argued, the integration of the Mizrahim into the Herut Party and the leadership of the Likud was a relatively late phenomenon. Throughout the 1950s and 1960s, the Likud maintained its character as the representative of the so-called fighting family, and as such was dominated by former members of Beitar and the Irgun, most of whom were of Eastern European descent.[80]

This analysis reinforces the importance of the question of the affinity between the Revisionist Movement and the Oriental communities during the Mandatory period in general and regarding the Arab Question in particular.[81] In the previous chapters we noted that the Revisionist Movement sought to emphasize the special bond that it claimed existed between Vladimir (Ze'ev) Jabotinsky (the founder and leader of the Revisionist Party) and the Sephardi and Oriental Jews. Before the 1931 elections to the Yishuv's third Assembly of Representatives, a list of candidates associated with Revisionist Zionism was formed comprising Sephardi and Oriental Jewish Communities supporters of Jabotinsky.[82] Jabotinsky was careful to recall this connection. In a letter to the World Confederation of Sephardi Jews, he declared: "I am pleased that my brothers from the Sephardi community and the other Oriental communities still recall the feelings of respect I have always had in my heart toward this part of our people—a part that is the true base and foundation of our ancient race."[83]

The formation of the list of candidates consisting of Sephardi and Oriental Jewish supporters of Jabotinsky challenged the traditional Sephardi position that was expressed by organizations such as the Association of the Pioneers of the

East regarding the Sephardim's ability to serve as a bridge for rapprochement between Jews and Arabs. In an article titled "Mizrahanut and Revisionism," published in *Doar Hayom* as part of the debate on the proposed Arab-Jewish conference of 1932 (see chapter 3) and as an answer to an article published by Eliyahu Sasson in *al-'Alam al-Isra'ili* on August 26, 1932 (claiming that there was a contradiction between being an Oriental leader and a Revisionist), Moshe Ben-'Ami, one of Jabotinsky's supporters, argued that there was no contradiction between Oriental Jews' support for the Revisionist Party and support for rapprochement between Jews and Arabs: "The view that a son of the Orient (*ben hamizrah*) cannot head a Mizrahi institution if he is a Revisionist is a reprehensible one. The affiliation of a son of the Orient with revisionist Zionism does not negate his potential or his right to aspire to mutual understanding with the Arabs."[84] Regarding the Arab Question, Ben-'Ami stated that "every Mizrahi Jew has his own worldview and each one serves his people according to his views and conscience."

Ben-'Ami, who used both Mizrahanut and Mizrahaniyut in his article to describe the meaning of Oriental Jewish identity, asked "what is the attitude of the Oriental Jews(*bney 'edot hamizrah)* on the Arab question?" He began his answer by noting that "those who consider Oriental Jews to be a party; those who consider them as an association that shares a particular political opinion; those who seek to attribute to them a fixed frame of mind and special qualities that are not influenced by their surroundings and by what has happened and is still happening in our world—all these are mistaken. In reality, the Oriental Jewish communities today belong to the different parties and streams just like the other sections of the Yishuv." For Ben-'Ami, the meaning of the support of the Oriental Jews for the Revisionist Party was that "Mizrahaniyut does not mean obsequiousness and concessions." Mizrahaniyut, according to Ben-'Ami, supports a firm stance regarding the homeland and revival, and therefore there was no contradiction between "Mizrahaniyut and Revizionism"[85]

Ben-'Ami sought to support his argument by discussing the results of the elections to the third Assembly of Representatives, which he claimed revealed a clear division in voting patterns among Oriental Jews, with 40 percent supporting the Revisionist Zionism, 40 percent supporting the World Confederation of Sephardi Jews, and 20 percent supporting Mapai. Defending Jabotinsky's political position on the Arab Question, Ben-'Ami argued that his opposition to negotiations with the Arabs was not due to hatred or a lack of desire for understanding between Jews and Arabs, but because no one could be found on the Arab side who supported understanding, and because Revisionist Zionism opposed the path of obsequiousness. Ben-'Ami also presented the revisionist position that Arabs would not be persecuted in the Jewish state and that their civil and religious rights would be protected.[86]

The call to support the Revisionist Party exploited the sense of discrimination on the part of the Zionist leadership, creating a distinction between "first-class citizens and second-class citizens," as noted in the manifesto published by the Sephardi list of candidates that was associated with Revisionist Zionism in the elections of January 1931. Moreover, "official Zionism has not only failed to take an interest in the Oriental Jews, but has turned its back on them, regarding them as stepchildren."[87] The claim that Mapai bore the main responsibility for the grave economic and cultural condition of the Oriental Jews, and particularly for the neglect of the frontier neighborhoods and the Oriental youth and for discrimination in various fields, was repeated throughout the Mandatory period in numerous discussions, speeches, and articles, particularly in *Hed Hamizrah*.[88]

The discussion concerning the political support of the Oriental Jews for the Revisionist Movement included the question of whether the Mizrahim played a significant role in the Irgun and Lehi. This question was reinforced by the rhetoric employed by Menachem Begin, as the leader of the Irgun. As we discussed above in this chapter, the initial response by the Irgun to Ben-Gurion's alleged comments about the involvement of Yemenite Jews in terrorism emphasized that the Irgun was proud of its Oriental members and its ability to recruit residents of the poor neighborhoods who were on the margins of society in the Yishuv. Begin repeated this point in his later speeches and after the establishment of the State of Israel—for example, in a Knesset session on December 8, 1964, and in a famous speech in Tel Aviv on June 27, 1981. At the height of the election campaign for the Knesset, Begin referred in his speech to the deaths of Moshe Barazani, a member of the Lehi who was born in Baghdad, and Meir Feinstein of the Irgun: "The members of our Mizrahi communities were heroic fighters, including in the underground. They include some of those who were hanged on the gallows and who continued to sing 'Hatikva' until the last moment of their life. They astonished the entire world with their exemplary heroism. . . . Ashkenazim? Iraqis? Brothers! Fighters!"[89]

The sociologist Shlomi Resnik examined the recruitment drives of the Irgun and the social background of its members. He found that under Begin's leadership, the number of members of the Irgun increased, leading to a change in the social profile of its activists. Graduates of the youth movements affiliated with the Revisionist Movement, such as National Hebrew Youth, Brit Hahashmona'im, or Beitar, were the primary source of recruits to the Irgun. Resnik found that the memberships of both the Irgun and Lehi were predominantly Ashkenazi. He estimated that 26.7 percent of the members of the Irgun and 25.5 percent of the members of the Lehi were Sephardim and Oriental Jews. Among activists in the two organizations who had been born in Palestine, the proportion of Sephardim and Oriental Jews was higher: 42 percent for the Irgun and 35 percent for the Lehi.[90] The Irgun historian David Niv supports these findings, noting that most of the members of the Irgun were of Ashkenazi origin. According to him, the proportion of Ashkenazim in most of the Irgun's branches was 65–75 percent, but in Jerusalem, the proportion was 50–60 percent.[91] Given these figures and the emphasis on the role of Oriental youth in the operations of the Irgun and Lehi, the question arises as to whether the involvement of the Oriental youth was also due to their belief in the idea of a joint Arab-Jewish struggle against the Mandatory government as a foreign colonial rule.

During the course of their violent campaign to end British rule, the Irgun and Lehi also argued that the British were fomenting conflict and division between Jews and Arabs. The Irgun saw the British policy of divide and rule as a classic colonialist tactic designed to encourage confrontation between different religious, national, and ethnic groups. On September 15, 1944, for example, the Irgun published a pamphlet addressed to the Arab population in Palestine advocating peace and fellowship between the two peoples: "We do not see you as enemies. We want to see you as good neighbors. We have not come to destroy you or to usurp the land you live on. There is room for you, too, in the Land of Israel, and for your children and grandchildren, as well as for millions of Jews who have no life other than in this land." The pamphlet explained the status Arabs would enjoy as a minority in a Jewish state: "The Hebrew government will grant you full equal rights: The Arabic and Hebrew languages will be the languages of the land; there will be no discrimination between Arab and Jew in securing a governmental or public position. The holy places of the Muslim religion will be under the supervision of your representatives."[92]

In August 1947, following the publication of the conclusions of the United Nations Special Committee on Palestine (UNSCOP), the Irgun distributed another pamphlet to the Arabs in Palestine: "The method used by the British enslavers to maintain their rule is an old and familiar one. This is the way of fomenting hatred between different sections of the population, so that they shed their blood in mutual clashes and weaken themselves by internal conflict."[93] Addressing the Arabs directly, the pamphlet continued: "Our Arab neighbors, do not be misled by the devilish game of the British enslavers. You know that we fight solely against the damned enslavers, and not against you." The Irgun even advocated a joint Jewish-Arab struggle: "Your interest and our common interest demands that you stand not against us, but with us in a decisive war against the British invader."[94]

However, the clearest call for anticolonialist Jewish-Arab cooperation was made not in Palestine, but in Cairo. On November 6, 1944, two Lehi activists, Eliyahu Hakim and Eliyahu Beit-Tzuri, assassinated Lord Moyne, the British minister of state in the Middle East. The assassination itself, and even more so the subsequent trial of Hakim and Beit-Tzuri in an Egyptian military court, was extensively covered in the global press.[95] The trial began on January 10, 1945 and lasted eight days. On March 22, the two men were executed. The trial, which was attended by dozens of foreign journalists, was held in a public hall in Cairo. One of the journalists who reported on the event was the American military correspondent and writer Gerold Frank, who published his recollections of the trial in a book.[96] The defense attorneys were prominent figures in the Egyptian legal scene, particularly Tawfiq Dus Pasha, who had served as a government minister and was a leading attorney.[97]

The international interest in the trial was not due solely to Lord Moyne's status as a senior British politician. The Hebrew and Arab press in Palestine also covered the trial extensively, and those present in the courtroom included 'Awni 'Abd al-Hadi, the leader of the Palestinian Istiqlal Party. The newspaper *Filastin* emphasized that this was the first major international trial held in Egypt since the 1936 agreement between Egypt and Britain. *Filastin* noted that the trial was conducted "in an Arab court, with Arab judges, in accordance with Arab laws, and in an independent Arab state where the law is free of any alien influence."[98] According to *Filastin*, the trial "has aroused pride among the Arabs and placed us on an equal footing with the most civilized nations of the world in terms of the honesty of justice and the pure application of the law." The manner in which the trial was conducted, and particularly the way the defense attorneys worked on behalf of the two Jewish defendants, were described by *Filastin* as proof that the Arabs were "a more noble, generous, and honest nation than the West—that West with the racial distinctions and unbridled nationalism that threw Europe into a barbaric war."[99] Journalists also focused on the response of the Egyptian public to the unique ideological stance presented by Hakim and Beit-Tzuri.[100]

Beit-Tzuri was born in Tel Aviv in 1922 to a father who had come from Minsk and a mother from a Sephardi family. He was educated at the Tachkemoni School in the city. His father, Yosef Moshe Beit-Tzuri, was well known among the Arab residents of Jaffa, where he served as director of the post office. In 1932 he and his family moved to Tiberias for four years.[101] During their stay in

Tiberias, Eliyahu gained a basic knowledge of Arabic. After the family returned to Tel Aviv, Eliyahu continued his high school education at Balfour School and was a member of the Maccabi youth movement. His schoolmates included Amichai Feiglin, who later served as the Irgun's operational commander; David Danon, a member of the Irgun and later a professor at the Weizmann Institute; and Uzi Ornan, a member of the Council for the Coalition for Hebrew Youth, which was better known as the Canaanite movement, and later a professor at the Hebrew University in Jerusalem.[102] Beit-Tzuri was influenced by the views of Yonatan Ratosh, the founder of the Canaanite movement, and joined the Council for the Coalition for Hebrew Youth and the National Cells (one of the Revisionist Party's youth movements).[103] After graduating from high school, Beit-Tzuri studied at the Institute for Oriental Studies in the Hebrew University of Jerusalem, where he acquired a knowledge of literary Arabic. At this stage he left the Irgun and joined the Lehi.[104]

Hakim was born in Beirut in 1925 and came to Haifa with his family at the age of seven. He attended the Alliance Israélite Universelle School and the Hebrew Reali School in Haifa before volunteering for the British Army during World War II. After serving in military bases in Egypt, he deserted and returned to Haifa in December 1943. Hakim also left the Irgun and was recruited to the Lehi by Ya'acov Banai, one of the senior operations officers in the organization.[105] His experience in the British army prior to his desertion, his knowledge of Arabic, and his involvement in a failed attempt to assassinate High Commissioner Harold McMichael all prepared Hakim for his ultimate mission. Despite the different backgrounds of Beit-Tzuri and Hakim, they were both well-educated urban youths who joined the Lehi. Their decision to join this underground organization can be explained, in part, by the strong anticolonial component in the Lehi's ideology.[106]

This anticolonial stance became apparent during the trial of Hakim and Beit-Tzuri and was highlighted in the news coverage of the event. The Egyptian public was particularly fascinated by Beit-Tzuri's remarks during his speech in his own defense. He attacked British imperialism and spoke in favor of the revival of the peoples of the Orient. He began his remarks by recalling that when he was twelve years old, he saw British police in Tel Aviv using violence to disperse a demonstration demanding open Jewish immigration. This incident led Beit-Tzuri to reconsider the legitimacy of British rule. His conclusion was unequivocal: "The Englishman may come to my country, be a policeman there, and act as he sees fit—since my country is held by a foreign government."[107] During the trial, Beit-Tzuri described the British policy as colonial imperialism and claimed that the Mandatory government had encouraged conflict and hatred between the two peoples: "British propaganda has accustomed the world to see the Palestine question as a conflict between Jews and Arabs, and the British as judges and regulators. It is inaccurate to see the issue in this manner. It is quite untrue! The Palestine issue is simply a confrontation between the Hebrew sons of the land, who are the owners of the land, and a government that is utterly alien to the land—the British regime."[108]

Beit-Tzuri's position, which strongly reflected the influence of the ideology of the Canaanite movement, was also reflected in his claim that his actions were motivated not by Zionism, but by the fact that as a "native of the country" (Ben Ha'aretz) he was fighting for the independence of his homeland: "It is a mistake to believe that we here represent Zionism. We, the Hebrew sons of the Land of Israel, have decided to secure our country's independence from the current regime. We are not fighting to implement the Balfour Declaration; we are not fighting for a National Home in accordance with the Mandate or otherwise. These do not interest us. We are fighting for the essence of the matter: for liberty. We want our Land of Israel to be free and independent."[109]

This position was emphasized by *Filastin*, which described Beit-Tzuri as one of the "sons of Palestine" (*abna filastin*).[110] This position was further emphasized in the remarks of the defense lawyer, who depicted the defendants as fighters against imperialism and British colonialism rather than as part of the Zionist struggle. After the announcement of the death penalty, which was perceived as resulting from British interference in the Egyptian judicial system, demonstrators in Cairo demanded the release of Hakim and Beit-Tzuri.[111] Indeed, fear that the assassination might influence Egyptian public opinion was one of the reasons for the execution of Beit-Tzuri and Hakim. Awareness of public opinion was apparent not only during the course of the trial and in the circumstances that led to the sentence, but also in a remark by Beit-Tzuri during his interrogation that he hoped that the jury would be composed of Arab citizens, since he was convinced that such jurors would prove sympathetic to his assassination of a British minister. During his interrogation, Beit-Tzuri explained that Arabs and Jews could live together in friendship and that the Arabs, particularly those in Palestine, supported the Stern Gang. For Beit-Tzuri, the assassination of Lord Moyne was the first stage in a global uprising.[112]

Canaanite ideology attached great importance to the national and territorial identity of the native of the land, immersed in his homeland, local geography, and the broader semitic domain. At the same time, the Canaanite interpretation of this identity negated the connection between nationhood and Judaism, and in this respect it was directly opposed to the idea of Zionism among Oriental Jews. Thus Beit-Tzuri represented a small cadre of educated Hebrew youths who grew up in the 1930s and found their place in the Lehi, viewing their struggle against the British as part of a broader struggle in the region as a whole.[113] From this standpoint, the assassination in Cairo was a step toward realizing the Lehi's ideal of cooperation with the Arab world against British imperialism.[114] The journal *Hahazit* (The front line), edited by Yisrael Eldad and Nathan Yellin Mor, provided an official interpretation of the assassination from the standpoint of the Lehi; like Beit-Tzuri, the journal argued that the assassination of Lord Moyne was an anticolonialist act. *Hachazit* described Lord Moyne's function as being to secure Britain's colonial rule in the Mediterranean and British economic interests in the region. According to the Lehi's position as expounded in the journal, the British sought to prevent the emergence of an independent Hebrew nation capable of "awakening the slumbering Orient from its sleep and restoring its sense of self-worth." Moyne's assassination was therefore intended to prevent Britain from realizing its desire for "a colonial population and colonial arrangements."[115] Members of the Lehi continued to apply this ideology in their political activities during the late 1950s and 1960s—for example, in the manifesto of the Semitic Action movement. Headed by Uri Avneri, Boaz Evron, and Nathan Yellin Mor, this group advocated the establishment of a Palestinian state alongside the State of Israel, as part of a regional federation.

Mista'arvim: The Arab Department of the Palmach

During the course of World War II, as the Yishuv mobilized to support the British war effort and as part of its preparations for a possible German invasion, the youth of the Yishuv were involved in new military and security organizations.[116] As noted above, the mobilization process highlighted the argument within the Yishuv about the status of the Sephardim and the Oriental Jews and their contribution to the national effort. During the war, however, the Irgun, Lehi, Haganah, and Palmach all intensified their efforts to recruit youths from the frontier neighborhoods to their ranks and special military intelligence units.[117] As Moshe Lissak noted, the labor movement criticized the separate political and social organizations of the Sephardim. Despite this criticism, special departments for the Oriental communities were established in the Histadrut and Mapai, as well as in their affiliated bodies, including the security organizations.[118]

As discussed above, the Sephardi elite demanded that the national institutions recognize their role as political, social, and cultural mediators between Jews and

Arabs. In contrast, the security organizations of the Yishuv found the Sephardi, Yemenite, and Oriental youth particularly suited to serve military purposes, disguised as Arabs. The question that needs to be considered is whether the recruitment of these youths into security organizations involved acts of disguise only, or whether it was also a reflection of their complex hybrid identity as natives of Palestine and the surrounding region, deeply embedded in Oriental culture and heritage. This hybrid identity, we argue, enabled these youths to cross from one society to the other, from one identity to the other, and from one side of the border to the other.[119]

In the spring of 1941, the Haganah established a Syrian Department on the initiative of the Political Department of the Jewish Agency, and in cooperation with British intelligence.[120] The department was an intelligence and commando unit that was intended to operate in Vichy-controlled Syria and Lebanon. Some of the members of the Syrian Department were Jews of Ashkenazi origin who had grown up in the mixed cities or worked as guards in Jewish agriculture settlements and had acquired a knowledge of Arabic.[121] However, the majority of the first members recruited into the department were of Oriental origin, in particular Damascene-born Jews. In September 1940 those members were sent to Beirut, Tripoli, and Damascus on intelligence and sabotage missions determined by the British army. This marked the beginning of a method of recruitment and activation through which additional groups of Mista'arvim, some of them natives of Palestine, were sent to Syria and Lebanon on military intelligence missions.[122]

In 1942, Yigal Allon, who was serving at the time as commander of the First Company of the Palmach, assumed command of the Syrian Department.[123] During his period in command, Allon focused mainly on developing a program of training and exercises for the Mista'arvim. In the summer of 1943, after the Haganah and the British army ended their period of cooperation, Allon initiated the formation of the Palmach's Arab Department. The department was staffed in part by some of those who had served in the Syrian Department, as well as by members of an intelligence department based on Mount Carmel. The new department was headed by Yerucham Cohen and was also known as the Shahar Department—"shahar" literally means "dawn," but the name was actually a bowdlerized allusion to the epithet "shchorim" (blacks), referring to the predominantly Oriental members of the department.[124] The Arab Department was a special unit that ran intelligence, patrol, and commando operations in Palestine and the Arab states until it was disbanded in 1950.[125]

Cohen, who headed the department between 1943 and 1945, was born in Tel

Aviv in 1916 to a family of Yemenite origin. He completed his high school studies at the Herzliya Gymnasium in Tel Aviv, where his father worked as a janitor; his family lived on the school grounds. Cohen brought considerable experience in intelligence and combat operations to his position in the department: he had worked with Arab laborers at a British army base in Palestine and been a member of the Special Night Squads responsible for protecting the oil line from Mosul to Haifa, under the command of Orde Wingate. In 1941 Cohen was among the first members of the Haganah's Syrian Department. During the 1948 war, he was the intelligence officer of the Palmach Brigade and adjutant to Allon, then commander of the Southern Front. As part of his duties, Cohen directed the Israeli negotiations with the besieged Egyptian troops in the Faluja enclave, including Gamal Abdel Nasser.[126] Cohen belonged to a significant cadre of Oriental members of the Palmach's Arab Department. Like their peers in the Irgun and Lehi, most of these activists had been raised in the frontier neighborhoods, alongside Arabs, or have been employed at places where both Arabs and Jews worked.

In her study of the Zionist use of force, Anita Shapira argued that most of the Jewish youths in the Yishuv grew up in a Jewish world in which Arabs played only a marginal role, and that the points of contact between Jewish and Arab youths were relatively limited.[127] This description is certainly accurate in the case of those who grew up in the rural collective settlements or in the Jewish colonies, but it is less true of the Oriental youth who grew up in the frontier neighborhoods of the mixed cities. This is clearly shown by the backgrounds of the members of the Palmach's Arab Department. According to Cohen, the recruiting efforts to the unit targeted "those with an Oriental appearance whose mother tongue is Arabic, and who lived in the peripheral neighborhoods of the cities with a mixed population, and were therefore thoroughly familiar with the Arab of the Land of Israel" and were "imbued with the characteristic qualities of the local Arabs."[128] Cohen explained that this meant that they lacked a high school education. One of these Oriental youth who were recruited for the Arab Department was Ya'acov (Ya'akuba) Cohen.

Ya'acov Cohen was one of the senior members of the Palmach's Arab Department, and he later occupied senior positions in the Intelligence Division of the Israeli Defense Forces (IDF). His biography illustrates the manner in which life in the impoverished neighborhoods of the mixed cities prepared Oriental youths for their function as Mista'arvim. Cohen was born in 1924 in the Nachalat Zion neighborhood of Jerusalem to a family of Persian descent. Like many of his comrades in the Arab Department, Cohen did not complete high school; instead, he started working to help his family, who faced severe financial difficulties. He joined the youth movement Hano'ar Ha'oved and participated in its training program at Kibbutz Kinneret. In 1942 he joined the Palmach and volunteered for the Arab Department. His training as a Mista'arev included listening to Friday sermons in mosques and working as a laborer in the port of Haifa, using the false identity of a Palestinian from Jaffa. Cohen continued to adopt a Palestinian Arab identity during his various intelligence activities. In the 1948 war he disguised himself as a Palestinian refugee and conducted intelligence operations in Beirut and Damascus.

Cohen described his life in the Nachalat Zion neighborhood—among Jews of Persian, Kurdish, and Syrian descent and in close proximity to the Arab villages of Sheikh Bader and Lifta—as characterized by neighborly relations between Jews and Arabs: "We felt at home in the village, including fighting, friendship, and thievery. . . . We learned their [the Arabs'] mentality and their customs. We were at home in their village and they were at home in our neighborhood."[129] He described the social and economic interactions he experienced during his childhood in the following terms: "When we were children we did not have clubs or playgrounds. These were our games. They [the Arabs] would come with donkeys loaded with bags of wheat and they would grind the wheat. We would help them, and so we found ourselves riding the donkeys and reaching their villages." He continued: "For example, on more than one occasion I ran away from school or stayed out of school and was afraid to come home. Or my father was mad at me. So I would go to them [the Arabs] and sleep there. I slept there quite often, even during the periods of rioting."[130]

However, the relations between people in the Nachlaot neighborhood and those in the nearby Arab villages also included elements of confrontation and violence. Cohen described the high level of anxiety in his neighborhood during the Arab Revolt—an anxiety that was intensified by the fact that some of the families in the neighborhood had relatives who were victims of the 1929 Hebron massacre. But the mukhtar of Sheikh Bader personally warned the residents of the Jewish neighborhood about possible attacks and did his best to protect them. When Cohen's father demanded that he hide under the bed in the event of an attack, Cohen replied: "I know the Arabs, their homes are like mine: no one will make me hide."[131] Cohen also offered his own explanation for the violence shown by Oriental youths toward Arab passers-by: "During the day we weren't afraid of the Arabs, but at night we were afraid of them. At night we always trembled in fear that they might attack. But during the day there was a kind of counter-reaction to this and we would abuse the Arabs. We used to make lots of trouble for them, overturning their stalls, tipping over their baskets of eggs. Today I think about how cruel we were in our actions toward them. But again, this was a kind of counter-reaction to our night-time fear of the Arabs as children."[132]

Cohen is only one example. Nissim 'Ataya also grew up in the Nachalat Zion neighborhood. There were many children in his family, and he was forced to quit school and work as a cobbler. Before joining the Palmach, 'Ataya served as a counselor in the youth movement Hano'ar Ha'oved, working with neglected youths in Jerusalem. In December 1947 he was sent to the village of Beit Nabala, disguised as an Arab barber, to monitor the movements of the Jordanian Legion. To this day the circumstances of his death and his place of burial remain unknown. David Mizrahi, who was also born in Jerusalem but grew up in Rehovot, had a similar background. He had to leave school and worked as a laborer in an orange packing factory in an orchard. In May 1948 Mizrahi was caught in Gaza during a controversial intelligence operation, and he was executed together with his friend Ezra Ifgin. Moshe 'Adaki, who was born in Cairo to a family of Yemenite origin and grew up in the Beit Shalom neighborhood of Jerusalem, also left school because his family faced extreme financial hardship.[133] He too found his place in the Palmach's Arab Department.

Another group of youths who served as Mista'arvim in the Palmach were Jewish immigrants who arrived in Palestine with their families from Arab and Muslim countries and settled, in most cases, in the border neighborhoods of the mixed cities. Other youths, lacking any profession or vocation, immigrated to Palestine alone, while their families remained in one of the neighboring countries. These youths were initially absorbed in the kibbutzim, but most of them eventually found their way to the border neighborhoods of the main cities. Youths who had been active in the Zionist youth movement Hehalutz in Damascus and in Iraq were particularly prominent among these recruits to the Arab Department.[134] Thus the pool of recruits for the Palmach's Arab Department included Palmach members of Oriental origin; a small cadre of Ashkenazim who had acquired a command of Arabic, such as Uri Thon, who grew up in Baghdad and Cairo; and youths from the frontier neighborhoods of the mixed cities.[135] A distinction could thus be made between youths from the economic and social elite of the Sephardi community and those who had grown up in economic and social deprivation. The Palmach commanders were not unaware of this distinction.[136]

In many respects, service in the Arab Department allowed young immigrants to maintain the hybrid Jewish-Arab identity they had acquired in their countries of origin. Thus, for example, the pseudonyms they adopted were often their

Arab childhood names in their countries of birth.[137] Yet service in the Palmach also enabled the youths to integrate themselves into the society of the Yishuv and adopt a Sabra identity. It is true that in a number of cultural areas, such as slang and music, the Palmach absorbed elements of their Arab culture that were subsequently passed on to Hebrew culture as a whole.[138] Nevertheless, the dominant cultural identity the Mista'arvim were expected to assume after completing their mission was a Hebrew, not an Arab, one. Their loyalty was not questioned, as they were committed to the Zionist project and the Yishuv. The members of the Arab Department were not immune to the demand to be integrated into Hebrew culture, or to the negative attitudes toward the Oriental communities. On various occasions, the members encountered a cool reception in the kibbutzim. Moreover, during their time in the kibbutzim they rarely developed social relations with the members of the host communities. The members of the department sought to explain this by noting that the kibbutz members were nervous about possible romantic connections between youths of Oriental descent and the women in the community. As Gamliel Cohen, one of the leading members of the department, noted years later, however, the underlying problem was the kibbutz members' feeling that the youths were alien and different. Cohen argued that the same attitude was apparent during the absorption of Oriental children in the kibbutzim, in comparison to the treatment of children of European origin.[139]

Encounters between members of the Arab Department and the Muslim and Christian Arab population also exposed their hybrid identity as they moved—in some cases for many years—between different communities and between their Hebrew and Arab identities. During operations outside the borders of Palestine, they were required to use a cover story that could explain their Palestinian Arabic dialect. Some of those stationed in Beirut or Damascus chose to present themselves as Palestinian refugees. Shimon Harosh (Horesh), for example, was born in 1926 in the Manshiyya neighborhood on the border between Tel Aviv and Jaffa and attended St. Joseph's School in Jaffa. In May 1948 he traveled to Lebanon and Damascus disguised as a Palestinian refugee from Safed.[140] Meanwhile, members of the Arab Department who were active among the Palestinian population and whose Arabic accent was that of a neighboring country often presented themselves as immigrant workers from Syria or Egypt.[141] The members of the Arab Department were also well aware of the sometimes considerable differences among the Arabic dialects of different areas within Palestine, as well as between the speech of urban dwellers and villagers.[142]

The Mista'arvim sent regular reports to the Palmach headquarters, and those were also forwarded to the Arab Bureau of the Political Department of the Jewish Agency and to the Haganah's Intelligence Service. The reports mentioned the suspicious attitudes prevalent among the Arab population toward Oriental and Yemenite Jews, who were often suspected of sabotage or intelligence activities. In addition, Palestinian Arab refugees in the Arab countries were suspected of being Jews in disguise. Such suspicion about the mixing (instead of the exchange) of identities between Jews and Palestinian Arabs, or between Jewish and Muslim Palestinian refugees, is a powerful illustration of the complexity of relations between the two peoples during the Mandatory period. The reports of the Mista'arvim thus enhance our understanding of attitudes among the Arab population in the mixed cities during the 1948 war and among the Palestinian refugees in the Arab countries. In most cases, the Mista'arvim became integrated into the lower socioeconomic classes within the Arab population and reported on the mood in these classes, rather than among the Arab elite.

The Mista'arvim of the Arab Department frequented streets and markets; sat in cafés; went to nightclubs; and worked in ports, factories, and car repair shops. They listened to Friday sermons in the mosques and participated in political demonstrations and public events. While their specific perspective and the aspects they chose to emphasize were based on their military roles, their reports nevertheless provide important insights into the prevailing mood and the impact of the security situation on daily life, as well as into the deteriorating relations between Jews and Arabs. In October 1947, shortly before the outbreak of war, members of the Arab Department were sent on reconnaissance missions in the main centers of the Palestinian population in Haifa, Safed, and Tiberias. Gamliel Cohen described his impressions from these missions in the following terms: "With a considerable measure of enthusiasm, I described the evidence of coexistence in Tiberias: Jews and Arabs sitting alongside each other around the tables at a restaurant on the shore of the Sea of Galilee, talking among themselves in Arabic peppered with Hebrew words." Tiberias was described as a city that was indifferent to the problems facing Palestine, where the residents sat on their balconies reading books; and as a city where Jews and Arabs met in the bathhouse and lived next to each other in the same buildings.[143]

The members of the Arab Department also provided personal testimony regarding the significance of the Palestinian Nakba. The fascinating testimony of the Mista'arev Havakuk (Hawla) Cohen presents the perspective of an Oriental Jew, disguised as a Palestinian Arab, reflecting on the experience of being a refugee during the 1948 war. Cohen was born in Yemen but was raised from the age of two in the Yemenite neighborhood in the east of Rishon Lezion. He learned Arabic from his Arab friends who worked in the orchards and vineyards around the colony.[144] Cohen was sent on a mission in the mixed neighborhoods of Haifa and the Arab sections of the city, disguised as an Arab. He wrote that on the Arab street it was possible to find "expressions of affection for Jews and a genuine desire to live with them in peace and fellowship."[145] On April 22, 1948, after the Haganah launched an offensive in Haifa, Cohen described the exchanges of gunfire in the Wadi Nisnas neighborhood and the reactions of the Arab residents with whom he was sitting in one of the city's cafés to the Haganah mortar attack. He then described the scenes at the eastern gate to the port of Haifa: "There we saw a sad and appalling sight. Hundreds of men, women, and children stood on the jetty waiting to board boats that were transferring them to Acre. Women, children, and the elderly were given first place."[146]

The next day, Cohen toured the mainly Arab downtown section of Haifa, which had by then been abandoned and was deserted. He was stopped by Haganah members and transferred to the Haganah base in Hadar Hacarmel together with other Arabs. With his comrade from the Arab Department, Yitzhak Shushan, Cohen boarded a bus for Beirut. The two men pretended to be Palestinian refugees from Haifa.[147] In Beirut Cohen met Shaul Carmeli, who had also been in downtown Haifa during the fighting and had boarded one of the ships heading to Beirut with Palestinian refugees.[148] Cohen spent several months in Beirut, mingling with young people and sports fans in the city. His acquaintances in Beirut included Palestinian refugees he had met in Haifa. He was known in the city as "the dark Palestinian."[149] After the war Cohen served in the Israeli military intelligence, and in 1951, at the age of twenty-four, he was killed in the Sdom area during an intelligence operation.

Cohen's reports show that his work went beyond intelligence operations in their narrow sense. His testimony is a useful source regarding the work of the Mista'arvim and the vacillating personal identity of the members of the Arab Department, and it also serves as historical evidence and testimony by virtue of the fact that they were intimately involved, both as actual participants and as documenters, in the changing public mood and atmosphere during the 1948 war. The activities and reports of Cohen and his comrades thus reveal that their work had an element of mediation between identities and cultures, as well as elements of documentation and commemoration. The man who was mainly responsible for training them for these activities, and who embodied the role of the Mista'arev as a cultural mediator, was Shimon Somekh, known as Sama'an (a nickname was taken from his family's original Arabic surname).

Arab Jews: Between Arab and Hebrew Identities

Somekh was one of the most senior and important figures in the Palmach's Arab Department.[150] He was born in Iraq in 1916 and completed his high school studies in Baghdad. He left home at the age of seventeen and, with his friend Rahamim Sbiro, set out in a taxi for Syria. From Damascus he reached Tel Aviv via Rosh Pina and Beit Shean. Sama'an worked in the orchards of Petach Tikva and began to study at Mikveh Israel agricultural school. He followed in the footsteps of his uncle Eliyahu Agassi, whose activities were discussed in detail in previous chapters, and moved to Haifa, teaching Arabic in the kibbutzim of the Jezreel Valley. This teaching program was funded, as discussed in chapter 4, by the Arab Bureau of the Political Department of the Jewish Agency, headed by Eliyahu Sasson. In 1942, while teaching in Kibbutz Mishmar Ha'emek, Somekh was recruited to the Palmach by Allon, and later he joined the Syrian Department. After the department was disbanded, he joined the Palmach's Arab Department and was appointed the chief instructor and head of training for the Mista'arvim. Somekh was effectively responsible for recruiting, training, and guiding the Mista'arvim; he formulated the basic principles shaping their work and its professional characteristics in military and intelligence terms.[151]

Somekh's "theory of the Mista'arvim" stated that a candidate for this work "must, above all, be a member of an Oriental Jewish community originating in one of the neighboring Arab countries or North Africa; his language and mother tongue should be Arabic; and he must have maintained contact with his Arab neighbors in his country of origin or lived alongside or among them."[152] This definition is very similar to the way the Iraqi-born writer and literary scholar Sasson Somekh defined an Arab Jew, even though the context is obviously very different.[153] The contents of the course for the Mista'arvim, as developed by Shimon Somekh, reflect the fact that the Mista'arev must be able to assimilate himself into a Muslim population, drawing on his familiarity with the foundations of Islam and the customs of rural and urban Arab society. For Somekh, a Mista'arev "is not merely a dark-faced youth with a mustache who speaks Arabic and appears in an Arab environment, drinking coffee, staying for a moment or two, and then moving off. Being a Mista'arev means appearing as an Arab in every respect, in language, conduct, residence, work, and leisure, with a suitable cover story and with documents supporting his biography and background."[154]

Testimonies of and interviews with the members of the Arab Department repeatedly emphasize Somekh's unique character and status in the department, as well as the influence he exerted on those he trained. Ya'akuba Cohen commented: "He was completely different from us. He was polite. He was always scrupulously well dressed. We were rough, very loud, and very wild: Israeli Sabras, noisy and disheveled. He was extremely courteous and came from a very well-placed and educated background. We were savage Palmachniks. But he fit in with us excellently. He didn't take part in our hijinks—he was much more reserved. Even his smiles were very cautious. Very polite and well mannered, he was an Arabic teacher."[155] In other words, he was the quintessential Arab Jew. Somekh was a teacher and guide, rather than a commander, and this was probably one of the reasons for the special status he enjoyed in the department, as well as for the fact that he was not appointed its commander. In a rare interview, Somekh used the metaphor of a teacher and his students to describe the way he trained the young recruits to the department, mentioning his own background as an Arabic teacher.[156] The education and social background of most of the members of the Arab Department, together with the unique nature of the Palmach, thus gave Somekh's role an educational, as well as a military, significance.

Somekh used his own cultural background in teaching and training the Mista'aravim. He was typical of the generation of Iraqi Jews born in the 1920s. Members of this group grew up under the benign regime of King Faisal I and were highly active in the social and cultural life of Iraq. During the 1930s and 1940s, as Arab nationalism became an increasingly powerful force as part of the anticolonial struggle, some members of this generation joined the Zionist underground movement, while others became active in the Iraqi Communist Party. The education and upbringing of this generation allowed those who immigrated to Palestine to find a place as Arabic-language teachers in the Yishuv. As mentioned above, Somekh's uncle Eliyahu Agassi encouraged him to work as a teacher in the kibbutzim in the Haifa District. And Sasson enabled Somekh to complete his studies in Islam with Sheikh Yahya al-Ansari.[157]

Somekh's relationship with Agassi and Sasson, two prominent figures in the field of Jewish-Arab relations during the Mandatory period, was possible thanks to his membership in Iraqi Jewish intellectual circles. Before leaving Baghdad, Somekh had been a member of the Ahi'ever Association.[158] This was a cultural society founded in the early 1930s by Jewish youths in Baghdad, most of whom attended the Shamash, Alliance Israélite Universelle, and Rachel Shahamon schools. The association sought to disseminate Hebrew culture and promote Zionist ideals among its members. It maintained a Hebrew library, held meetings, and ran physical training programs.[159]

The activities of the Ahi'ever association should be seen in the context of the broad-based Arab cultural resurgence in the 1920s among the Jews of Iraq. As Reuven Snir discussed in detail, this cultural revival was manifested in the growing involvement of Jewish intellectuals in shaping Arab culture, from a standpoint of close identification with an Iraqi national identity. This cultural background also facilitated the growth of the Ahi'ever association.[160] The association remained active until 1939, and its members were among the founders of the Hehalutz movement in Iraq.[161] As a product of this Zionist and cultural involvement, and with the encouragement of Reuven Shiloah, who taught Hebrew in Baghdad, and David Yellin, who met with the members of the association, some of them began to emigrate to Palestine.[162] As noted, these included Shimon Somekh and Rahamim Sbiro.

Another group of Ahi'ever members who left Iraq in 1934 included Ezra Meni, Shaul Sela, and Avraham Sharoni (also mentioned in chapter 3). Meni had served as the treasurer of the association; Sharoni had also served as its treasurer and its librarian. Both young men were graduates of Rachel Shahamon School.[163] After arriving in Palestine, Meni and Sharoni worked in the orchards of the Sharon region, like Shimon Somekh. They also taught Arabic in kibbutzim in the Jezreel Valley, the Jordan Valley, and at the Galilee High School in Tiberias. While working as an Arabic teacher, Sharoni was recruited into the Syria Department, and in 1942 he was sent to Beirut disguised as a representative of the Solel Boneh Construction Company.[164] In 1945 he began to study Arabic language and literature at the Hebrew University; he later held various positions, such as a teacher of Arabic at the Hebrew Reali School in Haifa. With his background as an Arabic teacher and a Mista'arev, Sharoni joined the Haganah's Intelligence Service and worked on wiretapping conversations between Palestinian leaders and leaders of Arab countries during the 1948 war.[165]

Former members of the Ahi'ever association and the Hehalutz movement in Iraq found therefore their place in the Yishuv not only in the Palmach's Arab Department, but also in Haganah's Intelligence Service. Meni and Sharoni (like Shaul Sela, another member of Ahi'ever who came to Palestine in the same group) moved from the wiretapping unit to the Intelligence Division of the IDF, where they served as senior Arabic-Hebrew translators. Sharoni later headed a team that wrote an Arabic-Hebrew dictionary of modern and classical literary Arabic. Meni taught Arabic at the Balfour School in Tel Aviv before joining the Haganah's Intelligence Service; in 1976 he was awarded the Israel Prize for linguistics for his dictionaries of Arabic military terms with Hebrew translations.[166]

Meir Dahan is another example of an Arabic teacher who taught in the kibbutzim of the Jordan Valley as part of the Jewish Agency program directed by Sasson, before later serving in the Haganah's wiretapping unit during the 1948 war. Dahan, however, was a native of Palestine. He was born in Tiberias in 1899 and was among the first to volunteer for the Jewish Brigade during World War I. In 1926, after completing his studies at the teacher training seminar in Jerusalem, Dahan taught Hebrew in Egypt, where he lived until 1942. After returning to Palestine he joined the kibbutz Kvutzat Kinneret and taught Arabic in the kibbutzim of the Jezreel Valley, at evening classes for policemen in Tiberias, and to Jewish mukhtars in the Galilee.[167] After returning from his protracted stay in Egypt, Dahan wrote of the need to encourage Jewish-Arab rapprochement. He advocated inviting Arabic teachers from the neighboring countries, particularly Egypt, to teach Arabic classes in Jewish elementary and high schools.[168]

Gil Eyal, who examined the phenomenon of the Mista'arvim as a manifestation of the hybrid Jewish-Arab identity, noted that Oriental immigrants from the Arab countries were unfamiliar with Palestinian Arab culture and society and with the patterns of Jewish-Arab coexistence in Palestine. In addition, Eyal argues that the familiarity of these young men with the Arab culture of their own countries of origin was also relatively superficial.[169] However, the personal backgrounds of the Mista'arvim—not only those who came from intellectual circles such as the Ahi'ever Association, like Shimon Somekh and Sharoni— show that the Oriental Jews who served in the Arab Department of the Palmach certainly viewed themselves as part of a cultural and communal expanse that served as the arena for extensive social, economic, and cultural contacts between Jews and Arabs. Indeed, some of the members of the Arab Department had a partial command of Arabic and of Muslim culture, and most of them had not completed their education, due to their economic circumstances. Nevertheless, their experiences as Oriental Jews who grew up in families that emigrated from Arab countries and lived in the frontier neighborhoods of the mixed cities enabled them to maintain, at least partially, their hybrid Jewish-Arab identity. It is therefore not surprising that the Mista'arvim focused their activities on the common Arab masses rather than the elite (despite Sasson's reservations about that approach).

In May 1987, former members of the Arab Department appeared on a panel that was held in the Intelligence Heritage and Commemoration Center in Israel. Among other questions, the panelists were asked whether it was not a historical tragedy that the Yishuv had made this social group that had at least the linguistic ability to engage in dialogue with Arabs instead fight against the Arabs.[170] The members of the department on the panel chose not reply to this question. They showed an unswerving devotion to Zionist ideals, their own military past, and the security missions they carried out. The unanswered question raised during the panel reflects what Yonatan Mendel refers to as a tension between "Arabic in the service of peace" and "Arabic in the service of security."[171]

But as we have seen, Shimon Somekh and Sharoni represented a group of Arab Jews who did not see any contradiction between the use of Arabic to promote peace and its use for security purposes. They are typical of a generation of Jews in the Middle East whose members were uprooted from their cultural and social milieu and who subsequently attempted to maintain a Jewish-Arab identify in Mandatory Palestine. These Jews and the people they trained, whether born in neighboring Arab countries or natives of Palestine, repeatedly crossed the local and regional borders between Jews and Arabs, borders along which they had been raised and with which they were thoroughly familiar. While doing so, they also crossed the bridges their mentors had struggled to maintain between Baghdad and Jaffa, the Arab Jew and the Hebrew Sabra, the frontier neighborhoods and the rural collective settlements, and Hebrew and Arab cultures.

Service in the Palmach's Arab Department and in the Haganah's Intelligence Service also facilitated the creation of a connection between the local space and the regional domain. Intelligence work not only involved translation, monitoring Arabic-language broadcasts, and reading Arab newspapers, but it also provided real contacts with the countries of the Levant beyond the borders of Palestine. At this time, prior to 1948, this regional domain still constituted a single, open expanse, but the young men who had left Iraq, Syria, and other Arab countries had no possibility of returning to their former countries of residence. They had lost their citizenship, their connections with their families had been disrupted, and had they returned as tourists they would have been arrested. Their activities as Mista'arvim thus offered them a chance to cross the borders in the region, often disguised, and to reconnect with their families or communities.

In many cases, the crossing of borders was intended to support the actions of the Zionist movement in Arab countries, to maintain contacts with Jewish communities in the Muslim lands, or to collect military intelligence. Other operations, however, sought to smuggle Jewish immigrants across borders, and these actions often included aspects of Jewish-Arab cooperation, albeit of an illegal character. Immigrants who reached Lebanon, Syria, and Iraq were taken by vehicles to the northern border area and were then smuggled into one of the kibbutzim in the Upper Galilee. An additional method of entry was by boat, from Beirut to Acre.[172] Some five thousand Jews came to Palestine during the 1940s using this route. Members of the Palmach's Arab Department cooperated with Arab smugglers, who took the immigrants very close to the border. The Mista'arvim were responsible for receiving the immigrants from the Arabs and gathering them at Kibbutz Ayelet Hashahar, from where they were dispersed among the kibbutzim of the Upper Galilee. A detailed discussion of this operation is beyond the scope of this book, but it deserves mention as a further example of the ways in which the borders in the Middle East were crossed, with cooperation between people on both sides as part of a smuggling chain that crossed boundaries and nationalities.[173]

The Oriental Neighborhoods and the Suburban Military Units

In the 1980s, Haim Hefer, one of the most famous writers and songwriters of the Palmach, offered the following description of the members of the Arab Department: "'You black guys'—that's what we called them, and we meant it admiringly. They really knew the land and its people, without borders or divides. They came to us from impoverished alleyways, borderline neighborhoods, and poor families. Yemenite immigrants, Sephardim, Iraqis, and Egyptians—we knew their background and their ethnic origin."[174] As we have seen, this is an accurate description of the background of most of the members of the Arab Department.

The Palmach made a concerted effort to recruit people from the frontier neighborhoods from 1942 to 1944. This effort came to be known as "the Popular Palmach" (as opposed to refined or elitist), and it resulted in the recruiting of dozens of young men and women from these neighborhoods into the Palmach's various units. The Palmach recruiters met with some 1,400 youths during the drive. The recruiters received assistance from the youth movement Hano'ar Ha'oved and the Tel Aviv Social Work Department. In the three main cities—Jerusalem, Tel Aviv, and Haifa—they visited factories where Oriental youths were employed; evening schools; and branches of Hano'ar Ha'oved in the neighborhoods of Tel Aviv, particularly in Kerem Hatemanim and Hatikvah. Most of the 150 recruits came from two distinct groups: members of Hano'ar Ha'oved and the children of new immigrants from Muslim countries who were not involved in any organized activities and were considered neglected youth. The recruits were absorbed into almost all the units of the Palmach but were grouped together in their own squads.[175]

The recruitment of members of Hano'ar Ha'oved to the Palmach was not free of stereotypical and paternalistic aspects. The Palmach activists involved in the recruitment drive described the Oriental youth as neglected, abandoned, uneducated, lacking Zionist awareness, and indifferent to the work of the Yishuv. These descriptions were consistent with the perception of urban youths as ideologically inferior to the pioneering youths in the rural collective settlements. The historian Shlomit Keren explains in her research on this issue that the Palmach commanders saw their work as nothing less than the rescuing of Oriental youths to channel them toward pioneering self-realization and draw them into the pioneering ideology and culture of the labor Zionist movement.[176] The Palmach recruiters and commanders described their encounters with the youths in the frontier neighborhoods as introductions to an alien and strange world. They felt that the Oriental youths suffered from an inferiority complex and maintained a Diaspora-like view of the world.[177] This attitude toward the new recruits, who were described as "the abandoned youths," was also manifested in the doubts expressed by some of the Palmach commanders about the ability of the Oriental youths to become integrated into the ranks of the Palmach.[178]

At the beginning of 1944, the youths recruited from the frontier neighborhoods were sent to a Palmach intake camp established in Kibbutz Ayelet Hashahar. The first company commander at the intake camp was Moshe Khalfon, the son of Abraham Khalfon (discussed in chapter 2), who served as the secretary of the municipality of Haifa, the secretary of the local Jewish community committee in that city, and chairman of the Council of the Sephardi Community in Haifa. Moshe Khalfon, who became one of the first recruits to the Palmach after studying at Kadoorie Agricultural School, described his trainees at the intake camp as primarily Yemenites from the neighborhoods of Tel Aviv and Jerusalem. They had been working for a living and had completed elementary, but not secondary, school. Khalfon wrote:

> Almost all the recruits show clear signs of abandonment and neglect. For years they have wandered around the streets of the cities, engaging in various and strange vocations without any supervision or care, and without any attention from the public. They grew up wild, subject to the influence of fleeting mood swings on the street, to superficial thought, and to a primitive understanding of political events. They were sometimes swallowed up in Beitar or the Palestine Communist Party and they could regularly be found in places of entertainment. . . . They were mature and had the wisdom of experience—mature before their time, from the street corners and sidewalks, in the suburbs, in the outskirts of the major cities. Jewish youths in their own Land, they were forgotten by the organized Yishuv and left to their own devices. Who would care for them and redeem them? How did

we permit ourselves to abandon our most important strength—thousands upon thousands of youths from the second generation?! It is impossible not to address this question to us all, to the Zionist movement and the Yishuv, to any feeling and thinking person among us![179]

These comments are reminiscent of the repeated claims during the Mandatory period of the connection between the neglect and abandonment of Oriental youth in the frontier neighborhoods and their lack of Zionist awareness and tendency to join the Irpun and Lehi organizations. Through its activities in the neighborhoods, the Palmach sought to prove that it was open to all sections of the Yishuv and to people from all classes and ethnic backgrounds. Khalfon and his comrades carried out their mission in a way that was very similar to the methods used by Somekh in the Arab Department, including similar patterns of counseling and Zionist education, as well as military training. The counselors did their best to give each recruit personal attention to encourage all of them to act out of a sense of conviction, rather than relying solely on military authority and army discipline. "We must love them and devote ourselves to them," Khalfon wrote. "We must understand them, build on their faith and affection, and step by step transcend with them."[180]

During the 1940s, youth were recruited from the frontier neighborhoods not only by the Palmach, but also by the Haganah. In Jerusalem, the efforts to reach out to the suburban youth, as the youths in the frontier neighborhoods were called, led to the formation of a Youth Battalion named the Judea Battalion, whose members were youths from the Hano'ar Ha'oved and the frontier neighborhoods in the city. The battalion had some 600 members, most of whom were Mizrahim. In Haifa, too, most of the members of Hano'ar Ha'oved who joined the Youth Battalions came from Oriental families in the frontier and mixed neighborhoods.[181]

In Tel Aviv, the suburban youth were recruited mainly to the Shahar Association (Agudat Hashahr), which initially operated as an autonomous body distinct from the Youth Battalions. The association's goal was "to penetrate the frontier neighborhoods and through cultural, educational, and sporting activities raise the standard of the local youth."[182] This approach to the frontier neighborhoods in quasimilitary terms and this view of their young people as in need of saving from their current social and cultural condition were far from unique at that time. The perception that this recruitment activity achieved both educational and political goals was embodied in the association's effort "to develop outreach activities in the Zionist field and to direct the youth to proper channels of self-fulfillment, thereby extracting them from the harmful influence of the secessionists and various hoodlums."[183]

The association worked with youth in the neighborhoods of Tel Aviv, including Kerem Hatemanim, Manashiyya, Montefiore, Florentine, Shapira, and Hatikvah. Like the original name of the Palmach's Arab Department (Shahar), the association's name also alluded to the epithet "blacks," reflecting its focus on members of the Oriental communities. The commander of the Shahar Association was Moshe Idelberg, a member of the Mapam Party and of the secretariat of the Tel Aviv Workers' Council, and the former Haganah commander in the Hatikvah neighborhood. The association worked with some 1,800 youths from the southern neighborhoods of Tel Aviv, and Idelberg explained that its goal was to educate the youths about citizenship, pioneering, and state security.[184] The youths were guided by volunteers and by instructors from the Youth Battalions, the Haganah's Field Corps, and the Palmach.[185] Dozens of youth clubs were established in the neighborhoods of Tel Aviv. The clubs offered lectures; cultural activities, such as attending concerts and plays; tours and outings around the country; and participation in sports events and physical training. The association aimed to reach out to some 14,000 youths in the neighborhoods of Tel Aviv, approximately 5,000 of whom were defined as neglected youth and were under the care of the Tel Aviv Social Work Department.[186]

The function of the Shahar Association of preparing Oriental youths in the frontier neighborhoods for service in Haganah units was reflected in the fact that some 800 of the association's members joined the Haganah, and later the IDF.[187] The Haganah organized its units in Tel Aviv to ensure that its members from the frontier neighborhoods were recruited into companies operating in the areas in which they lived. To do this, the Haganah received assistance from the neighborhood committees. Three suburban companies (*plugot haparvarim*) were formed and grouped into a battalion under the auspices of the Haganah's Field Corps.[188] One company was responsible for the area that included the neighborhoods of Hatikvah and Ezra; another operated in the Montefiore neighborhood; and the third was responsible for Kerem Hatemanim and Manashiyya.

In January 1948, most of the suburban companies of the Field Corps were merged into the 53rd Battalion of the Giv'ati Brigade, which was called the Suburbs Battalion.[189] Its commander was Yitzhak Pundak, who had served in the early 1940s as the Youth Battalions commander in Tel Aviv. The soldiers of the Suburbs Battalion were stationed along the front line between Jaffa and Tel Aviv. Their positions separated the two cities and essentially defined the area in which the soldiers lived. As the fighting intensified on both sides of the border, thousands of Jewish and Arab residents left their homes and became refugees. As residents of the peripheral and southern neighborhoods of Tel Aviv, the soldiers now found themselves fighting against their Palestinian neighbors for control of their shared domain. In the second stage of the war, after the surrender of Jaffa, the battalion fought against Egyptian forces on the southern front.[190]

The commemorative and documentary literature about the Suburbs Battalion repeatedly emphasizes the difficult economic background of the recruits and the function of the battalion as a melting pot in which Ashkenazim and Sephardim, new immigrants and natives, mingled together. This literature claims that the manner in which the soldiers of the battalion fought—and in some cases died, as in the battles of Negba and Nitzanim—reflects the successful Israeli concept of intermingling of the exiles (*mizug galuyot*) as well as the spirit of self-sacrifice among the soldiers from the frontier neighborhoods.[191] The biographies of the fallen members of the battalion generally describe youths who had worked for their living, most of whom had completed only elementary school, and who came from families with a large number of children. Ze'ev Shaham, the commander of the 1st Company in the Suburbs Battalion, described his soldiers as youths who "lived in the poor neighborhoods of Tel Aviv (Hatikvah, Shapira, and Kerem Hatemanim)" and who "have left a significant presence in the military cemeteries of the south and the Negev."[192]

Following their transition from the Shahar Association to the Suburbs Battalion, youth from the peripheral neighborhoods thus played a decisive role in the war in Jaffa and on the southern front. After facing criticism throughout the Mandatory period regarding their Zionist awareness and contribution to the Zionist struggle, they now became an integrated part of the 1948 Generation that fought to establish the State of Israel. In February 1949 one of the members of the Shahar Association who lived in Kerem Hatemanim wrote: "I looked over you, the ruins of Jaffa. From a high roof, I looked over the ruins of Jaffa. This Jaffa, my neighboring city, which was resoundingly defeated with no chance of revival. I looked at the ruins . . . at the destruction. . . . Now I feel no fear. I could stand tall and proud and raise my head."[193] So these youths, who had grown up in an area of confrontation and coexistence between Tel Aviv and Jaffa during the Mandatory period, now helped put an end to the area's existence and to any form of coexistence and neighborly relations in years to come.

Epilogue

The funeral of Avinoam Yellin was held in Jerusalem on October 24, 1937. Thousands of Jewish Jerusalemites honored one of the city's most prominent residents, who had been killed a few days before by a Palestinian assassin. Yellin had been shot outside his office in the British Mandatory government's Education Department. He was the son of David Yellin and the grandson of Rabbi Yehiel Michal Pines. Avinoam Yellin was born and raised in Jerusalem, was educated at Cambridge University, and had been a scholar of the Cairo Geniza and Arabic language and literature. He had also been a Hebrew and Arabic teacher and an inspector of Hebrew education for the British Mandatory government. Eulogies were delivered at Yellin's funeral by the Sephardi Chief Rabbi Ya'acov Meir; Yosef Yoel Rivlin, the president of the Association of Teachers; the translator Yitzhak 'Abadi; and the writer and scholar Yosef Meyuchas; among others.[1]

These eulogizers came from a circle of intellectuals, both Ashkenazim and Sephardim, who were born in Palestine. They mourned one of the leading exponents of the Jewish-Arab culture that had developed in the country during the latter years of the Ottoman era and in the Mandatory period. Yellin's funeral marked the gradual passing of the generation of Sephardi and Oriental leaders and intellectuals who had struggled to adapt to their evolving status among the Jewish population after World War I. This cadre of leaders had sought to enhance their political and social influence within the Yishuv, in part by emphasizing their historical role as mediators between Jews and Arabs. Yellin's life and the circumstances of his death epitomize a process of Jewish-Arab cultural dialogue side by side with the escalation of the Jewish-Arab conflict in Mandatory Palestine. It is this complex and nuanced dynamic that has been scrutinized in this book.

The Arab Revolt provided a powerful reminder of the impact of the national conflict in Palestine on the development of Jewish-Arab relations. As discussed in chapter 5, Itamar Ben-Avi's comment in 1936 about the need for "twin cities, not mixed cities," reflected the physical, economic, and social changes that occurred in the late 1930s, as well as the accompanying changes in attitudes about the intensifying conflict.[2] However, despite the growing trend toward segregation between the two national communities in Mandatory Palestine, Jews and Arabs continued to live with and alongside each other until the 1948 war. The frontier neighborhoods of the mixed cities, where most of the Oriental Jews lived, were characterized simultaneously by poverty, violence, and Jewish-Arab coexistence. These neighborhoods illustrated the conflict and segregation, on the one hand, and the cooperation and integration, on the other hand, that could be found primarily in the mixed cities. Within this everyday complex reality, Sephardi and Oriental Jews found themselves in a buffer zone between distinct national cultures and societies, and in a constant struggle between neighborly relations and national tension.

The 1930s saw a clear process of identification with the Zionist enterprise among Sephardi and Oriental Jews. In contrast, the cultural, economic, and social definition of the Sephardim was less clear, as were their patterns of collective political organization. The traditional tendency of the leaders of the Sephardi and Oriental Jewish communities in Palestine to refrain from using a categorical division between Jews and Arabs, between religious and secular Jews, and between those who did and those who did not possess a national conscience was also apparent in their attitudes about the culture and socioeconomic status of Oriental Jews. The socioeconomic condition of the Sephardi Jews and Jews who immigrated from Yemen and other Arab and Islamic countries illustrated the complex structure of the Oriental communities, with their distinct internal class distinctions and hierarchies. The unusual nature of that structure was particularly apparent when the Sephardi and Oriental elites in Jerusalem and other cities were compared to the Oriental Jews who lived alongside Arabs in the frontier neighborhoods and mixed cities. The living conditions and lifestyle of Oriental Jews in the latter group were closer to those of their Arab neighbors than to those of their fellow Jews. Accordingly, life on the border acquired not only a symbolic significance, but also a weight that stretched the overall fabric of Jewish-Arab relations in Mandatory Palestine. The border and frontier neighborhoods mirrored the peripheral status of Sephardi and Oriental Jews in the body politic of the Yishuv.

As this book has discussed, the leadership of the Oriental Jews was dominated by Sephardi Jews, who were natives of Palestine, and by Jews from Arab countries, who felt equally comfortable in Palestine and beyond its borders. This leadership developed during the Mandatory years, with the Association of the

Pioneers of the East serving as its main unifying organization. Despite the key role played by the Council of the Sephardi Community in Jerusalem, it was the Association of the Pioneers of the East that served as the core organization for Sephardi and Oriental political and social actions and for activities in a range of fields. The ethnic dimension of these activities undoubtedly limited the range of political actions open to the Association of the Pioneers of the East, and it also provoked fierce criticism from the Labor Zionist leadership of the Yishuv, including accusations of separatism and of jeopardizing the Zionist enterprise and the solidarity of the Yishuv. From the perspective of the Sephardi and Oriental communities, however, this type of organizational structure offered the potential to enhance their involvement in the politics of the Yishuv. The tendency to adhere to the familiar patterns of political action that emerged during the Ottoman period, based on the "politics of the notables" and on political contacts between officials and the leaders of the different religious communities, embodied a belief that this framework offered a chance to maintain cordial and peaceful relations between Jews and Arabs. Accordingly, it is not surprising that exponents of Palestinian nationalism embraced this approach, claiming that Oriental Jews were not supporters of Zionism and advocating that the various religious communities be unified under a Palestinian Arab nation based on loyalty to the common homeland.

In response to their inferior status in the institutions of the Zionist movement and the Yishuv following World War I, and with the intensification of the national conflict, the Sephardi and Oriental leaders sought to emphasize their suitability for the role of mediators between Jews and Arabs. The activists in the Association of the Pioneers of the East and other organizations expressed various opinions about the Arab Question. As we have seen, some of them identified with the right wing in the Yishuv, while others were affiliated with the labor movement. Nevertheless, they all believed in the ability of Oriental Jews to promote a rapprochement between Jews and Arabs in different fields, even though they differed in their political ways of achieving this goal.

Throughout the Mandatory period, the Council of the Sephardi Community in Jerusalem, the Association of the Pioneers of the East, and various other Sephardi and Oriental organizations consistently claimed that they were being excluded from the Yishuv institutions' process of making decisions about the Arab Question and from efforts to improve Jewish-Arab relations. However, various individuals, including key activists, were appointed to positions in the national institutions of the Yishuv that dealt with the Arab Question. These institutions included the United Bureau, the Arab Bureau of the Jewish Agency's

Political Department, the Arab Department of the Histadrut, and the Arab Department of the Palmach.

The creation and work of the Arab Department of the Palmach demonstrated the emergence of a new generation of Sephardi and Oriental Jews in the 1930s and 1940s and its members' involvement in the security apparatus of the Yishuv. The emergence of this generation also highlighted the power struggles between the Oriental and Sephardi components of the Middle Eastern Jewish communities and between the main centers of this population in Jerusalem and Tel Aviv. The 1930s and 1940s also saw efforts to enhance Zionist awareness, especially among Sephardi and Oriental youths, such as the attempts made to organize those youths in the Degel Zion youth movement and the Sephardi Labor Organization into organizations separate from those of the dominant Histadrut. These attempts at organization included calls to involve young people and workers in activities intended to strengthen the relations between Jews and Arabs, with particular emphasis on the importance of economic and social ties. The promotion of neighborly relations was a top priority of the Arab Bureau of the Jewish Agency's Political Department. Even though these activities had clear political and security objectives, they also had social and cultural goals and, in many ways, complemented each other.

The communal and religious organizations of the Sephardi and Oriental Jewish communities in Palestine and their relations with their Arab neighbors should also be viewed as a reflection of the patterns of affinity that existed between the Jewish communities and their non-Jewish neighbors in the Arab countries. Rapprochement between Jews and Arabs in Palestine was closely intertwined with the development of relations between Jews and Arabs in the Middle East as a whole. Indeed, throughout the Mandatory period, the Oriental Jewish community in Palestine maintained relationships with the Jewish communities in the neighboring countries. These relationships were based in part on ongoing Jewish immigration to Palestine from these countries and on family ties, religious contacts, and commercial relations. However, the Middle East also served as the arena for cultural bonds and exchanges, including the dispatch of activists from Palestine to the Jewish communities in the surrounding countries; the employment of teachers in schools; the publication of newspaper articles; and participation in the broader cultural and political discourse of the Middle East, in both Jewish and Arab contexts.

These affinities and contacts demonstrate the presence of a cultural community of educated Jews and Arabs who cooperated with each other and exchanged ideas through the Arabic and Hebrew newspapers in Palestine and the Arab countries.

Cultural links were also obvious in the lively debate in the Yishuv about the need for its official institutions to publish newspapers in Arabic and the importance of teaching Arabic to different audiences in the Yishuv. Such discussions also reveal the mediating role that Oriental and Sephardi Jews sought to play in cultural and other contacts between Jews and Arabs. However, they also expose the tension between the commitment to cultural and social rapprochement and the exploitation of these frameworks for security and political needs. In a mobilized society such as the Yishuv, there was inevitably a close link between cultural and educational activities and political and security objectives. The complicated patterns of cultural and political identity were thus manifested in the organizations of the Sephardi and Oriental Jewish communities in Palestine and in the way in which these communities regarded and debated the Arab Question.

The existence of a particular cultural and socioeconomic identity and its political and security aspects and manifestations, combined with the desire to play a mediating role between Jews and Arabs, were also apparent in the younger generation Sephardi and Oriental Jews, as many of those Jews chose to work in the security sphere. The involvement of many of them in military operations carried out by the Irgun and the Lehi, as well as in the Palmach's Arab Department, was primarily the result of the cultural and social affinity between Oriental Jews and Arabs. Thus, a group that considered itself responsible for creating bridges between Jews and Arabs now crossed those bridges for the purposes of sabotage and intelligence gathering. In doing so, however, and despite the clear national dimension of their activities, the Mista'arvim also crossed the very personal boundary between the Arab and Jewish dimensions of their own identities. Thus, their security activities were not devoid of a cultural dimension, as illustrated by the links between teaching Arabic and serving in the intelligence organizations of the Yishuv.

It is particularly important to note that most of the Arabized Jews who served in security-related missions had grown up in the frontier neighborhoods of the mixed cities. In these areas, socioeconomic deprivation and the proximity between Jews and Arabs created many opportunities for encounters between Jewish and Arab youths in Christian missionary schools, on playgrounds, and in many other shared sites. This environment shaped the personal and collective biography of the Oriental youths who were later recruited into the so-called black units of the Palmach and the Haganah. During their security service, these youths crossed existing ethnic borders, but they also played an important role in creating new boundaries between Jews and Arabs and between the State of Israel and its Arab neighbors.

Throughout the Mandatory period, the leaders of the Sephardi and Oriental Jewish communities in Palestine were conscious of the connection between their position on the Arab Question and the developing national conflict in Palestine, on the one hand, and the condition of their fellow Jews in the Arab countries, on the other hand. The leaders of the Jewish communities in the Arab countries were also aware of this connection and of the sensitive issue of the identification of Jews in these countries with the Zionist movement, particularly in the wake of Arab nationalism and the anticolonial struggle. The theme of rescuing the Jews of the Arab countries became a key component in Oriental Jewish discourse during the 1940s. One of the issues discussed in this context was whether the relationship between Muslims and Jews under Islam could be characterized as one of dialogue, coexistence, tolerance, and symbiosis. Another component of this discussion focused on the relations between Jews and Arabs in Palestine. Key Sephardi and Oriental figures sought to challenge the idyllic view of Muslim-Jewish relations and the accompanying claim that it was Zionism that had led to the deterioration of these relations in Palestine. This challenge was certainly due, to a large extent, to a political standpoint that sought to emphasize the Zionist credentials of Oriental Jews and their support for Zionism's goal of establishing a Jewish state. However, it also reflected a desire to emphasize that Oriental Jews, as a community deeply rooted in the history of the region, had had a more complex, nuanced, and often multifaceted experience of Jewish-Muslim relations than the idyllic claims of coexistence suggested. This experience, it was argued, made them ideal candidates to serve as mediators and promoters of a certain kind of coexistence and rapprochement between Jews and Arabs in the cultural, social, and political spheres alike. This discourse was particularly prominent during the twilight of the British Mandatory period, leading up to the outbreak of the 1948 war.

The establishment of the State of Israel sparked a revolutionary change in relations between Jews and Arabs, reversing their relative majority and minority statuses in a way that would shape the condition of Jews and Arabs in the Middle East for generations to come. The 1948 war and the establishment of the State of Israel were accompanied by a local and regional crisis whose ramifications continue to reverberate today. At the same time, the state of emergency of the early days of the State of Israel created new opportunities for the Sephardi and Oriental leadership.[3] The need to help restore the relations with the Palestinians who remained within the borders of the state, and the possibility of helping shape Israeli policy toward the Palestinian Arab minority, allowed Sephardi leaders once again to position themselves as mediators between Jews and Arabs.

However, the post-1948 political context had become radically different from the one discussed in this book. The potential improvement in the political status of the Sephardi and Oriental leaders at the time was also influenced by the immigration of hundreds of thousands of Jews from the Arab countries. The absorption of these Jewish refugees into Israel created a historic opportunity for encounters not only between the well-established Sephardi and Oriental Jewish communities in the country and the Jewish communities of the Arab lands and between the existing Yishuv and the new immigrants, but also between these immigrants and the Palestinian Arab citizens of Israel. The Sephardi and Oriental leaders thus gained access to new arenas of action and influence regarding Jewish-Arab relations and the absorption of Oriental immigrants.

In 1948, after the establishment of the State of Israel, the Israeli Ministry for Minorities was formed. The new ministry—which was led by Bechor-Shalom Sheetrit—included a department for the rehabilitation of the Arab population headed by Moshe Erem, a member of Mapam, as well as an education and outreach department headed by Yehuda Burla. Until it was dismantled in the summer of 1949, the Ministry for Minorities sought to address the urgent civil problems and the severe socioeconomic deprivation facing the Palestinian population in Israel. The officials of the ministry coordinated the response of the other government ministries in such areas as supplies, employment, health, social assistance, and cultural activities among the Palestinian citizens of the state.[4]

The Ministry for Minorities sought to realize the promise of minority rights as presented in Israel's Declaration of Independence and to improve the economic, social, and cultural life of the Arab minority. The ministry also strove to integrate Arab citizens into the life and institutions of the young state and to nurture Jewish-Arab relations. The dismantling of the ministry in the summer of 1949 marked the end of a power struggle between the ministry and the military government. The decision to abolish the ministry represented the victory of a policy that focused on strengthening the state's power over and control and supervision of its Arab minority. The ministry's responsibilities were transferred to the military government, the advisor for Arab affairs in the Prime Minister's Office, and the Minorities Department in the Ministry of the Interior. The Minorities Department was responsible for such tasks as registering the Arab population and distributing their identity cards, establishing local councils and governments in the Arab communities, and planning and developing cultural activities for the Arabs.[5]

A large proportion of the officials in the Minorities Department were Sephardi and Oriental Jews. One of the most notable of these was Avraham Malul,

Nissim Malul's son, who served as the minorities officer in Jaffa and later as a judge at the court in Acre.[6] Like other Sephardi members of his generation who worked among the Arab population in Israel as representatives of the Ministry for Minorities and the Minorities Department of the Ministry of the Interior, Malul demonstrated the continuation of the traditional belief among Oriental Jews that they were best placed to serve as mediators between Jews and Arabs. During the early years of the State of Israel, however, the type of mediation and bridging they were involved in differed dramatically from that type during the Mandatory period in terms of substance, patterns, and goals. Against the background of the fundamental change in the relations between Jews and Arabs, the Minorities Department was part of the control and supervision mechanisms imposed by the military government.

Another area of attention of the Sephardi leaders was the absorption of Jewish immigrants from the Arab countries into the State of Israel. However, the political attempts by the Sephardi and Oriental leaders to lead the immigrants from these countries and to help solve the problems encountered in their integration into Israeli society (the so-called ethnic problem) failed. The Sephardi and Oriental leaders participated in the first elections held in Israel at the beginning of 1949 in a joint party called the List of the Sephardim and Oriental Communities. However, the leadership was divided between its centers in Jerusalem and Tel Aviv and between supporters of Bechor-Shalom Sheetrit and of Eliyahu Eliachar.[7] The leaders of the organizations of the Oriental and Sephardi communities thus proved unable to facilitate the emergence of a political leadership acceptable to the new immigrants. At the same time, similar to the situation during the Mandatory period, Jewish immigrants from Arab countries joined institutions that focused on Jewish-Arab relations, such as the Histadrut's Arab Department. Oriental Jews, particularly from Iraq and Egypt, also joined the editorial boards of Arabic-language newspapers published in Israel.[8] Some were also employed in the radio station the Voice of Israel in Arabic or as Arabic teachers. Together with work in the Israeli intelligence services, such positions gave the immigrants ways to maintain their Jewish-Arab identity in the State of Israel. However, the question of Arab identity and culture and the perception that Oriental Jews could serve as a foundation for local and regional cooperation were largely forgotten in the Israeli melting pot, due in large measure to the dominant and ongoing presence of the Arab-Israeli conflict.

The circumstances surrounding the failure of the Sephardi and Oriental leadership to guide the absorption of Jewish immigrants from Arab countries in the 1950s and those surrounding the dismantling of the Ministry for Minorities after only one year of operation highlight the failure of the approach described by Eliachar in his comments to the United Nations Special Committee on Palestine in 1947 (also quoted in chapter 1). "Having been born in Oriental countries," Eliachar argued, "knowing their customs and languages, their mode of life and their ethics, the Sephardim are called upon to play a greater role in the establishment of harmony and peace through the Middle Eastern countries."[9] However, the argument that Oriental Jews had a historical claim to serve as a bridge between Jews and Arabs lost its validity after 1948. Indeed, to a large extent it was forgotten, as were the voices of the other inhabitants of the Middle East that had once echoed throughout the Levantine locales of the Mandatory period, albeit in a sometimes contradictory manner. Those Oriental Jews who viewed themselves both as natives of the Orient (Bney Ha'aretz) and as natives of the country found themselves displaced as the result of 1948 not only from the Orient but also from their historical position. At the same time the Sephardi and Oriental Jews who sought to cross the geographical boundaries and the boundaries of identity, also contributed, in different ways, to the creation of these boundaries. This book has thus brought these Oriental and indigenous forgotten voices back to center stage, explored and identified the seeming contradictions and ambivalence in their perceptions and identities, and highlighted the often-ignored fact that this Levantine and Mediterranean locale was historically shared by so many people as Oriental neighbors.

Notes

Introduction

1. "A New Spirit—An open letter from Israeli Descendants of the Countries of Islam." "Ruch Jadidah/Ruach Hadasha: Young Mizrahi Israelis' Open Letter to Arab Peers.

2. See, for example, Eyal, *Hasarat hakesem min hamizrah*, 22–23; Hochberg, "The Mediterranean Option"; Ohana, *The Origins of Israeli Mythology*, 182–221; A. Rubinstein, *From Herzl to Rabin*, 54–81; Tal, "Israel in or of the Middle East."

3. See, for example, Gorny, *Zionism and the Arabs*; Heller, *Mibrit shalom le'ichud*.

4. Irwin Cotler, "The Double Nakba," *Jerusalem Post*, June 30, 2008.

5. M. Cohen, "Islam and the Jews." See also Lewis, *The Jews of Islam* and *Islam in History*, 137–52.

6. Memmi, "Who Is an Arab Jew?" For a different version of this text, see Memmi, *Jews and Arabs*, 21–22. For more recent works on this issue, see, for example, Gilbert, *In Ishmael's House*; Weinstock, *Nokhekhut ko arukah*.

7. On the policy of the Zionist movement toward the Arab Question, see, for example, Gorny, *Zionism and the Arabs*; Mandel, *The Arabs and Zionism before World War I*; Shapira, *Land and Power*.

8. On the cultural connections between Palestine and the Levant, see, for example, Alcalay, *After Jews and Arabs*.

9. Tsur, "Hahistoriographya haisraelit vehabe'aya ha'adatit," 19.

10. Bar-On, "Hahistoriographya haisraelit shel hasihsukh haisraeli-'aravi"; Gelber, *Historia, zikaron veta'amula*, 400–403; Shapira, "Hahistoriographya shel hatziyonut vemedinat israel beshishim shnot medina."

11. Horowitz and Lissak, *Origins of the Israeli Polity*, 16–35. For more on the dual-society model and the social and economic differences between Jews and Arabs in Palestine, see Khalidi, *The Iron Cage*, especially. 1–31; Metzer, *The Divided Economy of Mandatory Palestine*.

12. Halamish, "Eretz Israel hamandatorit."

13. Lockman, "Railway Workers and Relational History," 604. For more on this issue, see, for example, Bernstein, *Constructing Boundaries*; Gozanski, *Hitpathut hakapitalism befalestina*; Lockman, *Comrades and Enemies*; Metzer, "Kalkalat eretz Israel beyemei

hamandat"; Segev, *One Palestine, Complete*; Shafir, *Land, Labor and the Origins of the Israeli-Palestinian Conflict*; Smith, *The Roots of Separatism in Palestine*.

14. Halamish, "Eretz Israel hamandatorit."

15. For studies that discuss the connections between Sephardi and Oriental Jews and the Arab Question, see, for example, Alboher, *Hizdahut, histaglut vehistaygut*; M. Behar and Benite, *Modern Middle Eastern Jewish Thought*; Bezalel, *Noladetem Ziyonim*; Haim, *Yihud vehishtalvut*.

16. Razi, "Yehudiot 'arviot?"

17. See, for example, Herzog, *'Adatiyut politit*; Kats, "Zikatam shel sefaradim ubney 'edot hamizrah batnu'ot hadatiyot leumiyot hamizrahi vehapo'el hamizrahi be'eretz Israel 1918–1947"; Levi, "Hape'ilut hapolitit vehairgun shel hakehila hasfaradit bayeshuv ubemedinat Israel, 1945–1955"; Lissak, "Habe'aya ha'adatit veirgunim 'adatiyim bitkufat hayeshuv"; Morag-Talmon, *Ha'eda hasfaradit bitkufat hayeshuv*.

18. On joint Ottoman citizenship, see Campos, *Ottoman Brothers*; J. Cohen, *Becoming Ottomans*.

19. Exceptions are Alboher, *Hizdahut, histaglut vehistaygut*; Bezalel, *Noladetem Ziyonim*; Haim, *Yihud vehishtalvut*; Kats, "Zikatam shel sefaradim ubney 'edot hamizrah batnu'ot hadatiyot leumiyot hamizrahi vehapo'el hamizrahi be'eretz Israel 1918–1947"; Levi, "Hape'ilut hapolitit vehairgun shel hakehila hasfaradit bayeshuv ubemedinat Israel, 1945–1955"; Razi, "Yehudiyot 'arviyot?" and *Yaldei hahefker*.

20. "Memorandum Presented to the Anglo-American Committee of Inquiry on Palestine by the Sephardic Communities in Palestine," February 1946, 6209/10, Jerusalem Municipal Archive, Jerusalem (hereafter JMA).

21. "Hayeshuv ha'ivri besof 1936," *Davar*, February 11, 1937.

22. "Be-1946 hegi'a mispar hayehudim be'eretz Israel le-592,000," *Hamashkif*, September 2, 1946.

23. Lissak, *'Iyunim behistorya hevratit shel Israel*, 43 and 48.

24. Klein, *Lives in Common*, ix–xi and 19–64.

25. For the different terminology that was used in different contexts, see "al-Mu'tamar al-'Arabi al-Yahudi," *Filastin*, August 2, 1938; "Mushkilat Filastin," *Filastin*, August 9, 1938; "Nahna wa-almadaris al-tanawiyah," *Filastin*, February 11, 1945; "Wataniyat al-mahajjir: yahud filastin," *Filastin*, May 30, 1931.

26. Avraham Elmaleh, "Histadrut halutzey hamizrah (hirhurim)," *Doar Hayom*, November 30, 1923. On the term "Musta'arvim," see Ben Zvi, *Mehkarim umekorot*, 15–20; Rozen, "Ma'amad hamusta'arvim vehayahasim bein ha'edot bayeshuv hayehudi be'eretz Israel mishalhey hameah ha-15 ve'ad shalhey hameah ha-17."

27. For more on the frontier, periphery neighborhoods in the mixed cities, see chapter 4.

28. See, for example, Abbasi, *Zefat bitkufat hamandat 1918–1948*; Bernstein, "South of Tel Aviv and North of Jaffa"; Goren, *Shituf betzel 'imut*; Helman, *Or veyam hekifuha*; Kidron, *Bein leom lemakom*; LeVine, *Overthrowing Geography*; Razi, *Yaldei hahefker*.

29. Several studies published in recent years demonstrate the exciting research direc-

tions that are being pursued. See, for example, Ben-Bassat, *Petitioning the Sultan*; Campos, *Ottoman Brothers*; Hillel Cohen, *Tarpat*; Gribetz, *Defining Neighbors*; Halperin, *Babel in Zion*; Jacobson, *From Empire to Empire*; Klein, *Lives in Common*; Lev Tov, "Biluim be-mahloket"; Noy, "Tzmihatan shel praktikot etnografiyot bekerev intelligentsia yehudit se-faradit umizrahit beyerushalyim beshalhey hatkufa ha'othmanit uthilat tkufat hamandat."

30. On the concept of hybridity in relation to the Sephardim, see Eyal, *Hasarat hakesem min hamizrah*, 31–36.

31. For a discussion of Arab-Jewish identity, see, for example, Chetrit, *Intra-Jewish Conflict in Israel*; L. Levy, "Historicizing the Concept of Arab Jews in the *Mashriq*"; Shenhav, *Hayehudim ha'aravim*; Shohat, "Sephardim in Israel; Snir, *'Arviyut, yahadut, tziyonut*; Tamari, "Ishaq al-Shami and the Predicament of the Arab-Jew in Palestine."

32. On the role of Sephardi Jews as mediators between Jews and Arabs, see Eyal, *Hasarat hakesem min hamizrah*, 33–36.

33. For more on this argument, see Shenhav, "Yehudim yotzeu arzot 'arav be'israel," 117–123.

34. Klausner, "Hamizrahi-hama'aravi," 226–27. Unless otherwise indicated, all trans-lations are ours.

35. See, for example, Kramer, introduction, 17–26.

36. For an example of an attempt to integrate Middle Eastern history with the history of Zionism, the Yishuv, and the State of Israel, see Lassner and Troen, *Jews and Muslims in the Arab World*.

37. Bar-On, "Hahistoriographya haisraelit shel hasihsukh haisraeli-'aravi," 315; Gelber, "Ketivet toldot hatziyonut," especially 81–82.

38. Moshe Mizrahi, director's commentary, *Habayit Berekhov Chelouche*. The movie focuses on Sephardi-Ashkenazi relations within the Arab-Jewish environment of the mixed neighborhoods.

ONE *The Road Not Taken: The Ethnic Problem and the Arab Question*

1. "'Letoldot histadrut halutsey hamizrah,' skira leshnat," 1923, 5–8, JMA 324/9. See also Haim, *Yihud vehishtalvut*, 174–78.

2. Berlowitz, *Lehamtsi erets lehamtsi 'am*, 21–122; Yardeni, *Ha'itonut ha'ivrit be'erets Israel bashanim 1863–1904*, 320.

3. Bezalel, *Nolatedem Ziyonim*, 365–66; Gorny, *Zionism and the Arabs*, 11–77. On the Sep-hardim and the Arab Question, see also Alboher, *Hizdahut, histaglut vehistaygut*, 99–106.

4. Haim, *Yihud vehishtalvut*, 174.

5. Quoted in "Ha'asefa haklalit shel halutsey hamizrah," *Doar Hayom*, February 12, 1924.

6. "Histadrutenu bishnat 1924," *Skira bimlot shev'a shanim leyesoda shel histadrut halutsey hamizrah*.

7. See, for example, the speech of Rabbi Ya'akov Me'ir at the thirteenth Zionist Con-gress in Carlsbad, Czechslovakia, in August 1923, in which he demanded that the Sep-

hardim become part of the political negotiations with the Arabs (*Histadrut halutzey hamizarah, skira leshnat 1923*, 31).

8. Haim, *Yihud vehishtalvut*, 179–96.

9. The journal *Mizrah Uma'arav*, edited by Abraham Elmaleh, was one of the main places where this ideology was discussed. See, for example, Burla, "Hasfaradim vethiyatenu hale'umit."

10. Moshe Atiash, "Histadrut hayehudim hasfaradim," *Doar Hayom*, October 17, 1922. See also Moshe Atiash, "Likrat kriat ve'ida 'olamit shel hayehudim hasfaradim,"*Histadrut halutzey hamizrah, skira leshnat* 1924, 49–53.

11. See, for example, Porath, *Tzmihat hatnu'a haleumit ha'arvit hafalastinit 1918–1929*, 41–49.

12. Ibid., 111–19.

13. Quoted in *Hazfira*, October 27, 1921. On the declaration of Weizmann, see Weizmann, *Trial and Error*, 305.

14. "Asefat hava'ad haleumi," *Doar Hayom*, August 12, 1921.

15. "Hayahadut hasfaradit vehamishlahat ha'aravit," *Doar Hayom*, September 8, 1921. See also, for example, the telegram sent by the Committee of Jews in Safed, September 1, 1921, and the telegram sent by the Council of the Sephardic Jewish Community in Jaffa, Central Zionist Archive, Jerusalem (hereafter CZA) L3/43.

16. "Histadrut halutzey hamizrah la'itonut hamekomit," JMA 6325/1330.

17. "Karoz el hador hatsa'ir beyerushalayim," *Histadrut halutzey hamizrah, skira leshnat* 1923, 45; "Hayehudim hasfaradim vehamishlahat ha'aravit," *Doar Hayom*, September 8, 1921.

18. "Histadrut halutsey hamizrah la'itonut hamekomit," JMA 6325/1330.

19. Shlomo Kalimi, "Bein sfaradim ve'aravim," *Doar Hayom*, September 5, 1921.

20. Quoted in *Doar Hayom*, September 5, 1921.

21. "Al-Yahud al-Sephardim," *Filastin*, September 3, 1921.

22. "Kriat ha'aravim el hayehudim yelidey ha'aretz," *Ha'aretz*, Februray 28, 1922. The item is also quoted in Assaf, *Hayahasim bein yehudim ve'aravim be'eretz israel 1860–1948*, 90.

23. "Hata'amula ha'aravit: Kriah leyelidey ha'aretz lehahrim et habhirot," *Ha'aretz*, February 20, 1923.

24. See the report to the Zionist Commission, April 17, 1920, CZA L3/43.

25. Lediveri hahashman dibuah," *Doar Hayom*, November 4, 1920.

26. Chief Rabbi Avraham Yitzhak Hacohen Kook, "letter to the editor," *Doar Hayom*, November 4, 1920.

27. Rabbi Hakham Bashi Nissim Danon, letter to the editor, *Doar Hayom*, November 5, 1920.

28. "Behistadrut hasfaradim," *Doar Hayom*, August 23, 1921.

29. "Le Raymond Poincaré, michtav galuy beshem va'ad histadrut hatse'irim hasfaradim be'erets Israel," *Doar Hayom*, August 25, 1921.

30. Y. Chelouche, *Parashat Hayai*, 323.

31. Ibid., 353.

32. Ibid., 366.

33. Bezalel, *Nolatedem Ziyonim*, 7 and 406–7.

34. On inclusive Zionism, see Jacobson, *From Empire to Empire*, 101–9.

35. Y. Chelouche, *Parashat Hayai*, 334.

36. See Haim, *Yihud vehishtalvut*, 69–73.

37. Letter from Eliyahu Meir Berlin to Yosef Sprinzak, undated, JMA 6325/1330.

38. See Porath, *Tzmihat hatnu'a haleumit ha'arvit hafalastinit 1918–1929*, 49.

39. See, for example, A. Rubinstein, *From Herzl to Rabin*, 54–81.

40. M. Behar and Ben-Dor Benite, *Modern Middle Eastern Jewish Thought*, especially xxi–xxxix.

41. See Bezalel, *Nolatedem Ziyonim*, 370–75 and 385–87.

42. Quoted in *Doar Hayom*, July 10, 1924.

43. Kimchi, *Ziyonut betsel hapiramidot*, 122–23. On the newspaper *Israel*, see Hilel, *Israel bekahir*.

44. On the delegations, see Haim, "Hayahasim bein hahanhaga hasfaradit beyerushalayim lebein kehilot yehudiyot bamizrah hatichon bein shtey milhamot 'olam."

45. "El tsirey haknesiya hatsiyonit ha-15," *Doar Hayom*, August 24, 1927.

46. Quoted in "Hasfaradim vehamosadot hatsiyonim," *Doar Hayom*, July 6, 1928. The Sephardi representatives at the meeting were Laniado, Yosef Meyuchas, Avraham Elmaleh, and Eliyahu Eliachar. On Meir Laniado, see Eliachar, *Lihyot 'im yehudim*, 119–20.

47. Alboher, *Hizdahut, histaglut vehistaygut*, 99–113.

48. Kats, "Zikatam shel sefaradim ubney 'edot hamizrah batnu'ot hadatiyot leumiyot hamizrahi vehapo'el hamizrahi be'eretz Israel 1918–1947," 217–25.

49. Morag-Talmon, *Ha'eda hasfaradit bitkufat hayeshuv*. See also Levi, "Hape'ilut hapolitit vehairgun shel hakehila hasfaradit bayeshuv ubemedinat Israel, 1945–1955."

50. "Tochnit ha'avoda shel halutsey hamizrah beyafo ubetel aviv," *Doar Hayom*, December 4, 1924.

51. "David Avissar"; "David Avissar-Leyovalo," *Davar*, July 15, 1938.

52. David Avissar, "Hatsa'a leshe'elat havana vehaskama 'im 'arviyey erets Israel," November 1929, JMA 6325/1330. See also M. Behar and Ben-Dor Benite, *Modern Middle Eastern Jewish Thought*, 114–18.

53. David Avissar, "Hatsa'a leshe'elat havana vehaskama 'im 'arviyey erets Israel," November 1929, JMA 6325/1330.

54. Ibid.

55. See Gorny, *Mediniyut vedimyon*, 50–52.

56. David Avissar, "Hashe'ela ha'aravit," 1923, JMA 6325/1330.

57. Ibid.

58. These issues will be addressed at length in chapter 3.

59. On the Sephardim and the third Assembly of Representatives, see Haim, *Yihud vehishtalvut*, 91–114.

60. Herzog, *'Adatiyut politit*. See also Lissak, "Habe'aya ha'adatit veirgunim 'adatiyim bitkufat hayeshuv."

61. "Miyehudi sfaaradi: Michtav galuy la'adon Greenbaum," *Doar Hayom*, December 18, 1934.

62. "Mehaat 'adat hasfaradim beyerushalayim neged divrey Greenbaum: Giluy da'at me'et va'ad 'edat hasfaradim beyerushalayim," *Doar Hayom*, December 31, 1934.

63. Ibid.

64. For more on the Liberal Party, see Haim, *Yihud vehishtalvut*, 197–99.

65. Meir Laniado, "Lama yisadnu et hamiflaga haliberalit," JMA 6220/18/171.

66. Ibid.

67. Ibid.

68. Ibid.

69. "Yeshivat hamiflaga haliberalit," October 5, 1936, JMA 6220/18/171.

70. "Kinus hasfaradim ve'edot hamizrah beyerushalayim," *Davar*, September 20, 1936.

71. "Yeshivat hanhalat hamo'atsa hapolitit," October 18, 1936, JMA 6220/18/171.

72. Ibid., November 15, 1936, JMA 6220/18/171.

73. Ibid

74. Ibid.

75. "Protokol yeshivat hanhalat hasokhnut hayehudit," October 21, 1936, CZA S/100.

76. Quoted in "Ha'edot shel hav'ad haleumi," *Davar*, December 31, 1936.

77. "Avraham Elmaleh." For more on Elmaleh, see chapter 3.

78. Elmaleh's public and intellectual work was varied and impressive, as can be seen in his many diverse publications. See Noy, "Tzmihatan shel praktikot etnografiyot bekerev intelligentsia yehudit sefaradit umizrahit beyerushalyim beshalhey hatkufa ha'othmanit uthilat tkufat hamandat," especially 98–143. See also Molcho and Gaon, *Minha le'avraham*.

79. Quoted in "Ha'edot shel hav'ad haleumi," *Davar*, December 31, 1936.

80. "Tazkir lava'ada hamalkhutit me'et ba'ei koah hayehudim hasfaradim ve'edot hamizrah," November 1936, JMA 6322/1271.

81. Ibid.

82. Ibid.

83. Ibid.

84. On Meyhuchas's cultural activities, see, for example, "Agadot ha'aravim 'al sefer bereshit: Tamzit hartsa'ato shel Yosef Meyuchas behalutsey hamizrah," *Doar Hayom*, August 29, 1924; Noy, "Tzmihatan shel praktikot etnografiyot bekerev intelligentsia yehudit sefaradit umizrahit beyerushalyim beshalhey hatkufa ha'othmanit uthilat tkufat hamandat," especially 27–62.

85. See, for example, Abraham Elmaleh, "Yosef Meyuchas: Shloshim le'ptirato," *Hatzofeh*, October 1, 1942.

86. Yosef Meyuchas, "Igeret el havrey hava'ada hamalchutit," December 20, 1936, Archive of the Sephardi Council, JMA 6322/1270.

87. Yosef Meyuchas, "'Al hayahasim 'im shchenenu," *Hed Hamizrah*, October 15, 1942.

88. Yosef Meyuchas, "Igeret el havrey hava'ada hamalchutit," December 20, 1936, Archive of the Sephardi Council, JMA 6322/1270.

89. Eliachar, *Lihyot 'im Falastinim*, 36–37.

90. Ibid.

91. Ibid.

92. Quoted in "Yeshivat hanhalat hamo'atsa hapolitit," October 18, 1936, JMA 6220/18/171.

93. "Protokol have'ida ha'artsit she hayehudim hasfaradim vebney 'edot hamizrah be'erets Israel," April 8, 1939, JMA 6225/12.

94. The organizations included the Association of Bucharian Immigrants, the Association of Syrian Immigrants, the Association of Persian Immigrants, the Association of Immigrants from Aram-Tsuba, and the Haifa Sephardi Community Committee.

95. At the end of the conference Elmaleh, Eliachar, Chief Rabbi Ben-Zion Meir Hai Uziel, Moshe Levy, and Moshe Chelouche were elected to the leadership of the organization. See "Protokol have'ida ha'artsit she hayehudim hasfaradim vebney 'edot hamizrah be'erets Israel," April 8, 1939, JMA /6225/12.

96. Quoted in ibid. For more on Eliachar's criticism of the London Conference see his *Lihyot 'im Falastinim*, 82–95.

97. Kimchi, *Ziyonut betsel hapiramidot*, 133.

98. Such as Yellin, Menashe Eliachar, Eliyahu Eliachar, Avissar, Laniado, Ya'akov Chelouche, and Meyuchas.

99. Gabouy, *Kedma Mizraha*, 17.

100. On Molcho's approach to immigration, see his "*Kedma Mizraha*: shalav baderekh." See also Heller, *Mibrit shalom le'ichud*, 143–47. On Molcho's biography, see Elmaleh, "Shishim shnot haim."

101. See, for example, Gordon, *Brit Shalom vehatsiyonut hadu-leumit*; Lavsky, *Before Catastrophe*, 162–80; Ratzabi, *Between Zionism and Judaism*.

102. Milson, "Reshit limud ha'aravit vehaislam baoniversita ha'ivrit."

103. Ben Hanania, "Hanispah hatarbuti harishon bearzot 'arav lifney kum hamedinah."

104. Evri, "Paneha hamerubot vehamishtanot shel ha'sfaradiyut' bemifneh hameah ha'esrim," 2–13 and 110–27.

105. Ben Hanania, "Hanispah hatarbuti harishon bearzot 'arav lifney kum hamedinah."

106. Yosef Rivlin, "Yehudim ve'aravim," *Hed Hamizrah*, November 6, 1942.

107. Ibid. *Hamizrah*, September 29, 1942.

108. Other ideas reflected in Rivlin's piece, including the beliefs that the common socioeconomic status of Oriental Jews and Arabs brings them together and that Oriental Jews have been politically radicalized, is discussed in chapters 4 and 5, respectively.

109. Yosef Rivlin, "Yehudim ve'aravim," *Hed Hamizrah*, November 6, 1942.

110. "Eliyahu Eliachar." For Eliachar's biography, see his *Lihyot 'im yehudim*.

111. Bartal, "Du kiyum nichsaf."

112. Bartal, *Kozak vebedui*, 167.

113. Eliachar, *Lihyot 'im Falastinim*, 60–57.

114. Ibid., 96–99.

115. Ibid., 26.

116. Ibid., 103–4.

117. Ibid., 22. For more on Eliachar's political outlook, see his "Ma'amado shel hatzibur hasfaradi be'eretz Israel me'az hachrazat balfour," 67–81.

118. Eliachar, *Lihyot 'im Falastinim*, 22.

119. On Eliachar's struggle to change the electoral system, see his *Lihyot 'im yehudim*, 275–81.

120. Herzog, *'Adatiyut politit*. On the Sephardim and the Yishuv's fourth Assembly of Representatives, see Haim, *Yihud vehishtalvut*, 115–45.

121. Sofer, *Zionism and the Foundations of Israeli Diplomacy*, 292–96.

122. David Abulafia was born in Gallipoli in 1893 and served as an officer in the Ottoman army during World War I. He graduated from the Faculty of Law at Istanbul University and worked as a lawyer after arriving in Palestine in 1921.

123. "Midavid Abulafia lehanhalat ha'ichud ha'olami shel hakehilot hasfaradim," March 25, 1946, JMA 6209/10. See also "Hafederazia ha'olamit shel kehikot hasfaradim beNew York memalet et yedey hamishlahat lehofi'a bishma," *Ha'olam Hasfaradi*, April 12, 1946.

124. "Memorandum Presented to the Anglo-American Committee of Inquiry on Palestine by the Sephardic Communities in Palestine," February 1946, JMA 6209/10.

125. "Hoda'at hamishlahat hasfaradit be'eretz israel bifnei va'adat hahakirah ha'anglo-america'it 'al eretz Israel," March 13, 1946, JMA 16209/10.

126. Ibid.

127. "Memorandum Presented to the Anglo-American Committee of Inquiry on Palestine by the Sephardic Communities in Palestine," February 1946, JMA 6209/10.

128. "'Edut f Jamal al-Husseini," *Davar*, March 13, 1946.

129. Ibid.

130. Yitzhak 'Abadi, "Hitahdut yehudit-'aravit," *Doar Hayom*, August 11, 1920.

131. Frumkin, *Derech shofet beyerushalayim*, 221.

132. Yitzhak 'Abadi, "Hitahdut yehudit-'aravit," *Doar Hayom*, August 11, 1920.

133. Ibid.

134. Quoted in "Yom etmol beva'adat hahakira," *Davar*, March 14, 1946.

135. Speeches of Meir Ginio, David Abulafia, Meir Laniado, Eliyaho Eliachar, and Moshe Ben-Ami to the National Conference of Sephardi Jews in Eretz Israel, December 22–23, 1946, JMA 6225/12.

136. Letter from David Remez, chair of the National Council, to the Council of the Sphardi Community in Jerusalem, June 13, 1947, JMA 6322/1280.

137. Discussion of the Sephardi council, June 25, 1947, JMA 6322/1280.

138. Quoted in "Doh mita'am va'ad ha'eda hasfaradit beyerushalayim," *Hed Hamizrah*, November 3, 1950.

139. Testimony of Eliyahu Eliachar, president of the Council of the Sephardi Community in Jerusalem, before UNSCOP, CZA S 75/5962.

140. Eliachar, *Lihyot 'im Falastinim*, 112–13.

141. Testimony of Eliyahu Eliachar, president of the Council of the Sephardi Community in Jerusalem, before UNSCOP, CZA S 75/5962.

TWO *Natives of the Orient: Political and Social Rapprochement*

1. On the effects and influence of 1929, see Hillel Cohen, *Tarpat*; Sela, "Meora'ot hakotel (1929)."

2. Hillel Cohen, *Tzva hatzlalim*, 18–19.

3. On the contacts between Weizmann and Arab leaders in the 1920s, see A. Cohen, *Israel veha'olam ha'aravi*, 178–88. For more on the political negotiations during the decade, see Caplan, *Futile Diplomacy*.

4. Hillel Cohen, *Tzva hatzlalim*, 19; Eliachar, *Lihyot 'im Falastinim*, 17–18; Yagar, *Toldot hamahlaka hamedinit shel hasokhnut hayehudit*, 111.

5. E. Rubinstein, "Hatipul bashe'elah ha'aravit beshnot ha'esrim vehashloshim," 213.

6. Gelber, *Shorshey hahavatzelet*, 52–53.

7. Ibid., 68; E. Rubinstein, "Hatipul bashe'elah ha'aravit beshnot ha'esrim vehashloshim," 79.

8. Minutes of the sixth meeting of the United Bureau, February 26, 1930, CZA S 25/10620.

9. Ibid.

10. Zaki Alhadiff to Frederick Kisch, August 26, 1930, CZA J105/27.

11. Zaki Alhadiff to the United Bureau, May 19, 1930, CZA J105/27.

12. On Levy and his work in Haifa, see S. Levy, "Mizihronotav."

13. E. Rubinstein, "Hatipul bashe'elah ha'aravit beshnot ha'esrim vehashloshim," 86.

14. An example is the Jewish leadership in Iraq—especially the position of Yehezkel Sasson, who served as the first minister of treasury in the Iraqi government in the 1920s. See Qazzaz, *Hayehudim be'iraq bameah ha'esrim*, 132–34 and 223–37.

15. Aharon Chaim Cohen, untitled testimony, July 1953, Haganah Archive (HA), Tel Aviv, 27.16.

16. See Hillel Cohen, *Tzva hatzlalim*, 39; Gelber, *Shorshey hahavatzelet*, 69.

17. E. Rubinstein, "Masa umatan 'im 'aravim: nisyonot nefel be-1930," 116.

18. 'Ovadia Kimchi, "Nisayon shel heskem bein yehudim le'aravim," *Hed Hamizrah*, May 5 and 12, 1950.

19. Hillel Cohen, *Tzva hatzlalim*, 26–27.

20. "Tohnit hahitahdut hashemit beshkhem," CZA J 105/8.

21. From Hasan Shalabi, Jawad Nashashibi, Mahmoud al-Budeiri, and Akram Tukan, "Hazmana le'asefa shel klub hahitahdut hashemit be April 15, 1930," CZA J 105/8; Hillel Cohen, *Tzva hatzlalim*, 26–27.

22. "Masa umatan leyisud klub meshutaf leyehudim ve'aravim," JMA 6322/1270.

23. From Muhamad Shahin to Haim Margaliot-Kalvarisky, August 13, 1930, CZA J 105/8.

24. Haim Cohen, untitled testimony, July 16 and 27, 1953, HA; Hillel Cohen, *Tzva hatzlalim*, 39; Gelber, *Shorshey hahavatzelet*, 69.

25. Ben-Gurion met with Mussa al-'Alami, 'Awni 'Abd al-Hadi, George Antonious, Riad al-Sulh, Shakib Arslan, and Ihsan bey al-Ja'abari. On Ben-Gurion's meetings, see Ben-Gurion, *Pgishot 'im manhigim 'aravim*.

26. Yitzhak Molcho in the Liberal Party's meeting, October 1936, minutes of the Liberal Party, JMA 6220/18/171.

27. Arlozoroff, *Yoman Yerushalayim*, 69, referring to October 6, 1931.

28. Gelber, *Shorshey hahavatzelet*, 119.

29. Elath, *Miba'ad le'arafel hayamim*, 185; Gelber, *Shorshey hahavatzelet*, 93.

30. Sasson, *Baderekh el hashalom*, 9–16.

31. The nature and importance of this encounter in Damascus will be discussed further in chapter 3.

32. Arlozoroff, *Yoman Yerushalayim*, 120, referring to November 24, 1931.

33. Ibid., 122–23.

34. Eliyahu Sasson, "Mizikhrinotay be'avar: Pgisha rishona 'im hamufti," *Bama'aracha*, October 1, 1962.

35. Eliyahu Sasson, "Hawla al-Mu'atamar al-Isra'ili al-Sharqi," *Al-'Alam al-Isra'ili*, June 20, 1932.

36. Sela, "Sihot umaga'im bein manhigim tziyonim lebein manhigim 'aravim falastinim 1933–1939," 7–10. See also Caplan, *Futile Diplomacy*.

37. On these meetings, see Sasson, *Baderekh el hashalom*.

38. Ibid., 355–58.

39. Danin, *Tziyoni bechol tna'i*, 160.

40. Sasson, *Baderekh el hashalom*, 76.

41. See, for example, Eliyahu Sasson's presentation in the Jewish Agency's executive session, May 13, 1943, CZA S 25/22162.

42. Eyal, *Hasarat hakesem min hamizrah*, 150–92.

43. Ibid., 44–60.

44. Ibid., 48.

45. According to Eyal, the knowledge acquired by the Arabists was intended to serve for mediation purposes between Jews and Arabs (ibid., 49).

46. Ibid., 17.

47. Uri Dromi, "Lo mizrahan ela ish hamizrah," *Ha'aretz*, January 1, 2007.

48. Memorandum from Eliyahu Sasson to David Ben-Gurion, "Hatza'ot lepe'ula bekerev ha'aravim ba'aretz uba'aratzot hashkhenot," April 21, 1939, CZA S 25/8163. See also Sasson, *Baderekh el hashalom*, 157–59.

49. Sasson, *Baderekh el hashalom*, 231–33 and 355.

50. Memorandum from Eliyahu Sasson to David Ben-Gurion, "Hatza'ot lepe'ula

bekerev ha'aravim ba'aretz uba'aratzot hashkhenot," April 21, 1939, CZA S 25/8163. See also Sasson, *Baderekh el hashalom*, 157–59.

51. Sasson, *Baderekh el hashalom*, 193–94.

52. From Eliyahu Sasson to Abraham Elmaleh, February 19, 1940, CZA S25/22197.

53. Kats, "Zikatam shel sefaradim ubney 'edot hamizrah batnu'ot hadatiyot leumiyot hamizrahi vehapo'el hamizrahi be'eretz Israel 1918–1947," 17–18.

54. From Kaplinsky to David Ben-Gurion, November 22, 1942, CZA S25/22034.

55. Minutes of the Committee of Investigation of the Relations between Jews and Arabs, CZA S25/22196.

56. Report from the Committee of Investigation of the Relations between Jews and Arabs to the Jewish Agency, August 19, 1942, CZA S25/22119.

57. On the importance of the League for Jewish-Arab Rapprochement, see Heller, *Mibrit shalom le'ichud*, 161–62.

58. "Hitya'atzut lepe'ula bekerev ha'aravim," May 13, 1943, CZA S25/22162.

59. Sasson, *Baderekh el hashalom*, 321–22.

60. Eliyahu Sasson, "Sikum pe'uloteha shel hamahlaka hamedinit bashetah ha'aravi bishnot hamilhama," June 6, 1943, CZA S25/22170.

61. lemoshe Shertok mehava'ada hamonizipalit shel hahisadrut, November 12, 1940, CZA S25/22135.

62. From the Histadrut Executive to Moshe Shertok, February 16, 1941, CZA S 25/22135.

63. One of the instructors in these courses was Meir Dahan, who is discussed in chapter 5. See minutes of the third meeting of the executive of the Institution of Arab Studies, October 5, 1944, CZA S25/22126; Eliyahu Sasson in a meeting about Arab affairs, May 13, 1943, CZA S25/22162; Miriam Glikson, untitled address at the end of the first course for the training of mukhtars, Nov. 12, 1944, S25/22167.

64. Danin, *Tziyoni bechol tna'i*, 154.

65. Hillel Cohen, *Tzva hatzlalim*, 182; Gelber, *Shorshey hahavatzelet*, 334.

66. Eliyahu Sasson, "Hatza'ot tochnit le'pe'ula lava'adot hayeshuviyot leyahasey shkhenim," December 6, 1942, CZA S25/22119.

67. From Eliyahu Sasson and Y. Golan to Moshe Shertok, September 14, 1942, CZA S25/22119.

68. On the work of the Arab Department of Hashomer Hatza'ir, see Nagri, "Hamahlaka ha'aravit shel hashomer hatza'ir," 100, and 118–23; Yahav, *Bishviley du hakiyum vehama'avak hameshutaf*, 63.

69. From Yehoshua Havoushi to Eliyahu Sasson, "Hava'adot leyahasey shkhenim betzfon hahoula," May 19, 1942, CZA S25/22168.

70. Yehoshua Havoushi, "Tafkidenu beshe'elat yahsey shkenim," CZA S25/22119.

71. Hillel Cohen, *Tzva hatzlalim*, 183; Yagar, *Toldot hamahlaka hamedinit shel hasokhnut hayehudit*, 304.

72. Minutes of the meeting of representatives from the Political Department with representatives from the Western Galilee, October 6, 1942, CZA S25/22119.

73. Yehoshua Havoushi to Eliyahu Sasson, "Hava'adot leyahasey shkhenim betzfon hahoula," May 19, 1942, CZA S25/22168–196.

74. Gelber, *Shorshey hahavatzelet*, 334.

75. Hillel Cohen, *Tzva hatzlalim*, 175.

76. See, for example, Michael Assaf, "Hitya'atzut lepe'ula bekerev ha'aravim," May 13, 1943, CZA S25/22162.

77. "Beinenu lebein ha'aravim besha'a zo," *Hatzofeh*, October 11, 1942.

78. Eliyahu Sasson, "Sikum pe'uloteha shel hamahlaka hamedinit bashetah ha'aravi beshnot hamilhama," June 6, 1943, CZA S25/22170.

79. See Herzog, *'Adatiyut politit*, 115–17.

80. Eliyahu Eliachar, "Yinaten ot hitnadvut lamitnadvim latzava haturki," *Bama'aracha*, January 7, 1962.

81. Chaim Shar'abi, "Ha'eda hateimanit bamilhama," *Davar*, May 11, 1945.

82. "Kinus histadrut ha'ovdim hasfaradim ba-23 beoctober 1942," *Hed Hamizrah*, November 6, 1942.

83. "Hasokhnut le'irgun bney 'edot hamizrah," *Davar*, September 1, 1942.

84. "Le'irguna shel ha'eda hasfaradit," *Hed Hamizrah*, August 14, 1942.

85. Mibechor Shalom Sheetrit lehanhalat hahistadrut uatziyouit, July 30, 1943, CZA S25/22170; minutes of the meeting of the Council of the Sephardi Community in Tel Aviv with Eliyahu Sasson, May 5, 1943, CZA S25/22170.

86. Levi, "Hape'ilut hapolitit vehairgun shel hakehila hasfaradit bayeshuv ubemedinat Israel, 1945–1955," 80.

87. Eliyahu Sasson, "'Al irgun 'edot hamizrah," *Hed Hamizrah*, September 29, 1942.

88. "Hafred umshol," *Hed Hamizrah*, September 11, 1942.

89. Quoted in a discussion on the strategies of work among the Arabs, May 13, 1943, CZA S25/22162.

90. "Kinus hano'ar hasfaradi mahlit 'al hakamat merkaz le'irguney hano'ar hasfaradi ba'aretz," *Hed Hamizrah*, January 29, 1943.

91. Moshe Chelouche, "Hahalom hafah le'metziut," *Histadrut ha'ovdim hasfrdim be'tel aviv: Hamifkad haklali harishon shel Degel Zion*, 2; Aryeh Turgeman, "Tafkid hano'ar besha'a zo," *Histadrut ha'ovdim hasfrdim be'tel aviv: Hamifkad haklali harishon shel Degel Zion*, 9.

92. "Moshe Chelouche."

93. Ram, *Hayeshuv hayehudi beyafo ba'et hahadasha*, 398.

94. "Degel Zion snif Tel Aviv," *Hed Hamizrah*, November 3, 1944.

95. "Basha'ar," *Bama'aracha: Dvar Merkaz Degel Zion be'eretz Israel*, May 1943.

96. Moshe Ben 'Ami, "Ha'ivri hatza'ir," *Doar Hayom*, December 11, 1928; "Misnif ha'ivri hatza'ir ledoctor Luria," CZA S2\573.

97. Yona Cohen, "Hinukh miktzo'i le'oley hamizrah," *Hatzofeh*, July 11, 1945.

98. See Shapira, *Hama'avak hanichzav*, 83.

99. On the Palestine Labor League, see Bernstein, "Brit po'aley eretz Israel"; Lockman, *Comrades and Enemies*.

100. On Burla's work in 1931, see Pinchas Lavon Archive of the Labor Movement, Tel Aviv (LA), 4-208-1-320.

101. Bernstein, "Yehudim ve'aravim be'mif'al nesher," 85.

102. A. Khalfon, "Heifa 'iri," 59.

103. A. Khalfon, "'Avoda letzido shel Hasan Shukri," 241–43. See also Goren, *Shituf betzel 'imut*, 46.

104. E. Rubinstein, "Yehudim ve'aravim be'iriyot eretz Israel (1926–1933)," 123.

105. Lockman, *Comrades and Enemies*, 103.

106. "Hamahlaka le'inyaney 'aravim, bulletin lemesirat yedi'ot 'al ma shetzarich la'asot benose hashe'ela ha'aravit," March 16, 1931, LA, 4- 208-1-320.

107. "Mehamahlaka ha'aravit shel hahistadrut lechaim Weizmann, 'al hashe'ela ha'aravit," LA, 4-208-1-320.

108. Lockman, *Comrades and Enemies*, 105.

109. Minutes of the Arab Department of the Histadrut, December 5, 1947, LA, 4--104–143–14.

110. Eliyahu Agassi, "Skira 'al pe'uloteha shel hamahlaka ha'aravit ubrit po'aley eretz Israel beheifa bishnat 1937," January 30, 1938, LA, - 250–27–2-119.

111. Nachmias, "Aravim veyehudim beshuk 'avoda dinami vesegregativi beheifa ha-mandatorit," 81.

112. Even Shoshan, *Toldot tnu'at hapo'alim be'eretz Israel, sefer shlishi*, 156–61.

113. See, for example, a meeting of the Arab Department of the Histadrut, May 18 1944, CZA S25/22124. On the Palestinian Arab Workers' Union, see Lockman, *Comrades and Enemies*, 50.

114. Eliyahu Agassi, "Skira 'al pe'uloteha shel hamahlaka ha'aravit vesnif brit po'aley eretz Israel beheifa lishnat 1937," January 30, 1938, LA, 4- 208-1-1287; Gelber, *Shorshey hahavatzelet*, 171; Abba Hushi, testimony from March 15, 1953, HA, 2271.

115. Lockman, *Comrades and Enemies*, 92–97, and "Patahnu et mohot ha'aravim," 113–14.

116. Lockman, *Comrades and Enemies*, 75.

117. On the Histadrut's policy of segregation, see Bernstein, "Brit po'aley eretz Israel."

118. See, for example, a meeting of the Arab Department of the Histadrut, May 18 1944, CZA S25/22124.

119. Osatzki-Lazar, "Mehistadrut 'ivrit lehistadrut israelit."

120. Letter from Eliyahu Agassi to Eliyahu Sasson, "Doch shnati mipe'uloteha shel brit po'aley eretz Israel beyerushalayim, May 1943–May 1944," CZA S25/2124.

121. Bernstein, "Brit po'aley eretz Israel," 249. See A. Cohen, *Israel veha'olam ha'aravi*, 306.

122. Lin, *Beterem se'ara*, 60–61.

123. Ya'akov Yesha'ayahu, "Histadrut ha'ovdim hasfaradim," *Kolenu: Biton histadrut ha'ovdim hasfaradim betel aviv*, 1947.

124. Haim, *Yihud vehishtalvut*, 202–7.

125. Turgeman, "Hasfaradim bama'aracha hale'umit."

126. Moshe Chelouche, "Dvarenu," February 1941, *Hed histadrut ha'ovdim hasfardim*, 5.

127. "Hamo'atza ha'artzit hashniyah shel histadrut ha'ovdim hasfaradim be'eretz Israel," *Hed Hamizrah*, November 6, 1942.

128. Quoted in ibid.

129. Gozanski, *Hitpathut hakapitalism befalestina*, 218.

130. "Histadrut ha'ovdim hasfaradim neged divrey hasitna shel 'iton hapo'alim ha'aravim," *Hed Hamizrah*, November 10, 1944.

131. "Ha'ovdim hasfaradim shechem ehad 'im kol helkey hauma," *Hatzofeh*, November 8, 1944.

132. "Kenes hano'ar hasfaradi mahlit 'al hakamat merkaz artzi le'irguney hano'ar hasfaradi ba'aretz," *Hed Hamizrah*, January 29, 1943.

133. "Histadrutenu le'or hamisparim," *Yedi'ot histadrut ha'ovdim hasfaradim be'eretz Israel*, November 1940, 12; "Mibifnim," *Kolenu: Biton histadrut ha'ovdim hasfaradim betel aviv*, April 1947, 2–3.

134. "Al Haperek: Parashat hasevel shel 'ovdei hanikayon, kenes mo'etzet hapo'alim hasfaradim betel aviv," *Yedi'ot histadrut ha'ovdim hasfaradim be'eretz Israel*, August 1943, 1; "Mibifnim," *Kolenu: Biton histadrut ha'ovdim hasfaradim betel aviv*, April 1947, 4–5.

135. "Bairgun ubatnu'a," *Bamitzpe: Biton histadrut ha'ovdim hasfaradim ubney 'edot hamizrah biyerushalayim*, September 1943, 15.

136. Haim, *Yihud vehishtalvut*, 120–21; "Nishbera hazit hamahrimim ba'edah hasfaradit," *Davar*, July 30, 1944; "Ha'ovdim hasfaradim mishtatfim babhirot," *Davar*, August 1, 1944.

137. "Mekoman shel 'edor hamizrah bayeshuv ubahistadrut," *Davar*, October 7, 1942.

THREE *Cultural Politics: Journalistic, Cultural, and Linguistic Mediation*

1. Haim Ben 'Attar, "'Al haeiva ha'aravit klapey hayehudim," *Haherut*, December 17, 1912.

2. These issues are discussed in length in Jacobson, *From Empire to Empire*, especially 82–116.

3. Ibid. See also Campos, "Between 'Beloved Ottomania' and 'the Land of Israel'"; Jacobson, "Sephardim, Ashkenazim and the 'Arab Question' in Pre-First World War Palestine."

4. The nature of the mediation process discussed in the two previous chapters differs from that of the one analyzed in this chapter, but there are clear links between all spheres of mediation, as will be shown below.

5. The term "cultural politics" is borrowed from a speech by Moshe Solovichki, director of the Department of Education in the National Council, at a party held as part of the Arabic teachers' conference (August 14–15, 1945, CZA J17/5853). See the detailed discussion on this term below.

6. For a discussion of the centrality of the print media in Palestine, see Ami Ayalon, *Reading Palestine*; Khalidi, *Palestinian Identity*.

7. See, for example, Hillel Cohen, *Army of Shadows*; Halperin, *Babel in Zion*, especially 162–74; E. Rubinstein, "Hadiyunim 'al hotza'at 'iton 'tziyoni'." On Jews writing in the Arabic press, see Snir, "'Mosaic Arabs' between Total and Conditioned Arabization," especially 277–78.

8. Halperin, *Babel in Zion*, 170.

9. For more on Malul and Moyal, see Campos, "Between 'Beloved Ottomania' and 'the Land of Israel,'" 474–77; Gribetz, "An Arabic-Zionist Talmud"; Jacobson, "Jews Writing in Arabic," 165–69, and *From Empire to Empire*, 120–22. On Moyal, see also a file on the Moyal family, CZA K13/91; Gaon, *Yehudei hamizrah be'eretz israel*, 381; "Shimon Moyal"; Yehoshua Ben Hanania, "Dr. Shimon Moyal vehabe'aya hayehudit 'aravit," *Hed Hamizrah*, October 10, 1944. On Esther Azhari Moyal's life and literary work as an Arab-Jewish intellectual in the Mashriq, see L. Levy, "Jewish Writers in the Arab East," 227–75, and "Partitioned Pasts." Levy presents her as an example of Arab Jewish modernity during the late Ottoman period. See also Yehoshua Ben Hanania, "Hasoferet Esther Moyal vetkufata," *Hed Hamizrah*, September 17, 1944; Snir, "'Mosaic Arabs' Between Total and Conditioned Arabization," 265–66.

10. In addition to Shimon Moyal, Esther Azhari Moyal and Malul, the association included Elmaleh, David Moyal, Yosef Amzalek, Yosef Eliyahu Chelouche, Ya'acov Chelouche, Moshe Matalon, David Hivan, and Yehoshua Elkayam. For more on the association, see Bezalel, *Noladetem Ziyonim*, 382–85; Y. Chelouche, *Parashat Hayai*, 166–70; Jacobson, *From Empire to Empire*, 106–7.

11. On *al-Akhbar*, see Malul's letter, September 10, 1919, CZA L4/927.

12. During his time in Iraq, Malul was in touch with the Jewish National Fund and suggested ways of enhancing the Zionist presence in Iraq. Among other things, he suggested the publication of an Arabic newspaper that would be affiliated with the Zionist movement. His ideas were rejected, and after a year and a half he was fired from the school. See Haim Cohen, *Hape'ilut hatziyonit be'iraq*, 80–81.

13. For more on Malul, see Ben Ze'ev, "Ha'askan veha'itonai Nissim Malul"; Gaon, *Yehudei hamizrah be'eretz israel*, 432–34; "Nissim Malul"; Yehoshua Ben Hanania, 'Ha'itonai hayehudi harishon," *Hapo'el Hatza'ir*, April 27 1959. In 1940 Burla sent a letter to Moshe Shertok, indicating that Malul's finances were in a very bad condition and asking for help in trying to find him a job, to rescue him from hunger. See letter from Yehuda Burla to Moshe Shertok, November 22, 1940, CZA S25\22165.

14. See, for example, the April 11, 1930, issue of *al-Salam*, published in Judeo-Arabic. For more on *al-Salam*, see CZA Z4/1250; JMA 4622/2.

15. Yehoshua, *Ta'arikh al-sihafa al-'arabiya al-filastiniya fi bidayat 'ahd al-intidab al-baritani 'ala filastin*, 209–10.

16. Discussion in the United Bureau, March 20, 1930, CZA S25/3131.

17. Hillel Cohen, *Tzva hatzlalim*, 30–33.

18. "Al-Salam hazar!," CZA J1\311.

19. Halperin, *Babel in Zion*, especially 166–74.

20. "Mushrash bamoreshet hayehudit uben bayit batarbut ha'aravit."

21. For more on Agassi, see Ben-Ya'acov, *Yehudei babel be'eretz israel meha'aliot harishonot 'ad hayom*, 390–94.

22. Report from Michael Assaf and Eliyahu Agassi to the Histadrut, January 24, 1938, CZA S25\9560.

23. Quoted in "Haqiqat al-Amr," CZA S25\9960.

24. Snir, "'Mosaic Arabs' Between Total and Conditioned Arabization," 277–78.

25. Quoted in Rubinstein, "Hadiyunim 'al hotza'at 'iton 'tziyoni'," 48–49.

26. See Jacobson, *From Empire to Empire*, especially 82–116.

27. Noy, "Tzmihatan shel praktikot etnografiyot bekerev intelligentsia yehudit sefaradit umizrahit beyerushalyim beshalhey hatkufa ha'othmanit uthilat tkufat hamandat," 127. The writers included Yosef Meyuchas, Hans Kohn, Yosef Yoel Rivlin, Yitzhak Shami, Shmuel Ben Shabat, Burla, and Malul (ibid., 137).

28. Eliachar, "Ma'amado shel hatzibur hasfaradi be'eretz Israel me'az hachrazat balfour," 71.

29. Snir ("'Mosaic Arabs' Between Total and Conditioned Arabization") analyzes the Jewish writers published in Arabic newspapers in Iraq, Egypt, Lebanon, Syria, Palestine, and North Africa and creates a typology of the different writers' cultural approaches.

30. Bashkin, *New Babylonians*, 166, 202.

31. Kimchi, *Ziyonut betsel hapiramidot*, 122–23. For more on *Israël*, see Hilel, *Israel bekahir*.

32. For a comprehensive analysis of the newspaper, see Bracha, "'Al-'Alam al-Isra'ili'."

33. Ibid., 84–89.

34. "Al-Mu'tamar al-'Arabi al-Yahudi," *Al-'Alam al-Isra'ili*, May 16, 1932. "Al-Isar'ilin al-Watani'in" can be translated and understood in different ways, based on the many meanings of the word *watani*. Based on the context of the different discussions and debates presented here, we treat this expression to mean the local, native Jews.

35. "Al-Mu'atamar al-Isra'ili al-'Arabi," *Al-'Alam al-Isra'ili*, June 20, 1932. It is worth mentioning that not all of these people were Zionist activists. Shaul, for example (who was born in 1904 in Iraq), was one of the country's prominent writers, poets, and translators. Like other Iraqi Jews, he viewed himself as a Jew of the East and as strongly connected to Iraq. Shaul stayed in Iraq after most members of the Jewish community had left the country and immigrated to Israel only in 1971, where he continued writing in Arabic about the experience of Arab Jews in Iraq. See Bashkin, *New Babylonians*, 24–26; Somekh, "Sifrut lelo kahal."

36. Moshe Glikson, "Al haperek: ve'ida 'aravit-israelit," *Ha'aretz*, May 26, 1932.

37. Born in Jaffa in 1901, Aharon Ya'akov Moyal was a lawyer and a member of the Association of the Pioneers of the East. Uziel immigrated to Palestine from Thessaloniki in 1914. He was exiled to Damascus during World War I. After his return he became a teacher, and later he studied and then practiced law. He was a member of the National Council and later of the Progressive Party.

38. Baruch Uziel, "Hasfaradim vehayahasim 'im shchenenu," *Ha'aretz*, June 2, 1932. See also: A. Y. Moyal, "Ha'edot hamizrahiyot vehave'ida ha'aravit-israelit," *Ha'aretz*, June 2, 1932.

39. Uziel, ibid.

40. See Eliachar, *Lihyot 'im yehudim*, 493.

41. In the original Hebrew, "Mi lamishma'at haleumit velathiya haamitit shel 'am Israel beartzo—eleynu!" (Nissim Malul, *Ha'aretz*, May 29, 1932).

42. See Y. Harel, *Zionism in Damascus*.

43. For a thorough summary and analysis of Elmaleh's life, see Molcho and Gaon, *Minha le'avraham*.

44. Y. Harel, "Mihurban yafo nivneta dameseq."

45. On Shami as a model of the Arab-Jewish hybrid identity, see Tamari, "Ishaq al-Shami and the Predicament of the Arab-Jew in Palestine."

46. Y. Harel, "Mihurban yafo nivneta dameseq," 197.

47. Ibid.

48. Y. Harel, "Kidma gdola." Rivlin was born in 1889 to a prominent family in Jerusalem. After he was recruited into the Ottoman army during World War I, he went to Damascus. He remained there after the war to serve as the director of the Hebrew School for girls. He returned to Jerusalem in 1922, pursued a PhD in Arabic and Islamic studies, and later became one of the founders of the Institute of Islamic Studies at the Hebrew University. Among his monumental projects was the translation of the Qur'an into Hebrew (1936). He was one of the young intellectuals who were active throughout the Mandatory period in strengthening the cultural contacts between Jews and Arabs in Palestine.

49. Sasson, *Baderekh el hashalom*, 9.

50. Y. Harel, "Leumiyut, tziyonut, 'itonut ve'sotzyalism bekerev yehudey dameseq tahat shilton Faisal," especially 141; Ran, "Eliyahu (Elias) Sasson."

51. Bracha, "'Al-'Alam al-Isra'ili,'" 22–23 and 53–54. See also L. Levy, "Historicizing the Concept of Arab Jews in the *Mashriq*."

52. The organizational history of the Sephardi community and local Jews in Mandatory Palestine is discussed in chapter 1.

53. Eliyahu Sasson, "Bayna al-Sephardim wa-Ashkenazim," *Al-'Alam al-Isra'ili*, December 22, 1927.

54. Ibid.

55. Eliyahu Sasson, "Al Mu'tamar al-Isra'ili al-Sharqi," *Al-'Alam al-Isra'ili*, June 27 1932.

56. Eliyahu Sasson, "Al-Mu'atamar al-'Arab al-Isra'ili," *Al-'Alam al-Isra'ili*, July 18, 1932.

57. Eliyahu Sasson, "Rad 'ala Maqal," *Al-Hayat*, May 21, 1930.

58. Eliyahu Sasson, "Al-Mawt 'ala Al-Din al-Sahih," *Al-Hayat*, May 23 1930.

59. Eliyahu Sasson, "Haim hava'ad ha'aravi meyatzeg ne'eman shel ha'am ha'aravi?," *Davar*, July 31, 1930 (this letter by Eliyahu Sasson to Zaki Shahin was published by Sasson in *al-Akhbar* and quoted in *Davar*).

60. "'Itonai yehudi 'aravi pone leshalom befalastin," *Davar*, August 3, 1930.

61. Eliyahu Sasson, "Hawla al-Tafahum al-Manshud," *Filastin*, July 31, 1930.

62. *Filastin*, August 1, 1930. This was also published as "Ma leyehudim velele'umiyut Yehudit," *Davar*, August 29, 1930.

63. Michael Assaf, "Delatroya benosah sefarad," *Davar*, January 25, 1928.

64. Eliyahu Sasson, "Al Mu'atamar al-Israe'ili al-Sharqi," *Al-'Alam al-Isra'ili*, June 27, 1932.

65. Eliyahu Sasson, "Mu'atamar al-Isra'ili al-'Arabi," *Al-'Alam al-Isra'ili*, July 18, 1932.

66. Michael Assaf, "Hawla al-Mu'atamar al-Yahudi al-'Arabi," *Al-'Alam al-Isra'ili*, July 18, 1932.

67. Eliyahu Sasson, "Hawla al-Mu'atamar al-Isra'ili al-Sharqi," *Al-'Alam al-Isra'ili*, July 22, 1932.

68. Eliyahu Sasson, "Hawla al-Mu'tamar al-Yahudi al-Sharqi," *Al-'Alam al-Isra'ili*, August 8, 1932.

69. Sasson, *Baderekh el hashalom*, 16.

70. Eyal, *Hasarat hakesem min hamizrah*, 48–50 and 52–57.

71. Letter from Gershon Barag to Yisrael Ben-Ze'ev, October 7, 1942, CZA J17/322.

72. Halperin, *Babel in Zion*, 198–99.

73. Goitein, "'Al hora'at ha'aravit," 13.

74. See Bezalel, *Nolatedem Ziyonim*, 255 and 386; Gribetz, *Defining Neighbors*, 185–98; Jacobson, "Jews Writing in Arabic"; Mendel, *The Creation of Israeli Arabic*, 16–27.

75. Halperin, "Orienting Language."

76. Mendel, *The Creation of Israeli Arabic*, 30.

77. Halperin, *Babel in Zion*, 198–200.

78. According to Menachem Klein, not only Sephardi or Oriental Jews constructed Arab-Jewish identity, but also Ashkenazi Jews who lived in close proximity to Arabs and spoke Arabic. Ben-Ze'ev may serve as an example of such an Ashkenazi Arab Jew. See Klein, "Arab Jew in Palestine."

79. Derri-Weksler wrote a fascinating microhistory of the Arab Library of so-called abandoned Palestinian books in Jaffa, collected by Ben Ze'ev, and the institutional struggles over its holdings. See Derri-Weksler, "Mizrahanut alternativit vehishtalvut bamerhav ha'aravi hamekomi," 2–5.

80. Ibid., 5–7; "Yisrael Ben Ze'ev"; Avidan Mashiach, "Doktor Yisrael Ben Ze'ev: Hiyuniyut hamizrah vetarbut hama'arav," *Herut*, February 11, 1964; "Hamitlamed ha'ivri harishon doctor bamichlala hamitsrit," *Doar Hayom*, February 7, 1927.

81. Kimchi, *Ziyonut betsel hapiramidot*, 162–63, and 166–69.

82. Derri-Weksler, "Mizrahanut alternativit vehishtalvut bamerhav ha'aravi hamekomi," 5–7; "Yisrael Ben Ze'ev"; Avidan Mashiach, "Doktor Yisrael Ben Ze'ev: Hiyuniyut hamizrah vetarbut hama'arav," *Herut*, February 11, 1964; "Hamitlamed ha'ivri harishon doctor bamichlala hamitsrit," *Doar Hayom*, February 7, 1927.

83. Yisrael Ben Ze'ev, untitled lecture at the Arabic teachers' meeting in Tel Aviv, July 3–4, 1939, CZA J17/319.

84. Halperin, *Babel in Zion*, 186.

85. Yisrael Ben Ze'ev, proceedings from a discussion regarding the teaching of Arabic, Education Department, Jerusalem, April 10–11, 1938, CZA J17/319

86. Shlomo Dov Goitein, untitled lecture at the Arabic teachers' meeting in Tel Aviv, July 3–4, 1939, CZA J17/319.

87. Arabic teachers in 1940, CZA J17/296; Proceedings of the Arabic teachers' meeting in Hebrew schools in Jerusalem, October 12, 1939, CZA J17/296; List of schools and Arabic teachers during 1945–1946, November 19, 1945, CZA J17/5853 (judging from the names, most teachers mentioned in this list were Oriental and Sephardi Jews, including Eliyahu Tzoreff, Avraham Ben Menashe, Ovadia Lalo, Ahron Moreh, Eliyahu Habuba).

88. Proceedings of the annual conference of Arabic teachers, August 3, 1944, CZA J17/319.

89. H. Shachter, "Hora'at ha'aravit bebatey sefer yehudim be'eretz israel," n.d., CZA J17/296.

90. See, for example, proceedings of the committee for the teaching of Arabic in Hebrew schools, March 22, 1931, CZA J17/249.

91. Halperin, *Babel in Zion*, 188.

92. Proceedings of the meeting of the curriculum committee, March 23, 1943, CZA, J17/322.

93. Michael Dana, untitled lecture at the Arabic teachers; meeting in Tel Aviv, July 3–4, 1939, CZA J17/319. See also "Sfarim 'ivriyim lelimud ha'aravit," *Davar*, January 9, 1947.

94. Shamosh, *Tmunot mishney ha'olamot*, 132–33.

95. Yitzhak Shamosh, untitled address to the second convention of Arabic teachers in the Kibbutzim, February 5, 1941, CZA J17/322

96. David Zvi Banet, untitled address to the committee of designing the curriculum for the Arabic teachers' course, March 24, 1943, CZA J17/322

97. Letter from Yisrael Ben-Ze'ev to Dr. Mosensohn, September 28, 1942, CZA J17/322.

98. Yisrael Ben-Ze'ev, untitled address to the annual conference of Arabic teachers, August 4, 1944, CZA J17/319.

99. Mendel, *The Creation of Israeli Arabic*, 29. Ben-Ze'ev, Elmaleh, Rivlin, and Eliyahu Habuba were among those who composed Arabic textbooks. Elmaleh also composed the first Arabic-Hebrew dictionary. In addition, other textbooks that were used were those composed by Arab writers, including Khalil al-Sakakini's *al-Jadid* and several textbooks from Egypt.

100. Mendel, *The Creation of Israeli Arabic*, 29. See also Yisrael Ben-Ze'ev, untitled address to the Arabic Teachers' meeting in Tel Aviv, 1939, 20, CZA J17/319. When discussing the problems with existing textbooks by Jews and Arabs alike, which were not completely appropriate for secondary schools, Ben-Ze'ev noted that the most important book was written by the teacher in the Jerusalemite Schneller School, Elias Nassarallah Hadad.

101. Mendel, *The Creation of Israeli Arabic*, 29–31.

102. Curriculum for the Arabic teachers' training courses, Jerusalem, January 19, 1944, CZA J17/296. On 'Adel Jabre, see Hajjar Halaby, "Out of the Public Eye."

103. Proceedings of the committee of designing the curriculum for the Arabic teachers' course, March 24, 1943, CZA J17/322.

104. Abraham Ohana, "Be'ayat limud ha'aravit bebatey hasefer ha'ivrim," *Hed Hamizrah*, September 18, 1943.

105. Shamir, "Kishrey hinuch vetarbut," especially 94–96.

106. Ibid., 96.

107. Derri-Weksler ("Mizrahanut alternativit vehishtalvut bamerhav ha'aravi hamekomi") discusses another library that Ben-Ze'ev wanted to establish in Jaffa, to contain books that were collected from other Arab libraries and individuals following the 1948 war. Derri-Weksler was not aware of the existence of the library in Jerusalem, but the records indicate that such a library did exist and operated in the 1940s under the leadership of Ben-Ze'ev.

108. Proceedings of the annual conference of Arabic teachers, August 4, 1944, CZA J17/319.

109. Yellin and Dushkin, proceedings from a meeting regarding the teaching of Arabic, Education Department, Jerusalem, April 10–11, 1938, CZA J17/319.

110. Eliyahu Habuba, untitled address to the annual conference of Arabic teachers, August 4, 1944, CZA J17/319. On Habuba in general, see "Eliyahu Habuba." On his textbooks and contribution to the teaching of Arabic in Hebrew schools, see Yehoshua Ben Hanania, "Sifrey limud 'ivr'im le'aravit," *Hed Hamizrah*, June 30, 1942.

111. Eliyahu Sasson to the secretariat of the Jewish Agency, January 20, 1941, CZA J17/322. See also letter from Eliyahu Sasson to the deputy director of the Department of Education, January 12, 1943, CZA J17/322. Sasson received many applications from native speakers of Arabic to become Arabic teachers. See, for example, CZA S25\22168

112. Halperin, *Babel in Zion*, 157.

113. Mendel, *The Creation of Israeli Arabic*, 31.

114. Michael Assaf, untitled address to the second convention of Arabic teachers in the kibbutzim, February 5, 1941, CZA J17/322.

115. Halperin, *Babel in Zion*, 152–62.

116. Eliyahu Agassi, untitled address to the second convention of Arabic teachers in the kibbutzim, February 5, 1941, CZA J17/322.

117. Eyal, *Hasarat hakesem min hamizrah*, 26.

118. On Shami, see Tamari, "Ishaq al-Shami and the Predicament of the Arab-Jew in Palestine."

119. Eliyahu Agassi, untitled address to the second convention of Arabic teachers in the kibbutzim, February 5, 1941, CZA J17/322.

120. Ibid.

121. Letter from Yisrael Ben Ze'ev to A. Arnon, December 21, 1942, CZA J17/322; letter from Yisrael Ben Ze'ev to Shimon Bejerano, January 5, 1943, CZA J17/322.

122. Mendel, *The Creation of Israeli Arabic*, 33–34.

123. Dr. Solovichki, director of the Department of Education in the Jewish National council, at a party held as part of the Arabic teachers' conference (August 14–15, 1945, CZA J17/5853).

124. Ben Ze'ev, at a party held as part of the Arabic teachers' conference (August 14–15, 1945, CZA J17/5853).

125. Moshe Smilanski, at a party held as part of the Arabic teachers' conference (August 14–15, 1945, CZA J17/5853).

126. David Moyal, at a party held as part of the Arabic teachers' conference (August 14–15, 1945, CZA J17/5853).

127. Yehoshafat Harkabi, at a party held as part of the Arabic teachers' conference (August 14–15, 1945, CZA J17/5853).

128. Derri-Weksler, "Mizrahanut alternativit vehishtalvut bamerhav ha'aravi hame-komi," 6–8.

129. In 1962 Agassi founded the Arab Publishing House, where he edited and published books for youth and adults, including many fables and folk tales from the Jewish community of Iraq. During the 1960s, he also edited Arabic children's newspapers. Hannah Amit-Kochavi created a typology of translators of Arabic literature into Hebrew between 1896 and 2009. The earliest translators lived in Jerusalem during the early twentieth century, were natives of Palestine, spoke Arabic, and had Arab neighbors. For more on the history of translation and translators of Arabic into Hebrew, see Amit-Kochavi, "The People behind the Words: Professional Profiles and Activity Patterns of Arabic Literature into Hebrew (1896–2009)"; Yardeni, *Ha'itonut ha'ivrit be'erets Israel bashanim 1863–1904*, 318–24.

130. Kayyal, "Targumey hasifurt ha'aravit le'ivrit," especially 176–77.

131. Shamir, "Kishrey hinuch vetarbut," 103.

132. Yosef Rivlin, "Yehudim ve'aravim," *Hed Hamizrah*, November 6, 1942.

FOUR *Mixing and Unmixing in the Oriental Ghettos*

1. "Hatzharat Moshe Levi hanivhar hayehudi le'iriyat yafo," *Iton Meyuhad*, June 29, 1934. This newspaper, which was established in 1933 presented itself as unaffiliated with any political party. It reported mainly on daily events, often of a sensational nature. On the newspaper, see Tzifroni, "Iton meyuhad- ha'olam betzahov."

2. Tivoni, *Kerem haya leyedidi*, 9–51. This book is a memoir of Levi's life, based on Levi's recollections, essentially told by Levi to Tivoni.

3. There is a detailed discussion on the location of the border between these neighborhoods below in the chapter.

4. Tivoni, *Kerem haya leyedidi*, 113.

5. Ibid., 166.

6. Ibid., 166–67.

7. Ibid., 171–73.

8. "Shum bahura mitel aviv lo hitnazra bashanim ha'ahronot," and Peg'a hanedunya dohef et habahurot hayehudiyot lizro'ot zarim,"*Iton Meyuhad*, December 26, 1942. On the role of the mukhtar in cases of conflicts among Jews and Arabs in the Yemenite Quarter and in cases of conversion of Jewish girls to Islam, see Tivoni, *Kerem haya leyedidi*, 168–72.

9. Letter from the Council of the Jewish Community in Hebron to the National Council, March 14, 1928, CZA J1/15.

10. For letters on different cases from 1929 and 1939, see unit 3, file 1929, Haifa Historical Society, Haifa (HHS). See also Razi, "Yehudiot 'arviot?," especially 147–57. For more on the relations between Arab men and Jewish women in Haifa, see Kidron, *Bein leom lemakom*, 65–66.

11. Tivoni, *Kerem haya leyedidi*, 168–71. Another case of a Jewish man who converted to Christianity as a result of hardships was described in "Mibagdad derekh hametzuka betel Aviv leagan hatvila," *Iton Meyuhad*, April 17, 1938.

12. Tivoni, *Kerem haya leyedidi*, 167.

13. Ibid., 161–62; see also 173–75. For more on the involvement of local Jews in the security apparatus, see chapter 5.

14. The term "frontier neighborhood" was commonly used in the Hebrew press and in Jewish political and public discourse during the Mandatory period. For more on this issue, see Bernstein, "South of Tel Aviv and North of Jaffa," 117.

15. This shift is very well portrayed and discussed in Klein, *Lives in Common*, especially 132.

16. On the term "ghetto" in its sociological meaning, see Wacquant, "Mahu ghetto?," especially 151–52.

17. Monterescu and Rabinowitz, "Introduction," 1.

18. Allegra, Casaglia, and Rokem, "The Political Geographies of Urban Polarization."

19. Quoted in ibid., 566. See also Tzfadia, "Mixed Cities in Israel," 153–56.

20. Monterescu and Rabinowitz, "Introduction," 5.

21. Karlinsky, "Jaffa and Tel Aviv before 1948," 139. In 1931, for example, when the last British census in Palestine was conducted, about 82 percent of the Arabs lived in Arab villages or towns, while about 50 percent of the Jewish population lived in mixed cities (Horowitz and Lissak, *Origins of the Israeli Polity*, especially 27–28).

22. Goren, "'Avoda meshutefet bein yehudim le'aravim behitpathut ha'aretz–haim titachen?'," especially 93–94.

23. Monterescu and Rabinowitz, "Introduction," 4.

24. Goren, *Shituf betzel 'imut*, 12.

25. Tzfadia, "Mixed Cities in Israel."

26. See, for example, Bernstein, *Nashim bashula'im*; Hart, *Krovim-rehokim*; Monterescu

and Rabinowitz, *Mixed Towns, Trapped Communities*; Sharfman, Nachmias, and Mansour, *The Secret of Coexistence*; Yazbak and Weiss, *Haifa before and after 1948*.

27. Monterescu and Rabinowitz, "Introduction," 11 and 14.

28. Nachmias, "Arabs and Jews in a Dynamic Job Market," 68.

29. Karlinsky, "Jaffa-Tel-Aviv Partitioned Urban Space during the Mandate" 2. Elsewhere Karlinsky calls this a divided model of urban coexistence ("Jaffa and Tel Aviv before 1948," 140).

30. See, for example, Hart, *Krovim-rehokim*; Klein, *Lives in Common*; LeBor, *City of Oranges*; Yazbak and Weiss, *Haifa before and after 1948*.

31. Abassi, "Mishpahat Tabari vehanhagat hakehila ha'aravit betveria beshalhei hatkufa ha'othmanit ubetkufat hamandat" and *Zefat bitkufat hamandat 1918–1948*.

32. This is the explanation offered in Tzfadia, "Mixed Cities in Israel."

33. Karlinsky, "Jaffa-Tel-Aviv Partitioned Urban Space during the Mandate," 11.

34. There are two recent exceptions. First, Menachem Klein focuses much of *Lives in Common* on the local, native identity of Arab Jews and on daily interactions between Jews and Arabs in Jaffa, Jerusalem, and Hebron. Second, in *"Haifa Umm al-Gharib,"* Regev Nathanson and Abbas Shiblak touch on the cultural proximity in terms of language, dress, and lifestyle between Arabs and Jews of Oriental descent, whom the authors refer to as *Yahud Awlad-'Arab*.

35. In Tiberias, Jews were 63 percent of the population in the late 1930s. By the end of the Mandatory period, 6,400 of the 11,000 residents of the city, or 58 percent of the population, were Jews. In Safed, the Jewish population fell from a majority of the city's population on the eve of World War I to 21 percent by the late 1930s ("Hayeshuv ha'ivri besof 1936," *Davar*, February 11, 1937). See also Ben-Artzi, *Lahapokh midbar lekarmel*, 334; Bezalel, *Noladetem Ziyonim*, 24 and 40; Klein, *Lives in Common*, 66 and 69.

36. Report of the community's committee, 1940, Haifa Municipal Archive (HMA), Haifa, 35–08–11. According to David Gurevich, Aaron Gertz, and Roberto Bachi, the Jewish community in Jerusalem in 1939 was 52.7 percent Ashkenazim, 13.1 percent Sephardim, and 34.2 percent Mizrahim; in Haifa in 1938 the proportions were 86.2 percent Ashkenazim, 12.3 percent Sephardim, and 1.5 percent Mizrahim; and in Tiberias in 1942 they were 27.4 percent Ashkenazim, 62.1 percent Sephardim, and 10.5 percent Mizrahim (*Ha'aliya, hayeshuv vehatnu'a hativ'it shel haukhlusin be'eretz israel*, 257). See also Haim, *Yihud vehishtalvut*, 32–33.

37. However, there were very small communities of Sephardi Jews living in agricultural settlements such as Pkiyin, which was the oldest Jewish agricultural settlement; and modern ones, like those established after the Zionist emigrations, such as Yavneel. See Bezalel, *Nolatedem Ziyonim*, 25–35.

38. Ibid., 21–23. Only a few Jews—not enough to be considered a community—lived at times in other Arab cities such as Jericho, Beer-Sheba, Lod, and Nazareth (ibid., 23).

39. H. Rokah, "'Al hikaltut hayehudim hamizrahim," *Davar*, May 17, 1936.

40. On the poor conditions in these neighborhoods and on the patterns of marriage and

birthrates among the Oriental Jews, see, for example, Bachi, *Hakira 'al ha'oni vehatzuna hayeruda bekerv yehudei yerushlayim*; "Doh shel *Va'ad hakehila*," 1940, HMA 35–08–11; Gurevich, Gertz, and Bachi, *Ha'aliya, hayeshuv vehatnu'a hativ'it shel haukhlusin be'eretz israel*, 237–38; "Hamiktzo'ot vetnaey ha'avoda shel ha'ovdim hamizrahim," *Davar*, August 24, 1939; Kark, Oren-Nordheim, and Eshel, *Yerushalayim vesvivoteha*, 128; "Totz'ot haseker shel 1937," *Davar*, February 21, 1938.

41. Vashitz, *Ha'aravim be'eretz israel*, 223.

42. Radai, *Bein shtey 'arim*, 173–74.

43. Avraham Zebrasky, "Eich neshaken et haplitim," *Yedi'ot 'Iriyat Tel Aviv*, 1936, 4–5.

44. Haim, *Yihud vehishtalvut*, 32–34; Kark, Oren-Nordheim, and Eshel, *Yerushalayim vesvivoteha*, 199–201.

45. Razi, *Yaldei hahefker*, 47–51 and 86–90.

46. On concerns about the abandoned children and their potentially bad influence on the children of Tel Aviv, see a letter from Hedvig Gelner to Israel Rokach, February 19, 1940, 4/1426, Tel Aviv Municipal Archive, Tel Aviv (hereafter TAMA). On children migrating from Tiberias to Tel Aviv in search of jobs, see a letter from Hedvig Gelner to S. Henrietta Szold, July 10, 1934, TAMA 4/2116. In 1939–40 hundreds of families migrated to Tel Aviv from Jerusalem and other cities (letter from Hedvig Gelner to the department of social work, October 18, 1940, TAMA 4/1426).

47. See a letter from the welfare department of the local Jewish community commit-tee of Tiberias to Rabbi Ya'akov Moshe Toledano, in Cairo, Feburary 3, 1935, 316.68.24, Tiberias Research Institute, Tiberias (TRI). See also a letter from the child welfare's department of the Tel Aviv municipality to the welfare department of the local Jewish community committee of Jerusalem, April 5, 1938, TAMA 4/1425. The phenomenon of abandoned wives was not limited to Mizrahi Jews, and it is known to be a typical phenomenon of immigration. For more on the abandoned women, see Alroey, "Nashim 'azuvot beshalhey hatkufa ha'othmanit vereshit hamandat"; Razi, *Yaldei hahefker*, 86–89.

48. Bernstein, "South of Tel Aviv and North of Jaffa," 116.

49. Aleksandrowicz, "Gvulot shel niyar," especially 174; Shavit and Biger, *Hahistorya shel tel aviv*, 1:59–61.

50. Aleksandrowicz, "Gvulot shel niyar," 176. This area was also known as Tin Town, due to its small tin-covered houses.

51. Y. Chelouche, *Parashat Hayai*, 20–21; Mori, "Yisuda vehipathuta shel shchunat kerem hatemanim betel aviv," especially 36–37. For a list of Jewish and Arab residents in Kerem Karton, see TAMA 4/2207.

52. Kerem Hatemanim and parts of Neve Shalom were incorporated into Tel Aviv in 1921, when Tel Aviv was recognized by the British authorities as a township. See "Letoldot gvuloteha she tel aviv," *Yedi'ot 'Iriyat Tel Aviv*, November–December 1943, 12. However, as will be discussed below, both Levi and representatives of Neve Shalom frequently requested that Tel Aviv incorporate all of the neighborhood. Most probably, at least in the case of Kerem Hatemanim and Karton, their official municipal separation was less

important than their spatial connection. For more on the appeals for the incorporation of the border neighborhoods into Tel Aviv, see in Goren, "Yehudey Yaffo veshe'elat hasipuah 1936–1939."

53. June 21, 1943, Jabotinsky Institute Archive (JIA), Tel Aviv, 10.8–4. For a list of the Jewish residents of Manshiyya, many of whom came originally from Syria, Yemen, Turkey, or Russia, see TAMA 4/4127. The same file contains letters from Jewish residents of Manshiyya who left their houses in the neighborhood during the 1940s because they feared the Arabs living in Manshiyya and nearby. The residents asked for assistance from the municipal government in finding alternative housing.

54. On Kerem Hatemanim and Karton, see B. Nimrod, "Bein kerem hatemanim lekarton," *Hed Hamizrah*, April 14, 1950. According to this article, there were around 2,000 residents in Kerem Hatemanim, and 4,000 in Karton. These numbers differ from the ones presented above.

55. Meir-Glitzenstein, *Yetziyat yehudei teman*, 55. See also "Hayeshuv ha'ivri besof 1936," *Davar*, February 11, 1937.

56. On the political organizations of the Yemenites, see Herzog, *'Adatiyut politit*, 54–75.

57. Ibid., 26.

58. Pomrak, *Chelouche*, 237.

59. Israel Rokach, "Takziva shel 'iriyat tel aviv lishnat haksafim 1949–1950," *Yedi'ot 'Iriyat Tel Aviv*, September 1949, 3–4.

60. Aleksandrowicz, "Gvulot shel niyar," 167, 174–78, and 185.

61. Goren, "Yehudey Yaffo veshe'elat hasipuah 1936–1939," 523; "Tel aviv doreshet sipuah hashkhunot," *Yedi'ot 'Iriyat Tel Aviv*, September–October 1947, 12.

62. Naor, *Social Mobilization in the Arab-Israeli War of 1948*, 118.

63. Bernstein, "South of Tel Aviv and North of Jaffa," 117–21; Aleksandrowicz, "Gvulot shel niyar," 170–80. See also Goren, "Yehudey Yaffo veshe'elat hasipuah 1936–1939," 508–11; LeVine, *Overthrowing Geography*, 114–17; Shavit and Biger, *Hahistorya shel tel aviv*, 99. According to a 1928 census, 1,762 Jews lived in the part of Neve Shalom that was in Tel Aviv, and 2,445 Jews lived in the part that was in Jaffa. According to the same census, 1,826 Jews lived in Harat al-Tank (Aleksandrowicz, "Gvulot shel niyar," 178). For a list of the neighborhoods included in Tel Aviv in 1921, see *Yedi'ot 'Iriyat Tel Aviv*, 1943, 12.

64. Goren, *Shituf betzel 'imut*, 61.

65. Rotbard, *'Ir levana, 'ir shhora*, 161–62.

66. For a list of Arabs living in Kerem Hatemanim/Karton, see TAMA, 4/2207.

67. Manshiyya Police Station, general information, June 21, 1943, JIA, kaf 4-10/8. See also Musih, "Malachim bishmey manshiyya," 33.

68. Rivka Aharonson, "Plitey manshiyya," *Davar*, May 10, 1936.

69. Musih, "Malachim bishmey manshiyya," 48.

70. "Lekah hape'ula," *Davar*, June 9, 1936.

71. For example, Chaim Alperin, the city inspector of Tel Aviv, commented in January 1948 about the Jewish refugees who had escaped from Manshyyia: "This human material

that forms the most painful problem represents no problem as long as it lives in the peripheral alleyways in poor housing conditions, far removed from cultural customs and in Arab homes, and does not become involved in the life of the city" (quoted in Naor, *Social Mobilization in the Arab-Israeli War of 1948*, 171–72).

72. Kidron, *Bein leom lamakom*, 294.

73. See, for example, various complaints about the conditions in Kerem Hatemanim and its ongoing neglect by both Jaffa and Tel Aviv: Levi to Wauchope, copy of memorandum sent in English to the mayor of Tel Aviv, August 24, 1936, TAMA, 4/2208; Levi to the mayor of Tel Aviv, November 23, 1937, TAMA 4/2208. In his writings, Levi does not distinguish between Kerem Hatemanim and Karton, referring instead to the Yemenite Quarter. See the Committee of Kerem Hatemanim (Karton Manshiyya Jaffa) to Israel Rokach, March 9, 1947, TAMA 4/2209.

74. For a detailed analysis of the appeal process and the negotiations with the British administration and decision makers, see Goren, "Yehudey Yaffo veshe'elat hasipuah 1936–1939," especially 511–30. Goren places much of the blame for the failure to annex the neighborhoods on the way the process was dragged out on the British Mandatory authorities.

75. The Office of Municipal Inspector to the secretary of Tel Aviv Municipality, March 7, 1927, TAMA 4/2207.

76. Abraham Barnett to the Tel Aviv municipality, November 12, 1936, TAMA 4/2208.

77. Committee of the Quarter of Neve Shalom to the Jewish Agency, August 16, 1939, TAMA 4/2208.

78. Bernstein, "South of Tel Aviv and North of Jaffa," 127.

79. See, for example, ibid. See also Bernstein, *Nashim bashula'im*, especially 51–83 and 166–217; Hart, *Krovim-rehokim*; Hillel, "Kishrey yom yom bein yafo vetel aviv bitkufat hamandat, heibetim shel tarbut, biluy upnay."

80. "Brit shalom bekerem hatemanim," *'Mishmar*, August 21, 1947.

81. Musih, "Malachim bishmey manshiyya," 30.

82. Ibid., 83–87.

83. The poultry market is described as a vibrant place, which attracted many residents of Tel Aviv who used to visit the Carmel market. See Y. Mastboim, "Ashkenazim kavshu et kerem hatemanim," *Iton Meyuhad*, April 20, 1945.

84. Tivoni, *Kerem haya leyedidi*, 176–77.

85. Geula H., "Isha mitlonenet," *Iton Meyuhad*, November 17, 1933. See also a letter from a resident of Kerem Hatemanim to the Tel Aviv municipality mentioning the poor sanitary conditions in the Hacarmel Market, May 28, 1936, TAMA, 4/2208. Note the mention of the location of the café in the heart of Tel Aviv: it was behind Cinema Allenby, one of the main cinemas in Tel Aviv. This location affected who frequented the café. Still, it was called an Oriental café and described as similar to the Arab cafés in Jaffa. On cafés in Tel Aviv with an Oriental nature as sites of crossing and interaction, see Bernstein, *Nashim bashula'im*, 67–74.

86. "Sha'a kala 'im zoleley kubeibot vesahkaney shesh besh," *'Iton Meyuhad*, July 26, 1946. On cinemas as a site for interaction, see Hillel, "Kishrey yom yom bein yafo vetel aviv bitkufat hamandat, heibetim shel tarbut, biluy upnay," 21–23.

87. Moshe Levi to the high commissioner of Palestine, August 24, 1936, TAMA 4/2208.

88. Helman, *Or veyam hekifuha*, 110.

89. Bernstein, *Nashim bashula'im*, 59–76.

90. "Yom hakippurim be'ir hakodesh yaffo," *'Iton Meyuhad*, October 4, 1933; "Yom kippurim betel aviv—yom 'kippurim' beyaffo," *'Iton Meyuhad*, September 20, 1934.

91. "Tiyul hatuf barehovot shel yaffo beyom hashabat," *'Iton Meyuhad*, March 8, 1940.

92. Bernstein, *Nashim bashula'im*, 188–92; *'Iton Meyuhad*, eve of Sukkot 1946; *'Iton Meyuhad*, October 26, 1946. See also Helman, *Or veyam hekifuha*, 166–69. Prostitution was a concern in Jerusalem as well. See, for example, "Haprizut be'ir hakodesh," *'Iton Meyuhad*, February 4, 1934; "'Anaf batey haboshet poreah beyerushalayim," *'Iton Meyuhad*, October 15, 1947.

93. "Irgun yehudi-'aravi lamilhama baprizut," *'Iton Meyuhad*, September 5, 1947.

94. Bernstein, *Nashim bashula'im*, 205–7.

95. "Hayeha vekitza hatragi shel harakdanit sarah, beyaffo," *'Iton Meyuhad*, May 16, 1947.

96. "Mumarim vehashudim betel aviv," January 2, 1948, HA, 112/1221. We thank Deborah Bernstein for drawing our attention to this document.

97. See Rotbard, *'Ir levana, 'ir shhora*.

98. See, for example, A. Khalfon, "Heifa 'iri," 60–64; Nuseibeh, *Zikriyat maqdisiya sirah d'atiya*, 43–45; interview of Nethanel Matalon, February 27, 2003, Oral History Project (OHP), Institute of Contemporary Jewry, Hebrew University of Jerusalem; lists of residents and landlords by streets in Kerem Hatemanim-Karton, February 1935–June 1936, TAMA 4/2207. See also Hasan and Ayalon, "Arabs and Jews, Leisure and Gender in Haifa's Public Spaces"; Klein, *Lives in Common*, 37–40.

99. Interview of Nethanel Matalon, February 27, 2003, OHP.

100. Sabbagh, *Palestine*, 178–79. Karl Sabbagh was the son of the famous broadcaster Isa Sabbagh, who worked for the BBC Arabic service during World War II (Nathanson and Shiblak, "*Haifa Umm al-Gharib*," 197).

101. Rozenfeld, *Mea shnot simha*, 5; Maman, *Noladeti ba'aretz hazot*, 88.

102. There were stories of such cases from the Mandatory period, too, like the one told by Ziona Tajer of her mother breast-feeding Arab children in Jaffa in the 1920s. See interview of Ziona Tajer, December 27, 1972, OHP. However, as mentioned, these were more common during the late Ottoman period. See, for example, Yehoshua, *Yerushalayim tmol shilshom*, 136.

103. Interview of Eliezer Matalon, May 11, 1992, OHP. Moshe Matalon founded the Hamagen Association in 1913 and was one of the leading Sephardi public figures in Jaffa who struggled for Jewish-Arab peaceful coexistence. See "Moshe Matalon."

104. Halperin, "Babel in Zion," 245–308.

105. Khaled, *My People Shall Live*. Khaled's description of her childhood should be read

in the context of the narrative of the making of a Palestinian freedom fighter, opposing her ideal early childhood with the bitter reality of a partitioned Palestine. The decision by the United Nations to partition the country marked "the turning-point in my relationship with Tamara" and was followed by Khaled's family's expulsion from Haifa in April 1948 and the *Nakba* of the Palestinian people (ibid.). In addition, as Manar Hasan and Ami Ayalon note, "both Arab and Jews tend to view pre-1948 daily realities through the loaded prism of subsequent events" ("Arabs and Jews, Leisure and Gender in Haifa's Public Spaces," 71). For an example of such a retrospective description, see Hazem Zaki Nuseibeh's account of his happy childhood days in Jerusalem before 1929, when "the ambiance of coexistence the city witnessed was similar to the calm before the storm, a storm that hit all the people of Palestine" (*Zikriyat maqdisiya sirah d'atiya*, 44; see also 43–45).

106. Al-Shukeiri, *Arba'un 'aman fi alhayah al'arabiyah waldawliyah*, 280–83.

107. See M. Cohen, "Islam and the Jews."

108. Karmi, *In Search of Fatima*, 41. See also Hasan and Ayalon, "Arabs and Jews, Leisure and Gender in Haifa's Public Spaces," 95; Klein, *Lives in Common*, 74–75; Nathanson and Shiblak, "*Haifa Umm al-Gharib*," 196.

109. Gayger, *Ehad mizikney Tzfat*, 211 and 267–68.

110. Klein, "Arab Jew in Palestine," especially 135–37.

111. Frumkin, *Derech shofet beyerushalayim*, 281, 323. See also Klein, *Lives in Common*, 52–54.

112. Yehoshua, *Yerushalayim tmol shilshom*, 138.

113. This issue is discussed thoroughly in Razi, *Yaldei hahefker* and "Subversive Youth Cultures in Mandate Tel-Aviv."

114. "Al be'ayat hahinuch veyaldey harehov," *Hed Hamizrah*, December 7, 1946.

115. Vashitz, *Ha'aravim be'eretz israel*, 236. For a detailed discussion of the discourse and praxis in the Jewish community regarding Jewish neglected children in Mandatory Palestine, as well as the involvement of the British authorities in the treatment of these children, see Razi, *Yaldei hahefker*.

116. The neighborhood was originally established in 1887.

117. 'Adaki, *Be'esh netsura*, 23. See also Klein, *Lives in Common*, 80–81; Shchori-Rubin and Schwartz, "Migrashei Hamishakim shel Guggenheimer-Hadassah," 79.

118. "Migrashey mishakim leyladim," *Doar Hayom*, January 22, 1934. See also a thank-you letter from the local Jewish community committee in Tiberias to the Guggenheimer playground committee, June 10, 1940, TRI, 839.896.12.

119. Letter from Mrs. R. Weitlas, chair of the Guggenheimer play committee in Jerusalem to the Jewish Agency, March 6, 1940, CZA S25/3055; Shchori-Rubin and Schwartz, "Migrashei Hamishakim shel Guggenheimer-Hadassah," 90–91. The authors also mention a program to establish a playground in Tiberias. Playgrounds were also opened in Rishon Lezion, Gedera, Rehovot, Ekron, Nes Ziona, and even in Mishmar Ha'emek, where the playground was open to Arab children from the neighboring villages.

120. See, for example, letter from the Jewish Agency to Mrs. R. Weitlas, chair of the Guggenheimer play committee in Jerusalem, April 4, 1940, CZA S25/3055. The letter

writer was concerned about the mixed nature of Jews and Arabs in the playgrounds not only on political grounds, but on moral ones.

121. Shchori-Rubin and Schwartz, "Migrashei Hamishakim shel Guggenheimer-Hadassah," 90–91.

122. See letter from Reuven Podhorzer, chair of Safed's community organization, to Mrs. R. Weitlas, chair of the Guggenheimer play committee in Jerusalem, March 1940, CZA S25/3055. Interestingly, it seems that the playgrounds were a very welcome addition to children's lives in Safed, which lacked recreational spaces. As Gayger described in his memoirs, "we children had to improvise solutions and alternatives. Abandoned spaces and wrecked houses . . . became our playgrounds" (*Ehad mizikney Tzfat*, 93).

123. Hadawi, "Sodomy, Locusts, and Cholera," 15–16. As seen elsewhere in this chapter, this is yet another example of a retrospective narrative told in light of future national developments.

124. "Mihayey hano'ar ha'oved," *Davar*, February 24, 1947.

125. On the membership of youths from Degel Zion in the Irgun, see interview of Menachem Yedid, JIA AI-16. Yedid, a native of Aleppo, was a member of Degel Zion who joined the Irgun. A member of the Herut Party, he later served in the Knesset.

126. On the history of the Arab scouts, see Degani, "They Were Prepared," especially 204. On the Zionist scouts, see Bar-Yosef, "Fighting Pioneer Youth," especially 44–47.

127. Avraham, "Hama'amats hahalutsi behadrachat dorenu hatza'ir," *Bama'aracha*, May 1943.

128. Dalia Karpel, "Bemoskva karu la yamina," *Ha'aretz*, December 7, 2004; Tamar Nesher, "Simha ha'aduma," *Makor Rishon*, November 5, 2004.

129. Ben Zaken, *Komonizm keimperialism tarbuti*, 103–11.

130. Palestine Royal Commission, *Report*, 341–42.

131. Halperin, "The Battle over Jewish Students in the Christian Missionary Schools of Mandate Palestine," especially 746–49. For more on the education system of Sephardi youth during the Mandate period, see Alboher, *Hizdahut, histaglut vehistaygut*, 139–58.

132. In 1925–26, out of the 26,832 Jewish students in Palestine, only 334 were studying in missionary schools, as opposed to 3,444 in schools run by Jewish philanthropic institutions (the French Alliance Israélite Universelle or the British Anglo-Jewish Association). In 1938–39 the number of Jewish students in missionary schools was estimated to be 773, and in 1941–42 it was 1,278 (or 1.4 percent of the Jewish students). See Halperin, "The Battle over Jewish Students in the Christian Missionary Schools of Mandate Palestine," 739.

133. Ibid., 750.

134. Quoted in ibid., 747.

135. Reports of the Council of the Sephardi Community in Haifa, HMA 8–215.

136. See, for example, an exchange about the case of Rachel Tadri, July 1939, TAMA 4/1772; a letter (regarding M. Mizrahi, who had immigrated from Iraq in 1931 and was considering sending his children to a missionary school) to the social work department at the Tiberias Municipality, November 27, 1938, TAMA 4/1772.

137. See, for example, the memoirs of Julia Chelouche (*Ha'etz vehashorashim*, 60).

138. Hasan, "Hanishkahot," 155.

139. See, for example, Eliachar, *Lihyot 'im yehudim*, 73.

140. Interview of Aharon Chelouche, 1994, OHP.

141. See a letter (complaining about the number of buses going from Tiberias to Al-Hama and the security concerns the writer had about Jews riding an Arab bus) to the Jewish community organization in Tiberias, January 27, 1942, TRI 306.61.24.

142. In 1936 the Khalfon family traveled to Al-Hama and stayed in a hotel among hundreds of Arab families. See Khalfon, "Heifa 'iri," 64.

143. For a list of businesses in Tiberias—including hotels, motels, stores, cafés, and bars—allowed to sell alcoholic beverages, see TRI 759.293.5.

144. See various letters of complaints from 1943–46 about Café Shor, Café Imperial, and Café Panorama, and the way they hurt the feelings of the Jewish residents to the Tiberias municipality, TRI 360.102.5.

145. Eliachar, *Lihyot 'im yehudim*, 70–71; Tuqan, *Derekh hararit, otobiyographya*, 16; Rozenfeld, *Mea shnot simha*, 15.

146. Hasan, "Hanishkahot," 100. On other areas of recreation in Haifa and Tiberias, see ibid., 104–7.

147. Hasan and Ayalon, "Arabs and Jews, Leisure and Gender in Haifa's Public Spaces," 84–85; Sharfman, "Hahayim beheifa hayu aherim."

148. Matalon, *Tel aviv*.

149. A letter from the head of the social division to Mr. Krinizi, the chair of Ramat Gan's municipality, July 24, 1945, TAMA 4/2155.

150. Gayger, *Ehad mizikney Tzfat*, 202–5.

F I V E   *Crossing the Lines: The Security Border between Jews and Arabs*

1. Shapira, *Land and Power*, 257.

2. "Halvayato shel Yisrael Hazan," *Doar Hayom*, April 19, 1936.

3. Niv, *Ma'arachot ha'irgun hatzva'i leumi*, 273.

4. Slutsky, *Sefer toldot hahaganah*, 2:632–36.

5. For a description of the funeral and the incidents in Jaffa at the time, see Kena'an, *Be'einey shoter falastini*, 75–86.

6. Golan, "Shikunam shel plitim yehudim mitel aviv bezman hamered ha'aravi hagadol."

7. For a discussion of the emphasis on buying Jewish products and its impact on Jewish-Arab relations, see Shoham, "Buy Local or Buy Jewish?"

8. See, for example, Chazan, *Metinut*; Shapira, *Land and Power*; Shavit, *Havlaga o tguva*.

9. For a discussion of the claim that the 1929 riots marked a turning point in the relations between the two peoples, see, for example, Kidron, "Hashpa'at totzoteyhem shel me'ora'ot 1929 'al heifa veyaffo/tel aviv"; "Me'oraot tarpat kenekudat mifne."

10. See, for example, Shapira, *Herev hayona*, 300.

11. Hillel Cohen, *Tarpat*, 300.

12. Menachem Raphael Cohen, "Lo hikartim," *Davar*, October 13, 1929. Also quoted in Hillel Cohen, *Tarpat*, 298–99.

13. David Siton, "Hagigim 'al hasifrut ha'aravit," *Bama'aracha*, September 1966.

14. Menachem Raphael Cohen, "Lo hikartim," *Davar*, October 13, 1929.

15. Itamar Ben-Avi, "Lekah 1936," *Doar Hayom*, April 26, 1939; "He'arat hama'arechet," *Doar Hayom*, April 26, 1939.

16. Slutsky, *Sefer toldot hahaganah*, 2:812.

17. Aharoni, *Be'ikvot hamufti 'im David Raziel*, 46.

18. "Yom zva'aa ba'aretz," *Hatzofeh*, July 26, 1938.

19. Slutsky, *Sefer toldot hahaganah*, 2:828.

20. Aharoni, *Be'ikvot hamufti 'im David Raziel*, 52.

21. Ibid., 8–9.

22. Y. Amrami interview of Ya'acov Sika Aharoni, July 18, 1993, JIA, ein-alef/68.

23. On the background of the members of the Mahatz unit, see *Aharoni, Be'ikvot hamufti 'im David Raziel*, 175–99.

24. Biger, "Binuya shel yerushalayim betkufat hashilton habriti 1917–1948."

25. The attack is described in length in Dror, "Hamistanen leyaffo, 1938."

26. Ibid., 101.

27. Ofir, *Rishoney etzel 1931–1940*, 166–70.

28. See, for example, 'Amidror (born Heller), *Bema'atzar bebeit lehem*, 51.

29. Lapidoth, *Hayom sarah haktana*, 19–22.

30. See, for example, *Filastin*, June 10, 1939.

31. "Rachel Habshush nidona lema'asar 'olam," *Davar*, June 13, 1939. See also *Filastin*, June 13, 1939.

32. From women's organizations to the chief military commander, September 1942, JIA, Gimel 6—4/11.

33. Geula Cohen, *Sipurah shel lohemet*, 276–98.

34. Hasson, *Hazaken veani*, 161. Hasson and this idea are discussed below.

35. "Lezecher ne'edarim," *Davar*, September 20, 1938.

36. Ofir, *Rishoney etzel 1931–1940*, 165.

37. See, for example, the leaflet "*Hashomer Hatza'ir* neged hamitpartzim."

38. Bernstein, *Nashim bashula'im*.

39. Singer, "Leretzah Esther Sheetrit."

40. Singer, '*Im hakorban harishon bemeora'ot heifa*.

41. Hanna Aramoni interview of Yitzhak Hasson, July 10, 1977, JIA ein-het- 6.

42. Hasson, *Hazaken veani*, 16.

43. Ibid.

44. "Giluy da'at ha'edah hasfaradit beyerushalayim," *Davar*, May 23, 1939.

45. "Lo Tirzah," *Davar*, July 7, 1939.

46. Eliachar, *Lihyot 'im Falastinim*, 66–68. See also "Le'inyaney hasha'a: terorism," *Hed Hamizrah*, March 10, 1944.

47. Chazan, *Metinut*, 234.

48. Rieger, *Hahinuch ha'ivri be'eretz Israel*, 1:216–18. See also Shapira, *Herev hayona*, 374.

49. For a discussion on restraint as a manifestation of a diasporic mentality, see Heshel Yeivin, "Pesh'a hadamim shel hasokhnut"; Shapira, *Herev hayona*, 329.

50. Binyamin and Peterzeyl, *Neged hateror*.

51. Thon, "Hinuch hano'ar be'edot hamizrah," 46–47.

52. Ibid., 47.

53. Berlowitz, "Hannah Thon."

54. Thon, "Hinuch hano'ar be'edot hamizrah," 49.

55. Ibid., 48.

56. For a comprehensive summary of this issue, see "Ben gurion veparashat hatemanim," file 193, container 33, Ben-Gurion Archive, Sede Boker (hereafter BGA).

57. Letter from David Ben-Gurion to the director of Agence France-Presse, January 22, 1947, CZA S 25/5654.

58. "Plitat kulmus o plitat pe," *Mishmar*, January 7, 1947.

59. "Temanim mesuyamim," *Herut*, January 4, 1947, issue 68, BGA, container 33, file 193.

60. "Biryonim ratzhu 'aravi betel aviv," *Mishmar*, August 18, 1947.

61. M. Tzadok, "Lehinukh hano'ar hatemani," *Davar*, February 6, 1947.

62. "She'arayim moha 'al pgi'ot hatzava," *Davar*, January 9, 1947.

63. Niv, *Ma'arachot ha'irgun hatzva'i leumi*, 372; Resnik, "Hamordim," 192.

64. "Hayehudim razhu et 'atzmam," quoted in *Davar*, August 13, 1947.

65. H. Sharabi, "Beshuley dvarim," *Davar*, January 6, 1947.

66. Council of the Sephardi Community in Jerusalem to the Jewish Agency, May 1, 1947, CZA S 25/5654.

67. "Haznahat haparvarim peroteha marim," *Mishmar*, January 2, 1947.

68. Ibid. The work of the youth movements in the frontier neighborhoods is discussed in chapter 4.

69. Dizengoff, "Ahrey zrikat hapzaza 'al yaldey bet hasefer."

70. "Behazit hamilhama bein hashomer hatza'ir latemanim," *Hatzofeh*, February 13, 1947.

71. "Hedey hatigra be'inyan kruz etzl benatanya," *Ha'aretz*, February 10, 1947.

72. "Behazit hamilhama bein Hashomer Hatza'ir latemanim," *Hatzofeh*, February 13, 1947; "Ma'asey por'ey etzel," *Mishmar*, February 13, 1947.

73. "El hano'ar ha'ivri," leaflet by the youth movements, April 1947, Hashomer Hatza'ir Archive, Giva'at Haviva (HHA); El po'aley eretz Israel - el miflagot hapo'alim," leaflet by the antifascist youth, HHA 1–3/29/1.

74. Irgun Tzva'i Leumi, statement, JIA, kaf-4—3/12.

75. Begin, *Bamahteret*, 345–46. For a discussion of an incident at the Hashomer Hatz'air club in February 1944 involving members of the Lechi, see Ben Tor, *Sefer toldot halehi*, 2:25.

76. "Yehe nishkenu tahor," *Davar*, March 17, 1947.

77. Ya'acov Riftin, "Dvarim bemo'etzet hashomer hatza'ir," *Mishmar*, March 14, 1947.

78. Yehuda Dranitzky, "Nehadesh et hatnufa hairgunit vehara'ayonit shel hahistadrut," *Mishmar*, June 30, 1947.

79. Goldstein, "Menachem Begin," 2–3.

80. U. Cohen and Leon, *Merkaz tnu'at haherut vehamizrahim, 1965–1977*, 26–28.

81. See Resnik, "Mahteret vepolitikah behevra mefuleget."

82. "El hasfaradim ubney 'edot hamizrah," *Doar Hayom*, January 2, 1931. A total of 47,552 voters participated in the elections for the third Assembly of Representatives, including 20,865 who voted for Mapai, 7,731 for the Revisionist Party, 1,610 for Sephardim-Mapai, 2,031 for the Sephardi Revisionists, 35 for the Sephardim-Poalei Zion Left, 2,235 for the Association of Sephardim, and 1,234 for the Yemenites. See "22.475 lemifleget po'aley eretz Israel mitoch 47.552," *Davar*, January 8, 1931.

83. Quoted in "Mijabotinsky lahitahdut ha'olamit shel hayehudim hasfaradim," October 11, 1928, JIA Alef-1 2/18/2.

84. Moshe Ben-'Ami "Mizrahanut verevizyonism," *Doar Hayom*, September 18, 1932.

85. Ibid.

86. Ibid.

87. "Mireshimat tomhey jabotinsky mibney 'edot hamizrah, el hasfaradim ubnei 'edot hamizrah," *Doar Hayom*, January 2, 1930.

88. See, for example, the responses to Berl Katznelson's article "Dalat ha'am," published originally in *Hapo'el Hatz'air* and reprinted in *Hed Hamizrah* on August 14, 1942. The responses included Ovadia Kimchi, "Berl Katznelson vedalat ha'am," *Hed Hamizrah*, August 28, 1942; S. Ben Moshe, "'Od 'al dalat ha'am,'" *Hed Hamizrah*, September 11, 1942; and I. Ben-Yitzhak, "Al haharda veha'ezra ledalat ha'am," *Hed Hamizrah*, August 15, 1942.

89. Quoted in Goldstein, *Gvura vehadara*, 309–10.

90. Resnik, "Hamordim," 189.

91. Niv, *Ma'arachot ha'irgun hatzva'i leumi*, 372.

92. JIA, Kaf 4–2/13.

93. "El shkenenu ha'aravim," JIA, Kaf 4–3/13.

94. Ibid.

95. See the newspaper cuttings collected in JIA, Kaf 5–1/3/4.

96. Frank, *The Deed*.

97. "Hapraklit hamitzri hayadu'a tawfiq dom pasha mevakesh rahamim lane'eshamim," *Hamashkif*, January 15, 1945.

98. "Hadihi akhlakna," *Filastin*, January 17, 1945, quoted in "Filastin 'al hamishpat," *Hamashkif*, January 18, 1945.

99. Ibid.

100. See Nedava, "Mishpat hakim vebeit tzuri bemitzraim."

101. "Yosef Bet Tzuri."

102. Evron, *Gidi vehama'aracha lepinuy habritim me'eretz israel*, 43.

103. Dotan, *Hamaavak 'al eretz israel*, 272.

104. For more on Beit-Tzuri, see JIA, Kaf 16–1/2.

105. See JIA Kaf 16–2/2. See also Ya'akov Markowizki, *Yamim shel dam vaesh: Pe'ilut halehi beheifa ha'aduma*, 2011, HHS46–54.

106. For more on the Lehi, see Heller, "Lehi bein yamin lesmol."

107. JIA Kaf 16–3/2.

108. Ibid.

109. Ibid.

110. Reuters News Agency, "Al-yawm al-thani lilmuhakamat quttal al-lord Moyne," *Filastin*, January 12, 1945.

111. "Min hamishpat 'ad hatliya," April 1945, JIA Kaf 5–1/3/4.

112. A copy of the report of the Commander of the Cairo Police on the interrogation of the detainees from the British National Archives (FO 371/41515) is included in "Hahitnakshut belord moyne: Hamismakhim," September 1973, JIA Kaf 16–5/2.

113. Among them was the poet and writer Moshe Giora Elimelech. See Yehuda Burla, "Meshorer bemadim," *Bama'aracha: Biton Degel Zion*, 1943.

114. Wasserstein, "Or hadash 'al retzah halord moyne."

115. *Hehazit: 'iton lohamey herut Israel* 15 (December 1944), JIA, Kaf 5–6/2.

116. On the Jewish mobilization to the British army during World War II, see, for example, Gelber, *Hahitnadvut umekoma bamediniyut hatziyonit vehayeshuvit 1939–1942*.

117. On the development of the intelligence units, see Gelber, *Shorshey hahavatzelet*.

118. Lissak, "Habe'aya ha'adatit veirgunim 'adatiyim bitkufat hayeshuv," 243. On the integration of Mizrahim into the Yishuv institutions, see Lissak, *Haelitot shel hayeshuv hyehudi be'eretz Israel bitkufat hamandat*, 108–12.

119. See Eyal, *Hasarat hakesem min hamizrah*, 26–31.

120. Gamliel Cohen, *Hamista'arvim harishonim*, 17–29.

121. Examples include Yosef Lazerovsky, a survivor of the 1929 massacre in Hebron, and Dan Hochman, the mukhtar of Kibbutz Hanita.

122. Bechar, "Re'shit hahista'arvut hameurgenet vehamahlaka hasurit," 17.

123. Shapira, *Yigal Allon*, 183.

124. Gamliel Cohen, *Hamista'arvim harishonim*, 37–39.

125. For more on the Arab Department, see Dror, *Hamista'aravim shel hapalmach*; Pail, "Palmach," 43–44.

126. For more on Cohen, see Y. Cohen, *Eich besurya za'ad hapalmach* and *Leor hayom ubamahshakh*.

127. Shapira, *Herev hayona*, 355.

128. Y. Cohen, *Leor hayom ubamahshakh*, 48–49.

129. Iza Dafni interview of Ya'acov Cohen, March–April 2001, Palmach Archive, Tel Aviv (PA). See also Dror, *Hamista'aravim shel hapalmach*, 38–42.

130. Iza Dafni interview of Ya'acov Cohen, March–April 2001, PA.

131. Ibid.

132. Ibid.

133. On 'Adaki's life, see his *Be'esh netsura*.

134. Weinberg, *The Diary of Shlomo Kostika*. Kostika's diary describes the path that he and other members of his generation followed from the Alliance Israélite Universelle School and the Hehalutz movement in Damascus to the Meah She'arim neighborhood of southern Tel Aviv, the youth movement Hano'ar Ha'oved, agricultural training on Kibbutz Hulata, and service in the Arab Department. See also Shenhav, *Hayehudim ha'aravim*, 7–9.

135. On Thon, see Ezra Greenbaum interview of Uri Thon, November 1989, PA. He was the grandson of Ya'acov Thon, who served as the deputy to Arthur Ruppin in the Eretz Israeli office and was one of the leaders of the Yishuv. Ya'acov Thon was a member of the Kedma Mizraha association; the views of his second wife, Hannah Thon, are discussed above in this chapter. Uri Thon was born in Nahalal. At the age of six his family moved to Baghdad, where his father managed a travel company. The family later moved to Cairo. See Gamliel Cohen, *Hamista'arvim harishonim*, 34–35.

136. Ezra Greenbaum interview of Danny Agmon, December 1990–January 1991, PA.

137. An example is Yair Harari, who was named Subhi Falah when he was born in Syria in 1923. See Avivi, "Lishon 'im haoyev," 58–59.

138. Almog, *The Sabra*, 98 and 198–201.

139. Gamliel Cohen, *Hamista'arvim harishonim*, 90 and 98.

140. Ibid., 155.

141. Ibid., 53.

142. Ezra Greenbaum interview of Gamliel Cohen, no date, PA.

143. Gamliel Cohen, *Hamista'arvim harishonim*, 148–49. See the reports on visits in Jaffa and Haifa, November 2, 1946, and June 16, 1947, PA box 3, file 3.3.

144. Y. Levy, "Kul kalb biji yomo," 30.

145. Quoted in Gamliel Cohen, *Hamista'arvim harishonim*, 122.

146. Quoted in ibid., 126.

147. R. Siton and Sasson, *Anshei hasod vehaseter*, 87–90.

148. Interview of Shaul Carmeli, transcript of the Mista'aravim Film based on a meeting held with the Arab Department members in May 12, 1987, PA.

149. Gamliel Cohen, *Hamista'arvim harishonim*, 221.

150. Bahar, "Avi hamista'arvim."

151. Gamliel Cohen, *Hamista'arvim harishonim*, 35–37; minutes of the Second Conference of Arabic Teachers in Collective Settlements Connected to the Political Department, February 10, 1941, HHA, 21–95/4/2.

152. Gamliel Cohen, *Hamista'arvim harishonim*, 39.

153. Somekh, *Baghdad etmol*. See also A. Behar, "Almog Behar 'im Sasson Somekh."

154. Gamliel Cohen, *Hamista'arvim harishonim*, 51.

155. Iza Dafni interview of Ya'acov Cohen, March–April 2001, PA.

156. Interview of Shaul Carmeli, transcript of the Mista'aravim Film based on a meeting held with the Arab Department members in May 12, 1987, PA.

157. Gamliel Cohen, *Hamista'arvim harishonim*, 35–37.

158. Ibid., 35.

159. Twena, "Tnu'at Ahi'ever hatzionit bebagdad," 3:102. For further details about the Ahi'ever Association, see Haim Cohen, *Hape'ilut hatziyonit bei'raq*, 64–66; Habas, *Ahim krovim-nidahim*, 112–14.

160. Snir, *'Arviyut, yahadut, tziyonut*, 29.

161. Haim Cohen, *Hape'ilut hatziyonit bei'raq*, 170.

162. Habas, *Ahim krovim-nidahim*, 114.

163. Twena, "Tnu'at Ahi'ever hatzionit bebagdad," 3:100.

164. Ilan, "Tivukh tarbuti," 198–99. On the work of Solel Boneh in Iraq and the meaning of Jewish-Arab identity see Shenhav, *Hayehudim ha'aravim*, 25–72.

165. Ilan, "Tivukh tarbuti," 198–99.

166. Ibid., 193–211.

167. "Meir Dahan."

168. Meir Dahan, "Yehudim ve'aravim: Sisma umetziut," *Hed Hamizrah*, October 23, 1942.

169. Eyal, *Hasarat hakesem min hamizrah*, 66–69.

170. The panel was organized as part of the production of a film about the Mista'arvim. See transcript of the Mista'arvim Film based on a meeting held with the Arab Department members in May 12, 1987, PA.

171. Mendel, "Re-Arabising the De-Arabised." For a further discussion of Mendel's analysis, see chapter 4.

172. Slutsky, *Sefer toldot hahaganah*, 3:168.

173. On cross-border smuggling, see Schayegh, "The Many Worlds of Abud Yasin."

174. Comments by Haim Hefer, transcript of the Mista'arvim Film based on a meeting held with the Arab Department members in May 12, 1987, PA.

175. Keren, "Hapalmach ha'amami- giyus no'ar hashkhunot 1942–1944." See also Levin, "Mif'al hagiyus."

176. Keren, "Hapalmach ha'amami- giyus no'ar hashkhunot 1942–1944," 162–66.

177. Allon, *Ma'arachot palmach*, 37.

178. Ibid., 33. See also "Megamot vema'as"; Slutsky, *Sefer toldot hahaganah*, 3:411–12.

179. Moshe Khalfon, "Min ha'avoda bakelet," *'Alon Hapalmach*, August 1944.

180. Ibid. In the original Hebrew: "Yesh le'ahavam, lehitmaser lahem, lehavinam, livnot 'al emunatam vehibatam, veshalav ahrei shalav lehit'alot yahad itam."

181. D. Koren, *Hagadn'a mehahaganah letzahal*, 128 and 148.

182. Kiriyati, "Agudat hashahar," June 10, 1947, 321/48/59, Israel Defense Forces and Defense Ministry Archive, Tel Hashomer (hereafter IDFA).

183. Ibid.

184. Moshe Idelberg to Ya'acov Dori, October 26, 1948, IDFA, 599/56/17.

185. D. Koren, *Hagadn'a mehahaganah letzahal*, 143.

186. Moshe Idelberg to Ya'acov Dori, October 26, 1948, IDFA, 599/56/17.

187. Ibid.

188. Kiryati Brigade, "Pkudat pe'ula bishkhunot hasfar," May 20, 1947, IDFA, 321/48/59.

189. E. Harel, *Lohamey hakrakh*, 285.

190. On Jewish war refugees from the frontier neighborhoods of Tel Aviv, see Naor, *Social Mobilization in the Arab-Israeli War of 1948*.

191. See, for example, Hashavya, *'Ad Halom: Gdud 53 hativat giv'ati tashah*; Pundak, *Gdud 53 (haparvarim) behativat giv'ati bemilhemet ha'atzmaut*.

192. Quoted in E. Harel, *Lohamey hakrakh*, 284. See also Ettinger, *Artzi at bocha ut-zoheket*, 112.

193. Aryeh Aviani, *Hashahar: 'Alon lehanikhey hashahar*, no. 3 (February 11, 1949), IDFA, 69/53/18.

Epilogue

1. "Halvayato shel Avinoam Yellin," *Davar*, October 29, 1937; "Avinoam Yellin." Shlomo Dov Goitein replaced Yellin as the inspector of Hebrew education.

2. Itamar Ben-Avi, "Lekah 1936," *Doar Hayom*, April 26, 1939.

3. On the political organizations of the Sephardi leadership in the early days of statehood, see Levi, "Hape'ilut hapolitit vehairgun shel hakehila hasfaradit bayeshuv ubemedinat Israel, 1945–1955," especially 164–79.

4. On the Ministry of Minorities, see, for example, A. Koren, "Kavanot tovot."

5. On the Minorities Department, see, for example, Osatzki-Lazar, "Hitgabshut yahasey hagomlin bein yehudim le'aravim bemedinat Israel," especially 109–17.

6. "Tafkidey mahleket hami'utim upe'uloteha," November 10, 1955, gimel-2213/12, ISA; "Pegisha shel ketziney hami'utim, mahleket hami'utim shel misrad hapnim," May 22, 1957, gimel-2217/12, ISA.

7. See Levi, "Hape'ilut hapolitit vehairgun shel hakehila hasfaradit bayeshuv ubemedinat Israel, 1945–1955," especially 136–63.

8. On the integration of Oriental Jews into the Arab press in the State of Israel during the early 1950s, see Kabha, "Yehudim mizrahim ba'itonut ha'aravit beisrael."

9. Testimony of Eliyahu Eliachar, president of the Council of the Sephardi Community in Jerusalem, before UNSCOP, CZA S 75/5962.

Bibliography

Archives and Collections (All in Israel)

Ben-Gurion Archive, Sede Boker (BGA)

Central Zionist Archive, Jerusalem (CZA)

Haganah Archive, Tel Aviv (HA)

Haifa Historical Society, Haifa (HHS)

Haifa Municipal Archive, Haifa (HMA)

Hashomer Hatza'ir Archive, Giva'at Haviva (HHA)

Israel Defense Forces and Defense Ministry Archive, Tel Hashomer (IDFA)

Israel State Archives, Jerusalem (ISA)

Jabotinsky Institute Archive, Tel Aviv (JIA)

Jerusalem Municipal Archive, (including the Sephardi Community Collection,) Jerusalem (JMA)

Oral History Project, Institute of Contemporary Jewry, Hebrew University of Jerusalem (OHP)

Palmach Archive, Tel Aviv (PA)

Pinchas Lavon Achive of the Labor Movement, Tel Aviv (LA)

Tel Aviv Municipality Archives, Tel Aviv (TAMA)

Tiberias Research Institute, Tiberias (TRI)

Yad Tabenkin Archive, Ramat Ef'al (YTA)

Newspapers and Bulletins

Al-'Alam al-Isra'ili

Al-Hayat

Al-Karmil

'Alon Hapalmach

Bama'aracha: Biton Degel Zion

Bama'aracha: Biton Hatzibur Hastarach ve'edot Hamizrah

Bamitzpe: Biton histadrut ha'ovdim hasfaradim ubney 'edot hamizrah beyerushalayim

Davar

Doar Hayom

Filastin

Ha'aretz Hahazit

Haherut

Hamashkif

Ha'olam Hasfaradi

Hapo'el Hatza'ir

Hatzofeh

Hazfira

Hed Hamizrah

Hed histadrut ha'ovdim hasfardim

Herut

'Iton Meyuhad

Jerusalem Post

Kolenu: Biton histadrut ha'ovdim hasfaradim betel aviv

Ma'ariv

Makor Rishon

Mishmar

Yedi'ot histadrut ha'ovdim hasfaradim be'eretz Israel

Yedi'ot 'Iriyat Tel Aviv

Unpublished Manuscripts

Bracha, Guy. "'Al-'Alam al-Isra'ili': Mekomo be'olam ha'itonut hayehudit veha'aravit bamizrah hatichon 'al rekahatmurut bakehilot hayehudiyot besurya velevanon, 1921–1948." PhD diss., Bar Ilan University, 2011.

Derri-Weksler, Aviv. "Mizrahanut alternativit vehishtalvut bamerhav ha'aravi hamekomi: Doctor Yisrael Ben Ze'ev, hasifriyah ha'aravit beyafo vehama'avak 'al sfarim falastinim 'netushim,' 1948–1952." MA thesis, Ben Gurion University of the Negev, 2013.

Evri, Yuval. "Paneha hamerubot vehamishtanot shel ha'sfaradiyut' bemifneh hameah ha'esrim." PhD diss., Tel Aviv University, 2013.

Halperin, Liora. "Babel in Zion: The Politics of Language Diversity in Jewish Palestine, 1920–1948." PhD diss., University of California, Los Angeles, 2011.

Hasan, Manar. "Hanishkahot: Ha'ir vehanashim hafalastiniyot, vehamilhama 'al hazikaron." PhD diss., Tel Aviv University, 2008.

Hillel, Maayan. "Kishrey yom yom bein yafo vetel aviv bitkufat hamandat, heibetim shel tarbut, biluy upnay." Seminar paper, Tel Aviv University, 2011.

Karlinsky, Nahum. "Jaffa-Tel-Aviv Partitioned Urban Space during the Mandate: An Alternative Perspective." Paper presented at the 27th Annual Conference of the Association for Israel Studies, Brandeis University, Waltham, MA, June, 2011.

Kats, Malka. "Zikatam shel sefaradim ubney 'edot hamizrah batnu'ot hadatiyot leumiyot hamizrahi vehapo'el hamizrahi be'eretz Israel 1918–1947: Datiyut, 'adatiyut ve'leumiyut bein megamot bidul lemegamot shiluv." PhD diss., Hebrew University of Jerusalem, 2008.

Lev Tov, Boaz. "Biluim bemahloket: Dfusey biluy vetarbut popolarit shel yehudim be'eretz Israel bashanim 1882–1914, kemeshakfey tmurot hevratiyot." PhD diss., Tel Aviv University, 2007.

Levi, Yitshak. "Hape'ilut hapolitit vehairgun shel hakehila hasfaradit bayeshuv ubemedinat Israel, 1945–1955." PhD diss., Hebrew University of Jerusalem, 1998.

Levy, Lital. "Jewish Writers in the Arab East: Literature, History, and the Politics of Enlightenment, 1863–1914." PhD diss., University of California Berkeley, 2007.

Musih, Norma. "Malachim bishmey manshiyya: 'Al shalosh praktikot she hahrava." MA thesis, Hebrew University of Jerusalem, 2010.

Nagri, Itai. "Hamahlaka ha'aravit shel hashomer hatza'ir: Nisayon leyisum ahva yehudit 'aravit." MA thesis, University of Haifa, 2004.

Noy, Amos. "Tzmihatan shel praktikot etnografiyot bekerev intelligentsia yehudit sefaradit umizrahit beyerushalyim beshalhey hatkufa ha'othmanit uthilat tkufat hamandat." PhD diss., Hebrew University of Jerusalem, 2014.

Osatzki-Lazar, Sarah. "Hitgabshut yahasey hagomlin bein yehudim le'aravim bemedinat Israel, ha'asor harishon 1948–1958." PhD diss., University of Haifa, 1996.

Resnik, Shlomi. "Mahteret vepolitikah behevra mefuleget: Hairgun hatzvai leumi mimahteret miflagtit lemiflaga bamahteret." PhD diss., Bar Ilan University, 1998.

Sharim, Yehuda. "The Struggle for Sephardic-Mizrahi Autonomy: Racial Identities in Palestine-Israel 1918–1948." PhD diss., University of California Los Angeles, 2013.

Books, Articles, and Online Items

Abassi, Mustafa. "Mishpahat Tabari vehanhagat hakehila ha'aravit betveria beshalhei hatkufa ha'othmanit ubetkufat hamandat." *Cathedra* 120 (June 1996): 189–200.

———. *Zefat bitkufat hamandat 1918–1948: 'Aravim veyehudim be'ir me'orevet.* Jerusalem, 2015.

'Adaki, Moshe. *Be'esh netsura.* Tel Aviv, 1975.

Aharoni, Ya'acov Sika. *Be'ikvot hamufti 'im David Raziel.* Ramat Gan, Israel, 2000.

Alboher, Shlomo. *Hizdahut, histaglut vehistaygut: Hayehudim hasfaradim be'erts Israel vehatnu'a hatsiyonit biymey hashilton habriti, 1918–1948.* Jerusalem, 2002.

Alcalay, Ammiel. *After Jews and Arabs: Remaking Levantine Culture.* Minneapolis, MN, 1993.

Aleksandrowicz, Or. "Gvulot shel niyar: Hahistoria hamehuka shel Neve Shalom." *Teorya Ubikoret* 41 (Summer 2013): 165–97.

Allegra, Marco, Anna Casaglia, and Jonathan Rokem. "The Political Geographies of Urban Polarization: A Critical Review of Research on Divided Cities." *Geography Compass* 6, no. 9 (2012): 560–74.

Allon, Yigal. *Ma'arachot palmach: Megamot vema'as.* Tel Aviv, 1965.

Almog, Oz. *The Sabra: The Creation of the New Jew.* Berkeley, CA, 2000.

Alroey, Gur. "Nashim 'azuvot beshalhey hatkufa ha'othmanit vereshit hamandat," *Israel* 15 (2009): 95–118.

Al-Shukeiri, Ahmad. *Arba'un 'aman fi alhayah al'arabiyah waldawliyah.* Beirut, 1967.

'Amidror (born Heller), Tzila. *Bema'atzar bebeit lehem.* Tel Aviv, 1962.

Amit-Kochavi, Hannah. "The People behind the Words: Professional Profiles and Activity Patterns of Arabic Literature into Hebrew (1896–2009)." *Translation and Interpreting Studies* 5, no. 1 (2010): 41–58.

Arlozoroff, Chaim. *Yoman Yerushalayim.* Tel Aviv, 1949.

Assaf, Michael. *Hayahasim bein yehudim ve'aravim be'eretz israel 1860–1948.* Tel Aviv, 1970.

"Avinoam Yellin." In *Encyclopedia lehalutsey hayishuv ubonav,* edited by David Tidhar, 2:895. Tel Aviv, 1947. Accessed March 24, 2016. http://www.tidhar.tourolib.org/tidhar/view/2/894.

Avivi, Shimon. "Lishon 'im ha'oyev." *Mabat Malam: Biton hamerkaz lemoreshet hamodi'in* 57 (November 2010): 58–61.

"Avraham Elmaleh." In *Encyclopedia lehalutsey hayishuv ubonav,* edited by David Tidhar, 1:513. Tel Aviv, 1947. Accessed March 24, 2016. http://www.tidhar.tourolib.org/tidhar/view/1/513.

Ayalon, Ami. *Reading Palestine: Printing and Literacy, 1900–1948.* Austin, TX, 2004.

Bachi, Roberto. *Hakira 'al ha'oni vehatzuna hayeruda bekerv yehudei yerushlayim.* Jerusalem, 1943.

Bahar, Yaron. "Avi hamista'arvim." *Mabat Malam: Biton hamerkaz lemoreshet hamodi'in* 64 (October 2012): 30–31.

Bar-On, Mordechai. "Hahistoriographya haisraelit shel hasihsukh haisraeli-'aravi." *Zion* 44 (2009): 311–37.

Bartal, Israel. "Du kiyum nichsaf: Eliyahu Eliachar 'al yahasey yehudim ve'aravim." In Eliyahu Eliachar, *Lihyot 'im Falastinim,* n.p. Jerusalem, 1975.

———. *Kozak vebedui: 'Am ve'eretz baleumiyut hayehudit.* Tel Aviv, 2007.

Bar-Yosef, Eitan. "Fighting Pioneer Youth: Zionist Scouting in Israel and Baden-Powell's Legacy." In *Scouting Frontiers: Youth and the Scout Movement's First Century,* edited by Nelson R. Block and Tammy M. Proctor, 42–55. Cambridge, 2009.

Bashkin, Orit. *New Babylonians: A History of Jews in Modern Iraq.* Stanford, CA, 2012.

Bechar, Yaron. "Reshit hahista'arvut hame'urgenet vehamahlaka hasurit." *Mikan Umisham* 16 (September 2012): 17–21.

Begin, Menachem. *Bamahteret: Ktavim.* Tel Aviv, 1978.

Behar, Almog. "Almog Behar 'im Sasson Somekh." *'Iton 77* 335 (December 2008): 20–24.

Behar, Moshe, and Zvi Ben-Dor Benite, eds. *Modern Middle Eastern Jewish Thought: Writings on Identity, Politics, and Culture, 1893–1958.* Waltham, MA, 2013.

Ben Hanania, Yehoshua. "Hanispah hatarbuti harishon bearzot ʻarav lifney kum hame-dinah." In *Minha leʼavraham: Sefer yovel lichvod Avraham elmaleh ben yerushalayim, hasofer veish hasefer, bimlot lo shivʼm shana,* edited by Yitzhak Raphael Molcho and Moshe David Gaon, 186–91. Jerusalem, 1959.

Ben Tor, Nechemiah. *Sefer toldot halehi.* Vol. 2. Tel Aviv, 2010.

Ben Zaken, Avner. *Komonizm keimperialism tarbuti.* Tel Aviv, 2006.

Ben Zeʼev, Yisrael. "Haʼaskan vehaʼitonai Nissim Malul." *Mahberet,* nos. 7–12 (1959): 146–48.

Ben Zvi, Yitzhak. *Mehkarim umekorot.* Jerusalem, 1965.

Ben-Artzi, Yossi. *Lahapokh midbar lekarmel: Hithavut hakarmel kemerhav nivdal beʼir meʼorevet, 1918–1948.* Jerusalem, 2004.

Ben-Bassat, Yuval. *Petitioning the Sultan: Protests and Justice in Late Ottoman Palestine.* London, 2014.

Ben-Gurion, David. *Pgishot ʼim manhigim ʼaravim.* Tel Aviv, 1972.

Ben-Yaʼacov, Abraham. *Yehudei babel beʼeretz israel mehaʼaliot harishonot ʼad hayom.* Jerusalem, 1980.

Berlowitz, Yaffa. "Hannah Thon: 1886–1954." *Encyclopedia.* Jewish Women's Archive. Accessed February 7, 2016. http://jwa.org/encyclopedia/article/thon-hannah-helena.

———. *Lehamtsi erets lehamtsi ʼam: Tashtiyot sifrut vetarbut bayetsira shel haʼaliya harishona.* Tel Aviv, 1996.

Bernstein, Deborah S. "Brit poʼaley eretz Israel: Irgunam shel poʼalim ʼaravim vemediniyut haʼavoda haʼivrit." *Megamot* 37, no. 3 (1996): 229–53.

———. *Constructing Boundaries: Jewish and Arab Workers in Mandatory Palestine.* New York, 2000.

———. *Nashim bashulaʼim: Migdar veleʼumiyut betel aviv hamandatorit.* Jerusalem, 2008).

———. "South of Tel Aviv and North of Jaffa—The Frontier Zone of 'In Between,'" in: *Tel Aviv, The First Century: Visions, Designs, Actualities,* edited by Maoz Azaryahu and S. Ilan Troen, 115–37. Bloomington, IN, 2012.

———. "Yehudim veʼaravim beʼmifʼal nesher." *Cathedra* 78 (December 1995): 82–106.

Bezalel, Itzhak. *Noladetem Ziyonim: Hasfaradim beʼeretz israel batsiyonut ubathiya haʼivrit batkufa haʼothmanit.* Jerusalem, 2007.

Biger, Gideon. "Binuya shel yerushalayim betkufat hashilton habriti 1917–1948." In *Yerushalyim batodaʼah ubaʼasiyah hatziyonit,* edited by Hagit Lavsky, 204–96. Jerusalem, 1989.

Binyamin, R. [Yehoshua Radler-Feldmann], and Yaʼacov Peterzeyl, eds. *Neged hateror: Maʼamarim, reshimot, giluyey daʼat.* Jerusalem, 1939.

Burla, Yehuda. "Hasfaradim vethiyatenu haleʼumit." *Mizrah Umaʼarav* 1, no. 2 (1920): 163–71.

Campos, Michelle U. "Between 'Beloved Ottomania' and 'the Land of Israel': The Struggle over Ottomanism and Zionism among Palestine's Sephardi Jews." *International Journal of Middle East Studies* 37, no. 4 (2005): 461–83.

———. *Ottoman Brothers: Muslims, Christians and Jews in Early Twentieth-Century Palestine*. Stanford, CA, 2011.

Caplan, Neil. *Futile Diplomacy: Arab Zionist Negotiations and the End of the Mandate*. London, 1986.

———. *Futile Diplomacy: Early Arab-Zionist Negotiation Attempts 1913–1931*. London, 1983.

Chazan, Meir. *Metinut: Hagisha hametuna behapo'el hatza'ir ubemapai 1905–1945*. Tel Aviv, 2009.

Chelouche, Julia. *Ha'etz vehashorashim*. N.p., 1982.

Chelouche, Yosef Eliyahu. *Parashat Hayai, 1870–1930*. Tel Aviv, 2005.

Chetrit, Sami Shalom. *Intra-Jewish Conflict in Israel: White Jews, Black Jews*. Princeton, NJ, 2010.

Cohen, Aharon. *Israel veha'olam ha'aravi*. Tel Aviv, 1964.

Cohen, Gamliel. *Hamista'arvim harishonim: Sipura shel hamahlaka ha'aravit shel hapalmach*. Tel Aviv, 2002.

Cohen, Geula. *Sipurah shel lohemet*. Tel Aviv, 1963.

Cohen, Haim. *Hape'ilut hatziyonit be'iraq*. Jerusalem, 1969.

Cohen, Hillel. *Army of Shadows: Palestinian Collaboration with Zionism, 1917–1948*. Berkeley, CA, 2008.

———. *Tarpat: Shnat haefes basikhsukh hayehudi-'aravi*. Tel Aviv, 2013.

———. *Tzva hatzlalim: Mashtapim falastinim besherut hatziyonut*. Jerusalem, 2004.

Cohen, Julia Philipps. *Becoming Ottomans: Sephardi Jews and Imperial Citizenship in the Modern Era*. Oxford, 2014.

Cohen, Mark R. "Islam and the Jews: Myth, Counter-Myth, History." *Jerusalem Quarterly* 38 (1986): 125–37.

Cohen, Uri, and Nissim Leon. *Merkaz tnu'at haherut vehamizrahim, 1965–1977: Mishutafut adnutit leshutafut taharutit*. Jerusalem, 2011.

Cohen, Yerucham. *Eich besurya za'ad hapalmach*. Tel Aviv, 1973.

———. *Leor hayom ubamahshakh*. Tel Aviv, 1979.

Danin, Ezra. *Tziyoni bechol tna'i*. Jerusalem, 1987.

"David Avissar." In *Encyclopedia lehalutsey hayishuv ubonav*, edited by David Tidhar, 2:577. Accessed March 24, 2016. http://www.tidhar.tourolib.org/tidhar/view/2/577.

Degani, Arnon. "They Were Prepared: The Palestinian Arab Scout Movement 1920–1948." *British Journal of Middle Eastern Studies* 41, no. 2 (2014): 200–18.

Dizengoff, Meir. "Ahrey zrikat hapzaza 'al yaldey bet hasefer." In *Sefer meora'ot tarzav*, edited by Bracha Habas, 388–89. Tel Aviv, 1937.

Dotan, Shmuel. *Hamaavak 'al eretz israel*. Tel Aviv, 1987.

Dror, Zvika. *Hamista'aravim shel hapalmach*. Tel Aviv, 1986.

Elath, Eliyahu. *Miba'ad le'arafel hayamim: Pirkey zichronot*. Jerusalem, 1989.

Eliachar, Eliyahu. *Lihyot 'im Falastinim*. Jerusalem, 1975.

———. *Lihyot 'im yehudim*. Jerusalem, 1981.

———. "Ma'amado shel hatzibur hasfaradi be'eretz Israel me'az hachrazat balfour."
Shevet Ve'am 1, no. 6 (1970): 67–84.

"Eliyahu Eliachar." In *Encyclopedia lehalutsey hayishuv ubonav*, edited by David Tidhar,
1:427. Accessed March 24, 2016. http://www.tidhar.tourolib.org/tidhar/view/1/427.

"Eliyahu Habuba." In *Encyclopedia lehalutsey hayishuv ubonav*, edited by David Tidhar,
12:4098. Accessed March 24, 2016. http://www.tidhar.tourolib.org/tidhar/view/12/4098.

Elmaleh, Avraham. "Shishim shnot haim: LeYitzhak Raphael Molcho ben hashishim."
Mahberet 3–4 (April–May 1953): 117–21.

Ettinger, Amos. *Artzi at bocha utzoheket: Sipuro shel zonik.* Tel Aviv 1991.

Even Shoshan, Zvi. *Toldot tnu'at hapo'alim be'eretz Israel, sefer shlishi.* Tel Aviv, 1966.

Evron, Yosef. *Gidi vehama'aracha lepinuy habritim me'eretz israel.* Tel Aviv, 2001.

Eyal, Gil. *Hasarat hakesem min hamizrah: Toldot hamizrahanut be'idan hamizrahiyut.* Tel
Aviv, 2005.

Frank, Gerold. *The Deed.* New York, 1963.

Frumkin, Gad. *Derech shofet beyerushalayim.* Tel Aviv, 1954.

Gabay, Moshe. *Kedma Mizraha.* Giv'at Haviva, Israel, 1984.

Gaon, Moshe David. *Yehudei hamizrah be'eretz israel—'Avar vehove.* Jerusalem, 1937.

Gayger, Benyamin. *Ehad mizikney Tzfat.* Minheret Hazman (Time Tunnel Project), Beit
Berl College. Accessed February 17, 2016. http://www.beitberl.ac.il/centers/minheret
_hazman/zichronot/DocLib/Benyamin%20Gayger.pdf.

Gelber, Yoav. *Hahitnadvut umekoma bamediniyut hatziyonit vehayeshuvit 1939–1942.* Vol.
1. Jerusalem, 1979.

———. *Historia, zikaron veta'amula: Hadisziplina hahistorit ba'olam uba'aretz.* Tel Aviv,
2007.

———. "Ketivet toldot hatziyonut: Me'epologetica lehitkahshoot." In *Bein hazon le-
rereizyah: Me'ah shnot historiographya tsiyonit, kovets ma'amarim*, edited by Yechiam
Weitz, 67–88. Jerusalem, 1997.

———. *Shorshey hahavatzelet: Hamodi'in bayeshuv 1918–1947.* Tel Aviv, 1992.

Gilad, Zrubavel, and Matti Meged, eds. *Sefer hapalmach.* Vol. 1. Tel Aviv, 1952.

Gilbert, Martin. *In Ishmael's House: A History of Jews in Muslim Lands.* New Haven, CT,
2011.

Goitein, Shlomo Dov. "'Al hora'at ha'aravit—1946." In *Hora'at ha'aravit kelashon zarah*,
edited by Jacob M. Landau, 11–34. Jerusalem, 1961.

Golan, Arnon. "Shikunam shel plitim yehudim mitel aviv bezman hamered ha'aravi
hagadol." *'Aley zayit veherev* 5 (2004): 57–82.

Goldstein, Amir. *Gvura vehadara: 'Oley hagardom vehazikaron haisraeli.* Jerusalem, 2011.

———. "Menachem Begin, tnu'at haherut vehameha'a hamizrahit: Bein vadi salib lapa-
nterim hashhorim." *Israel* 12 (2007): 1–38.

Gordon, Adi, ed. *Brit Shalom vehatsiyonut hadu-leumit: Hashe'ela ha'aravit keshe'ela yehudit.*
Jerusalem, 2008.

Goren, Tamir. "'Avoda meshutefet bein yehudim le'aravim behitpathut ha'aretz–haim titachen?' Shituf pe'ula bemo'etzet 'iriyat heifa betkufat hamandat." *Jama'aa* 12 (2004): 93–133.

———. *Shituf betzel 'imut: 'Aravim veyehudim bashilton hamekomi beheifa betkufat hamandat.* Ramat-Gan, Israel, 2008.

———. "Yehudey Yaffo veshe'elat hasipuah 1936–1939." *Zion* 79, no. 4 (2014): 507–30.

Gorny, Yosef. *Mediniyut vedimyon: Tochniyot federaliyot bamahshava hamedinit hatziyonit.* Jerusalem, 1993.

———. *Zionism and the Arabs, 1882–1948: A Study of Ideology.* New York, 1987.

Gozanski, Tamar. *Hitpathut hakapitalism befalestina.* Tel Aviv, 1986.

Gribetz, Jonathan M. "An Arabic-Zionist Talmud: Shimon Moyal's At-Talmud." *Jewish Social Studies* 17 no. 1 (2010): 1–30.

———. *Defining Neighbors: Religion, Race and the Early Zionist-Arab Encounter.* Princeton, NJ, 2014.

Gurevich, David, Aaron Gertz, and Roberto Bachi. *Ha'aliya, hayeshuv vehatnu'a hativ'it shel haukhlusin be'eretz israel.* Jerusalem, 1943.

Habas, Bracha. *Ahim krovim-nidahim.* Tel Aviv, 1953.

Hadawi, Sami. "Sodomy, Locusts, and Cholera: A Jerusalem Witness." *Jerusalem Quarterly* 53 (Spring 2013): 7–27.

Haim, Abraham. "Hayahasim bien hahanhaga hasfaradit beyerushalayim bien kehilot yehudiyot bamizrah hatichon bien shtey milhamot 'olam." *Shevet Ve'am* 2, no. 6 (1970): 60–68.

———. *Yihud vehishtalvut: Hanhagat hasfaradim beyerushalayim bitkufat hashilton habriti (1917–1948).* Jerusalem, 2002.

Hajjar Halaby, Mona. "Out of the Public Eye: Adel Jabre's Long Journey from Ottomanism to Binationalism." *Jerusalem Quarterly* 52 (Winter 2013): 6–24.

Halamish, Aviva. *Bemerutz kaful neged hazman: Mediniyut ha'aliya hatzionit beshnot hashloshim.* Jerusalem, 2006.

———. "Eretz Israel hamandatorit: Hevra dualit o metziut kolonialit?" *Zmanim* 92, Fall (2005): 1–25.

Halperin, Liora R. *Babel in Zion: Jews, Nationalism and Language Diversity in Palestine, 1920–1948.* New Haven, CT, 2014.

———. "The Battle over Jewish Students in the Christian Missionary Schools of Mandate Palestine." *Middle Eastern Studies* 50, no. 5 (2014): 737–754.

———. "Orienting Language: Reflections on the Study of Arabic in the Yishuv." *Jewish Quarterly Review* 96, no. 4 (2006): 486–89.

Harel, Eliyahu. *Lohamey hakrakh: Heil hasade shel tel aviv.* N.p., 1998.

Harel, Yaron. "Kidma gdola: Va'ad hatzirim vekehilat dameseq." *Pe'amim* 67 (1995): 57–95.

———. "Leumiyut, tziyonut, 'itonut ve'sotzyalism bekerev yehudey dameseq tahat shilton Faisal." *Pe'amim* 111–12 (2006): 103–43.

———. "Mihurban yafo nivneta dameseq: Hamifgash bein goley eretz israel lekehilat dameseq vetotsotav." *Zion* (1995): 183–207.

———. *Zionism in Damascus: Ideology and Activity in the Jewish Community at the Beginning of the Twentieth Century*. London, 2015.

Hart, Rachel. *Krovim-rehokim: Yahasei yehudim ve 'aravim beyafo vetel aviv, 1881–1930*. Tel Aviv, 2014.

Hasan, Manar, and Ami Ayalon. "Arabs and Jews, Leisure and Gender in Haifa's Public Spaces." In *Haifa before and after 1948: Narratives of a Mixed City*, edited by Mahmoud Yazbak and Yfat Weiss, 69–98. Dordrecht, the Netherlands, 2011.

Hashavya, Arye, ed. *'Ad Halom: Gdud 53 hativat giv'ati tashah*. Tel Aviv, 2005. *Hazaken veani: Sipuro ha'ishi shel rosh modi'in halehi*. Tel Aviv, 1993.

"*Hashomer Hatza'ir* neged hamitpartzim." In *Neged hateror: Ma'amarim, reshimot, giluyey da'at*, edited by R. Binyamin [Yehoshua Radler-Feldmann] and Ya'acov Peterzeyl, 93. Jerusalem, 1939.

Heller, Yosef. "Lehi bein yamin lesmol: He'arot lebikoret." *Cathedra* 71 (March 1994), 74–111.

———. *Mibrit shalom le'ichud: Yehuda Leib Magnes vehamavak lemedina du le'umit*. Jerusalem, 2003.

Helman, Anat. *Or veyam hekifuha: Tarbut tel aviv bitkufat hamandat*. Haifa, 2007.

Herzog, Hanna. *'Adatiyut politit: Dimuy mul metziut: nituah soziology-history she hareshimot ha "'adatiyot" leasefat hanivharim velakneset (1920–1984)*. Ramat Ef'al, Israel, 1986.

Heshel Yeivin, Yehoshua. "Pesh'a hadamim shel hasokhnut: Hafkarat hayeshuv he be'iyar tartzaz." In *Havlaga o tguva: Havikuach bayeshuv hayehudi 1936–1939*, edited by Yaacov Shavit, 87–95. Ramat Gan, Israel, 1983.

Hilel, Hagar. *Israel bekahir: 'Iton ziyoni bemizrayim haleumit, 1920–1939*. Tel Aviv, 2004.

Hochberg, Gil Z. "The Mediterranean Option: On the Politics of Regional Affiliation in Current Israeli Cultural Imagination." *Journal of Levantine Studies* 1, Summer (2011): 41–65.

Horowitz, Dan, and Moshe Lissak. *Origins of the Israeli Polity: Palestine under the Mandate*. Chicago, 1979.

Ilan, Naham. "Tivukh tarbuti: Avraham Sharoni min hamodi'in hatzvai el hamilon ha'aravi 'ivri." *Pe'amim* 122–23 (2009): 193–211.

Jacobson, Abigail. *From Empire to Empire: Jerusalem between Ottoman and British Rule*. Syracuse, NY, 2011.

———. "Jews Writing in Arabic: Shimon Moyal, Nissim Malul and the Mixed Palestinian/Eretz Israeli Locale." In *Late Ottoman Palestine: The Period of Young Turk Rule*, edited by Yuval Ben-Bassat and Eyal Ginio, 165–82. London, 2011.

———. "Sephardim, Ashkenazim and the 'Arab Question' in Pre-First World War Palestine: A Reading of Three Zionist Newspapers." *Middle Eastern Studies* 39, no. 2 (2003): 105–30.

Kabha, Mustafa. "Yehudim mizrahim ba'itonut ha'aravit beisrael." *Iyunim bitkumat Israel* 16 (2006): 445–61.

Kark, Ruth, Michal Oren-Nordheim, and Reuven Eshel. *Yerushalayim vesvivoteha: Rev'aim, shkunot vekfarim, 1800–1948.* Jerusalem, 1995.

Karlinsky, Nahum. "Jaffa and Tel Aviv before 1948: The Underground Story." In *Tel Aviv, The First Century: Visions, Designs, Actualities,* edited by Maoz Azaryahu and S. Ilan Troen, 138–64. Bloomington, IN, 2012.

Karmi, Ghada. *In Search of Fatima.* London, 2002.

Kayyal, Mahmoud. "Targumey hasifurt ha'aravit le'ivrit: Miorientalism lehitkablut." *Ha'ivrit* (2013): 175–92.

Kena'an, Habib. *Be'einey shoter falastini: Sipur leydata shel hahitnagdut hafalstinit.* Tel Aviv, 1982.

Keren, Shlomit. "Hapalmach ha'amami- giyus no'ar hashkhunot 1942–1944." In *Palmach: Shtey shibolim veherev,* edited by Yechiam Weitz, 153–84. Tel Aviv, 2000.

Khaled, Leila. *My People Shall Live: The Autobiography of a Revolutionary.* Edited by George Hajjar. 1973. Accessed February 17, 2016. http://www.onepalestine.org/resources /articles/My_People_Shall_Live.html.

Khalfon, Abraham. "'Avoda letzido shel Hasan Shukri." In *Heifa behitpathuta: 1918–1948,* edited by Mordechai Naor and Yossi Ben Artzi, 241–44. Jerusalem, 1989.

———. "Heifa 'iri." In *Haifa, oliphant vehahazon hatzioni,* edited by Yosef Nedava, 59–69. Haifa, 1978.

Khalidi, Rashid. *The Iron Cage: The Story of the Palestinian Struggle for Statehood.* Boston, 2006.

———. *Palestinian Identity: The Construction of Modern National Consciousness.* New York, 1997.

Kidron, Anat. *Bein leom lemakom: Hakehila ha'ivrit beheifa hamandatorit.* Jerusalem, 2012.

———. "Hashpa'at totzoteyhem shel me'ora'ot 1929 'al heifa veyaffo/tel aviv: Mabat mashve." *Israel* 22 (2014): 73–109.

Kimchi, Ruth. *Ziyonut betsel hapiramidot.* Tel Aviv, 2009.

Klausner, Joseph. "Hamizrahi-hama'aravi." In *Minha le'avraham: Sefer yovel lichvod Avraham Elmaleh ben yerushalayim, hasofer veish hasefer, bimlot lo shiv'm shana,* edited by Yitzhak Raphael Molcho and Moshe David Gaon, 226–28. Jerusalem, 1959.

Klein, Menachem. "Arab Jew in Palestine," *Israel Studies* 9, no. 3 (2014): 134–153.

———. *Lives in Common: Arabs and Jews in Jerusalem, Jaffa and Hebron.* London, 2014.

Koren, Alina. "Kavanot tovot: Kavim ledmuto shel misrad hami'utim, May 14 1948–July 1 1949." *Cathedra* 127 (April 2008): 113–40.

Koren, David. *Hagadn'a mehahaganah letzahal.* Tel Aviv, 1995.

Kramer, Martin. Introduction to *The Jewish Discovery of Islam: Studies in Honor of Bernard Lewis,* edited by Martin Kramer, 1–48. Tel Aviv, 1999.

———, ed. *The Jewish Discovery of Islam: Studies in Honor of Bernard Lewis.* Tel Aviv, 1999.

Landau, Jacob M., ed. *Hora'at ha'aravit kelashon zarah.* Jerusalem, 1961.

Lapidoth, Yehuda. *Hayom sarah haktana: Sipuran shel lohamot haetzel.* Tel Aviv, 2003.

Lassner, Jacob, and Ilan Troen. *Jews and Muslims in the Arab World: Haunted by Pasts Real and Imagined.* Lanham, MD, 2007.

Lavsky, Hagit. *Before Catastrophe: The Distinctive Path of German Zionism.* Detroit, MI, 1996.

LeBor, Adam. *City of Oranges: An Intimate History of Arabs and Jews in Jaffa.* New York, 2006.

Levin, Michael. "Mifal hagiyus." In *Sefer hapalmach,* edited by Zrubavel Gilad and Matti Meged, 1:277–78. Tel Aviv, 1952.

LeVine, Mark. *Overthrowing Geography: Jaffa, Tel Aviv, and the Struggle for Palestine, 1880–1948.* Berkeley, CA, 2005.

Levy, Lital. "Historicizing the Concept of Arab Jews in the *Mashriq.*" *Jewish Quarterly Review* 98, no.4 (2008): 452–69.

———. "Partitioned Pasts: Arab Jewish Intellectuals and the Case of Esther Azhari Moyal (1873–1948)." In *The Making of the Arab Intellectual (1880–1960): Empire, Public Sphere, and the Colonial Coordinates of Selfhood,* edited by Dyala Hamzah, 128-63. Milton Park, UK, 2012.

Levy, Shabtai. "Mizihronotav." In *Haifa, oliphant vehahazon hatzioni,* edited by Yosef Nedava, 78-174. Haifa, 1978.

Levy, Yosef. "Kul kalb biji yomo." *Mabat Malam: Biton hamerkaz lemoreshet hamodi'in* 60 (2011): 30–31.

Lewis, Bernard. *The Jews of Islam.* Princeton, NJ, 1984.

———. *Islam in History: Ideas, Men and Events in the Middle East.* Chicago, 1993.

Lin, Amnon. *Beterem se'ara: Yahasei yehudim ve'aravim bimdinat Israel.* Tel Aviv, 1999.

Lissak, Moshe. "Habe'aya ha'adatit veirgunim 'adatiyim bitkufat hayeshuv." In *'Iyunim behistorya hevratit shel Israel,* edited by Moshe Lissak, 239–55. Jerusalem, 2009.

———. *Haelitot shel hayeshuv hyehudi be'eretz Israel bitkufat hamandat.* Tel Aviv, 1981.

———, ed. *'Iyunim behistorya hevratit shel Israel.* Jerusalem, 2009.

Lockman, Zachary. *Comrades and Enemies: Arab and Jewish Workers in Palestine, 1906–1948.* Berkeley, CA, 1996.

———. "Patahnu et mohot ha'aravim: Hasiyah hatziyoni sozialisti vepo'aley harakevet be'eretz Israel 1919–1929." In *'Aravim veyehudim bitkufat hamandat: mabat hadash 'al hamehkar hahistory,* edited by Ilan Pappe, 103-24. Giv'at Haviva, Israel, 1995, 103–124.

———. "Railway Workers and Relational History: Arabs and Jews in British-Ruled Palestine." *Comparative Studies in Society and History* 35, no. 3 (1993): 601–27.

Maman, Adel. *Noladeti ba'aretz hazot: sipura shel adel maman lebeit toledano.* N.p., 2009.

Mandel, Neville J. *The Arabs and Zionism before World War I.* Berkeley, CA, 1976.

Matalon, Yivneel. *Tel aviv: Zichronot 1919–1939.* Accessed February 18, 2016. http://benyehuda.org/matalon_yivneel/telaviv.html.

"Megamot vema'as." In *Sefer hapalmach,* edited by Zrubavel Gilad and Matti Meged, 1:29. Tel Aviv, 1952.

"Meir Dahan." Kvutzat Kinneret commemoration (Yizkor) website. Accessed March 27, 2016. http://www.kinneret.org.il/kinneret/yizkorPage.asp?id=41.

Meir-Glitzenstein, Esther. *Yetziyat yehudei teman: Mivtza koshel vemitos mechonen.* Tel Aviv, 2012.

Memmi, Albert. *Jews and Arabs.* Chicago, 1975.

———. "Who Is an Arab Jew?" Accessed March 27, 2016. http://www.harissa.com/eng/whoisanarabjew.htm.

Mendel, Yonatan. *The Creation of Israeli Arabic: Political and Security Considerations in the Making of Arabic Language Studies in Israel.* London, 2014.

———. "Re-Arabising the De-Arabised: The Mista'arvim Unit of the Palmach." In *Debating Orientalism,* edited by Ziad Elmarsafy, Anna Bernard, and David Attwell, 94–116. London, 2013.

"Me'oraot tarpat kenekudat mifne." In *Yerushalyim batod'a uba'asiyah hatziyonit,* edited by Hagit Lavsky, 407–29. Jerusalem, 1989.

Metzer, Jacob. *The Divided Economy of Mandatory Palestine.* Cambridge, 1998.

———. "Kalkalat eretz Israel beyemei hamandat: Mabat 'al hitpathut hamehkar." In *'Iyunim bitkumat Israel (Kalkala vehevra bitkufat hamandat),* edited by Avi Bareli and Nahum Karlinsky, 7–58. Sede Boker, Israel, 2003.

Milson, Menachem. "Reshit limud ha'aravit vehaislam baoniversita ha'ivrit." In *Toldot haoniversita ha'ivrit beyerushalayim,* edited by Shaul Katz and Michael Hed, 1:575–88. Jerusalem, 1997.

Mizrahi, Moshe, dir. *Habayit Berekhov Chelouche.* Noah Films, 1973.

Molcho, Yitzhak. "*Kedma Mizrha*: Shalav baderekh." *Be'ayot* 5, no. 4 (1947): 143–47.

Molcho, Yitzhak Raphael, and Moshe David Gaon, eds. *Minha le'avraham: Sefer yovel lichvod Avraham Elmaleh ben yerushalayim, hasofer veish hasefer, bimlot lo shiv'm shana.* Jerusalem, 1959.

Monterescu, Daniel, and Dan Rabinowitz. "Introduction: The Transformation of Urban Mix in Palestine/Israel in the Modern Era." In *Mixed Towns, Trapped Communities: Historical Narratives, Spatial Dynamics, Gender Relations and Cultural Encounters in Palestinian-Israeli Towns,* edited by Daniel Monterescu and Dan Rabinowitz, 1–32. Burlington, VT, 2007.

———, eds. *Mixed Towns, Trapped Communities: Historical Narratives, Spatial Dynamics, Gender Relations and Cultural Encounters in Palestinian-Israeli Towns.* Burlington, VT, 2007.

Morag-Talmon, Pnina. *Ha'eda hasfaradit bitkufat hayeshuv: 'Adatiyut veleumiyut.* Jerusalem, 1991.

Mori, David. "Yisuda vehipathuta shel shchunat kerem hatemanim betel aviv." *Tehuda* 17 (1997): 35–42.

"Moshe Chelouche." In *Encyclopedia lehalutsey hayishuv ubonav,* edited by David Tidhar, 2:955. Accessed March 24, 2016. http://www.tidhar.tourolib.org/tidhar/view/2/955.

"Moshe Matalon." In *Encyclopedia lehalutsey hayishuv ubonav*, edited by David Tidhar, 7:2941. Accessed March 24, 2016. http://www.tidhar.tourolib.org/tidhar/view/7/2941.

"Mushrash bamoreshet hayehudit uben bayit batarbut ha'aravit." In *Sefer hashana shel ha'itonaim*, edited by Zisi Stavi, 337. Tel Aviv, 1983.

Nachmias, Eli. "Arabs and Jews in a Dynamic Job Market." In *The Secret of Coexistence: Jews and Arabs in Haifa During the British Mandate in Palestine, 1920–1948*, edited by Daphna Sharfman, Eli Nachmias, and Johnny Mansour, 1–70. Charleston, SC, 2007.

———. "'Aravim veyehudim beshuk 'avoda dinami vesegregativi beheifa hamandatorit." In *Tea 'al mirpeset hakazino: Du kiyum beheifa bitkufat hamandat habriti 1920–1948*, 23–111. Haifa, 2006.

Naor, Moshe. *Social Mobilization in the Arab-Israeli War of 1948: On the Israeli Home Front*. Rutledge, 2013.

Nathanson, Regev, and Abbas Shiblak. "*Haifa Umm al-Gharib:* Historical Notes and Memory of Inter-Communal Relations." In *Haifa before and after 1948: Narratives of a Mixed City*, edited by Mahmoud Yazbak and Yfat Weiss, 181–204. Dordrecht, the Netherlands, 2011.

Nedava, Yosef. "Mishpat hakim vebeit tzuri bemitzraim." *Bamahanayim*, no. 111 (1967): 186–93.

"Nissim Malul." In *Encyclopedia lehalutsey hayishuv ubonav*, edited by David Tidhar, 2:696. Accessed March 24, 2016. http://www.tidhar.tourolib.org/tidhar/view/2/696.

Niv, David. *Ma'arachot ha'irgun hatzva'i leumi: Hahaganah haleumit 1931–1937*. Tel Aviv, 1965.

Nuseibeh, Hazem Zaki. *Zikriyat maqdisiya sirah d'atiya*. N.p., 2009.

Ofir, Yehoshua. *Rishoney etzel 1931–1940*. N.p., 2002.

Ohana, David. *The Origins of Israeli Mythology: Neither Canaanite nor Crusaders*. Cambridge, 2012.

Osatzki-Lazar, Sarah. "Mehistadrut 'ivrit lehistadrut israelit: Hishtalvutam shel 'aravim ba'irgun 1948–1966." *'Iyunim Bitkumat Israel* 10 (2000): 383–89.

Pa'il, Meir. "Palmach: Yihudo hatzvai." In *Palmach: Shtey shibolim veherev*, edited by Yechiam Weitz, 35–64. Tel Aviv, 2000.

Palestine Royal Commission. *Report*. London, 1937.

Pomrak, Zvi Avraham. *Chelouche: Hatel avivi harishon*. Jerusalem, 2007.

Porath, Yehoshua. *Tzmihat hatnu'a haleumit ha'arvit hafalastinit 1918–1929*. Jerusalem, 1971.

Pundak, Yitzhak. *Gdud 53 (haparvarim) behativat giv'ati bemilhemet ha'atzmaut*. Tel Aviv, 2006.

Qazzaz, Nissim. *Hayehudim be'iraq bameah ha'esrim*. Jerusalem 1991.

Radai, Itamar. *Bein shtey 'arim: Ha'aravim hafalstinim beyerushalayim vebeyaffo, 1947–1948*. Tel Aviv, 2015.

Ram, Hana. *Hayeshuv hayehudi beyafo ba'et hahadasha: Mikehila sefaradti lemerkaz tzioni*. Jerusalem, 1996.

Ran, Yaron. "Eliyahu (Elias) Sasson—Mimeholeley hatnu'a hatziyonit bedameseq umovil ma'arehet hayahasim 'im ha'olam ha'aravi 'erev hakamata shel medinat israel." *Mikan Umisham* 2 (2005): 13–19.

Ratzabi, Shalom. *Between Zionism and Judaism: The Radical Circle in Brith Shalom 1925–1933*. London, 2002.

Razi, Tammy. "Subversive Youth Cultures in Mandate Tel-Aviv." In *Tel-Aviv, The First Century: Visions, Designs, Actualities*, edited by Maoz Azaryahu and S. Ilan Troen, 77–93. Bloomington, IN, 2012.

———. *Yaldei hahefker: Hahatzer ha'ahorit shel tel aviv hamandatorit*. Tel Aviv, 2009.

———. "Yehudiyot 'arviot? Etniut, leumiut vemigdar betel aviv hamandatorit." *Teoriya Ubikoret* 38–39, Winter (2011): 137–60.

Resnik, Shlomi. "Hamordim: Nituah sozyologi shel lohamey etzel bashanim 1944–1948." In *Hamordim: Ma'avak ha'etzel babritim 1944–1948: Diyun mehudash*, edited by Ya'akov Markowizki, 180–96. Jerusalem, 2008.

Rieger, Eliezer. *Hahinuch ha'ivri be'eretz Israel*. Vol. 1. Tel Aviv, 1940.

Rotbard, Sharon. *'Ir levana, 'ir shhora*. Tel Aviv, 2005.

Rozen, Minna. "Ma'amad hamusta'arvim vehayahasim bein ha'edot bayeshuv hayehudi be'eretz Israel mishalhey hameah ha-15 ve'ad shalhey hameah ha-17." *Cathedra* 17 (October (1980: 73–101.

Rozenfeld, Shlomi. *Mea shnot simha*. Kerem Maharal, Israel, 2011.

Rubinstein, Amnon. *From Herzl to Rabin: The Changing Image of Zionism*. Teaneck, NJ, 2000.

Rubinstein, Elyakim. "Hadiyunim 'al hotza'at 'iton 'tziyoni'—'aravi bishnot ha'esrim vehashloshim." *Kesher* 1, no.1 (1987): 45–54.

———. "Hatipul bashe'elah ha'aravit batkufa hamiyadit sheleahar meora'ot tarpat vehakamat halishka hameuhhedet shel hamosadot heyeshuvi'im: Hebetim medini'im." In *'Aravim veyehudim bitkufat hamandat: mabat hadash ' al hamehkar hahistory*, edited by Ilan Pappe, 65–102. Giv'at Haviva, Israel, 1995.

———. "Hatipul bashe'elah ha'aravit beshnot ha'esrim vehashloshim: Hebetim mosadi'im," *Hatziyonut* 12 (1987): 209–41.

———. "Masa umatan 'im 'aravim: Nisyonot nefel be-1930." *Yahadut Zmanenu* 7 (1992): 101–20.

———. "Yehudim ve'aravim be'iriyot eretz Israel (1926–1933)—Yerushalayim ve'iriyut aherot." *Cathedra* 51 (April 1989): 122–47.

"Ruh Jadidah/Ruah Hadasha: Young Mizrahi Israelis' Open Letter to Arab Peers." April 11, 2011. Accessed March 23, 2016. http://arabjews.wordpress.com./

Sabbagh, Karl. *Palestine: A Personal History*. London, 2006.

Sasson, Eliyahu. *Baderekh el hashalom*. Tel Aviv, 1978.

Schayegh, Cyrus. "The Many Worlds of Abud Yasin; or, What Narcotics Trafficking in the Interwar Middle East Can Tell Us about Territorialization." *American Historical Review* 116, no. 2 (2011): 273–306.

Segev, Tom. *One Palestine, Complete: Jews and Arabs under the British Mandate*. New York, 1999.

Sela, Abraham. "Meora'ot hakotel (1929)—Nekudat mifneh bayahasim bein yehudim le'aravim?" In *Yerusahalyim batoda'a uba'asiyah hatziyonit*, edited by Hagit Lavsky, 261–78. Jerusalem 1989.

———. "Sihot umaga'im bein manhigim tziyonim lebein manhigim 'aravim falastinim 1933–1939." *Hamizrah Hahadash* 23, no.1 (1973): 1–21.

Shafir, Gershon. *Land, Labor and the Origins of the Israeli-Palestinian Conflict*. Berkeley, CA, 1996.

Shamir, Shimon. "Kishrey hinuch vetarbut," *Cathedra* 67 (March 1993): 93–105.

Shamosh, Amnon. *Tmunot mishney ha'olamot*. Tel Aviv, 2011.

Shapira, Anita. *Herev hayona: Hatziyonut vehakoah 1881–1948*. Tel Aviv, 2002.

———. "Hahistoriographya shel hatziyonut vemedinat israel beshishim shnot medina." *Zion* 44 (2009): 287–309.

———. *Hama'avak hanichzav: 'Avoda 'ivrit 1929–1939*. Tel Aviv, 1977.

———. *Land and Power: The Zionist Resort to Force, 1881–1948*. Stanford, CA, 1999.

———. *Yigal Allon: Aviv haldo*. Ramat Gan, Israel, 2004.

Shara'bi, Rachel. *Hayishuv hasfaradi beyerushalayim beshalhei hatkufa ha'othmanit*. Tel Aviv, 1989.

Sharfman, Daphna. "Hahayim beheifa hayu aherim." *Biten ha'amuta leheker Haifa* 9 (May 2011): 6–9.

———, Eli Nachmias, and Johnny Mansour, eds. *The Secret of Coexistence: Jews and Arabs in Haifa During the British Mandate in Palestine, 1920–1948*, Charleston, SC, 2007.

Shavit, Yaacov, ed. *Havlaga o tguva: Havikuah bayeshuv hayehudi 1936–1939*. Ramat Gan, Israel, 1983.

———, and Gideon Biger. *Hahistorya shel tel aviv: Leydata shel 'ir*. Vol. 1. Tel Aviv, 2001.

Shchori-Rubin, Zippora, and Shifra Schwartz, "Migrashei Hamishakim shel Guggen-heimer-Hadassah." *Cathedra* 86 (January 1998): 75–98.

Shenhav, Yehuda. *Hayehudim ha'aravim: Leumiyut, dat ve'etniyut*. Tel Aviv, 2003.

———. "Yehudim yotzeu arzot 'arav be'israel: Hazehut hamefutzelet shel mizrahim bemehozot hazikaron haleumi." In *Mizrhim be'israel: 'Iyun bikorti mehudash*, edited by Yehuda Shenhav, Hanan Hever, and Pnina Mutzafi-Haller, 105–51. Jerusalem, 2002.

Shiloach, Amnon. "'Ezra aharon vehazemer ha'ivri hamizrahi bitkufat hayishuv." In *Yerushalayim betkufat hamandat: Ha'asiyah vehamoreshet*, edited by Yehoshua Ben Arieh, 450–72. Jerusalem, 2003.

"Shimon Moyal." In *Encyclopedia lehalutsey hayishuv ubonav*, edited by David Tidhar, 3:1219. Accessed March 24, 2016. http://www.tidhar.tourolib.org/tidhar/view/3/1219.

Shoham, Hizky. "Buy Local or Buy Jewish? Separatist Consumption in Interwar Palestine." *International Journal of Middle East Studies* 45, no. 3 (2013): 469–89.

Shohat, Ella. *Israeli Cinema: East/West and the Politics of Representation*. London, 2010.

———. "Sephardim in Israel: Zionism from the Standpoint of Its Jewish Victims." *Social Text* 19–20 (1988): 1–35.

Singer, Mendel. *'Im hakorban harishon bemeora'ot heifa.* Haifa, 1966.

———. "Leretzah Esther Sheetrit." In *Sefer meora'ot tarzav,* edited by Bracha Habas, 467–70. Tel Aviv, 1937.

Siton, Rafi, and Yitzhak Sasson. *Anshei hasod vehaseter: Me'alilot hamodi'in haisraeli me'ever lagvul.* Tel Aviv, 1990.

Slutsky, Yehuda. *Sefer toldot hahaganah: Mehaganah lemavak.* Vols. 2 and 3. Tel Aviv, 1963.

Smith, Barbara J. *The Roots of Separatism in Palestine: British Economic Policy: 1920–1929.* London, 1993.

Snir, Reuven. *'Arviyut, yahadut, tziyonut: Maavak zehuyot beyetziratam shel yehudei 'iraq.* Jerusalem, 2005.

———. "'Mosaic Arabs' Between Total and Conditioned Arabization: The Participation of Jews in Arabic Press and Journalism in Muslim Societies during the Nineteenth and Twentieth Centuries." *Journal of Muslim Minority Affairs* 27, no. 2 (2007): 261–95.

Sodit, Dror. "Hamistanen leyaffo, 1938." In *Neshek briti lemahsaney haetzel. Hamistanen leyaffo 1938. Minesharim kalu, me'arayot gaveru,* edited by Dror Sodit, 81–120. Tel Aviv, 1975.

Sofer, Sasson. *Zionism and the Foundations of Israeli Diplomacy.* New York, 1998.

Somekh, Sasson. *Baghdad etmol.* Tel Aviv, 2004.

———. "Sifrut lelo kahal: Sofrim yehudim kotvey 'aravit beisrael." *Gag* 4 (2001): 90–96.

Stavi, Zisi, ed. *Sefer hashana shel ha'itonaim.* Tel-Aviv, 1983.

Tal, David. "Israel in or of the Middle East." In *Israeli Identity: Between Orient and Occident,* edited by David Tal, 1–12. Routledge, 2013.

Tamari, Salim. "Ishaq al-Shami and the Predicament of the Arab-Jew in Palestine." *Jerusalem Quarterly* 21 (2004): 10–26.

Tidhar, David, ed. *Encyclopedia lehalutsey hayishuv ubonav.* Tel Aviv, 1947.

Tivoni, Shlomo. *Kerem haya leyedidi.* Tel Aviv, 1978.

Thon, Hannah. "Hinuch hano'ar be'edot hamizrah." In *Neged hateror: Ma'amarim, reshimot, giluyey da'at,* edited by R. Binyamin [Yehoshua Radler-Feldmann] and Ya'acov Peterzeyl, 46–49. Jerusalem, 1939.

Tsur, Yaron. "Hahistoriographya haisraelit vehabe'aya ha'adatit." *Pe'amim* 94–95 (2003): 7–56.

Tuqan, Fadwa. *Derekh hararit, otobiyographya.* Tel Aviv, 1993.

Turgeman, Raphael. "Hasfaradim bama'aracha hale'umit." *Kol,* April 1941, 7.

Twena, Abraham. "Tnu'at Ah'iever hatzionit bebagdad." In *Yahadut bavel: Golim vegeulim,* edited by Abraham Twena, 3:77–137. Ramla, Israel, 1973.

Tzfadia, Erez. "Mixed Cities in Israel: Localities of Contentions." *Israel Studies Review* 26, no. 1 (2011): 153–65.

Tzifroni, Gavriel. "Iton meyuhad- ha'olam betzahov." *Kesher,* no. 3 (May 1988): 107–12.

Vashitz, Yossef. *Ha'aravim be'eretz israel.* Merhavia, Israel, 1947.

Wacquant, Loïc. "Mahu ghetto? Bniya shel musag soziology." *Soziologya Israelit* 6, no. 1 (2004): 151–63.

Wasserstein, Bernard. "Or hadash 'al retzah halord moyne." *Zmanim* 7 (1982): 4–17.

Weinstock, Nathan. *Nokhekhut ko arukah: Keitsad ibed ha'olam ha'aravi vehamuslemi et yehudav.* Tel Aviv, 2014.

Weinberg, Moshe, ed. *The Diary of Shlomo Kostika.* Ramat Ef'al, Israel, 1989.

Weizmann, Chaim. *Trial and Error: The Autobiography of Chaim Weizmann.* London, 1950.

Yagar, Moshe. *Toldot hamahlaka hamedinit shel hasokhnut hayehudit.* Jerusalem, 2011.

Yahav, Dan. *Bishviley du hakiyum vehama'avak hameshutaf: yehudim ve'aravim bakalkala ubahevra.* 'Azur, Israel, 2008.

Yardeni, Gaia. *Ha'itonut ha'ivrit be'erets Israel bashanim 1863–1904.* Tel Aviv, 1979. Yazbak, Galia, Mahmoud, and Yfat Weiss, eds. *Haifa before and after 1948: Narratives of a Mixed City.* Dordrecht, the Netherlands, 2011.

Yehoshua, Ya'akov. *Hakhamim beyerushalayim hayeshana, 'isukam uparnasatam: Pirkey havay miyamim 'avaru.* Jerusalem, 1968.

——— *Ta'arikh al-sihafa al-'arabiya al-filastiniya fi bidayat 'ahd al-intidab al-baritani 'ala filastin.* Haifa, 1941.

———. *Yerushalayim tmol shilshom: Pirkey havay.* Jerusalem, 1977.

"Yisrael Ben Ze'ev." In *Encyclopedia lehalutsey hayishuv ubonav,* edited by David Tidhar, 1:378. Accessed March 24, 2016. http://www.tidhar.tourolib.org/tidhar/view/1/378.

"Yosef Bet Tzuri." In *Encyclopedia lehalutsey hayishuv ubonav,* edited by David Tidhar, 2:692. Accessed March 24, 2016. http://www.tidhar.tourolib.org/tidhar/view/2/692.

Index

Arab Jews. *See* Oriental Jews
Arab Revolt (1936–1939), 12, 39, 62–63,
  132–34, 135, 152–55, 164, 181–82, 229–
  30n71
Arabs: demographics, 226n21;
  employment, 68; living conditions,
  127–28; minority rights, 202–3. *See also*
  Arab-Jewish relations
Arab Spring, 1–2
Arab Worker's Congress, 82
Ard al-Yahud, 124, 157
Arlozoroff, Chaim, 60, 62
Ashkenazi Jews: Arabic, 109–10, 112,
  118, 222n78; Bney Ha'aretz term, 8;
  criticism of, 101–2; demographics, 7,
  227n36; as foreigners, 19, 21–22; im-
  migration, 7; as mediators, 11; mixing,
  141–42; Palmach, 182; security, 174
Assaf, Michael, 91, 103–4, 111, 115
Assembly of Representatives, 28, 32,
  46–49, 171, 172
Association of Sephardi Jews in Tel Aviv,
  47
Association of the Pioneers of the East,
  17–19, 20–21, 23–24, 29–32, 44–45, 78
'Ataya, Nissim, 182
Atiash, Moshe, 19
Avissar, David, 18, 29–32, 110

Balfour Declaration, 20–21, 22
Barag, Gershon, 106
Barnett, Abraham, 135
Barnett, Zerah, 130
Begin, Menachem, 173–74
Beitar movement, 145, 171
Beit-Shean, 126–27, 153
Beit-Tzuri, Eliyahu, 175–78
Ben-Ami, Moshe, 172–73
Ben 'Attar, Haim, 86–87
Ben-Avi, Itamar, 155
Ben-Gurion, David, 70, 93, 166–67

Ben-Ze'ev, Yisrael, 106, 107–14, 113, 116–
  20, 222nn78–79, 223n99–100, 224n107
Ben-Zvi, Yitzhak, 36, 56, 60, 91
Bney Ha'aretz (Natives of the Land) , 8,
  97. *See also* Oriental Jews; Sephardic
  Jews
Bney Hamizrah (Natives of the Orient),
  97. *See also* Oriental Jews
border crossings. *See* movement and
  border crossings
border neighborhoods. *See* frontier
  neighborhoods
Brit Shalom, 42–46
Burla, Yehuda, 79, 100

Canaanites Movement, 176, 177–78
Chelouche, Aharon, 147
Chelouche, Gavriel, 155
Chelouche, Moshe, 41, 76, 77, 82, 83
Chelouche, Yosef Eliyahu, 24–25
children: abandoned, 121–22, 129,
  228nn46–47; kibbutzim, 182, 183; labor,
  129, 228n46; mixing of, 139–47, 231n102,
  232n116, 232–33nn119–120, 233n122. *See*
  also education
cities, mixed: demographics, 127, 132,
  226n21, 227nn35–37, 229n63; illusion
  of mixing, 124–27, 155, 227n29; living
  conditions in, 127–28; mediation in,
  57–58; neighborhood committees
  in, 71–73, 115; scholarship on, 125–27,
  227n34; term, 125. *See also* frontier
  neighborhoods
class: and Arabic instruction, 116; Arab
  Revolt, 153, 229–30n71; frontier
  neighborhoods, 9, 127–28, 133, 139,
  146–47, 229–30n71; missionary schools,
  146–47; Palmach, 180, 182, 184; political
  parties, 47, 173–74; Sasson's focus on
  elites, 64; suburban military units, 195;
  terrorism, 164, 165, 170

Cohen, Aharon Chaim, 58, 59–60
Cohen, Aharon, 158
Cohen, Gamliel, 183, 184
Cohen, Geula, 160
Cohen, Havakuk (Hawla), 184–85
Cohen, Menachem Raphael, 153–54
Cohen, Ya'acov (Ya'akuba), 180–82, 186–87
Cohen, Yerucham, 179–80
colonialism. *See* anticolonialism
Committee of Investigation of the
    Relations between Jews and Arabs,
    68–69
Committee of Jews in Safed, 208n15
Committees for Neighborly Relations,
    71–73
Communism, 81, 145–46, 160, 187
conversion, 122–23, 226n11
Council of the Sephardi Community in
    Haifa, 47, 147
Council of the Sephardi Community in
    Jaffa, 208n15
Council of the Sephardi Community in
    Jerusalem, 18, 20, 33, 47, 52, 75, 163, 164,
    168
Council of the Sephardi Community in
    Tel Aviv, 75
cultural politics, 87, 218n5. *See also*
    mediation

Dahan, Meir, 188–89, 215n63
Damascus, 99, 100–101, 182
Dana, Michael, 111, 117
Danin, Ezra, 64, 71
Danon, Nissim (Hakham Bashi), 23
Degel Zion (youth movement), 77–78,
    145, 233n125
de Haan, Jacob Israël, 25
Doar Hayom (newspaper), 58, 143–44, 155,
    172
dual-society model, 5, 29–32, 124–27,
    227n29

Dubois, Louis-Ernest, 23
Dushkin, Alexander, 113

economics: Arab Department, 79,
    80–85; Arab Revolt effect, 153; Liberal
    Party, 33; and Peel Commission, 39;
    terrorism, 165; United Bureau, 54; work
    plans, 29, 30, 31, 66–67, 68. *See also* class
'Edot Hamizrah term, 6–7. *See also*
    Oriental Jews
education: Arab children, 57; Arabic
    language, 31, 70–72, 106–20, 186–87,
    188–89, 223n87, 223n99–100; Degel
    Zion, 77–78; exchanges, 112–13; as
    mediation, 31–32, 57, 106–14; missionary
    schools, 146–47, 233n132, 233n136;
    mixing in, 146–47; Peel Commission
    statements, 38, 39; Sephardi-Oriental
    Zionism, 31–32, 38; teachers' training,
    71; terrorism, 164, 166–67, 169; truancy,
    142–43
Egypt, 26, 63–64, 94, 108, 113, 175–78
Eliachar, Eliyahu: Association of the
    Pioneers of the East, 44–45; on bias,
    44–46; criticism of, 75, 76; on failure,
    204; on Jewish terrorism, 163–64,
    168; Peel Commission, 36, 38–40; Tel
    Aviv conference, 41; UNSCOP, 51–53;
    youths, 75–76
Elmaleh, Avraham, 8–9, 11, 36–38, 52, 94,
    99–100, 223n99
employment. *See* labor
Epstein, Eliyahu, 59, 60

Filastin (newspaper), 94, 175, 177
frontier neighborhoods: annexation and
    aid, 134, 135, 230n74; Arab Revolt in,
    152–53; class in, 127–28, 133, 139, 146–47,
    229–30n71; demographics in, 131, 132,
    229n54, 229n63; immigration, 128–30,
    132–33, 135, 153–55, 229n53, 229–30n71;

Levi in, 121–24; living conditions in, 127–28, 135, 139, 230n73; marginality, 130–39; mixing as illusion, 124–27, 227n29; mixing in, 135–49, 232n116, 232–33nn119–120, 233n122; overview, 9, 11; Palmach, 180, 182, 191–94; security and intelligence, 123, 136, 138, 151, 178–79, 180; term, 226n14; terrorism, 136, 164–71. *See also* cities, mixed

Frumkin, Gad, 142

Gayger, Benyamin, 141–42, 233n122
General Organization of Sephardi Jews, 18, 20
General Workers' Club, 79, 80
General Zionist Party, 28
generational tensions, 8, 12, 75–76
Glikson, Moshe, 97–98
Goitein, Shlomo Dov, 107, 109–10
Greenbaum, Yitzhak, 32–33

Ha'aretz (newspaper), 96, 97–98
Habshush, Rachel, 159, 165
Habuba, Eliyahu, 114, 223n99
Hadawi, Sami, 144
Haganah, 60, 72–73, 123, 184, 188–89, 194.
    See also intelligence; Irgun; Palmach
Haifa: Arab Revolt, 132–33;
    demographics, 127, 132, 227n36; internal migration, 129; labor organizations, 79–81, 82, 83; mixing in, 9, 143–44, 146–48; suburban military units, 191; tensions with other cities, 8–9; terrorism, 156–57, 160–61; youths, 75, 142. *See also* frontier neighborhoods
Haifa Workers' Council, 79
Hakim, Eliyahu, 175, 176–78
Hamagen Association, 89, 231n103
Hamizrahi movement, 28, 69
Hano'ar Ha'oved (youth movement), 145, 191–93

Harari, Yair, 239n137
Harkabi, Zidkiyahu, 73
Harosh (Horesh), Shimon, 183
Hashomer Hatza'ir (youth movement), 72, 82, 169, 170
Hasson, Yitzhak, 160, 162
Hassun, Philip, 79–80
Havoushi, Yehoshua, 72
Hebrew University, 42–43, 65, 107, 110
Hebron, 123, 127
Hed Hamizrah (newspaper), 94
Hefer, Haim, 191
Herut Party, 171
al-Hilu, Radwan, 145–46
Histadrut: Arabic language training, 71, 110; Arab relations, 54, 68, 78, 79, 80–85; Department of Oriental Jews, 85; Hano'ar Ha'oved, 145; newspapers, 91–92; Sephardi Labor Organization, 84. *See also* labor
Horovitz, Josef, 42–43
al-Husseini, Amin, 56, 57, 58, 59, 62, 63, 67, 73, 163
al-Husseini, Jamal, 22, 49–50
al-Husseini, Musa Kazim, 20
hybrid Arab-Jewish identity: and class, 116; newspapers, 92; overview, 9, 11–12; Sasson, 61, 65–66, 99–106; security and intelligence, 65, 150–51, 178–87, 203; terrorism, 151, 156–63

Ichud movement, 42, 43–46, 67, 76
Idelberg, Moshe, 194
immigration: Ashkenazi Jews, 7; bias, 32–33; frontier neighborhoods, 128–30, 132–33, 135, 153–55, 229n53, 229–30n71; post-1948, 202, 203–4; smuggling, 190–91; tensions, 42, 43, 45, 48, 84
Institute of Oriental Studies, 42–43, 65, 107, 110
Institution of Arab Studies, 71

intelligence: by Alafia, 81; analysis, 64–65; and Arabic, 65, 107, 110, 186–87, 188–89, 214n45; by Cohen, 58, 60; by Danin, 71–72; frontier neighborhoods, 123, 138, 180; hybrid identity, 65, 150–51, 179–87, 203; Jews in Arab countries, 182–83, 186–89, 203; labor organizations, 81, 82; mukhtars, 71, 123; neighborhood committees, 72–73; overview, 11; Sasson memo, 70; training, 185–87. *See also* Haganah; Palmach; security
intermarriage, 122–23
internal migration, 129–30, 228nn46–47
Iraq, 40, 63, 94, 182, 187–88, 190–91, 213n14, 220n35
Irgun, 123, 145, 156–61, 162, 166–70, 171–78, 233n125. *See also* Haganah
Izz a-Din al-Qassam, 151–52

Jabotinsky (Ze'ev), Vladimir, 171
Jaffa: border issues, 131–33; demographics, 132, 229n63; failed mediation, 24; Irgun, 156, 158; labor groups, 80; libraries, 222n79, 224n107; living conditions, 128; mixing in, 9, 146, 148; truancy, 142; youths, 75. *See also* frontier neighborhoods
Jerusalem: Arab Library, 113, 118, 224n107; Arab Revolt, 153; community centers, 166–67; demographics, 127, 227n36; internal migration, 129; labor groups, 80, 82–83; living conditions, 128; mixing in, 144, 146, 147, 148, 232n116; tensions with other cities, 8–9; youths, 76, 78. *See also* frontier neighborhoods
Jewish Agency: Arab Revolt, 62–63; bias, 28, 55; criticism of, 101; demographics, 7; immigration, 32–33; labor, 84–85; neighborhood committees, 71–73; newspaper funding, 94; Political Department, 55; United Bureau, 54–60,

94; UNSCOP, 52; work plans, 31, 66–71. *See also* Arab Bureau
Jews in Arab countries: call for action, 40; demographics, 127, 227n38; immigration, 128–29, 202, 203–4; intelligence and terrorism, 168, 182–83, 186–89, 203; Katawi on, 42; mediation, 46–53, 57; newspapers, 92–99, 203; UNSCOP, 51–53

Kalmi, Shlomo, 21, 55
Kalvarisky, Haim Margaliot-, 55, 59, 67
Kapeliouk, Menachem, 119
Karton Quarter. *See* Kerem Hatemanim
Katawi Pasha, Yosef, 41–42
Kedma Mizraha movement, 42
Kerem Hatemanim (Kerem Karton, Karton Quarter), 121, 124, 130–39, 152–53, 168, 228–29n52, 229n54, 230n73
Khaled, Leila, 140–41, 231–32n105
Khalfon, Abraham, 79–80, 81–82
Khalfon, Moshe, 192–93
kibbutzim, 72, 109, 114, 115, 116, 183, 188–89, 191, 192
Kimchi, 'Ovadia, 58–59
Klausner, Joseph, 11
Kook, Avraham Yitzhak Hacohen, 23

Labor Department (Jewish Agency), 84–85
labor: Arab workers, 68; bias, 43; children, 129, 228n46; groups, 78–85; internal migration, 129–30; newspapers, 91–92; terrorism, 163–64, 169; work plans, 68; youths, 77–78, 145. *See also* Histadrut
Labor Zionism, 24, 28, 29–32, 47, 161, 163–64, 169. *See also* Mapai
Laniado, Meir, 28, 33–36, 47–49, 50–51
League for Jewish-Arab Rapprochement, 42, 67
Lebanon, 64, 94–99, 179, 190–91

Neve Shalom, 121, 124, 130–39, 228–29n52, 229n63
newspapers: Arab, 26–27, 94–99, 220n34; Arabic-Zionist, 86–99; Iraq, 94; Jews in Arab countries, 92–99, 203; Moyne assassination, 175, 177–78; Revisionist Party, 173, 237n88; Sasson, 100–101; Zionism in, 21–22, 26–27, 208n9

Organization of Sephardi and Oriental Workers in Jerusalem, 82
Oriental Jews: demographics, 7, 127, 227nn35–36; scholarship, 2–3, 5–6, 15; as separate, 19; terms, 6–9, 97. *See also* Arabic; hybrid Arab-Jewish identity; Sephardic Jews

Palestine Labor League, 79, 80–81, 82, 91–92. *See also* Histadrut
Palestine Royal Commission. *See* Peel Commission
Palestinian Arab delegation (1921), 20–21
Palestinian Arab Workers' Society, 81
Palestinian Communist Party, 81, 145–46, 160
Palmach, 179–94, 238n121
Palmon, Yehoshua, 71, 72
Peel Commission, 35–40
periphery neighborhoods. *See* frontier neighborhoods
playgrounds, 143–44, 232n116, 232–33nn119–120, 233n122
Poincaré, Raymond, 23
Political Council of the Sephardi Community and Oriental Jews, 35
Political Department of the Jewish Agency, 55, 60, 66–73. *See also* Arab Bureau
prostitution, 133, 136, 137–38, 161

Raz, Ya'acov, 159
Rescue Committee, 76

Revisionist Zionism (Party and Movement), 12, 29, 172–74, 237n82
Riftin, Ya'acov, 170
riots, 54, 152–53. *See also* Arab Revolt (1936–1939)
Rivlin, Yosef Yoel, 43–44, 100, 110–11, 119–20, 221n48, 223n99

Safed, 127, 129, 143–44, 147, 148, 153, 227n35, 233n122
St. James Conference (1939), 41
al-Sakakini, Khalil, 50
Sasson, Binyamin (Salah), 52
Sasson, Eliyahu: Arab Bureau, 60–73; Arabic instruction, 111, 114–15, 116, 119–20; Arab-Jewish conference, 103–6; on Arab-Jewish relations, 101–3; background, 100–101; hybrid identity, 61, 65–66, 99–106; intelligence, 70; UNSCOP, 52; work plan, 66–71; youths, 74–76
Sasson, Moshe, 65
security: Arabic instruction, 65, 112, 114, 214n45; frontier neighborhoods, 123, 136, 138, 151, 178–79, 180; hybrid identity, 65, 150–51, 178–87; overview, 11, 12; WWII, 178–79. *See also* intelligence; Palmach
segregation, 126, 153, 155, 158. *See also* cities, mixed
Semitic Action movement, 178
separatism, 32–33, 34, 47, 98, 131
Sephardic Jews: demographics, 7, 127, 227nn35–36; research interest, 5–6, 15; as separate, 19, 21–22; tensions with Oriental Jews, 98; terms, 6–9, 97. *See also* Arabic; hybrid Arab-Jewish identity; Oriental Jews
Sephardi Labor Organization, 82–83, 84
Sephardi-Oriental Zionism, 24–26, 31–32, 37–38, 48–49

Shahar Association (Haganah), 193–94
Shahar Department. *See* Palmach
Shamosh, Amnon, 111, 119
Shamosh, Tuviya (Tawfiq), 91
Shamosh, Yitzhak, 42, 74, 76, 110–11
Sharoni, Avraham, 110, 188
Shaul, Anwar, 94, 220n35
Sheetrit, Bechor-Shalom, 73, 75, 202
Sheetrit, Esther, 161–62
Shertok (Sharett), Moshe, 52, 60, 62
Al-Shukeiri, Ahmad, 141
Singer, Mendel, 161–62
Sitton, David, 52, 94
Slonim, Meir, 146
Smilanski, Moshe, 117, 118
Solovichki, Moshe, 117
Somekh, Sasson, 186
Somekh, Shimon (Sama'an), 185–87
suburban military units, 191–95
Supreme Muslim Council, 102
Swartz, Rachel, 143
Syria: Communism, 145; independence
  movement, 62, 63, 67; newspapers,
  94–99; smuggling, 190–91; WWII, 179;
  youth groups, 145, 182, 239n134
Syrian Department. *See* Palmach

Tel Aviv: Arab Revolt, 132–33, 135;
  border issues, 131–33; Degel Zion,
  77–78; demographics, 132, 229n63;
  incorporation, 132, 134; internal
  migration, 129, 228nn46–47; labor
  groups, 82–83; mixing in, 136–38, 143–
  44, 148; neighborhood committees,
  73; 1939 conference, 41–42, 211nn94–
  95; suburban military units, 191,
  193–94; tensions with other cities,
  8–9; terrorism, 167, 168, 169; youths,
  74–75, 76, 77–78, 142. *See also* frontier
  neighborhoods; Kerem Hatemanim
terrorism: Arab, 136, 155; frontier

neighborhoods, 136, 155, 164–71; hybrid
  identity, 151, 156–63; Jewish, 156–61,
  166–70; reactions to, 163–64, 168,
  170–71.
Thon, Hannah, 164–66
Thon, Uri, 182, 239n135
Tiberias, 127, 129, 143–44, 147–48, 153, 155,
  227nn35–36, 228nn46–47, 232n119
Turgeman, Aryeh, 77, 82, 83
Turgeman, Raphael, 82–83
Tzabari, Simha, 145–46, 160

Union of Sephardi and Oriental Jews in
  the Land of Israel, 40–41
United Bureau, 54–60, 94
United Nations Special Committee on
  Palestine (UNSCOP), 40, 46, 51–53
Ussishkin, Menachem, 28
Uziel, Baruch, 98
Uziel, Ben-Zion Meir Hai, 36, 52, 69–70,
  152

Valero, Moshe, 42

Weizmann, Chaim, 20, 55, 58
World Confederation of Sephardi Jews,
  18, 27–28, 47, 209n46
World War I, 74, 99, 100
World War II, 73–74, 178–79
World Zionist Organization, 20, 24, 27,
  30, 55

Yahuda, Abraham Shalom, 43
Yehoshua, Ya'akov, 110–11
Yellin, Avinoam, 155, 196
Yellin, David, 55, 100, 113, 147
Yemen, 145
Yemenite Association, 131, 167–
  68
Yemenite Jews: demographics, 7;
  as distinct, 131; military service,

www.ingramcontent.com/pod-product-compliance
Lightning Source LLC
Chambersburg PA
CBHW032121020426
42334CB00016B/1026